WITHDRAWN
WRIGHT STATE UNIVERSITY LIBRARIES

ADMINISTRATIVE THEORY IN EDUCATION:

TEXT AND READINGS

Administrative Theory in Education: Text and Readings

FRANCIS GRIFFITH

PENDELL
PUBLISHING
COMPANY

LB
2805
.G73

International Standard Book Number: 0-87812-156-0
Library of Congress Catalog Card Number: 77-074528

© 1979 by
Pendell Publishing Company
Midland, Michigan

All rights reserved
Published 1979
Printed in the United States of America

To Kathryn

CONTENTS

List of Figures, Tables vi
Preface viii
Acknowledgements xv

Unit I **Changing Views of Organization and Their Administration**

Overview 3

Selected readings 34

Topics for discussion 35

Taylor and Mayo Compared . . . Reinhart Bendix .. 37

What is Meant by Organization and Its Principles? . . . James D. Mooney and Alan C. Reiley 44

Unhuman Organizations . . . Harold J. Leavitt 49

Unit II **The Behavior of Individuals in Organizations**

Overview 69

Selected readings 92

Topics for discussion 94

The Work Ethic is not Dead . . . Royal Bank of Canada 96

People . . . Robert Townsend 106

Beyond Theory Y . . . John J. Morse and Jay W. Lorsch 110

A New Dirty Word: Administrator . . . John White . 125

Unit III **Leadership**

Overview 131

Selected readings 140

Topics for discussion 142

Diagnosing Educational Leadership Problems . . . Philip E. Gates, Kenneth H. Blanchard, Paul Hersey 144

Unit III **Leadership (continued)**

Style or Circumstance . . . Fred E. Fiedler 155

How to Choose a Leadership Pattern . . . Robert Tannenbaum and Warren H. Schmidt 166

Misconceptions About Leadership . . . William W. Watson 181

Unit IV **Change**

Overview 193

Selected readings 200

Topics for discussion 201

Educational Change: Its Origins and Characteristics . . . Donald Orlosky and B. Othanel Smith 203

The Micropolitics of Innovation: Nine Propositions . . . Ernest R. House 212

Core Managerial Strategies Culled From Behavioral Research . . . George F. Truell 222

Unit V **Decision-making**

Overview 233

Selected readings 243

Topics for discussion 244

Decision Making by Management . . . Royal Bank of Canada 246

Decision-Making and Administrative Organization . . . Herbert A. Simon 256

A Means of Measuring Teacher Participation in Decision-Making . . . John K. Best 278

The Principal as a Counterpuncher . . . Ray Cross . 283

Unit VI **Communication Theory**

Overview 291

Selected readings 305

Topics for discussion 306

Unit VI **Communication Theory (continued)**

Dealing With Breakdowns in Communication — Interpersonal and Intergroup . . . Carl R. Rogers . . . 308

Serial Communication of Information in Organizations . . . William V. Haney . . . 312

Information, Communications, and Understanding . . . Peter F. Drucker . . . 327

Unit VI **Communication Theory (continued)**

Johnny, the Grad You Hired Last Week, Can't Write . . . Joseph A. Rice . . . 344

Is Listening Your Undeveloped Resource? . . . Roger Gray . . . 354

Speech Patterns of Administrators . . . Lena L. Lucietto . . . 362

Unit VII **Job Motivation and Morale Theories**

Overview . . . 373

Selected readings . . . 384

Topics for discussion . . . 385

The Herzberg Controversy: A Critical Reappraisal . . . Orlando Behling, George Labowitz, and Richard Kosmo . . . 387

Factors Affecting Teacher Morale F. C. Ellenburg . . . 394

Factors Which Affect Satisfaction and Dissatisfaction of Teachers . . . Thomas Sergiovanni . . . 402

Unit VIII **Evaluation of Teaching Competence**

Overview . . . 423

Selected readings . . . 433

Topics for discussion . . . 435

A Historical Approach to Teacher Evaluation . . . Michael L. Thompson . . . 436

Unit VIII **Evaluation of Teaching Competence (continued)**

An Uneasy Look at Performance Appraisal . . .
Douglas McGregor 442

In Defense of Performance Appraisal . . .
Harold Mayfield 452

Evaluate Teachers? . . . David Selden 464

LIST OF FIGURES AND TABLES

Unit II

Overview

1. Maslow's Hierarchy of Needs 71
2. Typical Role Set of a School Principal 84
3. Nomothetic and Idiographic Dimensions of Social Behavior 87
4. Varying Proportions of Role and Personality Components in Social Behavior 88
5. Getzels-Guba Model of Social Behavior 91

Beyond Theory Y - Morse/Lorsch

1. Study Design in "Fit" of Organizational Characteristics 113
2. Differences in Formal Characteristics In High-Performing Organizations 115
3. Differences in "Climate" Characteristics In High-Performing Organizations 120
4. Basic Contingent Relationship 121

Unit III

Diagnosing Educational Leadership Problems - Gates/Kenneth/Hersey

1. Basic Leader Behavior Styles 146
2. Situational Leadership Theory 147
3. Determining an Appropriate Leadership Style 149

Style or Circumstance - Fiedler

1. Group Situation Model 160
2. Group Situation 162

How to Choose A Leadership Pattern - Tannenbaum/Schmidt

1. Continuum of Leadership Behavior 169

Unit IV

Educational Change: Its Origin and Characteristics - Orlosky/Smith

1. Changes Listed According to Date of Origin Source, Rating of Success, and Focus of Change 205-206

Unit V

Overview

1. A Framework for Decision-Making 237

A Means of Measuring Teacher Participation In Decision-Making - Best

1. Decisional Situations 279
2. Frequency of Participation In Each Decisional Situation 280

3. Rank and Percentage of Teacher Equilibrium 281

Unit VI

Overview

1. A Model of the Communication Process 297
2. A Model of the Communication Cycle 298
3. The Abstraction Ladder 302

Unit VII

Overview

1. Continuum Assumption of Factors Causing Satisfaction and Dissatisfaction 374
2. Vroom's Motivational Model 379
3. The Dimensions of Morale 381

Factors Which Affect Satisfaction and Dissatisfaction of Teachers - Sergiovanni

1. The Continuum Assumption 403
2. Herzberg Hypothesis: Satisfaction Factors and Dissatisfaction Factors are Mainly Exclusive 404
3. Basic Design Features of Content Analysis.................. 409

Table 1. Percentages and Values of Chi Squared - First-Level Factors 410

Table 2. Percentages and Values of Chi Sqaured - Second-Level Factors 412

PREFACE

This book is intended for men and women preparing for administrative positions in education but it is hoped that practicing administrators will also profit from reading it.

Until recently textbooks in educational administration have emphasized techniques and procedures. Experience has shown, however, that the how-to-do-it approach is of dubious value. Techniques applicable to small schools may not work in large, those useful in rural and suburban schools may not be adaptable to urban schools, and those designed for elementary schools may not be applicable to secondary schools. Besides, techniques can be learned on the job more speedily and meaningfully than in a classroom.

Current emphasis in the preparation of school administrators is on the theoretical aspects of educational administration. The subject matter is the concepts which underlie and give meaning to practice and which generate new procedures. Paradoxically, the theoretical approach has proved to be the most pragmatic. "Theory," said John Dewey, "is in the end the most practical of all things."

Texts in the field are of two kinds: anthologies of articles by different authors or a sequential discussion of theoretical concepts by one or more authors in close collaboration. This book combines these two types into one by including both text and readings.

It consists of a number of units, each dealing with a major topic. Each unit is composed of an overview or background summary of what scholars have discovered or theorized about the topic, an annotated bibliography, a set of topics for classroom discussion, and several carefully selected articles which supplement the text or, in some instances, present a different point of view. Each article is preceded by an introductory summary and is followed by questions which test the reader's understanding or ability to apply the writer's suggestions.

Some of the most significant articles in administrative theory have been published in non-educational journals. They apply with equal validity to school administration, for there is a commonality of administrative patterns and principles in the fields of business management, education, medicine and public health, and public administration. The benefits to be derived from a cross-fertilization of ideas from these several fields are undeniable. For this reason many of the selected readings come from fields other than education. Significance, relevancy, recency, and clarity were among the criteria for selecting all the articles.

Administrative Theory in Education: Text and Readings is designed as a concise summary of some of the major developments in the field. I am indebted to Miss Bidabee Gloster for clerical assistance with the manuscript. I am also indebted to all the graduate students in my administration courses over a period of many years whose suggestions, questions, and objections have stimulated and clarified my thinking. Whatever merits this book has is due to them. For its shortcomings, I alone am responsible.

F.G.

ACKNOWLEDGMENTS

Unit I

"Taylor and Mayo Compared," by Reinhart Bendix, *Work and Authority in Industry,* published by John Wiley and Sons, Inc. Copyright © 1956, pp. 311-316. Reprinted by permission of author.

"What is Meant by Organization and its Principles?," from *Onward Industry! The Principles of Organization and Their Significance to Modern Industry,* by James D. Mooney and Alan C. Reiley. Copyright © 1931, by Mooney and Reiley; renewed 1959 by Ida May Mooney. Reprinted by permission of Harper & Row, Publishers, Inc.

"Unhuman Organizations," by Harold J. Leavitt, July-August 1962, *Harvard Business Review.* Copyright © 1962 by the President and Fellows of Harvard College; all rights reserved. Reprinted by permission of Harvard Business Review.

Unit II

Figure 3, "Nomothetic and Idiographic Dimensions of Social Behavior," adapted from J. W. Getzels and E. J. Guba, "Social Behavior and the Administrative Process," *School Review,* 65, pg. 429. Copyright © 1957, by The University of Chicago Press, and reprinted by their permission.

Figure 4, "Varying Proportions of Role and Personality Components in Social Behavior," adapted from J. W. Getzels and E. G. Guba, "Social Behavior and the Administrative Process," *School Review,* 65, pg. 430. Copyright © 1957 by The University of Chicago Press, and reprinted by their permission.

Figure 5, "Getzels-Guba Model of Social Behavior," by J. W. Getzel and H. A. Thelem, from *The Classroom as a Unique Social System,* 59th Yearbook, pg. 26, National Society for the Study of Education. Reprinted by permission of the publisher.

"The Work Ethic is Not Dead," by The Royal Bank of Canada, in *Monthly Newsletter,* September 1974. Copyright © 1974 by The Royal Bank of Canada. Reprinted by permission of The Royal Bank of Canada.

"People," by Robert Townsend, from pp. 137-143 in *Up the Organization,* by Robert Townsend. Copyright © 1970 by Robert Townsend. Reprinted by permission of Alfred A. Knopf, Inc.

"Beyond Theory Y," by John J. Morse and Jay W. Lorsch, May-June 1970, *Harvard Business Review.* Copyright © 1970 by the President and Fellows of Harvard College; all rights reserved. Reprinted by permission of Harvard Business Review.

"A New Dirty Word: Administrator" by John White, *Changing Education,* Winter, 1969, pp. 43-44, official publication of the American Federation of Teachers, AFL-CIO. Reprinted by permission.

Unit III

"Diagnosing Educational Leadership Problem," by Philip E. Gates, Kenneth W. Blanchard and Paul Hersey, in *Educational Leadership,* Volume 33, No. 5. Copyright © 1976 by the Association for Supervision and Curriculum Development, and reprinted by their permission.

"Style and Circumstance: The Leadership Enigma," by Fred F. Fiedler, from *Psychology Today*. Copyright © 1969 by Ziff-Davis Publishing Company. Reprinted by permission of Psychology Today magazine.

"Misconceptions about Leadership," by William W. Wayson, from *The National Elementary Principal,* Nov-Dec 1975. Copyright © 1975 by NAESP. Reprinted by permission of NAESP and the author.

"How to Choose a Leadership Pattern," by Robert Tannenbaum and Warren H. Schmidt, March-April 1958, *Harvard Business Review*. Copyright © 1958 by the President and Fellows of Harvard College; all rights reserved. Reprinted by permission of Harvard Business Review.

Unit IV

"Educational Change: Its Origins and Characteristics," by Donald Orlosky and B. Othanel Smith, from *Phi Delta Kappan,* March 1972. Copyright © 1972 by Phi Delta Kappan, Inc. and reprinted by their permission.

"The Micropolitics of Innovation: Nine Propositions," by Ernest R. House, from *Phi Delta Kappan,* January 1976. Copyright © 1976 by Phi Delta Kappan, Inc., and reprinted by their permission.

"Core Managerial Strategies Culled from Behavioral Research," by George F. Truell, *Supervisory Management,* January 1977. Copyright © 1977 by AMACOM, a division of American Management Associations. Reprinted by permission of the publisher from Supervisory Management.

Unit V

Figure I, "A Framework for Decision-Making," by William Strand, University of Arizona. Used by permission.

"Decision Making By Management," by The Royal Bank of Canada, *Monthly Newsletter,* Vol. 44, No. 1, January 1963. Copyright © 1963 by The Royal Bank of Canada. Reprinted by permission of The Royal Bank of Canada.

"Decision Making and Administrative Organization," by Herbert A. Simon, *Public Administration Review,* Winter, 1944, Vol. IV. Copyright © 1944 by Public Administration Review; all rights reserved. Reprinted by permission of Public Administration Review and Herbert A. Simon.

"A Means of Measuring Teacher Participation in Decision Making," by John K. Best, *The Clearing House,* September 1975, Vol. 49, pp. 26-27. Copyright © 1975 by The Clearing House. Reprinted by permission of Heldref Publications.

"The Principal As Counter-Puncher," by Ray Cross, from *The National Elementary Principal,* October 1971, pp. 43-45. Copyright © 1971 by NAESP. Reprinted by permission of NAESP and the author.

Unit VI

Figure 3, "The Abstraction Ladder," from *Language in Thought and Action,* 3rd ed., by S. I. Hayakawa. Copyright © 1972 by Harcourt Brace Jovanovich, Inc., and reprinted with their permission.

Figure 1, "A Model of the Communication Process," adapted from Claude E. Shannon and Warren Weaver, *The Mathematical Theory of Communication,* p. 98, Urbana, Ill: The University of Illinois Press. Copyright © 1949. Reprinted by permission of The University of Illinois Press.

"Dealing With Breakdowns in Communication — Interpersonal and Intergroup," reprinted from "On Becoming a Person," by Carl R. Rogers. Copyright © 1961 by Carl R. Rogers. Used by permission of Houghton Mifflin Company.

"Serial Communication of Information in Organizations," by William V. Haney, reprinted from "Concepts and Issues in Administrative Behavior," by Sidney Mailick and Edward H. Van Ness. Copyright © 1962, pp. 150-165. Reprinted by permission of Prentice-Hall, Inc., Englewood Cliffs, New Jersey.

"Information, Communications and Understanding," in *Technology, Management and Society* by Peter F. Drucker. Copyright © 1970 by Peter F. Drucker. Reprinted by permission of Harper & Row, Publishers, Inc.

"Johnny, the Grad You Hired Last Week, Can't Write," by Joseph A. Rice, *Supervisory Management,* September 1976. Copyright © 1976 by AMACOM, a division of American Management Associations. Reprinted by permission of the publisher from Supervisory Management.

"Is Listening Your Undeveloped Resource?" by Roger Gray, *The Hillsdale Report,* Vol. 12, No. 1. Copyright © 1973 by Hillsdale College, and is reprinted by their permission.

"Speech Patterns of Administrators," by Lena L. Lucietto, *Administrator's Notebook,* Vol. XVIII, No. 5, 1970. The *Administrator's Notebook* is published by the Midwest Administration Center of The University of Chicago, and is reprinted by their permission.

Unit VII

Figure 2, "Vroom's Motivational Model," adapted from Marvin D. Dunnette, "The Motives of Industrial Managers," *Organizational Behavior and Human Response,* May 1967, pg. 178. Dunnette developed the model from Victor H. Vroom, *Work and Motivation,* John Wiley and Sons, Inc., New York, 1964. Reprinted by permission John Wiley and Sons, Inc.

Figure 3, "The Dimensions of Morale," adapted from J. W. Getzels and E. G. Guba, "Social Behavior and the Administrative Process," *School Review,* 65. Copyright © 1957 by The University of Chicago Press, and reprinted by their permission.

"The Herzberg Controversy: A Critical Reappraisal," by Orlando Behling, George Labowitz and Richard Kosmo, *Academy of Management Journal,* March 1968, pp. 99-108. Copyright © 1968 by Academy of Management Journal and reprinted by their permission.

"Factors Affecting Teacher Morale," by F. L. Ellenburg, *Bulletin of the NASSP,* December 1972, pp. 37-44. Copyright © 1972 by the NASSP, and reprinted by their permission.

"Factors Which Affect Satisfaction and Dissatisfaction of Teachers," by Thomas Sergiovanni, *Journal of Educational Administration,* Vol. V, No. 1, May 1967. Copyright © 1967 by the Journal of Educational Administration, and is reprinted by their permission.

Unit VIII

"A Historical Approach to Teacher Evaluation," Michael L. Thompson, *The Clearing House,* November 1962. Copyright © 1962 by *The Clearing House*. Reprinted by permission of Heldref Publications.

"An Uneasy Look at Performance Appraisal" by Douglas MacGregor, May-June 1957, *Harvard Business Review*. Copyright © 1957 by the President and Fellows of Harvard College; all rights reserved. Reprinted by permission of Harvard Business Review.

"In Defense of Performance Appraisal", by Harold Mayfield. March-April 1960, *Harvard Business Review*. Copyright © 1960 by the President and Fellows of Harvard College; all rights reserved. Reprinted by permission of Harvard Business Review.

"Evaluate Teachers?" by David Seldon, *Changing Education,* Vol. 1, No. 2, Spring 1969. Reprinted by permission of David Seldon.

ADDITIONAL ACKNOWLEDGEMENTS

Brian Flynn for suggesting the universe as a model of a closed system.

Raymond Rhéaume for editorial assistance on systems theory.

Special thanks to Professor William Strand, University of Arizona, for permission to reprint his Framework for Decision-Making and for helpful suggestions about the decision-making process.

UNIT I

CHANGING VIEWS OF ORGANIZATIONS AND THEIR ADMINISTRATION

CHANGING VIEWS OF ORGANIZATIONS AND THEIR ADMINISTRATION

OVERVIEW

Administrative theory is not a new subject. From ancient times to the present men have speculated on the nature of organizations and the behavior of those who run them. With the exception of Machiavelli, however, the writers of previous centuries—Plato, Aristotle, Thomas More, and Edward Bellamy, to name just a few—were concerned with utopian rather than actual conditions. Machiavelli alone described realistically the use of executive power unrestrained by moral considerations. Contemporary writers on administrative theory try to reflect actuality. They are concerned with the way things are rather than the way they should be.

The modern study of administration began in 1887 when Woodrow Wilson, then an instructor in Princeton, advocated the scholarly study of administration, arguing that executive method should be based on stable principles rather than empiricism. His essay, "The Study of Administration," did not immediately effect any changes but eventually it stimulated others to search for principles upon which a science of administration could be founded.

The history of administrative theory can be divided into three periods: the Classical School, 1910-1930; the Human Relations School, 1930-1960; and the Behavioral School, 1960 to the present day. The dates are approximate rather than exact, and the movements are not sharply demarcated, for there is considerable commonality among them.

THE CLASSICAL SCHOOL, 1910-1930

The Classical School was composed of writers who achieved prominence during the first quarter of this century by attempting to explain the managerial task in rational terms only. They looked on individuals and segments of organizations as discrete units, and emphasized the formal organizational structure without recognizing that an informal structure co-existed with it. Usually they did not gather objective and verifiable evidence to sustain their propositions but developed their theories on the basis of their own experience. Their theories were not refined and their attitudes at times dogmatic. Nevertheless their insights were valuable in the sense that they laid the foundations upon which later scholars built.

a. Max Weber: The Merits of Bureaucracy

First in time and importance among the theoreticians of the classical school is the towering figure of Max Weber, a German historian and sociologist who held academic appointments at several German universities during the latter part of the nineteenth and the early part of the twentieth century. A champion of democracy, he helped shape the Weimar Constitution at the end of World War I. He died in 1920 at the age of 79 before he could realize his lifelong ambition to construct a general science of human behavior.

Weber lived during a period when the relatively simple social and political structures of the pre-industrial era were disappearing. As giant industrial corporations developed, labor strife increased and communism grew in influence as a political force. As Weber watched the rise of big business and the increasing complexity of government operations, he became fascinated with the phenomenon of bureaucracy.

Bureaucracy is a system of administration by means of departments or bureaus, each headed by a chief. Organizations dealing with great numbers of clients are generally structured and administered as bureaucracies. A bureaucratic organization creates a need for coordination to insure that the component units work smoothly together to achieve a common goal. Coordination, in turn, requires a hierarchical chain of authority, written records, uniform procedures, and other depersonalizing mechanisms.

Weber was the first to define and explicate bureaucracy. He used the term without the negative connotations it has today to denote an organization with certain structural features. He looked upon a bureaucracy as the most efficient kind of organization ever devised.

Its rationality appealed to him. Human behavior, he believed, should be rational and bureaucracy was the best type of organization for achieving rationality in group endeavors. An ideal bureaucracy was more just, impartial, and predictable than any other type of organization because it was impersonal and not subject to individual caprice. It was efficient because its administrators and technicians were highly skilled in their specialties.

Basic to the explication of bureaucracy is his concept of authority. He distinguished three kinds. Charismatic authority, relatively rare, is the influence exerted by an individual through his personality. Traditional authority is based on age and experience. Legalistic or administrative authority is based on law.

A charismatic organization results when followers institutionalize their leader's teachings to preserve and spread them. Some religious organizations are charismatic. An absolute monarchy in which a ruler's power is handed down to his descendents is an example of a traditional organization. A modern democracy, deriving its power from the expressed consent of the governed and existing to promote the common good, is a legal or rational organization. Many organizations employ all these legitimizations in seeking support from their members.

The ideal bureaucracy, according to Weber, has five basic characteristics:

1. ***Hierarchical structure***. Each subordinate is supervised by someone immediately above him in the line of command. Compliance is not left to chance.
2. ***Functional specialization***. Administrators are selected on the basis of demonstrated competence to perform the tasks of a particular position.
3. ***Prescribed competence***. Each incumbent has the responsibility and commensurate authority to carry out his functions. The limits, rights, and powers of his position are clearly defined to prevent overlap.
4. ***Written records***. Administrative decisions and rules are recorded. Records and files, sometimes disparagingly referred to as red tape, are essential for the interpretation and enforcement of rules.
5. ***Stable rules and policies***. Rules promote efficiency and insure con-

tinuity. They facilitate orderly, rational, and equal treatment of clients. Without them, administrators would operate inconsistently and on an ad hoc basis.

All bureaucracies are not alike although Weber made no distinction. A contemporary scholar distinguishes among them on the basis of their mode of control.[1] Coercive bureaucracies, prisons for example, compel compliance by force. Utilitarian bureaucracies such as business organizations obtain compliance by paying salaries. Normative organizations, such as professions, use symbolic controls like prestige. When a superintendent urges his teachers to give unstintingly of their energies in the service of youth because of their professional status, he is exercising normative control.

Among the claimed advantages of bureaucracies are efficiency, predictability, and impersonality. Bureaucracies serve large numbers of persons in an orderly and systematic way. Their personnel are trained and knowledgeable. Each worker is supervised by a superior who in turn is supervised by someone above him so that at every echelon there is a check on task performance. The boundaries of each position are clearly demarcated to preclude duplication of effort. Since bureaucracies operate on the basis of codified rules and policies, their decisions are predictable and free from prejudice and arbitrariness.

Some present-day scholars question whether bureaucracies do in fact possess the characteristics and advantages set forth by Weber. They offer empirical and logical evidence to support their contention that the assumptions of rationality, impersonality, infallibility of rules, unity of ends, and the existence of a single bureaucratic form are myths. To illustrate: school systems frequently behave illogically and different schools in the same system have different policies. School personnel disregard rules, show favoritism, and engage in internal struggles. These deviations are not exceptions to common practice but are characteristics of all organizations.[2]

Bureaucracies encourage conformity, a fear of deviating from established ways of doing things. They do not easily adapt to changing conditions. The bigger and more complex they are, the less adaptable they are. They cannot cope easily with emergencies or temper policies to special situations. When faced with problems different from those they customarily encounter,

---

[1] Etzioni, A., *Modern Organizations*, Englewood Cliffs, N.J : Prentice-Hall, 1964, pp. 59-60.

[2] Lane, W.R., Corwin, R.G., Monahan, W.G., *Foundations of Educational Administration*, New York: Macmillan, Chap. 8.

they move with ponderous slowness to solve them. For example, when poor black and Hispanic students entered large city school systems in great numbers during recent years, the schools for a long time did not make any concerted effort to adjust their curriculums and teaching methods to their needs but tried to carry on as they had in the past.

Communication in a bureaucracy is generally from the top down. High level administrators can send orders down the line with relative ease but it is difficult for a low-level employee to communicate with an administrator at the top because his message will be screened, diverted, or stopped somewhere along the chain of command.

Bureaucracies perpetuate themselves and often grow in size without a corresponding increase in productivity. Weber recognized this tendency. "Once it is fully established," he wrote, "bureaucracy is among those social structures which are hardest to destroy."[3]

Despite their deficiencies bureaucracies are essential for the conduct of public or semi-public business as the impartial instruments of large numbers of taxpayers or shareholders. They are here to stay. The problem is not how to eradicate them but how to make them more flexible and responsive.

School organizations are bureaucracies. The characteristics listed by Weber apply to individual schools as well as to school districts. There is a hierarchical structure: teachers, supervisors, principals, assistant superintendents, and superintendent. Appointment and promotion are presumably on the basis of merit. The staff is composed of specialists — kindergarten teachers, teachers of secondary school subjects, reading consultants, guidance counsellors, and so on. The responsibilities and authority of each position are clearly defined and adhere to the position rather than to the individual who occupies it. Policies adopted by the board of education and rules promulgated by the superintendent are stated in writing.

Yet school systems are not as rigidly bureaucratic as coercive or utilitarian organizations. At the top of a district's pyramidal structure is the superintendent whose position is ambiguous and whose power has been reduced by militant teacher organizations. Not long since the superintendent was regarded as the staff's professional leader and its spokesman at board of education meetings. Teachers never dealt directly with the board of education but always through their superintendent. Requests for salary increases

---

[3]Weber, Max, "Bureaucracy" in H.H. Garth and C.W. Mills, *From Max Weber: Essays in Sociology*, New York: Galaxy Books, 1958, p. 214.

and changes in working conditions were submitted to him for his approval and submission to the board. Nowadays teachers look upon their superintendent as the board's man. They bargain face to face with boards of education without his intervention.

Line and staff structure is not strictly observed. Parents, teachers, and pupils appeal directly to the principal without going through the chain of command. Supervisory authority is not exercised firmly. Teachers and other personnel are not held accountable for results. Rules are not firmly enforced. The boundaries between positions are not sharply drawn. Finally, the functions of the board of education are not altogether analagous to those of a board of directors of a bureaucratic industrial corporation.

b. Scientific Management: Getting the most out of workers

Scientific management is the name given to a movement led by Frederick W. Taylor, a mechanical engineer whose primary aim was maximizing profits and minimizing costs of production. He argued that this aim could be accomplished and workers' salaries raised at the same time.

Born in 1856 in a middle-class Philadelphia family, Taylor was obliged to forego a college education after graduation from high school because of impaired vision. Looking for a career that would not require too much reading, he began as a laborer in a small shop and within a period of eight years progressed through the stages of timekeeper, machinist, gang boss, foreman, and assistant engineer to chief engineer of the works. His eyesight improved and he was able to attend night classes at Stevens Institute where he eventually earned an engineering degree.

Aware that the methods used by workers were inefficient, he developed a managing technique which resulted in greater productivity and better worker-management relations. The technique involved a study of the most efficient method, the shortest time, and the best materials and tools for performing every job in the shop. It also included a new method of stimulating worker productivity, which Taylor called scientific rate-fixing, and a new allocation of responsibility between management and workers. Management was responsible for discovering the most efficient way of performing each operation and for training workers to use these ways. Management was also responsible for providing the most suitable materials and tools, and planning the best flow and sequence of work operations. Taylor demonstrated that his procedures resulted in greater productivity without increased exertion by the workers. By eliminating wasted time and energy and by simplifying movements, workers produced more with less effort. In essence, Taylorism was a new theory of motivation and a new theory of management.

Reformers began to apply the principles of scientific management to a variety of fields besides industry, among them religion, education, and the military profession. The movement spread to Europe during the first World War. In England the Fabian Society, an influential socialist organization, endorsed it and in France Premier Clemenceau ordered its application in military plants. Lenin, in 1918, urged the Russians to practice it. After the war the influence of the movement began to decline.

The effects of scientific management were not inconsequential. Some of its discoveries, like the touch system of typing, devised by one of Taylor's associates, have become permanent additions to modern life.

Principles of scientific management. Efficient management is a science. The laws, rules, and principles on which it is based are applicable to all kinds of human activities from simple individual acts to the complex activities of great corporations.

The principle object of management should be to achieve maximum prosperity for both employer and employee. For owners, maximum prosperity means higher dividends and the smooth functioning of every branch of industry. For employees, maximum prosperity means higher wages and the development of every worker to optimum efficiency so that he can perform the highest grade of work of which he is capable.

The interests of employer and employee are the same. Prosperity for the employer is coupled with prosperity for the employee. The prosperity of one cannot continue over a long period unless it is accompanied by prosperity for the other. If a concern is rightly managed, "it is possible to give the workman what he wants—high wages—and the employer what he wants—a low labor cost for his manufactures."[4] Both management and workers should strive, therefore, to train and develop every individual so that he can perform the highest class of work of which he is capable at the fastest pace and with the maximum of efficiency.

Why do workmen soldier on the job? First, because almost everyone has a natural inclination to take it easy. Secondly, because men, when they are engaged on the same job at a uniform salary, gradually but surely slow down their gait to that of the least efficient worker. They see no reason for exerting themselves when those who are lazy and who do only half as much work receive the same pay as they do. They believe that if an employer

[4] Taylor, Frederick Winslow, *The Principles of Scientific Management*, New York: Harper and Row, 1911, p. 10.

discovers that they can do more than they are doing he will sooner or later find a way of compelling them to do it without increasing their pay. Hence, they try to mislead and deceive him into believing that they are working to the limit of their capacity. They may even restrict the productiveness of the machines they are running when an increase in output could be achieved without additional effort on their part. Soldiering ceases when there is an intimate shoulder-to-shoulder relationship between management and workmen, and when wages are increased 30 per cent to 100 per cent under scientific management procedures.[5]

The elements which constitute the essence of scientific management may be summarized as:

> ***First:*** The development by management of the science of each work operation, with rigid rules for each worker's motions, and the perfection and standardization of all implements and working conditions.
> ***Second:*** The careful selection and training of all workers, and the elimination of all who refuse or are unable to adopt the best methods.
> ***Third:*** Constant help and watchfulness by management to insure that all work is done according to scientific principles and stimulation of productivity by paying each man a daily bonus for working fast and doing what he is told to do.
> ***Fourth:*** An almost equal division of work and responsibility between management and workmen. Managers work all day long side by side with the men, helping, encouraging, and smoothing the way for them.[6]
> ***Fifth:*** Definite tasks set each day for each worker. Workers receive daily written instructions describing "not only what is to be done, but how it is to be done, and the exact time allowed for doing it."[7] This "task idea" was the most prominent single element in scientific management, according to Taylor.

The application of the principles of scientific management depended on the use of several techniques or mechanisms. Foremost among them were time and motion studies which Taylor regarded as essential for developing a true science for a particular job. Efficiency experts carefully watched workmen as they performed each task, recording and timing their motions by stop watches. For greater accuracy, in some later studies, motion picture cameras were used and timing intervals measured in hundredths of a second.

---

[5] Ibid., p. 27.
[6] Ibid., p. 85.
[7] Ibid., p. 39.

Based on intensive and objective studies of a particular job, motions and tools were standardized. If better and faster methods were subsequently developed, they then became the standard and the older practices were discarded. Supervisors were responsible for enforcing standardized practices and preventing any deviation from them.

Instead of one supervisor or functional foreman, each workman had many different foremen over him, each responsible for a special aspect of the work. The inspector saw to it that he understood the drawings and instructions. The gang boss taught him how to set up the job in his machine and how to eliminate waste motion. The speed boss checked to see that the machine was run at the best speed. The repair boss gave instructions in the adjustment, cleanliness, and general care of the machine; the time clerk, about pay and written reports; the route clerk, about the sequence of jobs and the movement of work from one part of the shop to another. Finally, a disciplinarian "interviewed" him if he got into trouble with any of his various bosses.

Under the Taylor system, a shop — or, indeed, a whole works — was not managed by one individual but by a planning department. The daily routine of running the establishment was carried on by the various functional elements of this department so that the works would run smoothly even if the factory superintendent or his assistants were absent for an extended period of time. The leading functions of the planning department included, among others, a complete analysis of all work orders taken by the company, cost analysis, time and motion studies, standards, maintenance and improvement of system and plant, employment bureau, and pay department.

Scientific management in education.[8] Scientific management had a powerful impact on American education from 1910 to 1925. Articles in newspapers and periodicals, speakers at educational conventions, and policies adopted by school boards reflected a widespread impression that schools were inefficiently managed. Laymen and educators alike demanded that they be operated more efficiently and emphasized a pragmatic and utilitarian type of education rather than an intellectual and cultural. Critics charged that school curriculums were "theoretical, visionary, and impractical"[9] and demanded an extension of vocational education.

---

[8] The section which follows is based largely on Raymond E. Callahan, *Education and the Cult of Efficiency*, University of Chicago Press, 1962.

[9] Quoted in Callahan, p. 10.

Against such a barrage of criticism school superintendents were vulnerable because they lacked tenure. Their security depended on their ability to mollify an increasing number of voluble critics more than on their professional competence. In the clamor for efficiency many lost their positions. In 1913 the *American School Board Journal* reported that there were "wholesale changes in superintendencies and higher school positions" and "wholesale resignations, dismissals, and new appointments."[10]

With only a few exceptions, superintendents did not deny the charges of inefficiency leveled against the schools. Instead of rejecting the criticisms, they attempted to apply the principles of scientific management. They were aided in their efforts by one of the most influential organizations of that time, the National Society for the Study of Education, which devoted its entire 1913 yearbook to considering ways of applying Taylor's doctrines to city schools, and by the Department of Superintendence of the National Education Association which, in the same year, considered the question at great length at its annual convention.

Educational administrators responded to the demands for more efficient management by introducing new classroom methods and testing procedures. The new teaching methods were supposedly more productive than those of the past. The tests were standardized and designed to measure both subject matter and attitudinal changes. Educational objectives were re-examined. Curriculums were modified.Organizational patterns were changed. Supervision was made more "scientific" by the use of detailed rating devices to measure the efficiency of teachers and principals. Accounting methods were tightened and school budgets scrutinized to eliminate wasteful expenditures. Efficiency bureaus were established in large city systems. School surveys were conducted to determine areas of weakness. Between 1911 and 1925 so many surveys were conducted that, according to Raymond E. Callahan, "hardly a state or local school system in America was not surveyed."[11]

Among the educational innovations adopted in response to the demands for efficiency was the Gary Plan or platoon system. The Gary Plan was an organizational scheme designed for elementary schools. Schools were departmentalized and students moved from room to room at the end of each period. One advantage of the plan was that the regular program of studies was enriched by the addition of special subjects such as music, art, and nature study. Its main appeal, however, was that it resulted in financial saving because all classrooms were occupied all the time. When pupils were

---

[10] Quoted in Callahan, p. 54.

[11] Op. cit., p. 112.

not receiving instruction, they were in "study halls,"presumably receiving individual help, or in playgrounds and auditoriums. The school day was extended and schools were open year-round although the school year for individual students remained unchanged. The platoon system began to disappear after 1930 and is non-existent today.

Beginning about 1914, double and triple sessions were introduced into secondary schools, particularly in New York City, in the interests of economy and efficiency, and soon became an accepted pattern of organization. Some of New York City's high schools still operate on a double session basis.

The superintendency fell a victim to the cult of efficiency. Until the early part of the twentieth century, a superintendent was considered an educational leader, concerned primarily with the improvement of instruction. By 1925, however, the superintendency had become a managerial position rather than an educational one. Superintendents were looked upon as experts in the business aspects of education, the nuts and bolts of management, rather than as educators. This role change was in part the result of the increasing size and complexity of school systems, conflicting pressures from external sources, and the ever-increasing financial aspects of the position. As a consequence, training programs for school administrators stressed courses in school finance, building management, and public relations instead of philosophy and the liberal arts. Education was looked on as a business and the superintendent as a business executive.

The contemporary emphasis on accountability, behavioral objectives, merit pay, and competency-based certification may not be directly traceable to the scientific management movement but reflects its concern for measurable results and efficient operation. They are part of a pragmatic trend which has long been a characteristic of American society and which, since Taylorism, has been more and more evident in our educational system.

c. Henri Fayol: Getting the most out of management

Henri Fayol, like Taylor, was an engineer interested in increasing industrial efficiency. Unlike Taylor, he was concerned with the upper rather than the lower levels of management and with organizational concepts rather than techniques of production. Taylor's background was that of a shop foreman, which explains his interest in worker productivity, while Fayol's was that of a top administrator with almost absolute power over large numbers of subordinate managers.

Born in 1841 in France, Fayol became a mining engineer and achieved national recognition for his achievements. Withdrawing from engineering after twelve years, he spent the next sixteen as a geologist and the thirty years following that as the managing director of a metallurgical firm. Resigning that post, he became a cabinet minister in the government for seven years. He retired at 77 to establish the Center for Administrative Studies. In each of his careers he was eminently successful.

Drawing upon his extensive administrative experience, he set forth the guiding principles of a theory of administration in his internationally influential book, *General and Industrial Management*.[12] Perhaps his most significant contribution to administrative theory was his analysis of the administrative process into five major elements: planning, organizing, commanding, coordinating, and controlling. Typical activities:

Planning: Foretelling the future and preparing to meet its needs and opportunities.
Organizing: Constructing an organizational chart showing the duties of each position and its relationship to other positions; recruiting, selecting, and assigning personnel.
Commanding: Stimulating employees to do their best for the organization; issuing and enforcing regulations; eliminating unfit personnel; avoiding concern with detail.
Coordinating: Unifying efforts to achieve organizational goals.
Controlling: Rectifying weaknesses and preventing their recurrence; evaluating progress to see that all occurs according to predetermined plan; appraising things, people, and actions.

Fayol held that these elements are present in all business enterprises, no matter how small, and that their efficient exercise was essential to successful operation. Other writers have used his analysis as a basis for their own descriptions of the administrative process. In some cases their changes are not substantive but terminological. Luther Gulick, for example, described the work of an executive as planning, organizing, staffing, directing, coordinating, reporting, and budgeting.[13] A few years later Herbert A. Simon listed the elements as planning, budgeting, controlling, and coordinating.[14] About the same time the American Association of School Administrators set forth the elements as planning, allocation, stimulation, coordination, and evaluation. The substitution of stimulation for commanding and evaluation

[12] Fayol, Henri, *General and Industrial Management*, London: Pitman and Sons Ltd., 1949. Translated by Constance Storrs.

[13] Gulick, Luther, and Urwick, L., eds., *Papers on the Science of Administration*, New York: Institute of Public Administration, 1937.

[14] Simon, Herbert A., *Administrative Behavior*, 2nd. ed., New York: Macmillan, 1957.

for controlling suggests the influence of democracy. Fayol, who lived in the last half of the nineteenth and the early part of the twentieth centuries saw nothing uncongenial about associating commanding and controlling with management, but these terms grate on modern ears.

A contemporary writer, Edward H. Litchfield, has substantively modified Fayol's five-step description.[15] Litchfield regards administration as a cyclical process which starts with decision-making and proceeds through programming (making arrangements to effectuate decisions), communicating, controlling (following the plan agreed upon), reappraising, and formulating new decisions in the light of the reappraisal. Thus the administrative cycle begins and ends with decision-making. The elements are inextricably interrelated and the description of the process is applicable to individual, group, or organizational activity.

Fayol described fourteen principles upon which the soundness and good working order of an organization depend.[16] He cautioned that the principles were flexible and adaptable and should be applied with a sense of proportion.

1. Division of work: breaking down large tasks into their component parts and assigning workers to each part. The object of dividing work is to produce more and better work with the same effort.
2. Authority: the right to give orders and the power to exact obedience. Responsibility is a corollary of authority; wheresoever authority is exercised, responsibility arises.
3. Discipline: obedience, application, energy, behavior, and outward marks of respect. The best means of establishing discipline are through competent managers at all levels, fair and clear agreements between a firm and its employees, and the judicious application of sanctions (penalties).
4. Unity of command: employees receive orders from one superior only. Dual command — that is, two superiors wielding authority over the same person or department — is a source of conflicts.
5. Unity of direction: one head and one plan for a group of activities having the same objective. Unity of direction means coordination of strength and focussing of effort, and is provided for by a strong organizational structure.

---

[15] Litchfield, Edward H., "Notes on a General Theory of Administration", *Administrative Science Quarterly I*, No. 1, June 1956, pp. 3-29.

[16] Fayol, Henri, *General and Industrial Management*, London: Pitman and Sons Ltd., 1949. Translated by Constance Storrs. Chap. 4.

6. Subordination of individual interest to general interest: the interests of one person or group subordinate to those of the organization. This principle is effectuated by firmness and good example on the part of managers, fair agreements, and constant supervision.
7. Remuneration of personnel: the price of services rendered. Remuneration should be fair and afford satisfaction to employer and employee, but at the same time should not go beyond reasonable limits.
8. Centralization: always present to a greater or less extent. The question of centralization or decentralization is a simple question of proportion, a matter of finding the optimum degree for a particular organization. The objective to pursue is the optimum utilization of all the capabilities of the staff.
9. Scalar chain: the chain of superiors ranging from the ultimate authority to the lowest ranks. Since it may be disastrously lengthy in large concerns, managers should be permitted to short-circuit it so long as their actions are approved by their immediate superiors. "It is an error to depart needlessly from the line of authority, but it is an even greater one to keep to it when detriment to the business ensues."[17]
10. Order: a place for everything and everything in its place; a place for everyone and everyone in his place. The object of material order is to avoid the loss of material. The object of social order is to balance human requirements and organizational resources.
11. Equity: the combination of kindliness and justice. It does not exclude forcefulness or sternness. Its application requires much good sense, experience, and good nature.
12. Stability of tenure of personnel: time is required for an employee to get used to new work and succeed in doing it well. Insecurity of tenure is especially to be feared in large concerns, for much time is needed to get to know men and things in order to be in a position to decide on a plan of action, gain confidence in oneself, and inspire it in others.
13. Initiative: thinking out and executing. The initiative of all represents a great source of strength. Other things being equal, a manager able to permit the exercise of initiative on the part of subordinates is infinitely superior to one who cannot do so.
14. Esprit de corps: harmony and union among the personnel of a concern. Since differences and misunderstandings which a conversation can clear up grow more bitter in writing, communications should be oral whenever possible.

---

[17] Ibid., p. 31.

Application to education. The first to apply Fayol's analysis of the administrative process to education was Jesse B. Sears who substituted directing for commanding but otherwise made no major change.[18] Sears elaborated on each of the five elements and illustrated its application to educational administration. The A.A.S.A. formulation, mentioned before, is similar to Sears'.

Russell T. Gregg, who followed Sears, enumerated seven components: decision-making, planning, organizing, communicating, influencing, coordinating, and evaluating.[19] The use of influencing for commanding again illustrates how uncongenial the latter word is to administrators accustomed to a democratic climate. Gregg's most important contribution is his stress on the involvement of staff.

Fayol's five-step formulation is applicable to education as it is to industry and other fields but it may need to be adapted to particular situations, times, and circumstances. It is a scheme which can help school administrators form a concept of their role.

Beginning and experienced principals and superintendents can profit from a consideration of Fayol's fourteen principles. They are a distillation of experience and wisdom which, if adapted to circumstances and applied judiciously, can make smooth an administrator's road.

THE HUMAN RELATIONS SCHOOL, 1930-1960

A reaction against the doctrines and practices of scientific management began about 1930 generated by the growing strength and militancy of labor unions, the Hawthorne experiments of Elton Mayo, and theory and empirical evidence from the social sciences. John Dewey's writings extended the revolt into the field of education.

The human relations movement, as it was called, focussed attention on the human element in the work place. Labor is not a commodity to be bought and sold. Workers must be considered in the context of the work groups of which they are a part. Their relationships with their fellow workers and their bosses influence their behavior, morale, and productivity.

---

[18] Sears, Jesse B., *The Nature of the Administrative Process*, New York: McGraw-Hill, 1950.

[19] Gregg, Russell T., "The Administrative Process."In Roald F. Campbell and Russel T. Gregg, eds., *Administrative Behavior in Education*, New York: Harper and Brothers, 1957, Chap. 8.

The movement was interdisciplinary in nature. It was founded on new knowledge developed in the disciplines of psychology, group dynamics, sociology, political science, physiology, and labor economics. Drawn from these fields, such concepts as motivation, group behavior, the influence of groups on their members, role structures, power struggles between groups and individuals, and the resolution of conflict became the subject matter of the human relations school.

Among the leaders of the movement was Elton Mayo whose studies from 1927 to 1932 at the Hawthorne plant of the Western Electric Company in Chicago resulted in findings which brought into question some scientific management concepts. Although the company was considered progressive because of the pension plans, sickness benefits, and recreational and other facilities it provided, there was a great deal of dissatisfaction among its 30,000 employees. Tension was high and productivity low. Mayo was called in to investigate the causes.

Previous studies had been based on the assumption that a worker could be studied as an isolated unit whose efficiency was affected by wasteful movements, fatigue, and deficiencies in physical environment. Mayo's experiments demonstrated that these assumptions were not entirely true although there are situations where a worker may be studied in isolation and where physical conditions affect efficiency.

One typical experiment was designed to test the effect of improved illumination on output, the assumption being that the better the lighting the better the work. Two groups of employees were selected from the experiment, a control group and an experimental group. The illumination for the control group remained unchanged throughout the experiment while the illumination for the experimental group was increased in intensity at intervals. Predictably, the output of the experimental group increased. Unpredictably, the output of the control group went up also. Even when the illumination of the experimental group was lessened, output continued to increase. Clearly some force other than illumination was at work, a force which increased output no matter whether physical conditions were improved or worsened.

Researchers in the behavioral sciences have given the name Hawthorne effect to the impact of experimentation upon subjects. When some of the workers at the Hawthorne plant were made the center of attention and made to feel important, the researchers could not control the important variables and almost any change, beneficial or not, resulted in improved output.

Among the conclusions drawn from Mayo's researches:

1. Work is a group activity.
2. The social world of the adult is primarily patterned about work activity.
3. The need for recognition, security, and a sense of belonging is more important in determining workers' morale and productivity than the physical conditions under which he works.
4. A complaint is not necessarily an objective recital of facts; it is commonly a symptom manifesting disturbance of an individual's status position.
5. The worker is a person whose attitudes and effectiveness are conditioned by social demands from both inside and outside the work plant.
6. Informal groups within the work plant exercise strong social controls over the work habits and attitudes of the individual worker.[20]

The Hawthorne experiments disclosed a lack of systematic knowledge about work groups and their effects, beneficial and adverse, upon organizational objectives. They stimulated the development of the Human Relations movement by revealing the need of taking into account the attitudes of workers. The movement lost some of its appeal as time went on because it not infrequently led to lax administration and paternalism.

1. ***Motivation.*** The proponents of scientific management looked on man as an economic unit, a factor of production, an extension of a machine, motivated only by a desire for material gain. They did not recognize the truth of the biblical adage that man does not live by bread alone. The human relations theorists looked upon him as a complete human being with attitudes and needs which profoundly affected his work.

There are several kinds of human needs. Physiological needs are the most basic — air, food, shelter, and the like. Social needs such as companionship come into play after the physiological are satisfied. Psychological needs, including the need for recognition and the actualization of an individual's capacities, are motivators only after other needs are satisfied.

It follows, then, that employers must provide for the satisfaction of all human needs to obtain the most from their employees. When workers have the means of obtaining adequate food and shelter for themselves and their

---

[20] Miller and Form, *Industrial Psychology*, in Brown, J.A.C., *The Social Psychology of Industry*, Baltimore, Md.: Penguin Books, 1954, p. 85.

families, when they feel accepted and experience a sense of belonging, and when they enjoy the recognition and praise that follows accomplishment, they are more productive.

Low producers are not necessarily unmotivated. They may be motivated by other goals than the task at hand and changing the direction of their motivation presents a different problem from motivating those who are indifferent or phlegmatic.

Organizations have attempted to take care of their workers' social needs by recreational programs and other activities outside the lines of work. Such programs are not supervised by those responsible for supervising workers' on-the-job performance. While they have caused workers to regard their employing organizations favorably, they have not resulted in significantly increased output. More recent approaches include group decision-making and self-determination, which allow worker participation in management decisions and a larger degree of freedom in job performance. "General supervision" is substituted for close supervision. Other techniques include job rotation, job enlargement, and decentralization.

Motivation has been called the core of management.[21] It is still an unresolved problem although we have come a long way since the days of Taylor.

2. ***Organizational theory.*** The classical school paid attention only to the formal structure of an organization as shown on an organizational chart. An organizational chart is almost always pyramidal in form, showing the chief executive at the top with subordinate executives ranked beneath him. It is a diagram of the line and staff arrangement, span of control, channels of communication, boundaries of authority and responsibility, and the relationship of divisions, bureaus, and departments to one another.

The classical school failed to acknowledge the existence of an informal organization existing side by side with the formal. The informal organization does not appear on any organizational chart — indeed it would be difficult and sometimes impossible to diagram — but it exists nonetheless and plays an important part in the functioning of the formal organization. It consists of the social relationships among employees: the groups that travel to and from work, eat and drink or play bridge and poker together, or engage in other social activities.

---

[21] Likert, R., "Motivation: The Core of Management," New York: American Management Association, 1953.

The formal organization has an official origin. It is designed to accomplish a specific purpose and it continues to exist after its present membership has left. An informal organization is voluntary in origin, its purpose is not clear — at least to non-members, it has no hierarchy of positions, and it ceases to exist when its present membership has left.

A group may be composed of persons who share the same rest or lunch periods, or who are of the same age or sex, or who have similar interests, or who perform the same type of work or belong to the same department. A worker may belong to several groups and, if he does, the one with which he most closely identifies is his primary group.

Many workers get their satisfactions in the informal groups where they are treated as individuals, not cogs in a machine. The friendliness and recognition of their co-workers compensate for their impersonal treatment by the large and complex formal organization.

In these informal and shifting groupings, leaders arise. They are not elected or appointed, they have no legal standing, but they assume leadership roles on the basis of their colleagues' esteem, and together they constitute an informal authority structure.

The attitude of an employee's primary group, as voiced by the group leader, may determine whether an official directive will be supported or subverted, whether employees will cooperate with administrators, or whether work norms will be raised or lowered. The group can influence a member to interpret rules narrowly or broadly, to slow down or speed up, to comply or resist.

A skillful administrator knows the various informal organizations in his school or district and he knows their leaders. To insure their cooperation he "sounds them out" before initiating a new plan or policy. In discussions with them he hears opinions which might not be openly expressed in formal meetings. He uses them as channels of communication to scotch rumors and prevent misunderstandings. He recognizes that the informal organization adds a flexible dimension which enables the formal organization to adjust to special cases and situations.

3. ***Socially determined norms.*** To discover as much as possible about the restriction of output by employees, Mayo studied a group of fourteen workers engaged in wiring switchboards or, as they were then called, "banks". The group had its own natural leaders whose judgments were respected by the others. (The natural leaders were not those placed in authority by man-

agement.) The fourteen workers were paid on a piece-rate basis so that the more work a man performed the more salary he earned. Despite the financial incentive to earn more, each worker produced 6000 units a day, no more or less, although he was easily capable of producing 7000. When anyone produced more than his fellow workers, he was regarded as a rate-buster and soon forced back into line. On the other hand, if he produced fewer than 6000 units, he was looked upon as a slacker and forced to meet the quota the group had unofficially agreed upon. The informal organization had its own norms and would tolerate no deviation from them.

The bank-wiring experiment showed that an informal group can lower output. Another experiment, conducted in Southern California aircraft factories in 1943, showed that informal groups were instrumental in raising production and in decreasing absenteeism and labor turn-over.

These and other investigations show that workers respond to group influence. They act as members of a group, not as individuals. It follows, then, that administrators should not deal with workers as individual units, isolated from those they work with, but as members of work groups subject to group pressures.

4. ***Conflict.*** In every organization differences of opinion arise regarding policies and methods. How should antagonistic points of view be dealt with?

Mary Parker Follett, a social philosopher and student of management, adverted to this problem frequently in her lectures and articles. Miss Follett, born in 1868, was a prominent member of the human relations school whose reputation was such that she was engaged as a consultant by governmental and industrial organizations both in this country and England. Her humanitarian concerns and her stress on individual and social values impelled her to serve on commissions dealing with vocational education, minimum wages, and the League of Nations. Few would disagree with the observation of one critic that "her writing is filled with profound truth and practical help yet simple and direct."[22]

In the thinking of the classical school, conflict was to be avoided because its results were often disastrous. In Miss Follett's view, conflict was unavoidable but might have profitable results to both parties if properly handled.

---

[22] Merrill, Harwood F., ed., *Classics in Management*, New York: American Management Association, 1960.

> There are three ways of settling differences: by domination, by compromise, or by integration. Domination, obviously, is a victory of one side over the other. This is not usually successful in the long run for the side that is defeated will simply wait for its chance to dominate. The second way, that of compromise, we understand well, for that is the way we settle most of our controversies — each side gives up a little in order to have peace. Both these ways are unsatisfactory. In dominating, only one side gets what it wants; in compromise neither side gets what it wants. We are continually hearing compromise praised. That is the accepted, the approved way of ending controversy, yet no one really wants to compromise, because that means giving up part of what he wants. Is there any other way of dealing with difference?
>
> There is a way beginning now to be recognized at least and sometimes followed, the way of integration. Let me take first a very simple illustration. In a university library one day, in one of the smaller rooms, someone wanted the window open, I wanted it shut. We opened the window in the next room where no one was sitting. There was no compromise because we both got all we really wanted. For I did not want a closed room. I simply did not want the north wind to blow directly on me; and he, the man in the room with me, did not want that particular window open, he merely wanted more air in the room. Integration means finding a third way which will include both what A wishes and what B wishes, a way in which neither side has had to sacrifice anything.[23]

Solving differences by integration means progress. "In domination you stay where you are. In compromise likewise you deal with no new values. By integration something new has emerged, the third way, something beyond the either-or."[24]

Some years ago negotiations between a board of education and a teachers union reached an impasse over the issue of accountability. Both sides agreed that accountability was desirable but the board wished to initiate a rating system which the union objected to on the grounds that it was unfair and unworkable. After prolonged argument, both sides agreed to set up a commission to study the problem and to prepare a plan to be effectuated within a specified period. Neither side lost, neither won.

5. ***Communication.*** The classical organizational model conceived of

---

[23] Follett, Mary P., "Coordination." In Merrill, Harwood F., ed., *Classics in management*, American Management Association, 1960.

[24] Ibid.

communication mainly as the transmission of orders and information from higher to lower echelons. Little thought was given to the necessity of communication between ranks or from lower to higher ranks.

Communication in the human relations view is the lifeblood of an organization. Management must see to it that information flows freely, up, down, and horizontally through established networks of the formal organization and non-official networks of the informal organization.

Everyone affected by an action or policy should be made acquainted — preferably beforehand — with the reasons for it. The rationale for keeping employees informed is that desired behavioral response is more likely when everyone is aware of what is going on and the reasons therefor. It is not enough, of course, for employees to understand information transmitted to them; they must also accept it. This implies that they must have an opportunity to voice their opinions and questions, in face-to-face meetings if possible, and to have them listened to with an open mind.

6. ***Participation in decision-making.*** Large, complex organizations tend to be autocratic because of their rigid formal structure. Since the administrators responsible for their operation can compel obedience by various sanctions ranging from admonition to dismissal, subordinates are likely to remain silent when faced with decisions from above which they consider unwise and unfair.

Many studies have shown that participation in decision-making benefits both management and workers. Management benefits by tapping the experience and talents of workers whose ideas may strengthen the organization's functioning. Employees benefit by growing in maturity and responsibility. They identify themselves more closely with the organization and achieve a sense of belonging and recognition.

Insecure executives fear to practice participatory leadership because they look upon employees' questions and suggestions as personal criticism. Mature executives welcome the free exchange of comments as potentially helpful. They encourage the participation of personnel at all levels in the formulation of policies which directly affect them.

Democratic administration, the label given to participation in decision-making by individuals and groups, has been widely misunderstood and abused. It is not a laissez-faire procedure. It does not mean guiding persons to accept an administrator's viewpoint. It does not avoid the firm exercise of authority. It is not a means of avoiding unpleasant decisions.

In the name of democratic administration, subordinates have been allowed to decide issues of no importance to anyone or manipulated to adopt as their own decisions already made by management. The trappings of democracy — voting, the absence of formality, and committee procedure — have been substituted for the essence of democracy, a respect for every individual and a concern for his welfare.

Application to education. The Human Relations school came into prominence at a time when there was a growing unrest among educators with the mechanistic approach of scientific management. It coincided with the publication of John Dewey's *Democracy and Education* and the rise of the progressive educational movement which stressed the need for humane treatment of children and more participation by teachers in the direction of education.

Terms heretofore unheard of in educational thought, like morale, rapport, and democracy became catchwords. Administrators became concerned about the morale of their staffs and the rapport between teachers and pupils. Books and articles discussed democratic administration, democratic supervision, and democratic teaching. In the 1930's the National Education Association conducted a nationwide survey to determine whether pupils in all grades knew the meaning of democracy and turned up with the not unexpected finding that they had a good idea of the advantages of democracy but little notion of its responsibilities. Teachers welfare committees were formed in school districts to defend teachers' interests. Local and state teacher organizations grew in strength and claimed the right to participate in the formulation of policies which affected their membership.

Dewey held that an ideal school is a miniature society in which pupils are best prepared for life by living in a democratic climate. A school is democracy in microcosm and should reflect democratic principles in its structure and actions. Above all it should emphasize respect for individuality and increased freedom for teachers and students.

Perhaps because of their ambiguities, Dewey's teachings were oversimplified and misapplied. Democracy was originally a political concept, referring to a form of government in which those in authority derived their power from the free consent of the governed as expressed through the ballot box. Voting, which is an essential part of political democracy, is not an essential part of educational democracy. Educational problems cannot be solved by majority rule. A skillful administrator should always be receptive to advice and suggestion from every source but he is under no obligation to follow it if it is at odds with his own best thinking, the findings of research, or sound educational philosophy.

Another misconception arising from the human relations movement was that a contented staff was a productive staff. Principals became so concerned with the importance of maintaining good relations with their faculties that they sometimes shied away from taking decisive actions which might imperil their popularity. They tolerated incompetence and malingering or neglected class visitations rather than incur the ill-will of their staffs, even though the pupils were often the losers.

On the whole, though, the effects of the human relations movement on education were beneficial. The autocratic school administrator is no longer with us. Teachers and pupils enjoy more freedom than ever before and schools are happy places in which to learn and work.

THE BEHAVIORAL SCHOOL, 1960 TO THE PRESENT

The Behavioral or Structuralist School is a synthesis of scientific management and human relations with some important modifications and additional insights. It does not reject the contributions of previous schools but it does suggest some shortcomings in their positions. It uses the content and research methods of the behavioral sciences in its search for actuality.

The foremost writers of the behavioral school include Chester A. Barnard, who was president of the New Jersey Bell Telephone Company and the Rockefeller Foundation and author of *The Functions of the Executive,* an influential book which is widely regarded as a classic in the field; Herbert A. Simon, who analyzed organizational behavior from the standpoint of decision-making; Rensis Likert whose research indicates that high morale and high productivity can be equated only under certain conditions; and Chris Argyris, who has written and spoken extensively on the relationship between the individual and the organization. These and other writers of the behavioral school are concerned with actual conditions. Their writings are descriptive rather than prescriptive, a search for what is rather than what should be. They question such traditional concepts as the rationality of organizations and the identity of organizational and individual goals.

The behavioral school is not a unified body of thought. Different writers have different ideas and emphases. Organizations are studied from the standpoint of systems analysis: a method involving mutually dependent variables in simultaneous variation.

1. ***The concept of organization.*** Parsons defines organizations as social

units deliberately constructed to accomplish specific goals.[25] According to Etzioni, they are characterized by division of labor, a central authority (in some organizations, such as hospitals, there is a dual authority), and provisions for the replacement of personnel who leave or are removed.[26]

The existence of a single organizational purpose which employees labor to accomplish is an unjustified assumption. An organization is not a unity knit together by a single dominating goal. Employees are not affected by the broad purposes of an organization. They are conscious of the aims of their particular work unit but fail to perceive any commonality of purpose with other departments. According to Barnard: ". . . an organizational purpose has directly no meaning for an individual. What has meaning is the organization's relation to him — what burdens it imposes, what benefits it confers."[27] The individual's connection with the organization is contractual, an exchange of money or other rewards for services rendered. His dedication to the organization's goals is not necessary for its existence.

Barnard defines an organization as a system of consciously coordinated activities or forces of two or more persons. In this definition there is no suggestion that employees have common motives or are committed to organizational ends. Coordination can be achieved without any commitment on their part.

Argyris defines an organization even more realistically. In his tentative conceptual definition, an organization is:

1. a plurality of parts
2. each achieving specific objectives, and
3. maintaining themselves through their interrelatedness, and
4. simultaneously adapting to the external environment, thereby
5. maintaining the interrelated state of the parts.[28]

2. ***Extended scope.*** Administrative theory used to deal almost exclusively with industrial organizations but the behaviorists have broadened it to include the fields of public administration, medicine and public health, edu-

---

[25] Parsons, Talcott, *Structure and Process in Modern Societies*, Glencoe, Ill.: The Free Press, 1960, p. 17.

[26] Etzioni, Amitai, *Modern Organizations*, Englewood Cliffs, N.J.:Prentice-Hall, 1964, p. 3.

[27] Barnard, Chester, *The Functions of the Executive*, Cambridge, Mass.: Harvard University Press, 1938, p. 88.

[28] Argyris, Chris, "Understanding Human Behavior in Organizations: One Viewpoint," in Mason Haire, ed., *Modern Organization Theory*, New York: John Wiley and Sons, 1959, p. 125.

cation, religious sects, armies, political parties — in short, every kind of organization. The rationale for this extension of interest is that basic concepts and patterns of administration are common to all organizations regardless of their purpose.

3. ***Relationship between the formal and informal organization.*** The Human Relations movement revealed the existence of an informal organization existing synchronously with the formal organization and showed that in the informal organization workers found the friendliness, status, feeling of belonging, and other psychological satisfactions which the formal organization failed to provide. The behaviorists recognize the validity of these findings but argue that the presentation is imbalanced and inadequate — imbalanced because it plays down the role of the formal organization and inadequate because it glosses over many variables.

The ways in which the two organizations interact and their effects on each other need further investigation. Workers are often members of more than one informal group. A leader in one may be a follower in another. Leaders in the formal organization may also be leaders in the informal. Some groups cut across departmental and divisional lines, others include both workers and administrators. Some exist off-the-job and others on-the-job; some are work-related, others are not; some have ties with other organizations outside the work place. These and other aspects of the interrelationship of the two organizations are the subject of in-depth behavioral investigations using the research methodology of the social sciences.

4. ***Reward system.*** Workers receive economic, social, or symbolic rewards for their efforts. Disputing the claims of the scientific management school, human relations advocates argued that economic rewards such as salaries and bonuses were less potent incentives than non-economic rewards such as affection, recognition, and esteem. From the behavioral standpoint, both approaches are incomplete.

Studies show that blue-collar workers give up desirable jobs at low salaries for undesirable jobs at higher salaries. They forego challenging, congenial positions for dull, repetitive jobs which pay more. They do not want to be singled out for praise because they fear the unfavorable comments and resentment of their co-workers. On the other hand, symbolic rewards and status symbols such as titles, reserved parking spaces, and imposing private offices are more powerful motivators for professional and white-collar workers than economic rewards. Lawyers give up high incomes to become judges at lesser annual salaries because of the prestige that attaches to a judicial position.

5. ***Systems theory.*** A distinctive feature of the behavioral school is its reliance on systems theory and analysis as a means of studying organizations.

A system is a delimited group of interconnected and interrelated elements functioning as a unit to produce a total effect. Griffiths' definition of a system as "a complex of elements in mutual interaction" has the virtues of brevity and simplicity.[29] For example, an automobile is a mechanical system, a dog is a biological system, and a school is a social system.

A social system is a conceptualization, not a physical entity. A class is a social system consisting of students and teacher and their interrelationships. It is part of a larger social system, the department, which is part of another, the school, and so on. Group and personal behavior occur in the context of a social system. All except the smallest systems have subsystems and all except the largest have suprasystems.

For example, the school district as a suprasystem is composed of:

a. A client system: students.
b. A technical system: supervisors, teachers, paraprofessionals, and other operational personnel.
c. A managerial system: superintendent, central office staff, principals, and other administrators.
d. An institutional system: board of education and residents of the school district.[30]

Systems are classified as open or closed. A closed system is one which is isolated from its environment. It does not affect and is not affected by its surroundings. It is doubtful that any closed system exists since everything in some way affects, or is affected by, its environment. Perhaps the only example of a closed system is this universe, assuming that no other universe exists.

An open system interacts with its environment. It has an energy exchange with it. The classic example is a burning candle which consumes oxygen and gives off carbon dioxide.

---

[29] Griffiths, Daniel, "Administrative Theory and Change in Organizations," in Matthew B. Miles, ed., *Innovation in Education*, New York: Teachers College Press, 1964, p. 428.

[30] Adapted from R.L. Johns, "State Organization and Responsibilities for Education," in *Implications for Education of Prospective Changes in Society*, ed. Edgar L. Morphet and Charles O. Ryan, New York: Citation Press, 1967, pp. 20-22.

Open systems have a tendency to maintain themselves in steady states. They try to maintain equilibrium by self-regulating mechanisms. Thus, if a window is opened and a draft created, a candle will flicker but gradually stabilize itself unless the incoming air is so overpowering as to quench its flame. A principal who tries to inaugurate change may encounter resistance from faculty members who do not wish the usual equilibrium of the school to be disturbed.

It should be remembered, however, that a steady state is not necessarily a static state. Rather it is a state of dynamic equilibrium in which a school is responding to outside or inside pressures, or both, which seek to change its objectives, materials, and methods.

Another characteristic of open systems is equifinality. Indentical results can be obtained from different procedures and under different conditions. Thus two teachers using different methods can obtain similar results from two different groups of children.

Open systems are also characterized by feedback. Feedback is informational or evaluative data coming from within or without the system which is useful to the system and its subunits. It is output which is fed back as input to influence succeeding outputs. Effective principals provide for feedback processes to improve the functioning of their schools. Often, however, the feedback they receive is limited, biased, and inaccurate because of faulty feedback mechanisms.

The traditional method of studying an organization was mechanistic; it was divided into its component parts and each was studied separately on the assumption that the whole was the sum of its parts. But a system is more than the sum of the segments that compose it. An automobile, for instance, is more than all the mechanisms and structures which make up its engine and body. To understand an automobile, one must know the purpose for which it was designed, the order and interrelationship of its parts, and their relationship to each other and to the whole. Since the parts of an automobile are interdependent, the interaction contributes to the total performance.

For the mechanistic approach to social systems the behavioral school substitutes an organismic viewpoint, that is, a point of view which accentuates the wholeness of the organism and examines it scientifically. From this logico-mathematical standpoint, principles can be derived and theories formulated.

A social system consists of parts, interactions, and goals.[31] The basic parts are the individual, the formal organization, the informal organization, status and role patterns, and the physical environment of work. These parts are bound into a configuration called the organizational system by the processes of communication, balance, and decision-making.

The importance of communication has long been recognized. It is the lifeblood of an organization, for without it cooperative activity would be impossible. In the past, communication has been studied as public relations or as the vertical-horizontal, downward-upward, line-staff, and formal-informal flow of information. It was not usually conceived as a means of control or as a link holding the parts of an organization together. Contemporary writers consider communication as a stimulus for action and as a control and coordinating mechanism which binds an organization's decision centers into a coherent pattern. They discuss communication networks, information flow, feedback, and other topics arising from investigations in cybernetics.

Balance is defined as "an equilibrating mechanism whereby the various parts of the system are maintained in an harmoniously structured relationship to each other.[32] Quasi-automatic balance is the propensity of an organization to maintain a steady state. Organizations adapt without much difficulty to changes which are minor and within established procedures. Innovative balance refers to an organization's ability to adapt to changes outside the scope of existing programs and at the same time maintain internal harmony. It involves the quantity and variety of information present in a system at a particular time and its ability to "forget" previously learned solutions to change problems.

An organization is also held together by its decision-making process. March and Simon distinguish two classes of decisions, decisions to produce and decisions to participate in the system.[33] The former results from an interplay between an individual and the demands of the organization. Participatory decisions relate to the reasons why individuals remain in or leave organizations. Both depend, on the one hand, on the jobs which individuals hold and their expectations and, on the other hand, the organizational structure and expectations.

Of what value is systems theory to a school administrator? It is a model

---

[31] This paragraph and the next three are based on William G. Scott, "Organization Theory: An Overview and Appraisal" in Schoderbek, Peter P., *Management Systems*, New York: John Wiley and Sons, 1967, pp. 46-49.

[32] Ibid., p. 48.

[33] March, James G. and Simon, Herbert A., *Organizations*, New York: John Wiley and Sons, 1958, Chapters 3 and 4.

or conceptual analogue for examining the way a school functions. It indicates that a school is a suprasystem composed of interrelated and interdependent subsystems and that the boundaries of these subsystems must be clearly demarcated to prevent duplication and waste. The relationships and interdependencies among the subsystems makes the whole greater than the sum of its parts.

Systems theory is also a theory base for research, a framework around which an investigator can organize his observations and thinking. It is a guide by which school personnel can bring about curricular change and improve the quality of a school's service to its students and community. Finally, it is a method of budgeting and evaluation, of determining the financial needs of each component and of assessing the relationships between input and output.

Application to education. The impact of the behavioral approach on administrative practice in education has thus far been minimal, perhaps because it is relatively new. It has come to the fore only in recent years and many experienced schoolmen are not yet acquainted with its content and method.

Perhaps, too, it has failed to affect administrative practice because its synthesis has not yet been fully effectuated. The process of combining the findings from the social and behavioral studies and the findings of the scientific management and human relations schools into a coherent whole is still in progress and not yet complete.

New textbooks in educational administration and supervision are now written from a theoretical standpoint in contrast to the older type which were filled with how-to-do-its and tricks of the trade. The cookbook approach failed because procedures used successfully in one setting could not always be employed in another. More importantly, it lacked intellectual substance and did not develop educators capable of conceptualizing a school in its larger aspects and coping with the social forces operating upon it. The new texts are inter-disciplinary in nature, a fusion of several disciplines. Their effect will be seen in the course of time.

The behavioral school has, however, already influenced thinking about morale, leadership, change, and the interrelationship of the individual and the organization. More will be said about these topics in later units.

SCHOOLS OF ADMINISTRATIVE THEORY

	Classical School (1910-1930)	**Human Relations School (1930-1960)**	**Behavioral School (1960 to present)**
Proponents:	Weber, Taylor, Fayol	Mayo, Follett, Roethlisberger	Barnard, Simon, Etzioni
Representative Concepts:	1. The characteristics and merits of bureaucracy. 2. The elements of management. 3. The application of the principles of scientific management. 4. The formal organization. 5. Motivation by economic rewards.	1 The informal organization. 2. Socially determined norms. 3. Conflict resolution. 4. Communication. 5. Participative decision-making. 6. Motivation by non-economic rewards.	1. Realistic concept of organization. 2. Relationship between formal and informal organization. 3. Systems theory. 4. Role theory. 5. Integration of individual and organization. 6. Motivation by economic, social, and symbolic rewards.
Application:	Concerned with industrial plants and, to some extent, public administration.	Concerned with industrial and commercial enterprises and, to some extent, public administration.	Concerned with organizations of all types: industrial, military, business, religious, educational, etc.

SELECTED READINGS

Callahan, Raymond E., *Education and the Cult of Efficiency,* University of Chicago Press, 1962.

A detailed account of the effect of the scientific management movement on education in the period 1910 to 1930. The consequences for American education were tragic, as Professor Callahan's study convincingly shows.

Etzioni, Amitai, *Modern Organizations*, Englewood Cliffs, N.J.: Prentice-Hall, 1964.

A brief, readable, and scholarly work employing the structuralist or behavioral approach. Focuses on organizational goals, organizational structure, and the social environment of organizations.

Gilbreth, Frank B., *Principles of Scientific Management*, Easton, Pa.: Hive Publishing Company, 1973.

A facsimile reprint of a 1912 book. Written in catechetical style, it answers questions raised by magazine readers on scientific management.

Haber, Samuel, *Efficiency and Uplift*, University of Chicago Press, 1964.

A detailed and critical examination of scientific management in the Progressive Era, 1890-1920. Particularly valuable for its discussion of the work of the "reformers" who came under Taylor's influence.

Lane, W.R., Corwin, R.G., and Monahan, W., *Foundations of Educational Administration: A Behavioral Analysis*, New York: Macmillan, 1966.

An introductory text keyed to concepts and research findings in the social and behavioral sciences that are fundamental to the management of educational organizations. Among the topics given special emphasis are communication, internal control, evaluation, and morale.

Owens, Robert G., *Organizational Behavior in Schools*, Englewood Cliffs, N.J.: Prentice-Hall, 1970.

A summary of important findings in the behavioral sciences which can be used by school administrators in their professional practice. Each chapter gives a concise description of the "state of the art" in a particular area, emphasizes significant ideas or studies, and suggests implications for school administration.

Schoderbek, Peter P., ed., *Management Systems*, 2nd ed., New York: John Wiley and Sons, 1971.

A book of readings in the field of business management, many of which have applicability to education. The first section deals with theoretical constructs and cybernetics; the second, with information and information systems.

Simon, Herbert A., *Administrative Behavior*, New York: Macmillan, 1958.
Widely acknowledged as an important contribution to the study of formal organization and administration. Professor Simon's thesis is that decision-making is the heart of administration. His conclusions are generally applicable to all types of organizations.

Taylor, Frederick Winslow, *Scientific Management*, New York: Harper and Row, 1947.
Comprises in a one-volume edition Taylor's *Shop Management, Principles of Scientific Management*, and his *Testimony Before the Special House of Representatives Committee*.

TOPICS FOR DISCUSSION

1. What is wrong, if anything, about applying the principles of scientific management to education?

2. In contemporary education is a superintendent primarily an educator or a manager? Which should he be? What prevents him from conforming to a concept of his role as an educational leader?

3. Are Fayol's 14 principles applied by your school principal or superintendent? Explain. Fayol's list of principles is not exhaustive. Suggest and discuss at least one other principle.

4. Re-read the section dealing with the bureaucratic nature of school organizations, p. 4. Do you agree in whole or in part with it? Cite reasons and examples to justify your point of view.

5. Do the supervisors in your school follow a policy of close or general supervision? What are the practical effects of the policy they follow? Would you recommend a change? Why?

6. Discuss the informal organization in your school. Consider the network of groups that compose it, the interlocking memberships, and the group leaders and the nature of their leadership. Of what value is the informal organization? Does it have any undesirable features? If you were principal, what use, if any, would you make of it?

7. The participation of teachers in decision-making is a concept widely written about and approved in educational literature. Do teachers really want to participate, knowing the time and study that participation requires? If so, what kind of decisions should their involvement be limited to?

8. "The school is a social system." Explain.

9. How does your school superintendent use communication as a stimulus for action and as a means of control and coordination? Cite one or more examples to illustrate.

10. Illustrate quasi-automatic and innovative balance by reference to your school system.

11. Compare a textbook on school administration written before 1960 with the one written after 1970. What differences in subject matter and mode of treatment do you perceive?

12. From your reading of this chapter what new insights have you gained?

TAYLOR AND MAYO COMPARED

By
Reinhart Bendix

Taylor differed from Mayo on several major points, yet the two men shared certain beliefs. Both believed that management must base its practices on principles established by scientific study. They both held that a managerial elite can bring about harmony and increased industrial production. They also maintained that industrial conflicts are harmful and production restrictions by workers result from erroneous views clung to by management and labor.

Their differences are significant. Mayo believed that workers act in natural solidarity with their fellows. Managers need more than technical training; they must develop logical thinking and master human-social facts. They must be able "to assess and handle the concrete difficulties of human collaboration," and workers must feel that their labor is socially necessary. Change must arise from within as a result of an acknowledged need. Since management can only lead to the extent that it is accepted by workers, its major objective should be to foster cooperative teamwork among its employees.

Major contributions in the history of ideas often consist in an author's striking summary of old ideas. I believe this is true of Mayo's work. There are traces of the "New Thought" movement in his emphasis upon the strategic importance of mental and emotional factors in the make-up of managers and workers. Cooperation in industry is identified by Mayo with society's capacity to survive; and this belief is akin to, if not identical with, the ideal of cooperation which inspired the employee-representation plans and the open-shop campaign of the 1920's. Mayo's neglect of trade-unions and of their role in industry is well in line with the open-shop campaign also, for in this campaign employers were not only fighting unions, but also introducing many measures designed to forestall them by satisfying the demands of workers in line with managerial objectives.

"Taylor and Mayo Compared," by Reinhart Bendix, *Work and Authority in Industry,* published by John Wiley and Sons, Inc. Copyright © 1956, pp. 311-316. Reprinted by permission of author.

Some managers had also anticipated Mayo with regard to a reassessment of the motivation of workers. During the 1920's, several writers had pointed out that it was wrong to think workers were interested only in money. Instead workers wanted to feel they were doing something worth while and that they had the respect of others. Failure to take this into account would wreck even the best intentioned welfare plans. "I know of one plant in particular," wrote a manager in 1923, "where everything conceivable seems to have been provided for the workman, but which fails as an example of maximum achievement, because of a taint of patronization. This makes it lose whatever significance it might otherwise have. . . . We must remember that we are living in a democratic community. Managerial achievement in human organization is not dependent on mechanical devices nor routine methods. . . . We are leading men, not handling robots."[1]

In comments such as these there was an awareness of the human problems in labor management that had not been apparent before. Nevertheless, these were incidental remarks which could not make inroads upon the settled conviction that workers were wage-pursuing automata or at any rate that employers could consider them only as factors of production. Even the managerial emphasis upon the attitudes and feelings of workers was often little more than a reference to another cost factor, which had to be taken into account. Views like these were mere intimations of Mayo's contribution. For Mayo used scientific investigations to prove workers were not self-interested individuals but persons with attitudes and feelings which had to be considered in terms other than a test of their aptitudes for better job placement.

A comparison and contrast between Mayo and Taylor is most illuminating in this connection. Mayo certainly shared Taylor's belief in science as the foundation upon which an enlightened management should base its approach. Taylor had advanced the idea of a managerial elite, which by means of a "mental revolution" could increase wages as well as profits. To do so it had only to base its shop management and the selection and training of workers upon the results of scientific studies. Though Mayo did not accept Taylor's techniques, his conception of a managerial or administrative elite which would bring about industrial harmony and increased production had much in common with Taylor's idea of a managerial elite. Both men were concerned with discovering the causes of low productivity or of output restriction; both insisted that industrial conflicts were harmful and that the cooperation of employers and workers should be increased; and both attrib-

[1] *AMR*, Vol. XII, November, 1923, pp. 7-8.

uted the output restrictions of workers to the mistaken views of labor and management.

Nevertheless, Taylor differed from Mayo on certain major points. He thought workers were justified to restrict their output as long as their increased productivity was not reflected in higher earnings. In this respect Taylor was certainly not typical of the managers, whose ideas and practices he sought to influence. yet he and they were at one in their endeavor to test each worker as an individual, since in their judgment it was his aptitude for work which counted, not his relations to his fellow-workers. As a group, workers were regarded as intrinsically hostile to management, since they tended to promote both the organization of trade-unions and the output restriction which trade-unions encouraged.[2] In these respects Taylor and his followers continued the tradition of regarding each worker as a wage-maximizing individual in isolation.

Elton Mayo broke with that tradition. His research confirmed his belief that workers acted in natural solidarity with their fellows, not as isolated individuals. As a result of Mayo's work, there was a marked increase in the existing tendency of managers and their spokesmen to concern themselves with the attitudes and feelings of workers. Moreover, Mayo extended his analysis to the qualities and practices of management, and he reinterpreted the meaning of managerial authority in industry.

During the 1920's and 1930's, industrial psychologists had attempted to put the selection, training, and job placement of workers on a scientific basis. This concern with relative aptitudes for different work operations had led to speculations concerning the motivation of workers, but this had never gone much beyond a commonplace reflection of currently fashionable psychological theories. Mayo brought these trends together into a new and striking synthesis which he contrasted with the "rabble hypothesis" of economic theory. According to that hypothesis, (1) society consists of unorganized individuals, (2) every individual acts in a manner calculated to secure his self-interest, and (3) every individual thinks logically. In opposing these opinions Mayo pointed out that most people do not think logically or systematically most of the time. They do so rather when they meet a personal crisis, which they seek to meet by logical thinking only because they

---

[2]Taylor accepted these views of management, but he probably differed somewhat from the average manager by his insistence that the individual worker's cooperation with the tests of scientific management should be enlisted with the definite assurance of higher earnings, if productivity was increased as a result. According to Taylor's own testimony, there were many managers who were willing enough to systematize job placement through aptitude tests and training programs, but who were unwilling to reward higher output with higher earnings.

can no longer rely upon social routine. Thus, both logical thinking and the pursuit of self-interest appeared to Mayo as a measure of last resort "when social association has failed,"for such association makes logical thinking unnecessary and imparts to the individual socially sanctioned standards in lieu of his personally defined self-interest.[3] In this view economic self-interest appears as the exception rather than the rule; and the willingness of the worker to cooperate with management and increase his output is no longer conceived as a response to appropriate incentives. Instead the worker is seen as the product of personal sentiments and emotional involvements; his thinking is nonlogical, and his conduct on the job is determined by his "desire to stand well with [his] fellows."[4] It is apparent that this approach tended to intensify the managerial concern with the attitudes and feelings of workers at the same time that it de-emphasized the importance of their economic self-interest.

Mayo's second contribution consisted in providing a new vocabulary of motivation for the managerial interpretation of managers and workers. In the 1920's the ideal image of the salaried employee and manager had been contrasted with real wants of the worker, a contrast of images which seemed to exclude the worker from the promise of striving and success as he had never been excluded before. In lieu of the calculated pursuit of self-interest and the struggle for survival, and also in lieu of a career of "winning friends and influencing people," Mayo developed an image of man as a creature of sentiments and nonlogical thinking, whose one overriding motive was the desire to stand well with his fellows. This image was applied to employers and workers alike.

Nevertheless, the significance of these common human traits differed between these two groups, according to Mayo. Although "social routines" suffice for the most part in the life of the worker and "logical reasoning" comes into play only when he is conspicuously lacking in "human skill" or when he confronts an emergency, it *ought to be* the other way around as far as the administrative or managerial elite is concerned. Mayo was emphatic in demanding that the elite control its sentiments, develop logical thinking, and, hence, master the "human-social facts."

---

[3]Mayo, *Social Problems,* pp. 40-40. Cf. also Mayo's own summary, *ibid.,* pp. 111-12.

[4]It may be remarked that Mayo's view of the worker extends past tendencies of managerial thinking in so far as it sees him both as a product of his social environment and of his instinctual equipment. In Mayo's view human instincts are satisfied primarily in man's social environment, and he assigns to management the task of manipulating "human relations" in this environment so as to satisfy these instincts and obtain increased production. Cf. Mayo, *Social Problems,* p. 122, and *The Human Problems of an Industrial Civilization* (Boston: Division of Research, Harvard Business School, 1946), p. 185.

> We have failed to train students in the study of social situations; we have thought that first-class technical training was sufficient in a modern and mechanical age. As a consequence we are technically competent as no other age in history has been; and we combine this with utter social incompetence. This defect of education and administration has of recent years become a menace to the whole future of civilization. . . .

And he follows this indictment with his vision of the future:

> The administrator of the future must be able to understand the human-social facts for what they actually are, unfettered by his own emotion or prejudice. He cannot achieve this ability except by careful training — a training that must include knowledge of relevant technical skills, of the systematic ordering of operations, and of the organization of cooperation.[5]

Mayo made short shrift of the invidious distinction between the real wants of workers and the ideal qualities of employers.Unlike Taylor, he resolutely advocated an analysis of the wants and qualities of employers as well as of workers. He saw the individuals in both groups as creatures of sentiment and nonlogical thinking. The difference between them consisted simply in the capacity of an administrative elite to engage in logical thinking, to be independent from social routines, to free themselves from emotional involvement in order to "assess and handle the concrete difficulties of human collaboration." These were exceptional attainments by definition. Indeed, it may be noted that Mayo did not speak altogether of the same kind of "logical reasoning" when referring to the two groups of workers and managers. For in his critique of economics he speaks of logical thinking in terms of the calculated pursuit of self-interest, and this refers clearly to the masses of the people. But in his critical appraisal of the administrative elite he refers to a "logic of understanding" that is needed in order to "organize sustained cooperation." The implication is of course that the elite can understand the "nonlogic" of the masses, while the masses resort to logic only in emergencies and because of their lack of social skills. Yet, despite this dissimilarity between managers and men, Mayo looked upon both groups with the same scientific detachment. Different as the abilities are between managers and workers, both groups are properly the subject of scientific analysis which will ensure cooperation in economic enterprises. Henceforth, the managerial elite would no longer be the subject of moral exhortation, for its "virtues" were no longer the self-evident synonyms of success. Rather success and virtue had become synonymous with the "human-social skills"

---

[5] Mayo, *Social Problems*, pp. 120, 122.

which, according to Mayo, would result from the systematic training of the managerial elite of the future.

Mayo's third contribution involved a reinterpretation of managerial authority. The guiding consideration of his research had been to work toward a society in which it is "possible for the individual to feel, as he works, that his work is socially necessary; he must be able to see beyond his group to the society." Already in 1919 he had concluded that failure in this respect would make the disintegration of society inevitable.[6] Such rather portentous statements have recurred frequently in Mayo's work, and his researches make clear what they mean. In his earliest study of a Philadelphia textile mill the productivity of the spinning department increased most strikingly, not simply when various rest-pause arrangements were introduced, but when one of them was introduced in response to the particular wishes of the workers themselves. In the case of the Relay Assembly Test Room productivity increased, according to Mayo, because the cooperation of the workers had been obtained. They had had an opportunity to choose their fellow-workers and therefore constituted a team that worked without "coercion from above or limitation from below." These are positive instances of cooperation. But in his search for the factors which account for cooperation Mayo also came upon instances of noncooperation. In the analysis of a work group (the Bank Wiring Observation Room) he and his associates discovered conclusive evidence of informal group control over the work performance of individual group members.

Critics of Mayo and his school have pointed out that both the willing teamwork of the six relay assemblers and the output restriction of 14 workers in the Bank Wiring Room were instances of cooperation. But in a managerial context this objection is beside the point. As T.N. Whitehead has said:

> What is feared to integration within a small group is that it may organize itself in opposition to the larger whole — and this it certainly will do if its existence be threatened; but equally, a protected group will endeavor to satisfy its wider interests by collaborating with the organization of which it is a logical part. In this way, its loyalty will extend to the firm as a whole.[7]

What can managers do so that their work groups feel protected in their interests, what can they do so that individual workers will reassess their

[6] See pp. 129-130.

[7] T. N. Whitehead, *Leadership in a Free Society* (Harvard University Press, Cambridge, Mass., 1936), pp. 98-99.

personal and social involvements inside and outside the enterprise in such a way as to increase their productivity? Whitehead's answer to this question is, I think, representative of the "Mayo School."

> Change, to be acceptable to a group, must come from within, and must appear as the visible need of its present activities. . . . So management in industry can lead its groups to just that extent to which it is itself accepted by those groups, and it can lead no further; anything beyond that will be resisted as compulsive interruption to social living.[8]

And what Whitehead says of the work group applies to the individual as well. The change from output restriction to willing cooperation depends in both instances upon an indirect inducement. Hence, Mayo's view of the managerial task may be defined as the endeavor to provide an organizational environment in which employees can fulfill their "eager human desire for cooperative activity."[9] The major objective of management is to foster cooperative teamwork among its employees.

---

[8] *Ibid.*, p. 110.
[9] Mayo, *Social Problems*, p. 112.

QUESTIONS

1. Mayo says administrators must master social-human facts. Describe an educational situation of which you have first-hand knowledge and show how a school administrator failed or succeeded in assessing and handling the concrete difficulties of human collaboration.

2. Mayo argues that change must arise from within an organization as a result of an acknowledged need. Yet some important educational changes have resulted from external forces; for example, laws, judicial decisions, and pressure groups. Cite examples of change resulting from internal forces and others from external forces.

WHAT IS MEANT BY ORGANIZATION AND ITS PRINCIPLES?

By
James D. Mooney and
Alan C. Reiley

The authors of the following article were for years executives of General Motors in the area of exporting. Their work brought them into contact with business, government, and military organizations in many different countries.

As they see it, organization is the form taken by every human association to attain a common purpose. It is the channel through which the acts and policies of management become effective.

Management is the psychic principle, the force which actuates, directs, and controls the organizational plan and procedure. Organization is analogous to the human body and management is the psychic force which activates it.

Management is the technique of handling people. The technique of organization is that of relating specific duties in a coordinated scheme. Logically the technique of organization precedes that of management.

A technique can be acquired, especially if its underlying principles are known. As an industrial organization grows in size, a knowledge of principles becomes increasingly important to prevent disintegration or inertia. If these principles are identified, then individuals who fall far short of genius can apply them efficiently.

Every human society, however primitive, must have something in common, and it is as a means for the furtherance or the protection of these common interests that formal organizations appear. If, however, we search beneath such formal organizations for their psychic fundaments, we find them in full operation even in acts and objectives where only one person is

---

"What is Meant by Organization and its Principles?," from *Onward Industry! The Principles of Organization and Their Significance to Modern Industry,* by James D. Mooney and Alan C. Reiley. Copyright © 1931, by Mooney and Reiley; renewed 1959 by Ida May Mooney. Reprinted by permission of Harper & Row, Publishers, Inc.

concerned. Thus, we frequently speak of organizing one's self for a given purpose.

The very act of walking implies that the mind has defined its objective, the sentiment has affirmed it as a desirable objective, and that the will is moving toward the objective. It is impossible to exclude the idea of an objective, and of a definitely organized movement to attain it, from any psychic act, however casual or inconsequential.

When two persons combine for a given purpose, we have the same psychic fundaments, plus the principle which must underlie all associated effort. Let us again employ the simplest illustration. Two men unite their strength to move some object which is too heavy or bulky to be moved by one. Here we have associated effort, which is synonymous with organization, and likewise coordination, the first principle which underlies all such effort.

This simple illustration indicates clearly the exact definition of organization. *Organization is the form of every human association for the attainment of a common purpose.*

Organization has been termed the formal side of management; likewise the machinery of management, the channel through which the measures and policies of management become effective. There is truth in these descriptions, but not the whole truth. Again organization has been likened to the framework, the articulated skeleton of the business structure. Here again the simile is sound as far as it goes, but inadequate. It implies that organization refers only to the differentiation and definition of individual duties, as set forth in the familiar organization charts. But duties must relate to procedure, and it is here that we find the real dynamics of organization, the motive power through which it moves to its determined objective. Organization, therefore, refers to more than the frame or skeleton of the industrial edifice. It refers to the complete body, with all of its correlated functions. And it refers to these functions as they appear in action, the very pulse and heart beats, the circulation, the respiration, the vital movement, so to speak, of the organized unit. It refers to the coordination of all these movements as they combine and cooperate for the common purpose. This analogy between human group organization and the *biological organization* of the physical body has been noticed by several writers.

If the sphere of organization is so all inclusive, how then are we to define administration and management? Following the previous analogy, management is nothing less than the psychic principle itself. Management is the vital spark which actuates, directs and controls the plan and procedure of organization. With management enters the personal factor, without which nobody could be a living being with any directive toward a given purpose. The relation of management to organization is analogous to the relation of the psychic complex to the physical body. Our bodies are simply the means and the instrument through which the psychic force moves toward the attainment of its aims and desires. It is evident also that, in order to attain these objects, the body must be adequate to the performance of this instrumental function. This same instrumental adequacy is an absolute necessity in a business organization, and for the same reasons. Through this analogy we may see clearly the importance of formal organization in the pursuit of business objectives, and the need for its broader and more intensive study.

This description of the true relation between organization and management also indicates exactly what is meant by system in organization. As organization relates to procedure, involving the inter-relation of duties as well as duties in themselves, so system may be defined as the technique of procedure.

The introduction of the word "technique" gives us another slant on the relation of management to organization. It would appear from what we have already written that organization is in some way subordinated to management. In a practical sense so it is, for the instrument must always appear subordinate to that of which it is the instrument, and, furthermore, one important duty of management is to provide its own instrument, which means to organize. Yet in another sense the relationship is reversed. If the building presupposes the builder, or organizer, the function of management also presupposes the building, or something to manage. Let us therefore compare these two things in terms of technique.

The technique of management, in its human relationships, can be best described as the technique of handling or managing people, which should be based on a deep and enlightened human understanding. The technique of organization may be described as that of relating specific duties or functions in a completely coordinated scheme. This statement of the difference between managing and organizing clearly shows their intimate relationship. It also shows, which is our present purpose, that the technique of organizing is anterior, in logical order, to that of management. It is true that a sound organizer may, because of temperamental human failings, be a poor manager, but on the other hand it is inconceivable that a poor organizer can make a good manager, if he has any real organizing work to do.

All history bears witness to the reality of that something we have called organizing genius, a genius which is truly creative, like the genius manifested in the higher realms of creative art. Indeed organizing is an art, which means that, like every art, it must have its own technique, which in turn must be based on principles. That the great organizers of history applied these principles unconsciously proves nothing except that their technique was not acquired; it was inherent in their genius. Nevertheless all experience proves that a technique can be acquired, and the more readily if its underlying principles are known. This does not mean that a knowledge of these principles will make everyone who knows them an efficient organizer. To know principles is one thing, and to apply them efficiently is another. Nevertheless it stands to reason that a knowledge of these principles must be the first step in the acquisition of a sound organizing technique.

The importance of such knowledge is evident in the problems that now confront modern industry, among which that of growth through organization is the most important. An industrial organization may achieve a certain limited size through the business acumen of some individual, the genius of an inventor or scientist, or the knowledge of tools and production technique of some engineer. To expand this organization beyond a limited size, however, requires some experience and knowledge of the sheer technique of organization, and how its principles must be applied in order to provide for the necessary growth. As an industrial organization grows in size, a knowledge of these principles becomes increasingly important, for two reasons. If these principles are not understood and properly applied the organization either becomes threatened with disintegration, or it develops an increasing inertia which constitutes in itself an obstacle to further growth.

Far more conspicuous in the public eye, however, is the other side of the picture, furnished in the vastness of the leading units of modern industry. These institutions may be accounted for by that faculty we have called organizing genius; in fact this is the usual explanation. Nearly always, in these great institutions, there is some one individual whom popular belief identifies as the real architect and creator of the organized edifice. If we grant the soundness of this belief, then we cannot escape its implications, namely that industrial growth through organization must ever be dependent on that exceptional quality we call genius. The answer is that even organizing genius cannot create principles of organization; it can only apply them, and if these principles can be found and definitely identified then human qualities that fall far short of genius should be adequate for their efficient application.

QUESTIONS

1. It has been said that organization is not an end in itself but a means to an end. Is this statement consonant with the point of view offered by Mooney and Reiley? Explain.

2. "A technique can be acquired and the more readily if its underlying principles are known." What is the difference between a technique and a principle? Illustrate by describing a procedural technique and citing one or more principles which underlie it. Explain how a knowledge of principles may help generate techniques.

UNHUMAN ORGANIZATIONS

By
Harold J. Leavitt

"The theme here is not that human relations theory is either incorrect or immoral. My argument is that it is simply insufficient. It is too narrow a perspective from which to analyze the management of organizations." So states Mr. Leavitt in the introductory section of this article. He suggests that we re-examine our beliefs that organizations are essentially human, that their management is essentially a process of coordinating human effort, and that the best organization is one in which each member contributes his full potential.

A re-examination is necessary because in discarding Taylorism we may have thrown out some of its useful features and because we now have knowledge from the information and communication sciences which may make us question our present beliefs. Bits and pieces of research have resulted in some unexpected findings.

Large organizations should be viewed as differentiated sets of subsystems rather than as unified wholes. This view leads to a management-by-task outlook — the recognition that many subparts of an organization may perform many different kinds of tasks. It follows, then, that many different kinds of managerial practices are called for.

PARTICIPATION — FACT OR FANCY?

Even if we grant that people carry out solutions to business problems more eagerly when they have participated in the decision, does this mean that the solution itself is *better?* Most people seem to think so.

In the early days of industrial psychology, our outlook was much like the industrial engineer's. We were worried about how to define and describe jobs, how to design the physical work place so that people would be more productive. We ignored the feelings and social environments of people —

"Unhuman Organizations," by Harold J. Leavitt, July-August 1962, *Harvard Business Review*. Copyright © 1962 by the President and Fellows of Harvard College; all rights reserved. Reprinted by permission of Harvard Business Review.

worrying instead about things like eye-hand coordination and the effects of noise on performance.

That wave of activity was followed in the 1940's and 1950's by studies of the relationship between emotional and social factors, on the one hand, and productivity and morale, on the other. A large amount of evidence was accumulated revealing that people support what they help to create; that democratically run groups develop greater loyalty and cohesiveness than do autocratically run ones; and that strong identification with and commitment to decisions are generated by honest participation in the planning of those decisions.

In the last ten years, however, a third emphasis has been creeping into behavioral research about organizations — an emphasis on the thinking, analyzing, problem-solving side of human behavior. Earlier in this period, we had concentrated on the willingness of people to *use* the solution, not on the quality of the solution itself. A good solution to a problem, by definition, was one that worked; and could therefore only be a solution that people were willing to carry out; and therefore, in turn, only one in which they had participated. Our research proved the positive relationship between participation and willingness, all right; but sometimes we argued as though we had also proved that participative solutions were *better*, even when measured by some logical or economic yardstick, than solutions arrived at by a separate group of expert planners. We have argued, for example, that people close to the job know more about the job than anyone else. They do not make the kind of silly mistakes that experts unfamiliar with the dirty details might make, and they have more and better ideas than the experts anyway.

So we have tried to have the best of both worlds: workable solutions and logically better and more creative ones, too. But though we have made a good case for human workability, we may have been a little overzealous in laying full claim to creativity and quality, too.

The purpose of this article is to urge that we take another look at our beliefs about the place of people in organizations. They are beliefs that have matured, even oversolidified, in the 1940's and 1950's. And they are beliefs which, until the last couple of years, have seemed as safe and inviolate as the moon.

Let me emphasize from the start that although this article is a critique of

---

AUTHOR'S NOTE: This article draws on material presented at the Massachusetts Institute of Technology's Centennial Symposium on Executive Development in April 1961.

our "human relations" emphasis on people, I am not worried about "manipulation," "group-think," "softness," "conformity," or any of the other recent criticisms. In fact, most theories and techniques of human relations are, to my mind, both sound and progressive. *The theme here is not that human relations theory is either incorrect or immoral. My argument is that it is simply insufficient. It is too narrow a perspective from which to analyze the management of organizations.* But I am not suggesting that we turn back to the earlier and even narrower beliefs of "tough" management. What we have to do is to push beyond the plateau of present beliefs, which are becoming too deeply ingrained among managers and social scientists. Such beliefs now hold:

1. That organizations are and ought to be in their essence *human* systems.
2. Therefore, that the management of organizations is and ought to be in its essence a process of coordinating human effort.
3. Implicitly, that the best organization is the one in which each member contributes up to his "full potential"; and that the best individual manager is he who has set up conditions which maximize the creativity and commitment of his people.
4. And that management is a *unified* rather than a *differentiated* process; i.e., that good management at one level or in one locale of an organization ought to be essentially the same as good management at any other level or locale in that or any other organization. This idea is so implicit, so seldom said aloud, that I cannot be perfectly sure it is really there.

Incidentally, this fourth belief in some unifying essence was, I think, held to by earlier theorists about management, too. To early Taylorists, for example, "rationalization" of work was the pure essence of good management and was, in theory, applicable anywhere and everywhere from president to sweeper.

PARTICIPATIVE BELIEFS

For simplicity, let me refer to the first three of the above as "participative beliefs." They have one common integrating element — the idea that organizations are essentially human. It follows that we should begin our descriptions and analyses of organizations in human terms. They have a value element in common, too — a very strong one; i.e., not only are organizations best described in human units; they *ought* to be human. It is right, many of us believe, to think about organizations from a human point of view, because people *are* more important than anything. Moreover, we are blessed (according to these beliefs) by the happy coincidence that managerial practices which place human fulfillment first also happen to be the most efficient and productive practices.

I can offer no definitive evidence to prove that these beliefs are not straw men. It may be they are not really widely shared by social scientists, managers, consultants, and personnel people. If that should be the case, and they are only fat red herrings, then our re-examination may help to destroy them.

Reasons for Re-Examination

I urge that these beliefs be re-examined not so much because they are wrong, in any absolute sense, and certainly not because the beliefs that preceded them, especially the Tayloristic beliefs, were right. Essentially, the participative beliefs ought to be re-examined for two reasons.

(1) *In so eagerly demolishing Taylorism we may have thrown out some useful parts of the baby with the bath water. We may even be repeating some of the mistakes of Taylorism that we have taken such pains to point out.*

Incidentally Taylor made himself almost too clear a target for those who came later. He had no trouble at all organizing all sorts of humanistic people against him by making statements like this:

"Now one of the very first requirements for a man who is fit to handle pig iron . . . is that he shall be so stupid and so phlegmatic that he more nearly resembles . . . the ox than any other type . . . he must consequently be trained by a man more intelligent than himself."[1]

Such antidemocratic pronouncements probably contributed backhandedly to the oversolidification of the participative beliefs. For while part of the participative target was to improve management practice, part of it was also to win the war against "inhuman" scientific management.

Though it is clear that Taylorism has had some large and unforeseen costs, it also seems clear that present-day Taylorism, i.e., the ideas and techniques of industrial engineering, continue to be viable and almost invariably present in American firms. Human resistance to the techniques has been a real problem, but not always an insurmountable or economically intolerable one. And partially with the naive help of social scientists, the

[1] Frederick W. Taylor, *Scientific Management* (New York, Harper & Brothers, 1911), p. 59.

costs of Taylorism (the slowdown, for instance) have often been eased enough by psychological palliatives (like suggestion systems) to warrant their continued use.

Moreover, we may have overshot, in condemning Taylorism, by *appearing*, at least, to be condemning any *differentiation* of organizations that separates out planning functions from performing functions. We have urged more participation, more involvement, but we have not been very explicit about how far we want to go toward the extreme of having everyone participate in everything all the time.

(2) *We have new knowledge both from the information and communication sciences and the social sciences that may be applicable to organizational problems; and if we freeze on our present beliefs, we may not be able to incorporate that knowledge.*

Two relevant sets of ideas have been emerging over the last few years. One is the development of information technology, a science in which human beings need *not* be the fundamental unit of analysis. We cannot examine that in detail here.[2] The other set is the emerging findings from recent research on individual and group problem solving. This research in which human beings have indeed been the fundamental unit will be the subject of the rest of this discussion.

Self-Programing People

Some remarkably similar findings keep turning up in a number of different places. They look irrelevant at first, but I think they are really quite to the point. For instance, given a problem to solve, people try to develop a program that will solve not only the specific problem at hand but other problems of the same "class." If we give a true-false test, the subject not only tries to answer each question properly; he almost invariably sets up and checks out hypotheses about the order of true and false answers. If he hits the sequence "True, False, True, False," for example, he guesses that this is "really" an alternating series and predicts a "True" for the next one. This is a commonplace finding, known to baseball fans (i.e., the next pitch is "due" to be a fast ball) and gamblers and school kids, and even to social scientists.

[2]See Harold J. Leavitt and Thomas L. Whisler, "Management in the 1980's," HBR November-December 1958, p. 41; or H. A. Simon, "The Corporation: Will It Be Managed by Machines?" in *Management and Corporations,* 1958, edited by M. L. Anshen and G. L. Bach (New York, McGraw-Hill Book Company, Inc., 1960).

The point, which I believe is as fundamental as many other points psychologists have made about the nature of man, is that humans have strong and apparently natural tendencies to program themselves. In many cases a "solution" to a problem is really a program for solving all problems of that class.

The second finding is that the challenge, the puzzle, the motivational impetus for the problem solver also stems in part from this same need — the need to develop a general program. Moreover, when such a general program is discovered, then any particular task within the program is likely to become trivial and uninteresting. When we "understand" tick-tack-toe, the game stops being much fun.

Here is an example from an experiment that will come up again later:

Suppose we ask three people to play the "Common Target Game."[3] The three players are blindfolded and not allowed to talk with one another. At a signal from an instructor each is asked to put up any number of fingers. If each man puts up zero fingers, the sum of the three will of course be zero; and if each man puts up his maximum of ten, the total shown by the three will be 30.

Given these rules, we now set up the following task. The instructor will call out some whole target number between zero and 30. The cooperative objective of the three players (without knowing what the others have done) is to put up enough fingers so that the sum of the fingers will add up exactly to the target number. Thus, if the instructor calls out the number 16, each player tries to hold up enough fingers such that the three together hold a total of 16. They are then told what they actually hit; and if they miss, they try again until they hit that target. Then they are given a new target.

If we play this game for a while and tune in on the players' thoughts, it turns out that each player is busily thinking up general systems for deciding how many fingers to hold up. Usually he says something like this to himself: "There are three of us. Therefore it is probably sensible to start by dividing each target number by three. If the target is 16, we should each take five to begin with. Then we will have to decide who will take the extra one that is

---

[3] Research with this "Common Target Game" was started by Alex Bavelas of Stanford University. For a recent paper on its use see Harold J. Leavitt, "Task Ordering and Organizational Development in the Common Target Game," *Behavioral Science,* July 1960. Bavelas also inspired the communication experiment described later.

left over.'' He then goes on to think up additional sets of rules by which these leftovers can be allocated.

But what he has done in effect is to say this: ''Let us not treat each new target as a brand new problem. let us instead classify all possible targets into three simple categories: (a) *targets evenly divisible by three,* e.g., 15; (b) *targets divisible by three with one left over,* e.g., 16; (c) *targets divisible by three with two left over,* e.g., 17.''Our subject has now simplified the world by classifying all possible targets. No target is any longer novel and unique. It is now a member of one of these three classes.

Moreover, if the players can agree on one general program that permits them to hit targets on one trial, then they rapidly lose interest in the game — well before all targets have been tested. It is exciting, challenging, and disturbing only until a general program has been developed. Once they have developed it, the players can very easily instruct other people, or machines, to play the game according to the system they have developed.

These dual findings — programing oneself out of a challenging and novel situation, and then losing interest — keep showing up. And they keep reiterating the probably obvious point, so clearly observable in children, that people tend to reduce complexity to simplicity, and having done so find that the game isn't so much fun any more.

These findings lead me, very tentatively, to the generalization that high interest, high challenge, may be caused as much by the job at hand (is it already programed or not?) as by ''participation.'' The players in our game participated fully — but they got bored when required routinely to operate their program, despite the fact that it was their own baby. The fun was in the making.

If we make a big jump, we can then ask: is it reasonable to think that we can, in the real world, maintain a continuously challenging ''unprogramed'' state for all members of an organization? . . . especially when members themselves are always searching for more complete programs? . . . and while the demands made upon the organization call for routine tasks like making the same part tomorrow, tomorrow, and tomorrow that was made today?

The answer to this question is not obvious. In fact we have all witnessed the frequent demand of groups of workers for more and more highly detailed job definitions, on the one hand, accompanied by more and more complaints about ''deskilling,'' on the other. For instance, the airline pilot wants more and better ground-control programs to deal with increasing traffic; but once he gets them, he finds that the new programs also reduce the autonomy, the freedom, and the exercise of human judgment that make flying interesting.

Unhuman Teachers

Consider next the development and application of teaching machines — those simple, unsophisticated, mechanical gadgets which ignore the complexities of people, and which use feedback principles that are almost primitive in their simplicity.

With them, if the evidence is correct, we can teach spelling faster than most human teachers can, and perhaps languages too. We can instruct workers in complex machine operation, and often thereby enlarge their jobs. And girls can be taught to wire complex circuits as well as experts do simply by providing them with a sequential series of diagrams projected on a screen at the work place. The girl can control the diagram, moving back two pictures or foward four. Teach her to solder, give her the materials, and she can do the job — fast.

Her job has been enlarged, for she now wires the whole circuit (50 or 60 hours' worth) instead of one small piece. But there is no human interaction here — no patient human teachers; no great involvement; not even very much learning. For the crutch of the teaching machine stays there — always. She can lean on the diagrams next year if she should still want to, and she probably will.

It is beguilingly easy to demean or disavow such gadgets, to relegate them to low-class teaching of routines. It is especially easy to sweep them aside if we have been raised in the tradition of the participative beliefs. For even more than in management these beliefs prevail in education. "Real" teaching is, by current definition, a *human* process. How then can we take seriously devices which completely bypass the human teacher, which are not even in the same ball park with those problems that are believed to be at the very center of the teaching process, i.e., teacher-student rapport, teacher understanding of student personality, student dependency on the teacher?

It is not so much that teaching machines directly threaten present beliefs about teaching; it is rather than they simply bypass large parts of those beliefs. By treating teaching, naively perhaps, as something other than a human relations process, one simply does not face problems that arise as a consequence of human relationships.

Taking this view of things, one begins to wonder how many of the problems of teaching have been *caused* by the human teacher.

Which Kind of Structure?

A little over 12 years ago another area of research got under way at the Massachusetts Institute of Technology which dealt with communication nets and their effects on problem solving by groups. As this body of experimentation has built up, it too has added reason for uneasiness about the unshakability of the participative beliefs.

Let me review the experiments very quickly. They are quite simple in their conception and purpose. They ask how the structure of communication among members of a group affects the way that groups solves a given problem.

Suppose, for example, we connect up groups of five men so that they may communicate *only* through the two-way channels represented by the lines shown below. We can then ask whether comparable groups, working on the same problem, will solve it "better" in Network I than in Network II or Network III.

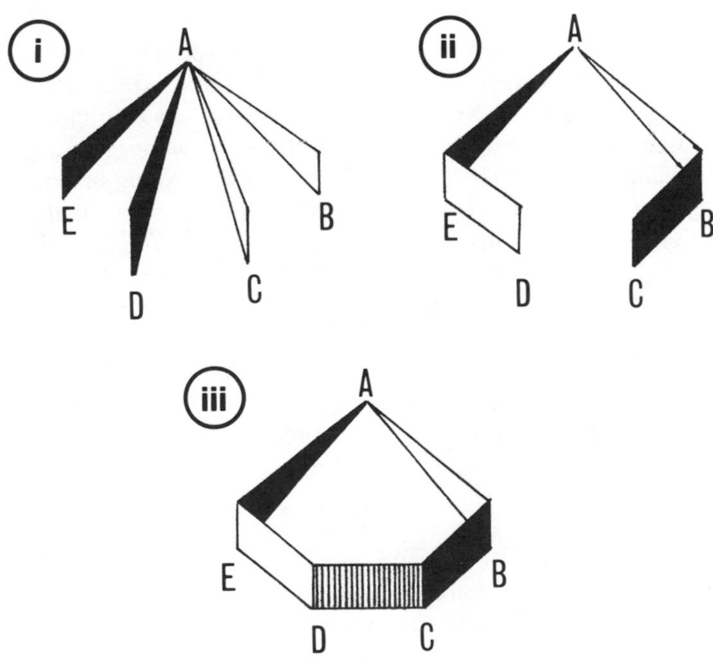

The men are put in booths so that they cannot see one another, and then given this simple problem to solve:

Each man has a cup containing five marbles of different colors. Only *one* corresponding color marble appears in *all* of the cups. The problem is to discover what that single color is, and to do it as fast as possible. Only written communications are allowed — only along the channels open in the particular network being tested. The job is not considered solved until all five men know what the common color is. The problem is used again and again for the same group in the same net, each time with new sets of marbles.

We can then measure the "efficiency" of each net by such factors as speed of problem solving, number of messages sent, number of errors made, clarity of organizational form, specificity of each job in the organization, and clarity of leadership. It turns out that on these simple tasks Network I is far more efficient than II, which in turn is more efficient than III. In other words, groups of individuals placed in Network I within a very few trials solve these problems in an orderly, neat, quick, clear, well-structured way — with minimum messages. In Network III, comparable groups solve the same problems less quickly, less neatly, with less order, and with less clarity about individual jobs and the organizational structure — and they take more paper, too.

However, if we now ask members of these three networks to indicate how *happy* they are in their jobs, we get the reverse effect. Network III people are happier, on the average, than II or I people (though the *center* man in Network I is apt to be quite happy). But since we are concerned with effectiveness, we may argue that happiness is not very important anyway. So let us go on to some other possible criteria of organizational effectiveness: creativity and flexibility.

We find two interesting things. First, when a bright new idea for improvement of operations is introduced into each of these nets, the rapid acceptance of the new idea is more likely in III than in I. If a member of I comes up with the idea and passes it along, it is likely to be discarded (by the man in the middle) on the ground that he is too busy, or the idea is too hard to implement, or "We are doing O.K. already; don't foul up the works by trying to change everything!"

Correspondingly, if we change the problem by introducing "noisy marbles"[4] (marbles of unusual colors for which there are no common names), then again we find that III has advantages over I. Network III is able to adapt to this change by developing a new code, some agreed-on set of names for the colors. Network I seems to have much greater difficulty in adapting to this more abstract and novel job.

So by certain industrial engineering-type criteria (speed, clarity of organization and job descriptions, parsimonious use of paper, and so on), the highly routinized, noninvolving, centralized Network I seems to work best. *But* if our criteria of effectiveness are more ephemeral, more general (like acceptance of creativity, flexibility in dealing with novel problems, generally high morale, and loyalty), then the more egalitarian or decentralized Network III seems to work better.

What shall we conclude? Using the common "efficiency" criteria, the Taylorists are right. But these are narrow and inhuman, and if we use creativity and morale as criteria, modern participative beliefs are right. But are we also to conclude that the criteria of creativity and flexibility and morale are somehow *fundamentally* more important than speed and clarity and orderliness?

Or shall we (and I favor this conclusion) pragmatically conclude that if we want to achieve one kind of goal, then one kind of structure seems feasible? If we want other criteria to govern, then another structure may make sense. Certainly it is reasonable to guess that in the real (as distinct from the laboratory) world, there will be locations and times which might make one set of criteria more important than the other even within the same large organization.

But participative managers, myself once included, will immediately go back to the happiness issue that I treated so cavalierly a few paragraphs ago. They will counter by arguing that Network I cannot work long — for the growing resistance and low morale it generates in its members will eventually cause it to burst.

The evidence is negative. The *relative* importance of this resistance is apparently small. There seem to be fairly cheap ways of compensating for the low morale, yet still keeping the organization going efficiently. To the best of my capacity to speculate, and also the best of my knowledge from extended runs (60 trials) of Network I,[5] it can keep going indefinitely, highly programed and unchallenging as it is to most of its members. Moreover, we

---

[4] Research on this part of the problem was conducted at M.I.T.'s Group Networks Laboratory by L. Christie, D. Luce, and J. Macy; see their *Communication and Learning in Task Oriented Groups,* Research Lab of Electronics, MIT (Tech Report No. 231, May 1952).

[5] A. M. Cohen, W. G. Bennis, and G. H. Wolkon, "The Effects of Continued Practice on the Behaviors of Problem Solving Groups," *Sociometry,* December 1961.

could probably automate Network I rather easily if we wanted to, and get rid of the human factor altogether.

Planned Decisions

In the Common Target Game mentioned earlier — the little game in which three players hold up fingers to try to sum to a target — some other interestingly odd results turn up. For one thing, we find that the game is solved better with an asymmetric system of rewards. If we offer only one player in the group a personal bonus depending on the number of fingers he contributes, groups seem to perform better than if we offer no rewards to anybody or equal rewards to everybody. In fact, if we offer everyone a personal payoff (1 point per finger, say), so that each man gets a reward in accordance with the size of his contribution, performance is not very good but *learning* is very fast. There is evidence, in other words, that competitive groups learn how to solve the problem very quickly, but then refuse to solve it that way because they are so busy competing.

One more finding: If groups simply play the game cooperatively, without any special payoff system, they almost never come up with the one cleanest and simplest solution to it. If, however, we ask them to sit down and plan *how* to play it, they almost always do come up with that neat and elegant system. (The simple, neat solution: A takes everything from 0 to 10; B adds everything from 11 to 20; and so on.)

Tentatively, then, we have these mildly disturbing findings:

- Differentiated groups (ones in which some members are rewarded differently from others) can perform better than undifferentiated groups — whether they be rewarded cooperatively only, or both cooperatively and competitively.
- Competitively motivated groups learn faster than cooperative ones; but their corresponding performance is dampened by their competition.
- Groups that "evolve" by working together directly on the problem come up with different, less clean, and less simple solutions than groups in which the planning and the performing phases of their activity are separated.

These results do not directly contradict any present ideas; but they suggest that manipulation of variables like competition or differentiation of roles may yield results we cannot easily fit into our well-organized and perhaps overly rigidified beliefs about the universal effectiveness of self-determination, wholehearted cooperation, and bottom-up planning.

What Kinds of Teams Win?

Finally, in some research we have been doing recently with the complex year-long business game that has been developed at Carnegie Institute of Technology, another similar finding has turned up.[6] We found that those teams had the highest morale and also performed best in which there was the greatest *differentiation* of influence among team members. That is, teams whose players saw themselves as all about equally influential were less satisfied and made smaller profits than teams whose players agreed that some particular individuals were a good deal more influential than others.

Now bringing the influence problem in at this point may be another red herring. But the optimal distribution of influence, and of power that produces influence, has been one of the problems that has plagued us industrial social scientists for a long time. Does participative management mean, in its extreme form, equal distribution of power throughout the organization? If not, then how should power be distributed? What is a "democratic" distribution? What is an autocratic one? I fear that none of us has satisfactorily resolved these questions. We have made some soft statements, pointing out that participation does not mean that everyone does the same job, and that the president ought still to be the president. But our specifications have not been clear and consistent, and we have never made a very good theoretical case for any optimal differentiation of power within an organization.

Again the finding is antiegalitarian, and in favor of differentiation. Yet egalitarianism of both communication and of power is often assumed to produce, through the participative beliefs, involvement, commitment, and morale.

IDEA OF DIFFERENTIATION

So it is developments in these two areas — the information sciences and bits and pieces of organizational research — that should, I submit, stimulate us to start re-examining our beliefs about the role of people in organizations. Together these developments suggest that we need to become more analytical about organizations, to separate our values from our analyses more than we have up until now; that we need also to take a more microscopic look at large organizations and to allow for the possibility of *differentiating* several kinds of structures and managerial practices within them.

---

[6] W. R. Dill, W. Hoffman, J. J. Leavitt, and T. O'Mara, "Experiences with a Complex Management Game," *California Management Review*, Spring, 1961, pp. 38-51.

Changes in this direction are, of course, already taking place but mostly at the research level (as distinct from the level of applied practice). In practice, participative management and the beliefs that accompany it are clearly very much on the rise. Efforts to promote more open communication across and up and down the organization are visible everywhere. There is not a first-rate business school in the country that does not place heavy emphasis on human relations in industry, with its implicit assumption of the essential role of people in problem solving. Although groups and committees are still dirty words in some industrial quarters, they are not nearly as dirty as they used to be. And certainly *decentralization* is an acceptable idea for almost every educated American executive.

But it is worth pointing out that, even at the level of current practice, participative ideas do not seem to be sweeping into the organization uniformly. In general, we have been concentrating more effort on developing participation at middle-management than at hourly levels — the Scanlon plan notwithstanding. We train supervisors, study R & D groups, counsel top management, and run sensitivity training programs for management groups, all on a large scale. Except for the Scanlon plan, it is not clear that we have moved very much beyond the suggestion system on the hourly worker front. But this is not because social scientists have not tried. They have tried very hard to bring the hourly worker into such activities. Sometimes they have been rebuffed by the workers or their unions, sometimes by managerial unwillingness to indulge in such "risky" experiments.

This differential emphasis on middle management as opposed to hourly workers is probably not a temporary accident. It represents, I believe, a general trend toward differentiating management methods at different organizational levels, roughly in accordance with the "programedness" of the tasks that those levels perform. It represents a new third approach to the problem of the routinization and programing of work.

The first approach was Taylor's: to routinize all work and, by routinizing, to control it. The second, the participative approach, was to strive to eliminate routine — to make all jobs challenging and novel. I suggest that the third approach — the one we are drifting into — is to do both: to routinize and control what we can; to loosen up and make challenging what we cannot. In so doing we may end up being efficient, and at once human and unhuman, depending on where, within the large organization, we choose to focus.

Consider, for example, recent thinking about the administration of research and development activities. Many observers have pointed up the growing tendency to free researchers, to deprogram them, to loosen their administrative bonds. Certainly the typical large and enlightened firm has moved in this direction, from a punch-the-time-clock attitude toward R & D (especially R) to looser controls and a freer environment.

WHAT DOES CHANGE MEAN?

I think most social scientists and personnel people have interpreted the change as a large breakthrough in the war against the whole tightly run autocracy of industrial organization. Loosening up of R & D, many feel, is just the first step toward loosening up the whole show. For our goal is not to eliminate the time clock in the lab; it is to eliminate all time clocks. The emancipated researcher is thus not a special case, but a model of the freedom that all members of an organization will ultimately enjoy.

This is a pleasant, democratic vision, but I don't believe it. Top management's willingness, under duress, to allow the R & D prima donna to behave like a prima donna can have another meaning. It can mean movement toward a more *differentiated* organization, with some parts of it very much loosened up while other parts become increasingly tight. While the creative researcher is being left free to create, the materials purchasing clerk must conform more tightly than ever to the new computer controlled program he has been handed.

I submit that the facts we have all observed fit together better when thus interpreted as signals of increasing differentiation.

By this third interpretation, we are not seeing in R & D the growth of participative management as such, but the growth of management-according-to-task; with the use of those administrative tools, participative or otherwise, that seem best adapted to the task at hand.

If this interpretation is correct, we should be seeing less and less uniformity in managerial practice; more of a class system, if you like — though a fluid one — in which the rules governing everything from hours of work to methods of evaluation to systems of compensation may vary from one group to another within the same parent organization. And, further, the many variations will be understandable in large part if one looks first at the tasks that each group is trying to accomplish, and secondly at the tools, psychological and technical, that are at the moment available for working on those tasks.

By this interpretation, too, growing differentiation should create some nasty problems in its own right. Differentiation should make for more problems of communication among sets of subgroups each governed by different rules. Mobility from one subgroup to another should become more difficult. And so on.

Let us, if you will permit me to press the point, suppose such problems do arise. What might we do to solve them? If we jump off from our participative beliefs, we move almost naturally toward a search for ways of increasing communication among groups, and opening mobility pathways as widely as possible. Jumping off from a more analytic base, however, we might stop and ask: Is communication among these groups useful? How much? For what? And how much mobility?

Perhaps only a thread of communication will be needed — perhaps no mobility across groups at all. But without further speculation I suggest that more and more we are differentiating classes and subclasses of tasks within organizations, so that questions about how much we use people, the kinds of people we use, and the kinds of rules within which we ask them to operate, all are being increasingly differentiated — largely in accordance with our ability to specify and program the tasks which need to be performed and in accordance with the kind of tools available to us.

CONCLUSION

The main purposes of this article, then, have been to ask for a reexamination of the "participative beliefs" about management, and to urge a consideration of the idea of differentiation.

In asking for a second look at the participative beliefs, I have tried not to associate myself with some others who are asking for the same thing but for quite different reasons. I do not want a return to tough management. Nor am I worried about groups replacing individuals. In my opinion the participative beliefs represent a great advance in management, one that needs now only to be placed in perspective.

In our eagerness over the last couple of decades to expand and test our new and exciting findings about participation, we may have made two serious but understandable and correctable mistakes: we have on occasion confused our observations with our values; and we have assumed that our participative beliefs represented the absolute zero of management — that there was no more basic level.

But though I believe in the values associated with the participative beliefs and in their great practical utility for solving huge present and future problems of human relationships, I ask that we try to fit them into the still broader perspective on organizations that is being generated out of the communication and systems sciences, and out of our rapidly growing understanding of the processes of thinking, organizing, and problem solving.

One way of setting these beliefs into a different perspective may be, I submit, by viewing large organizations as differentiated sets of subsystems rather than as unified wholes. Such a view leads us toward a management-by-task kind of outlook — with the recognition that many subparts of the organization may perform many different kinds of tasks, and therefore may call for many different kinds of managerial practices.

QUESTIONS

1. In what way is human relations theory insufficient, according to Prof. Leavitt? Give reasons for agreeing or disagreeing with his point of view.

2. Explain and illustrate what is meant by a management-by-task outlook in a school district setting. What kind of managerial practices are called for if such an outlook is adopted?

UNIT II

THE INDIVIDUAL AND THE ORGANIZATION

THE BEHAVIOR OF INDIVIDIALS IN ORGANIZATIONS

OVERVIEW

Several scholars have focused their attention not only on the behavior of organizations but also on the behavior of individuals within them. These writers have provided helpful insights but no one has yet developed a complete theoretical construct to account for the variety of individual behavior.

Speculations may be classified in three categories depending on whether they emphasize the personality of the individual, the nature of the occupation, or the interaction between the organization and the individual. These divisions are not mutually exclusive; there is considerable overlap among them.

PERSONALITY AS A DETERMINANT OF INDIVIDUAL BEHAVIOR

Maslow's Hierarchy of Needs. Abraham Maslow classified human needs in a pyramidal order, placing the most basic at the bottom of the pyramid and the least potent at the top. Until the most elemental needs are met — air, water, food, and shelter — it is useless to attempt to motivate an individual by appeals of a higher order. Human beings are not motivated by higher needs until their survival needs have been satisfied. A child who goes to school hungry has little interest in learning; his primary concern is for food. After survival needs are met, an individual looks for security. He needs to feel protected, safe from violence and terror.

When the physical requirements of survival and security have been assured, an individual looks for social satisfactions. He wants the company of friends. He has an urge to become associated with others, to belong, to feel wanted and loved.

A new level of needs arises when his social needs have been met. He desires to earn the esteem of others and to feel important because of his achievements. His ego demands gratification and self-respect.

The highest level of needs relates to self-actualization. The drive to develop one's abilities to the maximum and to become as fully realized a person as one is capable of becoming is present as a motivating force only when all previous needs have been satisfied. "What a man can be, he must be."[1]

One critic charges that self-actualization is a vague term for which there is no experiential or empirical validity. It is "drenched in value connotations both of what people are like and of what they can become."[2] Yet Maslow described the self-actualizing person in clear terms as one who perceives and is comfortable with reality. He recognizes his own abilities and limitations, and accepts himself as realistically as he accepts others and the world about him. He is problem-centered, self-directing, and continually and freshly appreciative. He is effective in interpersonal relations and empathizes with all mankind.[3]

It is interesting to note that those who are considered to have achieved self-fulfillment come from cultural and scientific fields and not from politics

---

[1] Maslow, Abraham H., *Motivation and Personality,* New York: Harper and Bros., 1954, p. 91.

[2] Bennis, Warren, "The Problem: Integrating the Organization and the Individual," in William G. Monahan, *Theoretical Dimensions of Educational Administration,* New York: Macmillan, 1975, p. 326.

[3] Maslow, Abraham H., "Self-Actualizing People — A Study of Psychological Health," Personality Symposium No. 1, 1950.

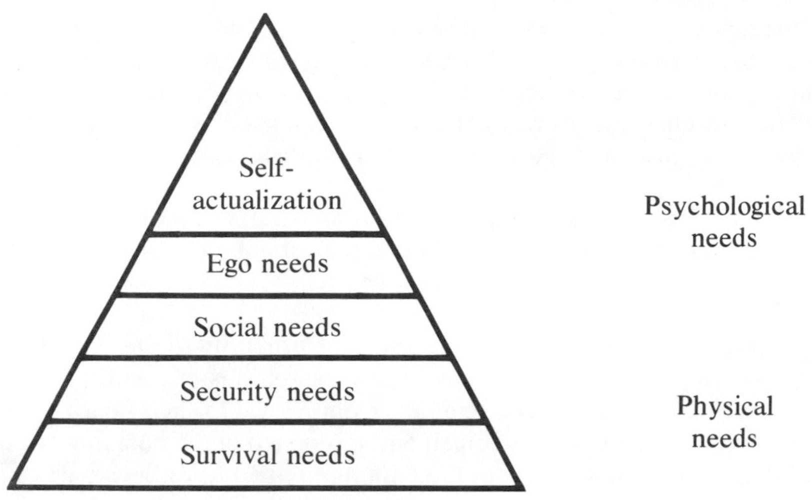

Figure 1

MASLOW'S HIERARCHY OF NEEDS

and management. They are philosophers, religious leaders, artists, musicians, poets, authors, and scientists, but not political leaders or businessmen.

In Maslow's formulation, needs are arranged in an order of potency. The physical needs are prepotent to the psychological. A satisfied need is no longer a motivator. A higher order of need does not become a motivator until the next lower order has been satisfied.

Maslow admits, however, that this schema is not applicable to all persons and situations. For example, some people need self-esteem more than they need love, and martyrs throughout history have sacrificed their lives rather than abandon the principles in which they believed.

Basic needs are generally met in all but the most undeveloped countries. The social programs of our nation and other developed countries are designed to meet the physical needs of millions, to provide them with adequate food, housing, medical care, and protection. Yet we still continue to use these elemental needs to motivate action and participation. In the teaching profession, for example, salaries and fringe benefits cease to be primary motivators once they have reached a level befitting professional workers. When teachers and administrators earn wages commensurate with their training and the importance and dignity of their calling, they look for other satisfiers. Achievement, recognition, the work itself, and the acceptance of responsibility are more powerful motivators than economic rewards.

Locals and cosmopolitans. School administrators and teachers may be classified on the basis of their professional orientation as locals and cosmopolitans.[4]

Locals are persons whose orientation is primarily to the school district in which they work. They remain with it for reasons of security. They are concerned with local practices and problems; loyal to their board of education, superintendent, and principal; and interested in the community and its traditions. Often they reside in the community and have been part of it for years, and their acquaintances are for the most part local residents.

But locals are not so much defined by geography — they may move from district to district — as they are by the breadth of their concerns. They are locals because their focus is on the local organization rather than on an institution which transcends the local scene. While active in community organizations and local teachers' groups, they show little interest in state or national educational associations and rarely attend their conventions. They do not subscribe to or read professional journals in their field.

Cosmopolitans are primarily oriented to their profession rather than to the organization which employs them. They are concerned about problems which transcend the district in which they work, problems which may be national or international in nature. They may be long-time residents of the community in which they are employed but their concerns extend beyond community boundaries. They remain with the local organization to pursue their commitment to the profession. The circle of their professional acquaintances extends to other states and even to other countries. They are active in state and national associations, frequently attend educational meetings and conventions, and regularly read professional journals. They are oriented not to the local situation but to their specialized subject field and profession.

It would appear that college and university faculty members are more often cosmopolitans than elementary or secondary school teachers. There

---

[4]Gouldner, Alvin W., "Cosmopolitans and Locals: Toward an Analysis of Latent Social Roles," *Administrative Science Quarterly,* II (Dec. 1957, March 1958), pp. 281-306 and 440-480.

are, however, no objective data to substantiate this impression.

Indifferents, ambivalents, and upward mobiles. Robert Presthus states that members of an organization accommodate to its demands in three ways — indifference, ambivalence, and upward mobility.[5]

Indifferents look upon their jobs merely as means to obtain off-job satisfactions. They evidence no real interest in the employing organization, pay only lip service to its values, and actually are alienated from it although they may conceal their alienation by "going through the motions." They insist on receiving the same pay as their colleagues although they perform at a marginal level at best and involve themselves with the organization as little as they can. It may be conjectured that they experience feelings of autonomy by withholding themselves.

Ambivalents constitute a small, perpetually disturbed minority who can neither renounce their claims for status and power nor play the disciplined role that would enable them to cash in on such claims. They resist and fear authority but at the same time they may readily submit to it. They want success, self-realization, and security but are unwilling to pay the price in dependency, submission, and sustained effort. Like the cat in the adage, they would fain fish eat but are loath to wet their feet.

Upward mobiles react positively to the requirements of the bureaucratic structure. They identify strongly with the organization, derive satisfaction from involvement with it, internalize its values, and regard their superiors with respect and admiration. Their loyalty is firm and their morale high, and when they are required to accommodate or sacrifice, they conform readily and without restraint. Upward mobiles get along well with their superiors and subordinates, and are never intentionally rude. They perceive the impressions they are making on people and adjust their behavior accordingly. But there is nothing insincere in their interpersonal relationships; on the contrary, they are sensitive to the feelings of others. Always there is the correct response, the appropriate reaction, the thoughtful act. The order, security, and prestige of a bureaucratic career appeals to them, and they are willing to work hard to succeed.

Indifferents, ambivalents, and upward mobiles are not ideal types but rather points on a continuum ranging from complete alienation at one end to total involvement at the other. School administrators and those preparing for

---

[5] Presthus, Robert, *The Organizational Society,* New York: Vintage Books, 1962.

administrative positions in the schools are usually upward mobiles.

Theory X and Theory Y. Maslow's theory of the hierarchy of needs underlies two theories of human behavior which Douglas M. McGregor has called Theory X and Theory Y.[6]

Essentially Theory X rests on the lower order of human needs. It proposes the notion that the average person dislikes work and will avoid it if he can. He is lazy, passive, resistant to change, and reluctant to assume responsibility. Consequently, he needs to be coerced, controlled, directed, and threatened with punishment to make him put forth adequate effort toward the achievement of organizational objectives. He prefers to be told what to do. He avoids responsibility and has little ambition. Above all, he wants security. Unquestionably, some individual behavior is explainable in these terms but there is increasing evidence that Theory X is not widely applicable and that it is out of line with observable facts and research findings.

Theory Y rests on Maslow's higher order of human needs. It replaces direction and control with the principle of integration and assumes that man is active, wishes to grow, and become more and more useful to the organization of which he is a part. The assumptions underlying it may be summarized as:

1. The expenditure of physical and mental effort in work is as natural as play or rest. The average individual does not inherently dislike work. Depending on controllable conditions, work may be a source of satisfaction or dissatisfaction.
2. External control and the threat of punishment are not the only means by which individuals are motivated to work toward organizational objectives. Man will exercise self-direction and self-control in the pursuit of objectives to which he is committed.
3. Commitment to objectives is related to the rewards associated with their achievement. The most significant of such rewards, for example, the satisfaction of the ego and self-actualization needs, can be direct products of effort directed toward organizational objectives.
4. The average human being learns, under proper conditions, not only to accept but to seek responsibility. Avoidance of responsibility, lack of ambition, and emphasis on security are consequences of experience, not inherent human characteristics.

---

[6]McGregor, Douglas, *The Human Side of Enterprise,* New York: McGraw-Hill, 1960, pp. 45-8.

5. The capacity to exercise a relatively high degree of imagination, ingenuity, and creativity in the solution of organizational problems is widely, not narrowly, distributed in the population.
6. Under conditions of modern industrial life, the intellectual potentialities of the average human being are only partially utilized.[7]

Which theory is "right?" If we accept Theory X, then communication will be largely one-way, from the top down, and nothing will go up except reports. The top levels of administration will make all decisions and determine the strategies to be carried out by middle management. "All we ask of the men," Henry Ford once said, "is that they do the work which is set before them."

Theory Y implies two-way communication and participation in goal-setting, planning, and decision-making at each level. It is more optimistic about the possibility for human growth and development than Theory X, and more concerned with self-direction and self-responsibility. But does Theory Y function at all levels or only in the upper echelons of administration? Can we expect low-level employees — maintenance men, assembly-line workers, and others engaged in simple repetitive tasks — to be motivated from within and to participate in decision-making?

McGregor advocates Theory Y because, ideally, it influences every individual to identify himself with the organization's objectives, to consider his job significant, and to realize that to do it effectively he needs the support of his superiors. They in turn look upon the giving of support as their prime responsibility.

Perhaps both theories are "right." In certain circumstances there is a need for direction, control, and close supervision to insure productivity and guard against wasteful effort. In other circumstances it is desirable to engage in collaborative activity, delegate responsibility and authority, and encourage independence of action.

More important than choosing one theory over the other is the need for every administrator to make his assumptions about human nature explicit. He must carefully examine his assumptions about what makes people behave as they do because his assumptions reflect his value system and determine his managerial style and practices.

Place bound and career bound superintendents. In a widely publicized

---

[7] Ibid. (With some slight textual changes.)

study of school superintendents, Richard O. Carlson says that the place where a superintendent is employed affects his administrative style. The place, in turn, is influenced by his own career aspirations, the way he achieved the superintendency, and the expectations of his clientele.[8]

Carlson classifies superintendents into two categories. A place bound superintendent is one who has risen through the ranks in his home district. He has lived in the community a long time, participated in its activities, and is well known to its residents. A career bound superintendent is a stranger to the district in which he holds his position. He has moved from place to place, each time presumably to more challenging responsibilities. He has no known commitments and is neither helped nor hindered by a set of social relationships.

These dissimilarities affect administrative behavior particularly with respect to change. Carlson's research shows that place bound superintendents are slow to adopt new educational practices. They are unwilling to rock the boat, preferring to keep things on an even keel, making ad hoc adjustments when necessary but not introducing major innovations. Career bound superintendents, on the other hand, introduce major changes within their first few years in office and move to other districts after the changes have taken hold.

Why do superintendents become place bound or career bound? Are there fundamental differences in their personality structures and professional backgrounds? To find answers to these questions Carlson used a battery of self-descriptive instruments to assess the attitudes, interests, values, aspirations, biographical backgrounds, leadership, and social activity of a large sample of Oregon, Pennsylvania, Massachusetts, and West Virginia school superintendents.

One self-descriptive instrument was the Adjective Check List which consists of 300 adjectives which describe socially desirable attitudes.[9] Participants in the survey were asked to check those they considered self-descriptive. Career bound and place bound superintendents differed in the frequency with which they checked certain adjectives. For example, career bound superintendents checked *confident, optimistic, idealistic, poised, progressive, spontaneous, suggestible,* and *wise* more frequently than did the place bound group. On the other hand, place bound superintendents

---

[8]Carlson, Richard O., *School Superintendents: Careers and Performance,* Columbus, O.: Charles E. Merrill Pub. Co., 1972.

[9]Gough, Harrison G., *Adjective Check List Manual,* Palo Alto, Cal.: Consulting Psychologists Press, 1965.

checked *silent* more frequently than did the career bound superintendents. The differences in choices were considered statistically significant.[10]

There were significant differences, too, in the professional backgrounds of the two types. The average place bound superintendent decided to become a superintendent when he was about eight years more advanced in age than his career bound counterpart. At the time of his decision he held a lower level administrative position. His aspirations escalated to the next higher position, from that to the one above, and so on to the superintendency. The career bound superintendent, on the other hand, determined to become a superintendent shortly after entering the teaching profession. The inference drawn from this comparison is that career bound superintendents are more confident, an inference confirmed by the Adjective Check List.

Place bound superintendents became superintendents because they happened to be at the right place at the right time. "The job turned up and there I was," said several place bound superintendents. Career bound superintendents managed their careers to reach the superintendency.

Place bound superintendents were selected for their positions because of their knowledge of local conditions and their past performance, and because the boards of education wanted to continue existing policies and practices. Career bound superintendents were selected because of their experience and education, and the desire of the board for action, for example, the improvement of the curriculum or the implementation of a building program. Boards of education were more likely to pick a career bound applicant if the previous incumbent's record was unsatisfactory.

In his summary of findings, Carlson concludes that the variable of origin is a potent predictor of administrative style in superintendents. Using the criteria of friendship choices, professional visibility, accuracy of judgment, and cosmopolitism, he found that place bound superintendents had lower status among their peers, were less involved in the social network of superintendents, and less active in their immediate geographic areas and in the areas outside their home district as well.

An interesting sidelight of Carlson's study is that the superintendents as a total group were of high caliber. They were concerned with people and sensitive to their feelings. In the performance of their duties they showed themselves to be tolerant, responsible, conscientious, capable, and interested in dealing with broad matters of policy.

---

[10]CASEA-ERIC/CEA News Bulletin, Eugene, Oregon: University of Oregon, Spring 1969.

Carlson implies that career bound superintendents move from district to district because of an altruistic desire to improve education. But they may be motivated instead by ambition, a desire for increased power, and a hankering for a higher salary. They become superintendents in small districts, introduce current educational fads, and then hop to greener pastures before the merits of their innovations can be assessed. They are able to obtain more lucrative and influential positions on the basis of these innovations. After they leave, the innovations are found unproductive and relegated to the educational scrapheap, but the man who introduced them is no longer around to face criticism.

Superintendents who flit from post to post are not necessarily abler and wiser than those who remain with a community and grapple with its problems, sometimes successfully and sometimes unsuccessfully, but always with concern for those who have reposed their trust in them. A hit-and-run superintendent is no asset to a school district or to the teaching profession.

THE OCCUPATION AS A DETERMINANT OF INDIVIDUAL BEHAVIOR

Professionals and non-professionals. Profession is an ambiguous term. It is used in so many senses and applied to so many pursuits that its meaning has become clouded. To distinguish between professional and non-professional occupations, the National Education Association has drawn up the following criteria:

1. A profession involves activities essentially intellectual.
2. A profession involves a body of specialized knowledge.
3. A profession requires extended professional (as contrasted with solely general) preparation.
4. A profession demands continuous in-service growth.
5. A profession affords a life career and permanent membership.
6. A profession sets up its own standards.
7. A profession exalts service above personal gain.
8. A profession has a strong, closely knit, professional organization.[11]

Although not listed above, a code of ethics is also a distinguishing characteristic of a profession. The NEA Code of Ethics of the Teaching Profession consists of a series of principles relating to the conduct of teachers and administrators in dealing with students, fellow teachers, the

[11] National Education Association, "The Yardstick of a Profession," *Institutes on Professional and Public Relations,* Washington, D.C., 1948, p. 8.

community, and the profession; it is also concerned with professional employment practices. NEA membership requirements include the obligation to abide by the code.[12]

Judged by these criteria, teaching is a profession although some observers believe that much remains to be achieved. People generally accord teaching professional status although they do not rank it as high as medicine, law, the ministry, engineering, chemistry, architecture, or dentistry, perhaps because these professions have more stringent admission procedures and longer periods of preparation.

The teaching profession does not yet have a controlling voice in the certification of teachers and the evaluation of their performance. Rarely does it discipline individuals for unethical conduct or failure to meet acceptable standards of proficiency. Its sanctions include reprimand, censure, suspension, and expulsion from NEA membership, none of which prohibits an individual from employment as a teacher. Lawyers and physicians guilty of unprofessional conduct may be prohibited from practicing by their respective professional organizations although such action is infrequent.

A profession is self-regulating and self-governing, and its members exercise a high degree of independence, responsibility, and initiative. Skilled, semi-skilled, and unskilled workers are not bound by the same high standards of personal conduct or work performance; they are generally supervised more closely and restricted in the exercise of independent judgment.

The influence of the organization. Of the many writers on organizations, none has concerned himself more with the effect of the work situation upon individual development than Chris Argyris, professor of education and organizational behavior at Harvard. According to Argyris, every person is capable of self-actualization. When an individual fully develops his potentialities, both he and the organization in which he works are the beneficiaries. Unfortunately, organizations are usually so structured and managed that they inhibit individual self-fulfillment.[13]

---

[12] National Education Association, NEA Handbook for Local, State, and National Association, Washington, D.C., 1966.

[13] For a more detailed exposition of Argyris' theory, cf. Chris Argyris, "The Individual and Organization: Some Problems of Mutual Adjustment" in *Administrative Science Quarterly,* II (June 1957); *Integrating the Individual and the Organization,* New York: John Wiley and Sons, 1964; and D. S. Pugh, D. J. Hickson, and C. R. Hinings, *Writers on Organizations,* Baltimore, Md.: Penguin Books, 1976.

The problem is threefold. It involves the strivings of the individual for maturity, the interpersonal effectiveness of those around him, and the nature of the organization.

What is known and agreed upon about the individual component? From birth to maturity an individual develops
. . . from a state of being passive as an infant to a state of being active as an adult.
. . . from dependence towards relative independence. Relative independence is the ability to "stand on one's own two feet" and at the same time to acknowledge healthy dependencies, that is, those that help him to be creative and to develop. The individual frees himself from parental domination and adopts his own set of behavioral determiners.
. . . from limited behaviors to many different behaviors.
. . . from erratic, casual, shallow, quickly dropped interests to more stable, deeper interests.
. . . from short-time perspective to longer-time perspective. An infant's behavior is largely determined by the present; and an adult's by the past and future.
. . . from a subordinate social position to an equal or superordinate social position relative to his peers.
. . . from a lack of self-awareness to self-awareness and self-control. The adult who successfully controls his own behavior develops a sense of integrity and feelings of self-worth.

No one develops at the same rate in each of these seven dimensions or achieves maximum development in all. Progress in each varies with the individual and with the same individual at different times.

Argyris' research shows that lack of interpersonal competence both by workers and administrators also prevents individuals from developing to maturity. Employees concern themselves only with their relatively trivial work difficulties and look upon their employment as an unhappy interlude between non-work periods. They perform repetitious tasks listlessly, show little interest in improving their skills, and are concerned only with personal gain, rarely with organizational health. While they may show no active dissatisfaction, they also show little enthusiasm and are content to be passive and dependent.

Their immediate supervisors fail to stimulate initiative or encourage collaborative planning. They display little genuine concern for the personal well-being of those they supervise and regard with suspicion and distrust any suggestion for change. Individuals and departments follow their own goals and ignore wider organizational interests, often to each other's detriment.

Faced with this lack of healthy interpersonal relationships among workers and lower level managers, top executives become even more autocratic and directive. They devise new controls which turn out to be self-defeating because they restrict the flow of descriptive non-evaluative feedback essential for organizational growth. In such an organizational climate, infantile attitudes and behaviors are fostered.

The nature of the formal organization prevents individuals from achieving self-fulfillment. If the formal organization is defined by the principles of task specialization, unity of direction, chain of command, and span of control, then employees work in a situation in which they tend to be dependent, subordinate, and passive to a leader. Specialization inhibits self-actualization because it does not provide the "endless challenge" which healthy personalities want. Unity of direction inhibits self-actualization because employees do not set their own goals but work towards those defined and controlled by someone else. The chain of command principle inhibits self-actualization because it requires individuals to be dependent upon, passive, and subordinate to control, direction, and coordination. Finally, the span of control principle, which states that administrative efficiency is increased by limiting a leader to supervising no more than five or six subordinates whose work interlocks, places great emphasis on close supervision. Close supervision makes subordinates dependent and passive — in other words, immature.

Based on his analysis, as summarized above, Argyris formulates three propositions:

1. There is a lack of congruency between the needs of healthy individuals and the demands of the formal organization.
2. The results of this disturbance are frustration, failure, short-time perspective, and conflict.
3. The nature of the formal principles of organization cause the subordinate, at any given level, to experience competition, rivalry, and intersubordinate hostility, and to develop a focus toward the parts rather than the whole.

How do employees adapt to these conditions? Some leave the organization. Others climb the organizational ladder. Many manifest defense reactions such as day-dreaming, aggression, gold-bricking, cheating, making errors, and so on.

Management then responds by increasing pressures and controls, and also by increasing the number of pseudo-participation and communication programs.

Is there a way out of this circular process? Top executives must increase their interpersonal competence. Jobs can be enlarged so that they give an individual more control over what is done in his own sphere of activities and require more use of his intellectual and interpersonal powers. Organizations must have different structures for different purposes so that if an observer wished to see the organizational chart he would be asked "For what type of decision?"

INTERACTION AS A DETERMINANT OF INDIVIDUAL BEHAVIOR

To explain the relationship between organizational and individual behavior, Jacob W. Getzels and Egon G. Guba have formulated a model which has been the theoretical basis of extensive research for more than a decade.

An understanding of systems theory and role theory is necessary for an understanding of the model. The essentials of systems theory have already been described (pages 29-32). A summary of the elements of role theory follows.

Role theory. Role theory is a conceptual framework for analyzing individual behavior in an organizational setting.

The word role comes from theatrical usage. A dramatist devises lines for a character to utter and prescribes the actions he must perform but the actor who portrays the character adds his own insights. A role is an actor's interpretation of a character in a drama. His interpretation is determined by his own understanding, his director's requirements, and the way his fellow actors portray their roles. Thus, many actors have played Hamlet yet it is unlikely that there have ever been two identical interpretations. Hamlet has been portrayed as a hero, a vacillating student, an impetuous youth, a neurotic, and even as a homosexual, without any change in lines or action.

As used in the study of administration, a role is not the same as a position. A *position* is a point on an organizational chart to indicate a set of responsibilities and powers. Each position is governed by rules, expectations, and demands vis-à-vis other positions related to it. A position does not become a role until it is occupied. A *role,* then, is the dynamic aspect of a position.

A role is defined in terms of expectations. It has certain privileges, responsibilities, and powers, and when a role incumbent exercises them he is said to be performing his role.[14] The expectations define for an incumbent what he should or should not do as long as he is an incumbent of the particular role. In this sense, role expectations tend to be externally defined.[15] For instance, a school superintendent and a school faculty expect a newly appointed school principal to perform certain duties. Teachers expect children to behave in certain ways while in school. A wife expects her husband to undertake certain responsibilities at home with regard to their children. Roles in other words serve as norms to guide the behavior of role incumbents.[16] Institutions use positive and negative sanctions to insure compliance with roles.[17]

Roles are complementary and interlocking. Each role derives its meaning from other related roles. For instance, a student's role is defined in terms of his teacher's role, and a teacher's role is defined in terms of his student's. A student perceives his role to be that of a learner and his teacher perceives his role to be that of a director of learning. A principal's role is expressed in terms of his teacher's expectations, and the converse is also true.

The rights of one role incumbent become the obligations of another. A student has the right to receive instruction and his teacher has the obligation to provide it; a teacher has the right to be obeyed and the student has the obligation to obey. A role, then, is a prescription for the role incumbent and for the incumbents of other related roles. It determines what an incumbent must do and what incumbents of other related roles within and without the institution must do. Complementary roles fuse into interactive units and this complementarity makes it possible for us to conceive of an institution as having a characteristic structure.[18]

The *role set* of a position consists of all its complementary roles. It comprises a pivotal role incumbent together with those who communicate their expectations to him. (Figure 2)

---

[14] Getzels, Jacob W. and Thelen, Herbert A., "The Classroom Group as a Unique Social System," in *The Dynamics of Instructional Groups: Sociopsychological Aspects of Teaching and Learning,* Fifty-ninth Yearbook of the National Society for the Study of Education, Part II, edited by Nelson B. Henry, University of Chicago Press, 1960, p. 66.

[15] Ibid., p. 71.

[16] Guba, Egon G., "Role, Personality, and Social Behavior," Unpublished paper. Bureau of Educational Research and Studies, Ohio State University, Sept. 1958.

[17] Ibid.

[18] Getzels and Thelen, op. cit., p. 66.

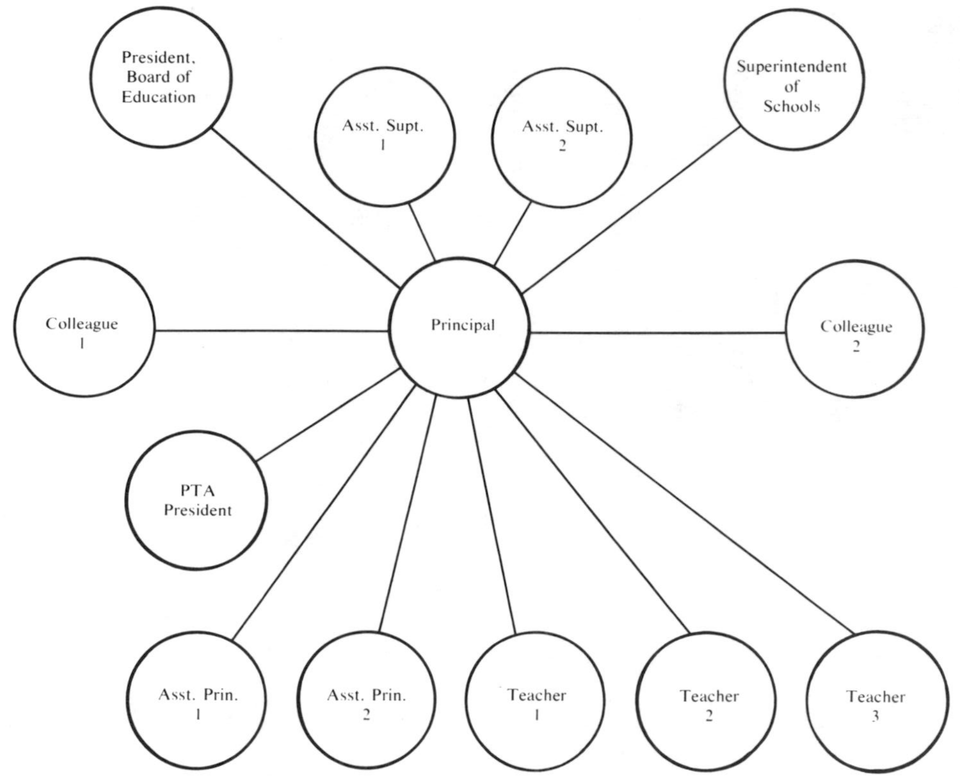

Figure 2

TYPICAL ROLE SET OF A SCHOOL PRINCIPAL

Figure 2 suggests how role conflicts and ambiguities can develop. The principal's concept of his role may be different from that held by some or all the other members of his role set, or the expectations of the various members of his role set may differ so widely from one another that his role is ambiguous.

A *prescribed role* consists of a set of expectations that incumbents of complementary positions have toward a role incumbent. A *subjective role* consists of expectations which a role incumbent has of his own behavior when he interacts with the occupants of complementary positions. An *enacted role* consists of the behaviors which a role incumbent engages in when interacting with those in complementary positions. In other words, a prescribed role is the way others see it; a subjective role is the way the incumbent sees it; an enacted role is the one actually performed.

Role conflicts are of three types. *Intrarole conflict* results when a role incumbent comes up against incompatible role expectations from occupants of complementary positions. For example, a principal may expect a guidance counsellor to deal with infractions of school discipline while the counsellor may believe that the enforcement of discipline is incompatible with his guidance role. *Personality-role conflict* results when an individual's personality prevents him from fulfilling his role. For example, a soft-spoken, shy young woman might find a position in a correctional institution incompatible with her personality. *Interrole* conflict occurs when an individual occupies two or more competing roles simultaneously. A teacher, for instance, may be a taxpayer, a member of a political party, and a father. If he works in one school district and resides in another, he may experience a conflict when he votes on the school budget. As a teacher he favors higher salaries for teachers but as a taxpayer he wants to hold down taxes. As an enrolled party member he is expected to vote for his party's nominees even though they are opposed to increased aid to education. As a father he may be dismayed at the incompetence of his child's school principal but reluctant to protest because of his professional affiliation. When individuals are faced with an interrole conflict, they may resolve it by assigning certain roles priority over others. They establish a hierarchy of roles based on their own needs and the legitimacy of the role expectations.

Role expectations are anticipatory and normative. A teacher anticipates certain reactions to his behavior; if he tells his students to perform a certain assignment or report to him at a specified time, he expects them to obey. Such actions, especially when they are frequent, tend to become obligatory; that is, students are not only expected to perform them but required to. To put it differently: a role incumbent not only anticipates compliance but believes that the occupants of complementary roles are obligated to comply and is disturbed when they do not.

Of what value is role theory to a school administrator? It helps him analyze what goes on in a school district, school, or even classroom. If he realizes that his own role performance is influenced by the expectations of those holding complementary roles and that role expectations tend to be normative, his own role conflicts may be lessened or resolved. An indispensable requirement for the resolution of role conflict is that it be made overt. It cannot be handled effectively unless brought out into the open and examined objectively. Then means for resolving it can be devised.

The Getzels-Guba model. The Getzels-Guba model is an attempt to understand the nature of social behavior and to predict and control it.

Social systems have certain imperative functions such as governing, educating, and policing, which are said to be institutionalized. The agencies which carry out these functions are called institutions (e.g. legislatures, schools, and law enforcement bodies) and they reflect the values of the larger society of which they are a part. They are structured so that they perform their functions in an orderly manner under the direction of human beings.

Every social system, then, is composed of two classes of phenomena which may be envisioned as independent of each other yet at the same time interacting. First, there are the institutions, composed of roles and expectations, established to achieve the system's goals. These constitute the normative or nomothetic dimension of activity. Thus the school as an institution may be viewed as composed of such roles as principal, assistant principals, guidance counsellors, teachers, and students.

Secondly, there are individuals with distinctive personalities and need-dispositions who inhabit the institutions. These constitute the idiographic or personal dimension of activity. No two principals, for example, are alike in the way they administer their schools. Each stamps his role with his own pattern of attitudes and motivations — in short, with his personality — and administers his school in a way different from other principals in the same district, even though all are bound by the same board of education policies.

Personality is the totality of an individual's characteristics, especially as they concern his relations to other people. It is "the dynamic organization within the individual of those need-dispositions that govern his unique reactions to the environment."[19] Need-dispositions are tendencies to act towards objects in certain ways and to expect certain consequences from these actions.[20]

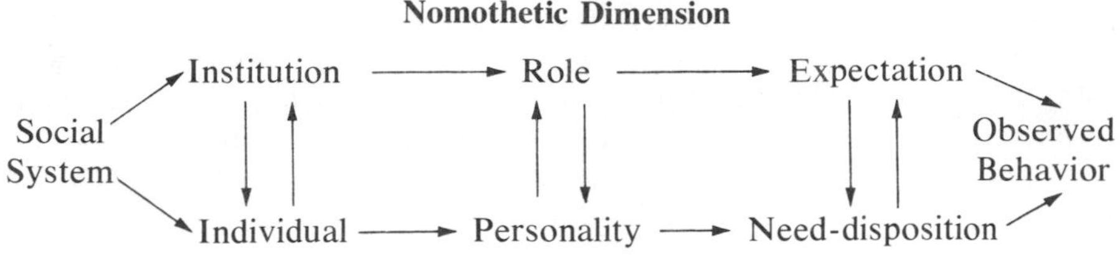

Figure 3

NOMOTHETIC AND IDIOGRAPHIC DIMENSIONS OF SOCIAL BEHAVIOR

Adapted from J. W. Getzels and E. G. Guba, "Social Behavior and the Administrative Process," *School Review,* 65, 1957, p. 429.

A social system — whether it is as large as a state or nation or as small as a class or group — is defined in terms of two dimensions, the nomothetic and the idiographic. On the nomothetic axis a social system is defined by its institutions, each institution by its roles, and each role by the expectations attaching to it. On the idiographic axis a social system is defined by the individuals who compose it, each individual by his personality, and each personality by its need-dispositions. Observe that each unit in the model (Figure 3) is an analytic unit for the term preceding it.

Any given act derives from the simultaneous interplay of both dimensions. Social behavior, in other words, is the outcome of an attempt by an individual to meet his role and its expectations in a way that accords with his personality and his need-dispositions. In algebraic terms, $B = f(R \times P)$, where B is observed behavior, R is a given institutional role defined by the expectations attaching to it, and P is the personality of the particular role incumbent defined by his need-dispositions.

Some administrators may consistently emphasize the nomothetic dimension, "going by the book" and permitting no deviation from established procedures and policies. Others may consistently emphasize the idiographic

---

[19] Getzels and Thelen, op. cit. p. 66.

[20] Adapted from Parsons, T. and Shils, E. A., *Toward a General Theory of Action,* Harvard University Press, 1951, as quoted in Getzels and Thelen, op. cit., p. 68.

dimension, permitting teachers maximum freedom in teaching methods and curriculum adaptations, even when they deviate from district regulations. Still others may vary their emphasis from one dimension to another depending on the specific act, the specific role, and the specific personality involved. Role and personality factors enter into almost every social act but the proportion of each varies in different situations.

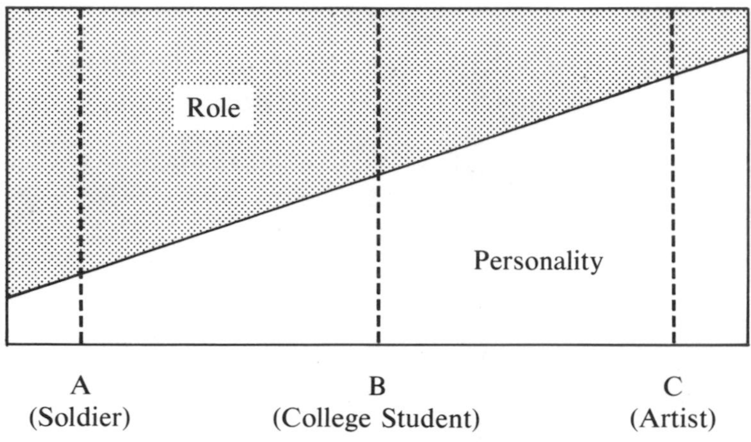

Figure 4

VARYING PROPORTIONS OF ROLE AND PERSONALITY COMPONENTS IN SOCIAL BEHAVIOR

Adapted from J. W. Getzels and E. G. Guba, "Social Behavior and the Administrative Process," *School Review,* 65, 1957, p. 430.

As shown in Figure 4, the behavior of a soldier (line A) is largely determined by the requirements of the army; he has little freedom for the expression of his own personality. The nomothetic dimension in this case overweighs the idiographic. On the other hand, an artist's social behavior is determined in large measure by his personality (line C); he has considerable freedom for creative activity because his role imposes few constraints upon him. A college student might range somewhere between the soldier and artist (line B) with respect to institutional restrictions and individual freedom.

The nomothetic dimension is the sociological level of analysis and the idiographic is the psychological. Besides these two dimensions there are three others: the anthropological, biological, and transactional.

An institution may be thought of in anthropological as well as sociological terms. It is imbedded in a culture with certain mores and values, and role expectations are related to them. Schools are not moated off from the surrounding culture; they are part of it. To illustrate: many communities have objected to courses of study, books on school library shelves, articles in student publications, and remarks by teachers because they consider them subversive of values inculcated by home or church.

An individual may be thought of in biological terms as well as personalistic. His personality is imbedded in a biological organism with certain constitutional abilities and potentialities which interact with the psychological or idiographic dimension. Thus a teacher's personality may be adversely affected by the condition of his health.

Finally, there is a transactional dimension which is a blend of the nomothetic and idiographic. It is not a compromise but an intelligent application of the two as occasion demands. Role and personality are maximized as the situation requires. The transactional dimension is oriented to a specific situation rather than to either an individual or institution. It is an attempt at both individual integration and institutional adjustment, the socialization of personality and the personalization of roles. It tries to balance the emphasis on the performance of role requirements and the expression of personality needs.

In its search for this balance, a group develops a climate made up of the intentions of its members. It takes into account their common or deviant perceptions, and their explicit or implicit agreements on how to deal with them. The group is of crucial importance, for it can impose institutional requirements on its members or support them in expressing their personal standards.

Thus a teacher may deal with a student's misbehavior strictly or leniently depending on the circumstances — the gravity of the offence, the intentions and previous record of the offender, and so on. A teachers' union may respond differently to the same breach of contract in different schools, justifying its lack of consistency on the circumstances in each case. A work crew paid on a piece work basis may impose strict production norms on its members or permit deviations from the norms by explicit or implicit agreement.

Commitment or identification is the congruence between needs-dispositions and goals; belongingness is the congruence between needs-dispositions and role expectations; and rationality is the congruence between role expectations and goals. In other words, commitment refers to the extent to which a role incumbent integrates institutional goals with his own needs; belongingness refers to the extent to which he satisfies role expectations and personal needs-dispositions simultaneously; and rationality refers to his perception of the logical appropriateness of his role expectations with institutional goals.

The complete Getzels-Guba model may now be presented (see next page).

Of what value is the Getzels-Guba model to school administrators? It is an aid in discovering and dealing with sources of conflict:

1. Conflict between the cultural values of the community and school expectations. Example: A community may object to a school's sex education program, the discussion of certain controversial issues, or the study of literature which questions traditional moral standards.
2. Conflict between role expectations and the need-dispositions of the incumbent of the role. Example: A classroom group may expect a particular student to behave in a way contrary to his individual dispositions. If the student fulfills the group's expectations, his personal integrity may be damaged, yet if he chooses to satisfy his personal needs, he may experience an unsatisfactory role adjustment.
3. Role conflict. When a role incumbent must conform simultaneously to a number of expectations that are mutually exclusive or contradictory, adjustment to one set of expectations makes it difficult or impossible to adjust to another. Role conflicts are of several types:
    a. Disagreement within the referent group defining the role. Example: University professors may object to classroom visitations by their department chairman as an affront to their professional status. The chairman, on the other hand, is expected by the dean of faculty and the university president to observe teachers and evaluate their teaching effectiveness.
    b. Disagreement among several referent groups, each having a right to define expectations for the same role. Example: A superintendent is expected by the board of education to act as its representative and reduce expenses by decreasing the size of the teaching staff. The teachers, on the other hand, expect the superintendent to act as their professional leader by reducing class size, thus increasing educational costs.

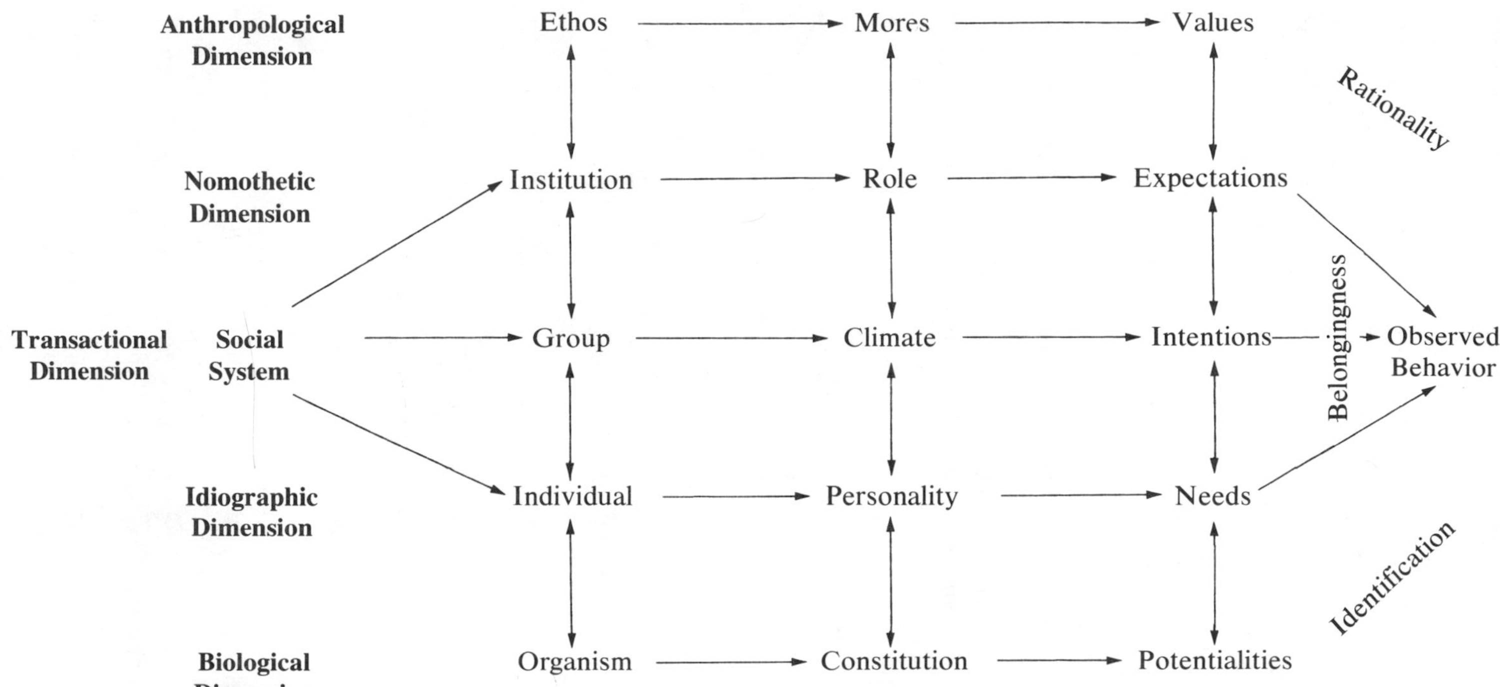

Figure 5

GETZELS-GUBA MODEL OF SOCIAL BEHAVIOR

Source: Jacob W. Getzels and Herbert A. Thelen, *The Classroom as a Unique Social System,* 59th Yearbook, National Society for the Study of Education, Nelson B. Henry, Ed., p. 66.

c. Contradiction in the expectations of two or more roles which an individual is occupying at the same time. Example: A teacher is expected to attend parent-teachers association meetings, committee meetings, and professional association meetings on his own time. Her husband, however, believes she has a prior responsibility to take care of the home and children. Attending the meetings may get in the way of her home responsibilities.
d. Personality conflict arising within the role incumbent because of opposing needs and dispositions. Personality conflict is independent of a situational setting but it may keep an individual at odds with the institution because it prevents him from performing his role. Example: A teacher who is fearful and tense may at the same time have a strong drive to dominate his associates and students with the result that he is continually causing friction which requires corrective action by his school superiors.

The Getzels-Guba model is often used as a conceptual framework in educational research. Its repeated use over more than a decade suggests that it is helpful in clarifying the complex relationships and conflicts which confront administrators.

A school administrator has the task of integrating organizational requirements with individual needs so that both the organization and individual benefit. The Getzels-Guba model may help him discover possible points of conflict and suggest modes of solution.

SELECTED READINGS

Carlson, Richard O., *School Superintendents: Careers and Performance,* Columbus, Ohio: Charles E. Merrill Pub. Co., 1972.

A research report on the characteristics, motivations, and managerial styles of school superintendents. Carlson contrasts two types, the place bound and career bound, with respect to the circumstances which lead to their selection, their adoption of educational innovations, and the effect of their stay in office upon the choice of their successor.

Johnson, David W., *Social Psychology of Education,* New York: Holt, Rinehart, Wilson, 1970.

Succinctly presents aspects of social psychological theory and research pertinent to education and provides the conceptual framework and cognitive tools needed to diagnose educational problems from a social psychological point of view. Chapters on role theory, interpersonal expectations and academic performance, and group norms are particulary useful.

Lipham, James M. and Hoeh, James A., *The Principalship: Foundations and Functions,* New York: Harper and Row, 1974.

The first two sections of this book utilize administrative theory as a basis for developing a competency-based approach to the principal's role. The chapters on social systems theory, organization theory, and role theory are particularly helpful. The third and final section deals with the principal's relation to the staff, pupils, and community.

Maslow, Abraham H., *Motivation and Personality,* New York: Harper and Row, 2nd ed., 1976.

In this revision of his 1954 classic, Maslow has updated and extended his original thesis on human motivation. He emphasizes the psychology of health, clarifies the meaning of self-actualization, and applies his teachings to theories of personality, personal growth, and general psychology.

Morrison, A. and McIntyre, D., ed., *Social Psychology of Teaching,* Baltimore, Md.: Penguin Books, 1972. (Paperback)

A selection of 23 articles dealing, *inter alia,* with theoretical approaches, the teacher's role, and classroom communication. Intended for a British readership, some of the articles may not be pertinent to the American scene but the one by J. W. Getzels and H. A. Thelen in which they apply the Getzels-Guba model to a classroom situation is worth studying.

Stinnett, T. M., *Professional Problems of Teachers,* 3rd ed., New York: Macmillan, 1968.

Although intended for new entrants to the teaching profession, this book is also of value to experienced teachers and administrators. Stinnett discusses the development of the American educational system, teaching as a profession, personnel policies, and working conditions. He stresses professional autonomy, the standards which the profession itself must establish, and collection action.

TOPICS FOR DISCUSSION

1. Using a slightly altered needs hierarchy developed by Porter in which physiological needs are deleted and autonomy needs added, Trusty and Sergiovanni report that while teachers are generally well satisfied with the fulfillment of lower order needs, they are appreciably less satisfied with the fulfillment of higher order needs. (Cf. Francis M. Trusty and Thomas J. Sergiovanni, "Perceived Need Deficiencies of Teachers and Administrators: A Proposal for Restructuring Teacher Roles," *Educational Administrative Quarterly,* Vol. 2, 1966, pp. 166-180.) Report on this research. What implications does it have for school administrators?

2. Assuming that you are well acquainted with all or most of the teachers in your school, classify them as indifferents, ambivalents, or upward mobiles and report on the number in each category. (It goes without saying that you should not mention names or describe any person in such a way that he may be identified.) If one category exceeds the others to a marked degree, can you offer an explanation?

3. Does your school principal consistently follow Theory X or Theory Y, or does he vary between one and the other as circumstances change? Cite instances. What would be the effect on the faculty if he were to use Theory Y exclusively?

4. Would you classify your school superintendent as place bound or career bound? Why? Does his administrative behavior confirm or negate Carlson's findings with respect to the adoption of new educational practices by place bound and career bound superintendents?

5. Are unionization and professionalism compatible? Do teachers' unions adversely affect the movement of teaching towards full professional status?

6. Argyris claims that increased interpersonal competence and job enlargement will help reduce conflict between the formal organization and the individual. Do the school administrators you know show a lack of interpersonal competence? Can the principle of job enlargement be applied to teaching? How?

7. Illustrate the meaning of *interrole conflict, personality-role conflict,* and *intrarole conflict* by referring to your experience as a teacher or administrator. How did you resolve each conflict?

8. Apply the Getzels-Guba model to any one of the following situations:

   a. A family you know.
   b. An algebra class.
   c. An art class.
   d. Parental complaints that the social studies course of study does not adequately show the contributions of a particular ethnic or racial group to our country's growth.
   e. The observed behavior of your school principal as seen by the superintendent, teachers, and community.
   f. A school which is the subject of community controversy.

THE WORK ETHIC IS NOT DEAD

By
The Royal Bank of Canada

Work is one of the conditions of being alive but it has changed in form and significance. Some of the unrest among workers is caused by the fact that we have not the compelling urgency of our forefathers. Young and old are willing to invest their efforts in work but they are demanding a pay-off in satisfaction. Work, not workers, must change.

The work ethic holds that work is good in itself. People are stimulated to work by the thought of a desirable end.

Machines have made our lives easier but at the same time have stripped work of meaning and psychological significance. The problem of fitting jobs and workers in a meaningful relationship perplexes management and unions.

People increasingly desire jobs that satisfy their social, ego, and creative needs as well as provide food and shelter. They want to be recognized, to belong, to become, and to have jobs which give them purpose in life. Ego needs can be satisfied by increasing a worker's decision-making authority and giving him an opportunity for creative expression. Job rotation and job enlargement may satisfy the worker's hidden hunger for recognition, responsibility, and achievement. When workers share in planning their work, they reach personal goals in the process of meeting the organization's objectives.

Not all responsibility rests on management. Every worker has obligations to himself and his employer.

THE WORK ETHIC IS NOT DEAD

No one has ever repealed the Law of Work, but it is in process of amendment. From the obscure life of organs within the body to the building of moon landing-craft, work is one of the conditions of being alive, but we need to keep up with changes in its form and significance.

"The Work Ethic is Not Dead," by The Royal Bank of Canada, in *Monthly Newsletter,* September 1974. Copyright © 1974 by The Royal Bank of Canada. Reprinted by permission of The Royal Bank of Canada.

Everyday work is some purposeful activity that requires the expenditure of energy with some sacrifice of leisure.

Sir William Osler, great Canadian physician and professor of medicine, whose book *The Principles and Practice of Medicine* is still a textbook after 82 years, believed "work" to be the master word in the ongoing life. It is the touchstone of progress, the measure of success, and the fount of hope. It is directly responsible, he said, for all advances in medicine and technology.

Not everyone is happy in his work. Job dissatisfaction is increasing. Workers are being infected by an uneasiness whose spread is challenging our assumptions about work and forcing us to make new definitions of jobs.

Some of the unrest and confusion is caused by the fact that we have not the compelling urgency of our forefathers. They had to work hard to survive: we have securities of this and that sort to make sure that we do not starve to death.

The late Dr. D. Ewen Cameron, internationally recognized psychiatrist who became the director of McGill University's Allan Memorial Institute in Montreal, wrote in his book *Life is for Living* (The Macmillan Co., 1948): "For half a century we have heard the most moving of lamentations from employers over the passing of the old time worker, the fellow who really loved his work, who hung around until he was satisfied that the job was done, who would think out ways to do it better. This kind of worker has not disappeared from the job; it is his kind of job that has done the disappearing."

Intelligent people, when they talk about the need for work, are not talking about returning to the twelve hour a day use of picks and shovels or wheelbarrows or horse-drawn scrapers in place of steam or diesel shovels, bulldozers and tractors.

Young and old are willing to invest their effort in work, but they are demanding a bigger pay off in satisfaction.

That workers find fault with their jobs is not a new phenomenon. What is new is the variety of their complaints and their increased determination to do something about removing the cause.

The development of a new respect for work and the promotion of a better understanding between those who perform the work and those who employ such workers is rapidly becoming one of the supreme tasks of employer statesmanship.

Some business executives have come to the conclusion that work, not workers, must change, and that leads them to the administration of strong medicine: the restructuring of jobs.

All the change that has been brought about by economic and mechanical progress cannot be looked upon as being against the workers' interest. Though the production technology has made man an appendage of tools and machines, and has weakened his journeyman's pride and autonomy, it has brought the price of automobiles, washing machines, cameras and refrigerators within his reach.

This gratification of his material desires by the mass production economy made man free to become aware of his dormant and unfulfilled psychological needs.

A Code of Values

The work ethic, the code of values that says you must work, is rooted in the Puritan way of life. The pilgrims who came to this continent in the 17th century filled their children's minds with copy-book maxims about the devil finding work for idle hands to do. They did this for the very good reason that in pioneer days hard and continuous work was necessary to keep parents and children from perishing. The urge to work was strengthened by the ambition to improve their level of living that animated the immigrants.

The work ethic goes further than this. An ethic is a body of moral principles that determines the course of a person's life. The work ethic holds that work is good in itself; that a man or a woman not only makes a contribution to society but becomes a better person by virtue of the act of working.

There must be work done by our hands, or none of us could live; there must be work done by our brains, or the life we live will not be enjoyable. A person is participating in the process of living only when he is doing something.

A second-century author whose pen name was Koheleth said: "Whatsoever thy hand findeth to do, do it with thy might, for there is no work in the grave, whither thou goest."

All work is not of the sort at which one wears an apron or overalls. Work is done by an artist or a writer just as by a stonemason or a machinist. Mary Roberts Rinehart, author of sixty full-length novels besides short stories and plays, did a book about her craft in which she warned *Writing is Work*. Kepler's calculations of planetary motions, Newton's meditations on the law of gravitation, and Selye's revolutionary concept of stress, were work, though they caused sweat of the brain and not of the body.

One motive that stimulates people to work is the thought of a desirable end. There is no job in the world so dull that it would not present fascinating angles to someone who was interested in the outcome.

A research scientist found that the human motivators were, in ascending order, possibility of advancement, responsibility, the work itself, recognition, and sense of achievement. Well-balanced people may be satisfied with the simple joy of doing something well. A man chipping rocks may be soaked in pity because of the drudgery, while the man working beside him may be proud that he is helping to build a cathedral.

A New Environment

Machines, allied with chemistry and biology, have given, to a vastly increased population, an abundance and variety of commodities and amenities, together with a lightening of toil, such as our ancestors in their most hopeful visions could never have imagined.

As societies advanced in making and obtaining good things, the expectations of their people rose, so that now many suffer a feeling of scarcity and deprivation. Consequently, they are more demanding about the content of their jobs.

It would be perverse to maintain that the fullness of life that is within reach of most civilized people could exist without the complex mechanical paraphernalia used in industry and science. It would be equally wrong to deny that in the process of streamlining, co-ordinating, integrating and adjusting industrial work to the machine, that work has become all but clean-stripped of meaning and of psychological significance for the worker.

Jobs seem to have been carved up with an eccentric jigsaw to suit the needs of new processes. As Dr. Cameron pictured it, they are broken down according to what the machine can do; the left-over fragments and the nursemaiding of the machine are given to the worker.

We cannot escape the law of life that what has not been produced cannot be consumed. Without machinery, productivity could not have risen to its present heights. Without this growth there would have been no marked increase in income, no marked decrease in the hours worked, and there would not be enough goods to supply the demand for them.

The change to machine production from the old craft manner of working, a change that people's minds were ill-prepared to handle, has caused stress of this and that sort. A precise, conscientious, meticulous individual is apt to break down if placed in repetitive jobs which call for work at speeds beyond his natural tempo and that employ only a limited part of his mental equipment.

The sort of union to be effected between the new jobs and workers is the problem that perplexes both management and unions. Monetary incentives will spring first to mind, but there is plenty of evidence to indicate that a full pay envelope does not settle all wants.

Someone once got the bright idea of attaching to every machine in a factory a meter that ticked up the wages of the worker in the same way as a taxi meter ticks up the fare. It was found that the workers soon lost interest in the meters; they decided it was better, safer, and more interesting to keep their minds on their jobs.

A Hidden Hunger

Workers may carry placards on which are printed demands for more pay, more leisure, and more comforts, but most of these are the surface indicators of a nagging hidden hunger. People increasingly desire jobs that satisfy creative needs as well as provide food and shelter.

The hidden hunger has to do with the need for recognition. A group of girls was studied. They reacted with increased production to every change in working conditions (temperature, lighting, seating, etc.) including those that were for the worse. What was important to them was not the improvement of conditions but the gesture of interest.

A person wants to be, to belong, and to become. He needs to feel that he is worthwhile, doing a worthwhile job. "Let my life mean something," is his request.

His ideal job would give him a purpose in life and make him part of a world-wide society of workers. He would be proud of his work: he would have a chance to develop and to show off his strongest skills and talents; his interest and abilities would be stimulated through a variety of tasks; he would be given freedom to make decisions.

Increasing a worker's decision-making authority satisfies his ego needs. When a corporation allowed its salesmen to set their own work standards and quotas their sales increased 116 per cent over groups not given this freedom.

Opportunity for self-expression is desired. Work of any kind, manual or brain, can be made the intimate expression of oneself. Without the opportunity to live up to his fullest possibilities a worker shrinks and dwindles. He loses his dignity as an individual.

Satisfying the Hunger

While keeping in mind the necessary connection between work and reward, there are some lines of action that may be taken to satisfy the worker's hidden hunger.

Job rotation means that the worker moves from one task to a related task within his group. Job enlargement has the worker assume several related tasks. Job enrichment makes use of more of the employee's capabilities and allows him to accept accountability for arranging his job. It expands the worker's personality by adding the managerial functions of planning and controlling to the actual doing of the job.

Making a wheelbarrow can be a satisfying job, but not if your part of the job consists only in inspecting the ball-bearings. To make a whole piece of pottery with your own hands is to live again through a heartwarming triumph of early mankind: you become a more or less conscious creator, a person who dominates intractable elements and resistant forces.

To make up natural units of work means to put the components of a job into a group so as to form a single responsibility.

Professor Frederick Herzberg made interesting discoveries about worker morale in a study in 1955. One major firm that drew upon his research changed the jobs of 120 girls, broadening their responsibility so that they could research, compose and sign letters without having them checked by a supervisor. The result was a drop in labour turnover of 27 per cent; 24 clerks did the work of 46; and $558,000 was saved in labour costs in eighteen months.

Democratic Leadership

Few advanced managers need to be convinced of the need for job enrichment: their quest is for ways in which to put the idea into effect. Some managers have found the secret: they make every worker a boss of something, and so allow him to feel a personal glow of pride in every achievement.

A supervisor can provide the conditions that stir the employee's desire to achieve. He can remove the road blocks preventing individuals from gaining satisfaction on the job. This does not mean that he should be permissive or lax or that he should abdicate his authority. He should develop in himself a democratic leadership style that encourages the employees to participate in planning and organizing their work. When this is properly done, the workers reach their personal goals in the process of meeting the firm's objectives.

Enlightened managers are increasingly aware of the inevitability of democracy as the pattern for a healthy society and of the importance of their role in supporting it. Under it, first-line supervisors become more than mechanical men carrying out executives' orders. Their own jobs are enriched, and they become more "resource persons and co-ordinators" than merely overseers.

Youth has its Say

Management has to work today with a more mobile and a better educated work force than was ever before available. Young people entering employment are likely to be more independent than were their elders, more accustomed to comforts, less respectful of codes of dress, speech and personal appearance, and more forthright in presenting their opinions.

They not only want to know what is expected of them, and what standards they must meet, but to have a hand in setting those standards. An essay in *Time* warned that some of them may be too educated, too expectant, and too anti-authoritarian for many of the jobs that the present economy offers them.

The advent of these young people to the work force is a fact of life to be reckoned with. They want significant jobs from the very beginning of their careers. They have high expectations for job satisfaction. Their fathers, with scars of the great depression still giving them twinges of pain, value job security very highly, but for the young there has to be more to a job than assurance that they will eat regularly.

During the first half of the century it was not uncommon for municipalities seeking to attract factories to advertise "abundance of cheap labour." They were admitting the fact that their men and women had not been educated beyond the doing of rough and routine tasks. Today, everyone is educated, not only in school and university but by newspapers, magazines, books, television and radio. Courses in all kinds of crafts and arts are available to any adult people who wish to employ their evenings in personal betterment.

The challenge facing employers is to work toward making the jobs suitable to the requirements of this new pattern.

The Worker's Responsibility

Not all the responsibility rests upon management. Every worker has obligations to himself and to his employer.

Work is an individual thing, even if one does it in company with a gang or a group or on a production line. It is a person's own, to do well or ill, to improve or debase.

A progressive worker is miles apart from the person who depends upon luck or a union or his personal winning ways to get him what he wants out of life. A good apple-polisher is not always a good grower of apple trees.

There are some basic truths that should be known to all workers and prospective workers, even though at times they seem to be obscured by passing events.

You should know what your job requires of you and where you stand in it. You have to conform to the rhythm of the plant or office: if you are a member of a rowing crew you cannot show rugged individuality in the way you dip your oar even if you are convinced that your way will push the shell along faster. You are entitled to hold your job only so long as you fill your position efficiently.

It is worth while to use all your equipment and to develop new skills, and thus make work exciting and absorbing. Everyone should remain in a state of growth and interest. Sir William Van Horne, who progressed from railway telegraph operator to push through the Canadian Pacific Railway to completion and to end his working life as president of the board of directors, said "What interests a man cannot be called work."

If your interest seems to be dwindling, do a little self-analysis. Have you kept up so as to remain capable of handling the job efficiently? Is your education adequate to enable you to cope with new and complex situations? Does your personality enable you to work smoothly with other people? Are you satisfied that the job you are doing is useful to society?

In addition to the care lavished on raising the standard of living we need a movement to raise the standard of thinking. No one will deny that some jobs are more interesting than others, but it is also true that one mind is more interested and thinks on a higher level than another.

The animal part of man's nature prompts him to avoid difficulties, to follow the lines of least resistance, to be satisfied with existing; but every mature human being feels the need to stretch his mind, to be intellectually aware, to replace the brute instincts with responsible action.

On being a Craftsman

A craftsman is one who is skilled in his job. All work, on however lowly a plane, can be pleasurable if skill is used in its performance. Even in nailing two boards together one may take pride in hitting the nail on the head.

Respect for quality performance is the chief attribute of the craftsman. His respect for his job becomes self-respect and contributes to the dignity of his life.

Taking pains with a job is somewhat akin to genius in its effects. President Abraham Lincoln was invited to "make a few appropriate remarks" at the dedication of the Gettysburg National Cemetery. In typical Lincoln effort for excellence he used care and work in his preparation, although his address contained only 265 words. Instead of a routine and formal statement he gave the world something very beautiful.

Conscientious completeness turns out a product that gives the worker satisfaction and pride. A craftsman in any line should bear in mind the doctor whose prayer was that he might never become slovenly in his work or so disinterested as to make a habit of prescribing "the mixture as before."

To contend that the element of drudgery can be wholly eliminated from work would be ridiculous. But it can be ameliorated. Work is what we make it: it can be worthy and satisfying whether it be putting nuts on bolts, building a house, managing an enterprise, painting a portrait, conducting research, or rendering professional service.

A person can put the stamp of his own spirit upon his work so that it becomes uniquely his. Fellow street-sweepers were discussing one their number after his death. One man said: "What impressed me was his interest in doing a good job; look at the way he took special pains to sweep clean around lamp posts. You could always tell a lamp post that Charlie had swept around."

Analyse your successes, however small, so that you discover or rediscover your skills and satisfactions. The person who is dissatisfied with his job but neglects to learn the possibilities that life holds out to him through work, or who is slothful about doing something to improve his position in life, is like a man who is trying to score a goal in a game he dislikes.

When Opportunity Knocks

When opportunity for advancement or improvement in your job knocks at your door she is usually wearing overalls. The pursuit of happiness means work; freedom means being able to work for things you want; independence means standing on your own feet free from dependence on the bounty of others; self-respect is the result of working for what you get.

Man has to work because work is an economic necessity (unless he is content to live on the dole); because it is a social obligation (unless he is content to be graded with the beasts), and because it is a basic human right (if he wishes to gain a sense of self-fulfillment).

The value of work is a personal thing. What we do may matter little in the history of the world, but it matters very much to ourselves that we should have some work to do. Otherwise, much of life will pass us by.

Nowhere in all the world can we find a more impressive monument to hard work coupled with vision, thrift and courage, than the civilization which flourishes in Canada.

QUESTIONS

1. "A full pay envelope does not satisfy all wants."
   Aside from adequate salaries and satisfactory working conditions, what needs do teachers and administrators have which should be satisfied?

2. "Every mature human being feels the need to stretch his mind."
   Should a superintendent or principal try to motivate his staff to stretch their minds? How?

PEOPLE

By
Robert Townsend

The former president of Avis explains the difference between Theory X and Theory Y in popular terms and illustrates them by a personal reference.

Like it or not, he says, the only practical act is to adopt Theory Y assumptions and get going.

There's nothing fundamentally wrong with our country except that the leaders of all our major organizations are operating on the wrong assumptions.[1] We're in this mess because for the last two hundred years we've been using the Catholic Church and Caesar's legions as our patterns for creating organizations. And until the last forty or fifty years it made sense. The average church-goer, soldier, and factory worker was uneducated and dependent on orders from above. And authority carried considerable weight because disobedience brought the death penalty or its equivalent.[2]

From the behavior of people in these early industrial organizations we arrived at the following assumptions,[3] on which all modern organizations are still operating:

1. *People hate work.*
2. *They have to be driven and threatened with punishment to get them to work toward organizational objectives.*
3. *They like security, aren't ambitious, want to be told what to do, dislike responsibility.*

You don't think we are operating on these assumptions? Consider:

1. *Office hours nine to five for everybody except the fattest cats at the top. Just a giant cheap time clock. (Are we buying brains or hours?)*

---

[1] By all the evidence, the other industrialized countries are as bad off, but no worse; their major institutions are operated on the same silly assumptions.

[2] Dismissal and blacklisting brought starvation to an industrial worker; excommunication brought the spiritual equivalent of death to a churchgoer.

[3] Douglas McGregor (see Bibliography) called these three assumptions "Theory X." Organizations that run on these premises — the hierarchies — are Theory X outfits.

"People," by Robert Townsend, from pp. 137-143 in *Up the Organization*, by Robert Townsend. Copyright © 1970 by Robert Townsend. Reprinted by permission of Alfred A. Knopf, Inc.

2. *Unilateral promotions. For more money and a bigger title I'm expected to jump at the chance of moving my family to New York City. I run away from the friends and a life style in Denver that have made me and my family happy and effective. (Organization comes first; individuals must sacrifice themselves to its demands.)*
3. *Hundreds of millions of dollars are spent annually "communicating" with employees. The message always boils down to: "Work hard, obey orders. We'll take care of you." (That message is obsolete by fifty years and wasn't very promising then.)*

Back off a minute. Let's pretend we know everything man knows about human nature and its present condition here, but nothing about man's organizations and the assumptions on which they're based. These things[4] we know about man:

1. *He's a wanting animal.*
2. *His behavior is determined by unsatisfied needs that he wants to satisfy.*
3. *His needs form a value hierarchy that is internal, not external:*
   (a) *body (I can't breathe.)*
   (b) *safety (How can I protect myself from . . . ?)*
   (c) *social (I want to belong.)*
   (d) *ego (1. Gee, I'm terrific. 2. Aren't I? Yes.)*
   (e) *development (Gee, I'm better than I was last year.)*

Man is totally motivated by each level of need in order — until that level is satisfied. If he hasn't slept in three days he's totally motivated by a need for sleep. After he has slept, eaten, drunk, is safe, and has acceptance in a group, he is no longer motivated by those three levels of needs. (McGregor's examples: The only time you think of air is when you are deprived of it; man lives by bread alone when there is no bread.)

We know that these first three need levels are pretty well satisfied[5] in America's work force today. So we would expect man's organizations to be designed to feed the ego and development needs. But there's the whole problem. The result of our outmoded organizations is that we're still acting as if people were uneducated peasants. Much of the work done today would be more suitable for young children or mental defectives.

---

[4] McGregor again.

[5] This book does not come to grips with the problem of America's 20 million poor: it deals with the 80 million psychiatric cases who do have jobs.

And look at the rewards we're offering our people today: higher wages, medical benefits, vacations, pensions, profit sharing, bowling and baseball teams. *Not one can be enjoyed on the job.* You've got to leave work, get sick, or retire first. No wonder people aren't having fun on the job.

So what are the valid assumptions for present-day circumstances? McGregor called them "Theory Y":

1. *People* don't *hate work. It's as natural as rest or play.*
2. *They don't* have *to be forced or threatened. If they commit themselves to mutual objectives, they'll drive themselves more effectively than you can drive them.*
3. *But they'll commit themselves only to the extent they can see ways of satisfying their ego and development needs (remember the others are pretty well satisfied and are no longer prime drives).*

All you have to do is look around you to see that modern organizations are only getting people to use about 20 per cent — the lower fifth — of their capacities. And the painful part is that God didn't design the human animal to function at 20 per cent. At that pace it develops enough malfunctions to cause a permanent shortage of psychoanalysts and hospital beds.

Since 1952 I've been stumbling around building and running primitive "Theory Y" departments, divisions, and finally one whole "Theory Y" company: Avis.

In 1962 after thirteen years Avis had never made a profit.[6] Three years later the company had grown internally (not by acquisitions) from $30 million sales to $75 million sales, and had made successive annual profits of $1 million, $3 million, and $5 million. If I had anything to do with this, I ascribe it all to my application of Theory Y. And a faltering, stumbling, groping, mistake-ridden application it was.

You want proof? I can't give it to you. But let me tell you a story. When I became head of Avis I was assured that no one at headquarters was any good, and that my first job was to start recruiting a whole new team. Three years later, Hal Geneen, the President of ITT (which had just acquired Avis), after meeting everybody and listening to them in action for a day, said, "I've never seen such depth of management; why I've already spotted three chief executive officers!" You guessed it. Same people. I'd brought in only two new people, a lawyer and an accountant.

---

[6]Except one year when they jiggled their depreciation rates.

Bill Bernbach used to say about advertising effectiveness: "Ninety per cent of the battle is what you say and 10 per cent is what medium you say it in." The same thing is true of people. Why spend all that money and time on the *selection* of people when the people you've got are breaking down from under-use.

Get to know your people. What they do well, what they enjoy doing, what their weaknesses and strengths are, and what they want and need to get from their job. And then try to create an organization around your people, not jam your people into those organization-chart rectangles. The only excuse for organization is to maximize the chance that each one, working with others, will get for growth in his job. You can't motivate people. That door is locked from the inside. You *can* create a climate in which most of your people will motivate themselves to help the company reach its objectives. Like it or not, the only practical act is to adopt Theory Y assumptions and get going.

It isn't easy, but what you're really trying to do is come between a man and his family. You want him to enjoy his work so much he comes in on Saturday instead of playing golf or cutting the grass. . .

QUESTIONS

1. Look around your school faculty and see whether Townsend is right when he says that modern organizations are only getting people to use about 20 per cent of their capacities. How might a top-level administrator release the undeveloped potential of his staff?

2. You can't motivate people, says Townsend. How then can a school executive create a climate in which teachers will motivate themselves to help the school reach its goals?

BEYOND THEORY Y

By
John J. Morse and Jay W. Lorsch

Both Theory X and Theory Y work well in some situations but not in others. There is no one best organizational approach. Predictable tasks are best carried on under Theory X; problem-solving tasks under Theory Y.

Contingency Theory, which goes beyond Theory Y, seeks a fit between task, organization, and people. It assumes that all workers want to achieve a sense of competence. The sense of competence motive can be fulfilled in different ways but is most likely to be fulfilled when the organization is tailored to fit the task and people. When a worker achieves one competence goal, he sets a new higher one for himself.

Some implications of Contingency Theory are set forth but further study is necessary.

BEYOND THEORY Y

During the past 30 years, managers have been bombarded with two competing approaches to the problems of human administration and organization. The first, usually called the classical school of organization, emphasizes the need for well-established lines of authority, clearly defined jobs, and authority equal to responsibility. The second, often called the participative approach, focuses on the desirability of involving organization members in decision making so that they will be more highly motivated.

Douglas McGregor, through his well-known "Theory X and Theory Y," drew a distinction between the assumptions about human motivation which underlie these two approaches, to this effect:

Theory X assumes that people dislike work and must be coerced, controlled, and directed toward organizational goals. Furthermore, most people prefer to be treated this way, so they can avoid responsibility.

"Beyond Theory Y," by John J. Morse and Jay W. Lorsch, May-June 1970, *Harvard Business Review*. Copyright © 1970 by the President and Fellows of Harvard College; all rights reserved. Reprinted by permission of Harvard Business Review.

Theory Y — the integration of goals — emphasizes the average person's intrinsic interest in his work, his desire to be self-directing and to seek responsibility, and his capacity to be creative in solving business problems.

It is McGregor's conclusion, of course, that the latter approach to organization is the more desirable one for managers to follow.[1]

McGregor's position causes confusion for the managers who try to choose between these two conflicting approaches. The classical organizational approach that McGregor associated with Theory X does work well in some situations, although, as McGregor himself pointed out, there are also some situations where it does not work effectively. At the same time, the approach based on Theory Y, while it has produced good results in some situations, does not always do so. That is, each approach is effective in some cases but not in others. Why is this? How can managers resolve the confusion?

A New Approach

Recent work by a number of students of management and organization may help to answer such questions.[2] These studies indicate that there is not one best organizational approach; rather, the best approach depends on the nature of the work to be done. Enterprises with highly predictable tasks perform better with organizations characterized by the highly formalized procedures and management hierarchies of the classical approach. With highly uncertain tasks that require more extensive problem solving, on the other hand, organizations that are less formalized and emphasize self-control and member participation in decision making are more effective. In essence, according to these newer studies, managers must design and develop organizations so that the organizational characteristics *fit* the nature of the task to be done.

While the conclusions of this newer approach will make sense to most experienced managers and can alleviate much of the confusion about which approach to choose, there are still two important questions unanswered:

---

[1] Douglas McGregor, *The Human Side of Enterprise* (New York, McGraw-Hill Book Company, Inc., 1960), pp. 34-35 and pp. 47-48.

[2] See for example Paul R. Lawrence and Jay W. Lorsch, *Organization and Environment* (Boston, Harvard Business School, Division of Research, 1967), Joan Woodward, *Industrial Organization: Theory & Practice* (New York, Oxford University Press, Inc., 1965); Tom Burnsman; G. M. Stalker, *The Management of Innovation* (London, Tavistock Publications, 1961); Harold J. Leavitt, "Unhuman Organizations," HBR July-August 1962, p. 90.

1. How does the more formalized and controlling organization affect the motivation of organization members? (McGregor's most telling criticism of the classical approach was that it did not unleash the potential in an enterprise's human resources.)
2. Equally important, does a less formalized organization always provide a high level of motivation for its members? (This is the implication many managers have drawn from McGregor's work.)

We have recently been involved in a study that provides surprising answers to these questions and, when taken together with other recent work, suggests a new set of basic assumptions which move beyond Theory Y into what we call "Contingency Theory: the fit between task, organization, and people." These theoretical assumptions emphasize that the appropriate pattern of organization is *contingent* on the nature of the work to be done and on the particular needs of the people involved. We should emphasize that we have labeled these assumptions as a step beyond Theory Y because of McGregor's own recognition that the Theory Y assumptions would probably be supplanted by new knowledge within a short time.[3]

The Study Design

Our study was conducted in four organizational units. Two of these performed the relatively certain task of manufacturing standardized containers on high-speed, automated production lines. The other two performed the relatively uncertain work of research and development in communications technology. Each pair of units performing the same kind of task were in the same large company, and each pair had previously been evaluated by that company's management as containing one highly effective unit and a less effective one. The study design is summarized in *Exhibit I*.

The objective was to explore more fully how the fit between organization and task was related to successful performance. That is, does a good fit between organizational characteristics and task requirements increase the motivation of individuals and hence produce more effective individual and organizational performance?

An especially useful approach to answering this question is to recognize that an individual has a strong need to master the world around him, including the task that he faces as a member of a work organization.[4] The accumulated feelings of satisfaction that come from successfully mastering one's

---

[3] McGregor, op. cit., p. 245.

[4] See Robert W. White, "Ego and Reality in Psychoanalytic Theory," *Psychological Issues*, Vol. III, No. 3 (New York, International Universities Press, 1963).

environment can be called a "sense of competence." We saw this sense of competence in performing a particular task as helpful in understanding how a fit between task and organizational characteristics could motivate people toward successful performance.

Exhibit I

STUDY DESIGN IN "FIT" OF ORGANIZATIONAL CHARACTERISTICS

Characteristics	Company I (predictable manufacturing task)	Company II (unpredictable R&D task)
Effective performer	Akron containers plant	Stockton research lab
Less effective performer	Hartford containers plant	Carmel research lab

Organizational Dimensions

Because the four study sites had already been evaluated by the respective corporate managers as high and low performers of tasks, we expected that such differences in performance would be a preliminary clue to differences in the "fit" of the organizational characteristics to the job to be done. But, first, we had to define what kinds of organizational characteristics would determine how appropriate the organization was to the particular task.

We grouped these organizational characteristics into two sets of factors:

1. Formal characteristics, which could be used to judge the fit between the kind of task being worked on and the formal practices of the organization.
2. Climate characteristics, or the subjective perceptions and orientations that had developed among the individuals about their organizational setting. (These too must fit the task to be performed if the organization is to be effective.)

We measured these attributes through questionnaires and interviews with about 40 managers in each unit to determine the appropriateness of the organization to the kind of task being performed. We also measured the feelings of competence of the people in the organizations so that we could link the appropriateness of the organizational attributes with a sense of competence.

Major Findings

The principal findings of the survey are best highlighted by contrasting the highly successful Akron plant and the high-performing Stockton laboratory. Because each performed very different tasks (the former a relatively certain manufacturing task and the latter a relatively uncertain research task), we expected, as brought out earlier, that there would have to be major differences between them in organizational characteristics if they were to perform effectively. And this is what we did find. But we also found that each of these effective units had a better fit with its particular task than did its less effective counterpart.

While our major purpose in this article is to explore how the fit between task and organizational characteristics is related to motivation, we first want to explore more fully the organizational characteristics of these units, so the reader will better understand what we mean by a fit between task and organization and how it can lead to more effective behavior. To do this, we shall place the major emphasis on the contrast between the high-performing units (the Akron plant and Stockton laboratory), but we shall also compare each of these with its less effective mate (the Hartford plant and Carmel laboratory respectively).

Formal Characteristics

Beginning with differences in formal characteristics, we found that both the Akron and Stockton organizations fit their respective tasks much better than did their less successful counterparts. In the predictable manufacturing task environment, Akron had a pattern of formal relationships and duties that was highly structured and precisely defined. Stockton, with its unpredictable research task, had a low degree of structure and much less precision of definition (see *Exhibit II*).

Akron's pattern of formal rules, procedures, and control systems was so specific and comprehensive that it prompted one manager to remark:

"We've got rules here for everything from how much powder to use in cleaning the toilet bowls to how to cart a dead body out of the plant."

In contrast, Stockton's formal rules were so minimal, loose, and flexible that one scientist, when asked whether he felt the rules ought to be tightened, said:

Exhibit II

DIFFERENCES IN FORMAL CHARACTERISTICS IN HIGH-PERFORMING ORGANIZATIONS

Characteristics	Akron	Stockton
1. Pattern of formal relationships and duties as signified by organization charts and job manuals	Highly structured, precisely defined	Low degree of structure, less well defined
2. Pattern of formal rules, procedures, control, and measurement systems	Pervasive, specific, uniform, comprehensive	Minimal, loose, flexible
3. Time dimensions incorporated in formal practices	Short-term	Long-term
4. Goal dimensions incorporated in formal practices	Manufacturing	Scientific

"If a man puts a nut on a screw all day long, you may need more rules and a job definition for him. But we're not novices here. We're professionals and not the kind who need close supervision. People around here *do* produce, and produce under relaxed conditions. Why tamper with success?"

These differences in formal organizational characteristics were well suited to the differences in tasks of the two organizations. Thus:

Akron's highly structured formal practices fit its predictable task because behavior had to be rigidly defined and controlled around the automated, high-speed production line. There was really only one way to accomplish the plant's very routine and programmable job; managers defined it precisely and insisted (through the plant's formal practices) that each man do what was expected of him.

On the other hand, Stockton's highly unstructured formal practices made just as much sense because the required activities in the laboratory simply could not be rigidly defined in advance. With such an unpredictable, fast-changing task as communications technology research, there were numerous approaches to getting the job done well. As a consequence, Stockton managers used a less structured pattern of formal practices that left the scientists in the lab free to respond to the changing task situation.

Akron's formal practices were very much geared to *short-term* and *manufacturing* concerns as its task demanded. For example, formal production reports and operating review sessions were daily occurrences, consistent with the fact that the through-put time for their products was typically only a few hours.

By contrast, Stockton's formal practices were geared to *long-term* and *scientific* concerns, as its task demanded. Formal reports and reviews were made only quarterly, reflecting the fact that research often does not come to fruition for three to five years.

At the two less effective sites (i.e., the Hartford plant and the Carmel laboratory), the formal organizational characteristics did not fit their respective tasks nearly as well. For example, Hartford's formal practices were much less structured and controlling than were Akron's, while Carmel's were more restraining and restricting than were Stockton's. A scientist in Carmel commented:

"There's something here that keeps you from being scientific. It's hard to put your finger on, but I guess I'd call it 'Mickey Mouse.' There are rules and things here that get in your way regarding doing your job as a researcher."

Climate Characteristics

As with formal practices, the climate in both high-performing Akron and Stockton suited the respective tasks much better than did the climates at the less successful Hartford and Carmel sites.

Perception of structure. The people in the Akron plant perceived a great deal of structure, with their behavior tightly controlled and defined. One manager in the plant said:

"We can't let the lines run unattended. We lose money whenever they do. So we make sure each man knows his job; knows when he can take a break, knows how to handle a change in shifts, etc. It's all spelled out clearly for him the day he comes to work here."

In contrast, the scientists in the Stockton laboratory perceived very little structure, with their behavior only minimally controlled. Such perceptions encouraged the individualistic and creative behavior that the uncertain, rapidly changing research task needed. Scientists in the less successful Carmel laboratory perceived much more structure in their organization and voiced the feeling that this was "getting in their way" and making it difficult to do effective research.

Distribution of influence. The Akron plant and the Stockton laboratory also differed substantially in how influence was distributed and on the character of superior-subordinate and colleague relations. Akron personnel felt that they had much less influence over decisions in their plant than Stockton's scientists did in their laboratory. The task at Akron had already been clearly defined and that definition had, in a sense, been incorporated into the automated production flow itself. Therefore, there was less need for individuals to have a say in decisions concerning the work process.

Moreover, in Akron, influence was perceived to be concentrated in the upper levels of the formal structure (a hierarchical or "top-heavy" distribution), while in Stockton influence was perceived to be more evenly spread out among more levels of the formal structure (an egalitarian distribution).

Akron's members perceived themselves to have a low degree of freedom vis-à-vis superiors both in choosing the jobs they work on and in handling these jobs on their own. They also described the type of supervision in the plant as being relatively directive. Stockton's scientists, on the other hand felt that they had a great deal of freedom vis-à-vis their superiors both in choosing the tasks and projects, and in handling them in the way that they wanted to. They described supervision in the laboratory as being very participatory.

It is interesting to note that the less successful Carmel laboratory had more of its decisions made at the top. Because of this, there was a definite feeling by the scientists that their particular expertise was not being effectively used in choosing projects.

Relations with others. The people at Akron perceived a great deal of similarity among themselves in background, prior work experiences, and approaches for tackling job-related problems. They also perceived the degree of coordination of effort among colleagues to be very high. Because Akron's task was so precisely defined and the behavior of its members so rigidly controlled around the automated lines, it is easy to see that this pattern also made sense.

By contrast, Stockton's scientists perceived not only a great many differences among themselves, especially in education and background, but also that the coordination of effort among colleagues was relatively low. This was appropriate for a laboratory in which a great variety of disciplines and skills were present and individual projects were important to solve technological problems.

Time orientation. As we would expect, Akron's individuals were highly oriented toward a relatively short time span and manufacturing goals. They responded to quick feedback concerning the quality and service that the plant was providing. This was essential, given the nature of their task.

Stockton's researchers were highly oriented toward a longer time span and scientific goals. These orientations meant that they were willing to wait for long-term feedback from a research project that might take years to complete. A scientist in Stockton said:

"We're not the kind of people here who need a pat on the back every day. We can wait for months if necessary before we get feedback from colleagues and the profession. I've been working on one project now for three months and I'm still not sure where it's going to take me. I can live with that, though."

This is precisely the kind of behavior and attitude that spells success on this kind of task.

Managerial style. Finally, the individuals in both Akron and Stockton perceived their chief executive to have a "managerial style" that expressed more of a concern for the task than for people or relationships, but this seemed to fit both tasks.

In Akron, the technology of the task was so dominant that top managerial behavior which was not focused primarily on the task might have reduced the effectiveness of performance. On the other hand, although Stockton's research task called for more individualistic problem-solving behavior, that sort of behavior could have become segmented and uncoordinated, unless the top executive in the lab focused the group's attention on the overall research task. Given the individualistic bent of the scientists, this was an important force in achieving unity of effort.

All these differences in climate characteristics in the two high performers are summarized in *Exhibit III* (see next page).

As with formal attributes, the less effective Hartford and Carmel sites had organization climates that showed a perceptibly lower degree of fit with their respective tasks. For example, the Hartford plant had an egalitarian distribution of influence, perceptions of a low degree of structure, and a more participatory type of supervision. The Carmel laboratory had a somewhat top-heavy distribution of influence, perceptions of high structure, and a more directive type of supervision.

Competence Motivation

Because of the difference in organizational characteristics at Akron and Stockton, the two sites were strikingly different places in which to work. But these organizations had two very important things in common. First, each organization fit very well the requirements of its task. Second, although the behavior in the two organizations was different, the result in both cases was effective task performance.

Since, as we indicated earlier, our primary concern in this study was to link the fit between organization and task with individual motivation to perform effectively, we devised a two-part test to measure the sense of competence motivation of the individuals at both sites. Thus:

The *first* part asked a participant to write creative and imaginative stories in response to six ambiguous pictures.

The *second* asked him to write a creative and imaginative story about what he would be doing, thinking, and feeling "tomorrow" on his job. This

Exhibit III

DIFFERENCES IN "CLIMATE" CHARACTERISTICS IN HIGH-PERFORMING ORGANIZATIONS

Characteristics	Akron	Stockton
1. Structural orientation	Perceptions of tightly controlled behavior and a high degree of structure	Perceptions of a low degree of structure
2. Distribution of influence	Perceptions of low total influence, concentrated at upper levels in the organization	Perceptions of high total influence, more evenly spread out among all levels
3. Character of superior-subordinate relations	Low freedom vis-a-vis superiors to choose and handle jobs, directive type of supervision	High freedom vis-à-vis superiors to choose and handle projects, participatory type of supervision
4. Character of colleague relations	Perceptions of many similarities among colleagues, high degree of coordination of colleague effort	Perceptions of many differences among colleagues, relatively low degree of coordination of colleague effort
5. Time orientation	Short-term	Long-term
6. Goal orientation	Manufacturing	Scientific
7. Top executive's "managerial style"	More concerned with task than people	More concerned with task than people

is called a "projective" test because it is assumed that the respondent projects into his stories his own attitudes, thoughts, feelings, needs, and wants, all of which can be measured from the stories.[5]

The results indicated that the individuals in Akron and Stockton showed significantly more feelings of competence than did their counterparts in the lower-fit Hartford and Carmel organizations.[6] We found that the organization-task fit is simultaneously linked to and interdependent with both individual motivation and effective unit performance. (This interdependency is illustrated in *Exhibit IV*.)

Putting the conclusions in this form raises the question of cause and effect. Does effective unit performance result from the task-organization fit or from higher motivation, or perhaps from both? Does higher sense of competence motivation result from effective unit performance or from fit?

Our answer to these questions is that we do not think there are any single cause-and-effect relationships, but that these factors are mutually interrelated. This has important implications for management theory and practice.

Exhibit IV

BASIC CONTINGENT RELATIONSHIP

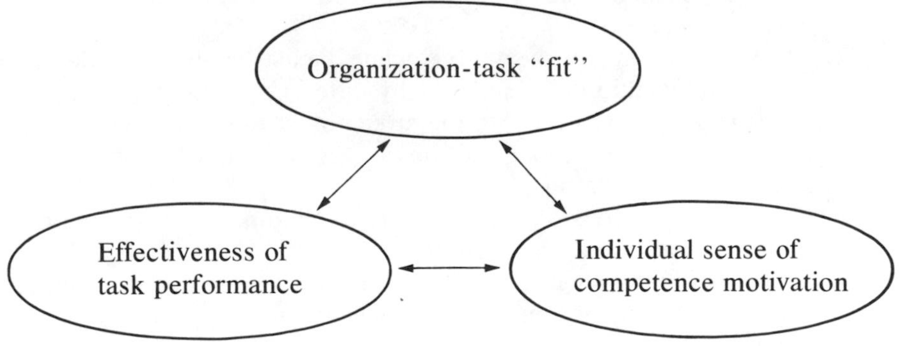

[5] For a more detailed description of this survey, see John J. Morse, *Internal Organizational Patterning and Sense of Competence Motivation* (Boston, Harvard Business School, unpublished doctoral dissertation, 1969).

[6] Differences between the two container plants are significant at .001 and between the research laboratories at .01 (one-tailed probability).

Contingency Theory

Returning to McGregor's Theory X and Theory Y assumptions, we can now question the validity of some of his conclusions. While Theory Y might help to explain the findings in the two laboratories, we clearly need something other than Theory X or Y assumptions to explain the findings in the plants.

For example, the managers at Akron worked in a formalized organization setting with relatively little participation in decision making, and yet they were highly motivated. According to Theory X, people would work hard in such a setting only because they were coerced to do so. According to Theory Y, they should have been involved in decision making and been self-directed to feel so motivated. Nothing in our data indicates that either set of assumptions was valid at Akron.

Conversely, the managers at Hartford, the low-performing plant, were in a less formalized organization with more participation in decision making, and yet they were not as highly motivated like the Akron managers. The Theory Y assumptions would suggest that they should have been more motivated.

A way out of such paradoxes is to state a new set of assumptions, the Contingency Theory, that seems to explain the findings at all four sites:

1. Human beings bring varying patterns of needs and motives into the work organization, but one central need is to achieve a sense of competence.
2. The sense of competence motive, while it exists in all human beings, may be fulfilled in different ways by different people depending on how this need interacts with the strengths of the individuals' other needs — such as those for power, independence, structure, achievement, and affiliation.
3. Competence motivation is most likely to be fulfilled when there is a fit between task and organization.
4. Sense of competence continues to motivate even when a competence goal is achieved; once one goal is reached, a new, higher one is set.

While the central thrust of these points is clear from the preceding discussion of the study, some elaboration can be made. First, the idea that different people have different needs is well understood by psychologists. However, all too often, managers assume that all people have similar needs. Lest we be accused of the same error, we are saying only that all people have a need to feel competent; in this *one* way they are similar. But in many other dimensions of personality, individuals differ, and these differences will determine how a particular person achieves a sense of competence.

Thus, for example, the people in the Akron plant seemed to be very different from those in the Stockton laboratory in their underlying attitudes toward uncertainty, authority, and relationships with their peers. And because they had different need patterns along these dimensions, both groups were highly motivated by achieving competence from quite different activities and settings.

While there is a need to further investigate how people who work in different settings differ in their psychological makeup, one important implication of the Contingency Theory is that we must not only seek a fit between organization and task, but also between task and people and between people and organization.

A further point which requires elaboration is that one's sense of competence never really comes to rest. Rather, the real satisfaction of this need is in the successful performance itself, with no diminishing of the motivation as one goal is reached. Since feelings of competence are thus reinforced by successful performance, they can be a more consistent and reliable motivator than salary and benefits.

Implications for Managers

The major managerial implication of the Contingency Theory seems to rest in the task-organization-people fit. Although this interrelationship is complex, the best possibility for managerial action probably is in tailoring the organization to fit the task and the people. If such a fit is achieved, both effective unit performance and a higher sense of competence motivation seem to result.

Managers can start this process by considering how certain the task is, how frequently feedback about task performance is available, and what goals are implicit in the task. The answers to these questions will guide their decisions about the design of the management hierarchy, the specificity of job assignments, and the utilization of rewards and control procedures. Selective use of training programs and a general emphasis on appropriate management styles will move them toward a task-organization fit.

The problem of achieving a fit among task, organization, and people is something we know less about. As we have already suggested, we need further investigation of what personality characteristics fit various tasks and organizations. Even with our limited knowledge, however, there are indications that people will gradually gravitate into organizations that fit their particular personalities. Managers can help this process by becoming more aware of what psychological needs seem to best fit the tasks available and the organizational setting, and by trying to shape personnel selection criteria to take account of these needs.

In arguing for an approach which emphasizes the fit among task, organization, and people, we are putting to rest the question of which organizational approach — the classical or the participative — is best. In its place we are raising a new question: What organizational approach is most appropriate given the task and the people involved?

For many enterprises, given the new needs of younger employees for more autonomy, and the rapid rates of social and technological change, it may well be that the more participative approach is the most appropriate. But there will still be many situations in which the more controlled and formalized organization is desirable. Such an organization need not be coercive or punitive. If it makes sense to the individuals involved, given their needs and their jobs, they will find it rewarding and motivating.

Concluding Note

The reader will recognize that the complexity we have described is not of our own making. The basic deficiency with earlier approaches is that they did not recognize the variability in tasks and people which produces this complexity. The strength of the contingency approach we have outlined is that it begins to provide a way of thinking about this complexity, rather than ignoring it. While our knowledge in this area is still growing, we are certain that any adequate theory of motivation and organization will have to take account of the contingent relationship between task, organization, and people.

QUESTIONS

1. From your own observation and experience, would you agree that predictable tasks are best carried on under Theory X and problem-solving tasks under Theory Y? Do teachers have to perform any predictable tasks? If so, should they be performed under the Theory Y concept?

2. Assuming that the Contingency Theory is valid, what are its implications for students, teachers, and administrators?

A NEW DIRTY WORD: ADMINISTRATOR

By
John White

Organizations seduce their personnel into identifying with them. When they identify with the employing organization, individuals compromise their principles and lose their individuality.

Promotion within an organization takes place until a person reaches his level of incompetency. The incompetent is more concerned with hiding his inadequacy than achieving the organization's goals. Insecurity is thus added to incompetency.

An adminis-traitor is characterized by incompetence, insecurity, and emphasis on system; an educator, by his concern for education.

A NEW DIRTY WORD: ADMINISTRATOR

The greatest hindrance to education is an administrator. Do not confuse an administrator with an educator. Administrators are a dime a dozen, but a real educator is rare. There are some people who leave the level of classroom teaching for greater responsibility, authority, and prestige of an administrative level, but nevertheless keep sight of their original values and goals — the improvement of human beings through education. These people remember why they first felt the call to teach. They remember the dream and the ideal which drew them to work with growing children. They sought promotion not for better pay or more power but simply because it offered wider opportunity to improve human minds. Such people are called educators; they are the most valuable people in the world.

All the rest are administrators. With varying degrees of mediocrity, they stumble along their shortsighted way, holding back positive innovation, rebuffing valuable change, and always, always wasting their efforts on trying to make the system run smoothly. What does an administrator strive for? The well-oiled machine, the neat little empire. Never mind the *purpose* of an educational system. Don't bother him with a lot of nonsense about concern

---

"A New Dirty Word: Administrator" by John White, *Changing Education*, Winter, 1969, pp. 43-44, official publication of the American Federation of Teachers, AFL-CIO. Reprinted by permission.

for students or with silly notions about making the world a better place. The administrator doesn't have time for it. He's busy perfecting a perpetual-motion machine in which routine is the mainspring and regulation is the driveshaft. The administrator aims at complete conformity and precision. Force the students to fit the system; standardize all individuality. His dream (O, the beauty of it all!) is to have a school completely free of students and staff, with waxed floors perpetually shiny and desks eternally in place.

How does a man get this way? Psychologists offer us a partial explanation: the organization man. One of the subtle but very real dangers of working for an organization is that, as a man rises in the organizational structure, he tends to identify himself with that structure. He immerses himself in the corporate image. Bit by bit, he surrenders his individuality; more and more, he becomes an extension of the organization. The end product is a neatly packaged item indistinguishable from countless other mass-produced humanoids.

Originally, our man was recognizable as a teacher. But for one reason or another — money, prestige, power — he sought promotion to higher levels. He got to it, but at the price of brainwashing himself and sacrificing his uniqueness. Over and over again, he has compromised his principles and suppressed his criticism in order to cultivate the proper image. Don't rock the boat; don't make waves; it disturbs the organizational millpond.

So, as he becomes integrated with the system, and rises to the top, his loyalty shifts. Whereas he first joined the educational structure for noble reasons which were centered outside the system, now he tends to be more concerned with the system itself. As a teacher, his concern was for education. He understood that school systems are only a *means* set up to achieve an *end* of literate, thinking, inquiring people. This was his loyalty.

As an administrator, however, he is less able to get into the classroom, less and less able to teach and observe. He's busy with business meetings; he's busy scheduling; he's busy regulating; he's busy trying to make the school more efficient. All these activities are necessary, of course, and even commendable — that is, until he loses sight of why they are necessary. When a man's emphasis and ultimate concern become focused on the system, rather than on the purpose for which the system was devised, then he has truly become an administrator. This is the point at which he ceases to be of value to education.

There is one other aspect of organization which accounts for much of the inertia in education today. A Canadian professor named Peter recently proposed a theory, called the Peter Principle, which attempts to explain incompetency in organizations.

Briefly it is this. An organization is a many-leveled structure with fewer positions available on each higher level. Promotion to those higher positions is based upon proving one's competency. So long as a person shows that he is competent, that he is capable of handling greater responsibility and workload, he will probably be promoted. But when it is clear that a man cannot do any better and will not succeed on a higher level, he is not promoted. Therefore he has risen in the hierarchy to a position he is not capable of adequately handling. He has reached his level of incompetency.

Then what happens? He stays there, of course! What organization ever demotes an employee? And so, all over the world, wherever there are organizations, one can find positions filled by men who are not fit for the job. They have risen to their level of incompetency, and there they stay.

What happens when a man functions in an inadequate, inefficient manner? Just look at any organization. There he is, the frustrated incompetent who knows he'll never rise higher, who knows he's not doing his job as well as possible. Ego becomes of primary importance to someone in such an insecure position, and so he begins to protect it with a lot of stupid little routines and regulations that are supposed to show others how well he can work. He dazzles them with his paperwork; he snows them with his administration. Make yourself look good by making others look bad, right? So he shoots down all suggestions and rejects all recommendations — or else claims them as his own. And, of course, he can try to get subordinates from getting wise to his incompetency by snarling at them so they don't bring around any more ideas for change which might upset his comfortable routine.

What has been said here? 1) In general, organizations tend to seduce their personnel into identifying with the organization. This encourages compromise of principles and loss of individuality for "the good of the system." 2) Promotion within an organization takes place until a person reaches his level of incompetency. Then a person is left to fill a position he is not capable of filling, so he becomes concerned with protecting his image rather than attaining the aims of the organization. This adds insecurity to incompetence.

Emphasis on system instead of goal, incompetence, insecurity. Put them all together, they spell ADMINIS-TRAITOR — a word that every person in education would do well to ponder. Where does the emphasis of a man's efforts lie? On administration or on education? One includes the other, but not vice versa. Every person in education should be an *educator,* but unfortunately, it just isn't so. Which are you?

QUESTIONS

1. Explain why you agree or disagree with Mr. White's belief that school systems seduce their personnel into identifying with them and that this encourages compromise of principles and loss of individuality.

2. Does the Peter Principle operate in school systems?

UNIT III

LEADERSHIP

LEADERSHIP

OVERVIEW

Business has long been interested in the phenomenon of leadership, much longer than education. Although students of business administration have investigated the theoretical and practical aspects of leadership for almost half a century, only during the last 20 years or so have school administrators recognized that leadership is a crucial question in education and that at every echelon, from the lowest to the highest, the selection and training of potential leaders, and their performance after they assume leadership roles, are matters of paramount concern.

A fair amount of writing about leadership, particularly in the field of business, has been inspirational and hortatory, based largely on personal experience. It is easy to denigrate the popularly written books and articles on leadership, yet they have influenced thousands beneficially. They are not helpful to serious students because they are based on opinion rather than on hard evidence resulting from scholarly inquiry.

The trait approach. The earliest approach to the systematic study of leadership consisted of a search for the traits which characterize leaders and set them apart from followers. The traitists hypothesized that effective leadership could be explained solely in terms of personality. They tried to identify the personal qualities which propelled individuals to leadership roles. Different researchers turned up with different lists of characteristics which they said leaders should possess, for example integrity, courage, imagination, dependability, foresight, intelligence, initiative, and sociability.

Basic to the trait approach was a definition of leadership as a combination of personal qualities which enables an individual to induce others to follow his direction in the accomplishment of an objective. Leadership was an influence process operating in one direction only, from leader to followers.

If the trait theory of leadership is valid, it follows that school administrators should seek out individuals with specified traits and train them to be leaders. Which traits? Stogdill's extensive review of the literature disclosed contradictory findings.[1] Thus with respect to age, six studies reported that effective leaders are generally younger but ten reported that they are older and seventeen reported that age must be considered in relation to the situation. Studies which sought to relate energy, emotional stability, intelligence, self-confidence, and other characteristics to leadership ability also resulted in contradictory results.

It is difficult to define each trait so that there is common agreement and no overlapping. Definition by synonyms is not helpful. To define self-confidence, for example, as self-reliance merely substitutes one verbal symbol for another. Unless self-confidence is defined operationally as a set of observable actions, it may mean different things to different persons.

The trait approach has contributed some findings which throw some light on the nature of leadership. Recent research shows that leaders differ from followers in self-oriented, task-oriented, and socially-oriented traits.[2] From a standpoint of self-orientation they tend to self-assured, physically active, verbally fluent, original, adaptable, independent, and tolerant of stress, ambiguity, and uncertainty. They are a cut above the average intelligence of the group they lead. Followers tend to distrust a leader whose

[1] Stogdill, R.M., "Personal Factors Associated With Leadership: A Survey of the Literature," *Journal of Psychology*, vol. 25, 1948, pp. 35-37.

[2] Stogdill, R.M., Nickels, W.G., and Zimmer, A., *Leadership: A Survey of the Literature on Characteristics, Attitudes, and Behavior Patterns*. Unpublished report, Greensboro, N. Car., Smith-Richardson Foundation, 1971.

intelligence is far beyond theirs, perhaps because they do not understand him or fear he does not understand them. No relationship between leadership and physique, extroversion, or emotional stability has yet been shown.

From a standpoint of task orientation, leaders exhibit a high level of responsibility, drive for production, and persistence in the face of obstacles. With respect to social orientation, they display a marked degree of sociability, administrative ability, and diplomacy. They are cooperative and able to enlist the cooperation of others.

It appears, then, that several clusters of traits distinguish leaders from followers, yet there is also evidence that a pattern of traits acceptable in one situation may not be acceptable in others.

Followers prefer leaders whose values and personality characteristics are similar to theirs, and they tend to be more productive under such leaders. This conclusion cannot be taken as uniformly true because satisfaction and productivity are contingent not only on leader-follower homogeneity but also on task demand and group structure. Moreover, groups are not always homogeneous and consequently their members hold different expectations of a leader's personality and the requirements of his role.

Trait theorists stressed the role of the leader and minimized that of his followers. Since they looked on leadership as one-directional, they implicitly approved a form of leader dominance which restricted follower initiative. Today leadership is not regarded as a one-way influence process but as a two-way interaction in which followers condition and limit a leader's responses. Admittedly, in this two-way interaction, the strongest influence is from leader to follower.

Although it is undeniable that personality is an element in the emergence and acceptance of leaders, the trait approach is of limited usefulness. Even if we could determine beyond doubt the traits necessary for leadership, we would not know the proper mix, that is, how much of this and how much of that trait are essential. Besides, some may possess leadership traits and yet not be leaders and, conversely, some may be leaders who lack them. The traits of leadership, if there are such, may be acquired after an individual has assumed a leadership role.

Trait research has not been helpful in selecting leaders. A survey of 52 studies in which personality scores were correlated with various measures of supervisory and executive success found the correlations impractical for selecting, placing, or promoting individuals in government and industry.[3]

Groups differ, and a leadership trait cluster acceptable to one may be unacceptable to another.

Different positions also make different demands. One may require a leader to initiate and maintain social interactions, and another may require individual and isolated activity such as paper work. Some lower echelon leaders handle technical details effectually but are uncomfortable and ineffective in high level positions in which they must deal with general and abstract ideas. To improve leader selection, the characteristics of both the leader and the position must be considered.

The sociological approach. While not denying the importance of personality traits, sociologists sought an explanation of leadership in the situation in which it emerges. In different situations different clusters of traits appear. The captain of a football team exhibits a different mix of leadership qualities from those of a school superintendent or bank president. Patterns of leadership traits vary in different contexts.

Leadership cannot be studied apart from the group in which it is exercised. It is found in a group. Robinson Crusoe was not a leader until Friday came along. Traits cannot be studied in isolation but only in relation to other traits and to the situation in which they appear. Leadership is a group phenomenon which varies from situation to situation and even within the same situation at different times. Individual leaders emerge because their peers respect their insights and judgment.

Leaders are influenced by their followers. Those who are led exert an upward influence on those who lead. They perceive their actions and the context in which they appear, and in the light of their perceptions accept or reject the leader behavior. Leadership occurs only when subordinates obey. The essence of leadership is shared dependence: the leader and his subordinates depend on one another but all the subordinates depend more on the leader than he depends on any one of them.

Group characteristics most closely associated with leadership are size, homogeneity, flexibility, stability, viscidity or cohesiveness, and hedonic tone or the satisfaction that individuals experience from being members of a group.[4] Sociological investigations into leadership have for the most part

---

[3]Ghiselli, E.E. and Barthol, R.P., "The Validity of Personality Inventories in the Selection of Employees." *Journal of Applied Psychology*, 37: 18-20; 1953.

[4]Hemphill, J.K., *Situational Factors in Leadership* (Columbus, O.: Bureau of Business Research, College of Commerce and Administration, The Ohio State University, 1949).

involved small ad hoc groups only, usually in controlled settings, and it is questionable whether the findings of small group research are applicable to others types of leadership situations. Small laboratory groups have no traditions, the motivation to lead is slight, outside pressures are missing, and the influence of small numbers on the leader may be weak. In real life, as a group becomes larger it makes more demands on the leader, and the members become more tolerant of decisions and directions which he makes without their involvement.

The situational study of leadership offers little help in the study of educational administration. There is such a variety of situational contexts that training institutions cannot determine what type of experience will be most valuable to prospective administrators. Experience in one type of situation, or even in a few types, may not be representative of what the trainee will ultimately need.

The contingency model of leadership. The contingency model of leadership, developed by Fred E. Fiedler after more than 15 years of research, combines the trait and situational approaches. Fiedler claims that leadership is explainable in terms of the following dimensions arranged in descending order of importance:

1. The leader-member personal relationships
2. The degree of task structure
3. The leader's position power

Group situations are ranked according to their favorableness to the leader; that is, the degree to which the situation enables the leader to exert influence over the group. If a leader's followers rate him high on the first dimension, if they perceive the group task to be highly structured, and if they attribute to his position a great deal of power and authority, the situation is favorable. If they consider all three dimensions low, the situation is unfavorable.

The task-directed type of leader is most effective in very favorable *and* very unfavorable situations. Fiedler explains that ". . . in the very favorable situations in which the leader has power, informal backing, and a relatively well-structured task, the group is ready to be directed, and the group expects to be told what to do. Consider the captain of an airliner in its final landing approach. We would hardly want him to turn to his crew for a discussion on how to land."[5]

[5] Fiedler, Fred E., *A Theory of Leadership Effectiveness*, New York: McGraw-Hill, 1967, p. 147.

Fiedler also cites an example to explain why the task-directed type of leader is also effective in an unfavorable situation. If the disliked chairman of a group planning an office party asks too many questions about what the group ought to do, he may be told that "we ought to go home."[6]

The human relations type of leader performs best in mixed situations where he has only moderate influence over the group; for example, in committees composed of professionals in which the task is not completely structured and the leader lacks power and authority over his associates.

A leader's effectiveness is contingent upon the situation. This implies that an organization can improve a leader's effectiveness by changing his authority, task, and even interpersonal relations within his group members. Fiedler says: ". . . good leadership performance depends as much upon the organization as it does upon the leader."[7]

The behavioral approach. The traitist and situational approaches sought to establish a casual relationship between leadership and sociological factors. The behavioral approach makes no attempt to discover behavioral determinants. It recognizes that leaders possess personal qualities and function in situations, but it focuses on observed behavior and does not look for causes. As objectively as possible it describes what leaders do.

Behavioral studies at present concentrate on those who hold top-level positions in formal organizations but as more information about leaders is gathered and a stronger conceptual framework constructed, behavioral research will undoubtedly extend to leaders of informal organizations.

In the behavioral approach, *leader behavior* is used instead of *leadership*, a substitution which indicates a shift from a value-laden term to an objective analysis of observed behavior. The behavioral study of leadership deals directly with observable phenomena and makes no assumptions about their causes. It differentiates between a description of how leaders behave and the evaluation of their performance.

By analyzing data obtained from an instrument called the Leader Behavior Description Questionnaire (LBDQ), Andrew Halpin and B. James Winer isolated two categories or dimensions of leader behavior, Initiating Structure and Consideration. Initiating Structure refers to a leader's be-

---

[6] Ibid., p. 147.

[7] Fiedler, Fred A., "Style or Circumstance: The Leadership Enigma," *Psychology Today*, March 1969, 62-73.

havior in organizing his work group, setting up channels of communication, and delineating methods of procedure. Consideration refers to behavior indicative of friendship, mutual trust, respect, and warmth between the leader and members of his group.

There are three forms of the LBDQ, each composed of 30 short descriptive statements of the way leaders behave. One form, in which group members describe their leader's behavior, is referred to as LBDQ-Real, Staff. A second, in which leaders describe how they think leaders *should* behave is designated as LBDQ-Ideal, Self. A third, in which group members describe how they believe a leader should behave is termed LBDQ-Ideal, Staff. The instrument can be used with military, industrial, educational, and other groups.

Respondents check one of five adverbs to show the frequency with which a leader engages in each form of behavior: always, often, occasionally, seldom, or never. Each item is scored on a scale of 4 to 0. Fifteen of the items deal with Initiating Structure and 15 with Consideration. Sample items:

He criticizes poor work.
He works without a plan.
He lets staff members know what is expected of them.
He finds time to listen to staff members
He refuses to explain his actions.
He is friendly and approachable.

Effective leader behavior is associated with high performance on both Initiating Structure and Consideration. Leaders who score high on Consideration but low on Initiating Structure are ineffective, for they minimize the importance of efficiency and productivity. Those who score low on Consideration but high on Initiating Structure are also ineffective, for they stress efficiency and productivity at the expense of morale and good human relations. Those who score low on both Initiating Structure and Consideration can scarcely be called leaders, for they preside over group chaos.

The LBDQ has been extensively used in studies of leader behavior in the field of education as well as in industry, business, and the military profession. According to Halpin, "Followers tend to agree in describing the same leader, and the descriptions of different leaders differ significantly."[8]

---

[8] Halpin, A.W., *Manual for the Leader Behavior Description Questionnaire*, Mimeo. (Columbus, O.: Bureau of Business Research, College of Commerce and Administration, Ohio State University, 1957.)

In recent years Ralph M. Stogdill has questioned whether two factors are sufficient to account for all the observable variance in leader behavior. Using a new theory of role differentiation and group achievement as a base, Stogdill hypothesized that twelve variables operate in the differentiation of roles in social groups and developed 12 subscales to measure each of the variables. Each subscale is composed of either five or ten items, making a total of 100. The new instrument, known as LBDQ-Form XII, although still in an experimental stage, seems more promising and sophisticated than the original LBDQ. It is easily administered. As few as four respondents will provide a satisfactory index score of a leader's behavior and additional respondents beyond ten do not significantly increase the stability of the index scores. Stogdill defines the subscales as follows:

1. ***Representation*** — speaks and acts as the representative of the group. (5 items)
2. ***Demand Reconciliation*** — reconciles conflicting demands and reduces disorder to system. (5 items)
3. ***Tolerance of Uncertainty*** — is able to tolerate uncertainty and postponement without anxiety or upset. (10 items)
4. ***Persuasiveness*** — uses persuasion and argument effectively; exhibits strong convictions. (10 items)
5. ***Initiation of structure*** — clearly defines own role, and lets followers know what is expected. (10 items)
6. ***Tolerance of freedom*** — allows followers scope for initiative, decision, and action. (10 items)
7. ***Role Assumption*** — actively exercises the leadership role rather than surrendering leadership to others. (10 items)
8. ***Consideration*** — regards the comfort, well being, status, and contributions of followers. (10 items)
9. ***Production emphasis*** — applies pressure for productive output. (10 items)
10. ***Predictive Accuracy*** — exhibits foresight and ability to predict outcomes accurately. (5 items)
11. ***Integration*** — maintains a closely knit organization; resolves intermember conflicts. (5 items)
12. ***Superior Orientation*** — maintains cordial relations with superiors; has influence with them; is striving for higher status. (10 items)

The behavioral approach has provided new insights into the nature of leadership. It has shown, for example, that the leader-follower relationship is a mix of personal and situational elements which do not operate singly but in patterns and clusters; that followers and leaders may not perceive these patterns and clusters clearly; and that the extent of misperception is related to organizational, group, or individual variables.

Leadership styles. Leader roles may be classified as autocratic, democratic, or laissez-faire.

An autocratic leader is one who determines all goals, policies, and means. He dictates activity steps, one at a time, so that there is always a large degree of uncertainty about future steps. He criticizes and praises the work of subordinates in personal terms. He engages in group participation when demonstrating but otherwise does not stimulate group activity.

A democratic leader involves group members in the determination of policies affecting their welfare and assists them to make decisions. He criticizes and praises objectively, focusing on facts rather than personalities. The members gain activity perspective through discussion and look upon the leader as a fellow-worker and resource person.

A laissez-faire leader allows complete freedom for group and individual decision and action. He withdraws from group activities, makes no attempt to appraise or control them, and comments upon them only when requested.

The classification of leaders as autocratic, democratic, or laissez-faire is of limited helpfulness in the study of educational administration. Today's social and political climate is such that authoritarian leaders simply could not function in schools. Teachers are too well trained and their organizations too militant to tolerate autocratic behavior by school executives. The external and internal pressures of modern education would swamp any principal or superintendent who conceived of his role as a withdrawing or laissez-faire leader. School administrators generally regard themselves as democratic, veering as occasion demands towards an autocratic or laissez-faire stance but never for long.

The behavioral approach rejects the autocratic-democratic-laissez-faire typology as not helpful and identifies three other styles instead. These styles, based on the Getzels-Guba model of the organization as a social system, are nomothetic, idiographic, and transactional. (For a description of the Getzels-Guba model, see page 91.)

The nomothetic or normative style emphasizes institutional requirements, that is, established rules, regulations, and procedures. A nomothetic leader "goes by the book". He insists on demonstrable results and stresses the quantity and quality of work expected by the organization from each member. On the LBDQ he would rank high in Initiating Structure.

The personal or idiographic style emphasizes the needs and personality of each member. An idiographic leader is concerned with promoting good human relations and providing for the satisfaction of individual needs. On the LBDQ he would rank high in Consideration.

The transactional style varies as circumstances change. Under one set of circumstances a transactional leader might move toward the nomothetic style and under another to the idiographic style.

Behavioral researchers have found the nomothetic-idiographic-transactional classification useful in analyzing, understanding, and predicting leader behavior.

SELECTED READINGS

Association for Supervision and Curriculum Development, *Leadership for Improving Instruction, Yearbook*, Washington, D.C.: ASCD, 1960.

The contents, to which more than 200 contributed, include the identification and development of educational leaders and a concept of democratic leadership.

Charters, Werrett Wallace, *Teacher Perceptions of Administrative Behavior*, St. Louis: Washington University, 1964.

Reports research findings on teachers' attitudes towards leader behavior of administrators.

Cummings, L.L., "The Manager as Leader," in Hack. G.G., Gephart, W.J., Heck, J.B., and Ramseyer, J.A., eds., *Educational Administration*, 2nd ed., Boston: Allyn and Bacon, 1971.

Leadership is defined as the process of interaction wherein one person influences the thoughts, feelings, and behavior of another person or persons in the pursuit of a common goal. Discusses four leadership styles: production-centered versus employee-centered; authoritarian-democratic-laissez-faire; boss-centered versus subordinate-centered; and initiating structure-consideration.

Cunningham, L.L. and Gephart, W.J., eds., *Leadership: The Science and Art Today*, Itasca, Illinois: F.E. Peacock Publishers, 1973.

Seven papers delivered at the twelfth annual Phi Delta Kappa symposium on educational research, each followed by a commentary and some by a transcript of subsequent discussion. The topics include general theory and research in leadership, the trait approach, research strategies, and the selection, training, and career development of educational leaders.

Fiedler, Fred E., *A Theory of Leadership Effectiveness*, San Francisco: McGraw-Hill, 1967.

The author bases his recommendations for the placement and training of leaders on research showing that leader effectiveness depends on leader-member relations, task structure, and the leader's position in the group-task situation.

Gibb, C.A., ed., *Leadership: Selected Readings*, Baltimore: Penguin Books, 1969.

A compilation of articles dealing with psychological elements in leadership, the role and personality of the leader in different group settings, and research findings in leadership.

Gross, N. and Herriot, R.E., *Staff Leadership in Public Schools: A Sociological Inquiry*, New York; John Wiley and Sons, 1965.

Report of a national study of elementary school principals. When principals conform to a concept of their role as one which stresses instructional leadership, their staffs benefit from and approve their efforts.

Halpin, A.W., *Theory and Research in Administration*, New York: Macmillan, 1966.

Summarizes the substantive findings of a group of studies in which the LBDQ was used, including two which deal directly with school superintendents. Acknowledges that the dimensions of initiating structure and consideration do not exhaust the field but holds that they should be taken in account in evaluating leadership skills.

Lane, W.R., Corwin, R.G., and Monahan, W.G., *Foundations of Educational Administration*, New York: Macmillan, 1967.

Chapter 12, "Scope and Character of Administrative Leadership," stresses the sociological conditions which influence leadership. The question posed is: Under what conditions can a leader best lead? The conditions involve mobility patterns, crises, organizational size, security of position, and the leader's awareness of organizational goals.

Stogdill, Ralph M., *Handbook of Leadership*, New York: The Free Press, 1974.

An organized inventory of all the published research findings on leadership. The most scholarly and comprehensive book of leadership yet published.

Sugden, Virginia, ed., *Common Patterns and Principles of Administration*, Hempstead, N.Y., Hofstra University, 1970.

Analyzes the professional literature in the fields of business, education, medicine and public health, and public administration to identify common patterns and principles of administration.

TOPICS FOR DISCUSSION

1. "Leaders are born, not made." Is this statement true? Does every normally intelligent person have leadership potential? If so, how can it be developed?

2. Is leadership restricted to those in administrative or supervisory positions or does it also reside in rank and file teachers? Explain and illustrate.

3. Do administrators have a responsibility for identifying and developing the leadership capacities of staff members? Justify your point of view.

4. Explain and illustrate a commonality of leadership principle and practice in the fields of business administration, educational administration, medicine and public health, and public administration. (Suggestion: Refer to Chapter VII of *Common Patterns and Principles of Management*, Virginia Sugden, Ed., Hofstra University, N.Y.)

5. What is symbolic leadership? Is the concept of symbolic leadership important in educational administration? (Suggestion: Refer to *Symbolic Leaders: Public Dramas and Public Men* by Orrin Edgar Klapp, Aldine Publishing Co., Chicago, Ill., 1964).

6. Discuss a recent leadership study in educational administration with particular attention to the significance of its findings. (Suggestion: For reports of research consult *Dissertation Abstracts*, University of Michigan, Ann Arbor, Mich.)

7. From all that you have read and discussed about leadership, what can you put into practice as a school administrator?

8. Aristotle said that a good leader has *ethos* or moral character, the source of his ability to persuade, *pathos* or the power to move people emotionally, and *logos* or the ability to move people intellectually. Name some leaders who, in your judgment, meet Aristotle's requirements. Justify your selection.

9. Halpin's study showed that school boards prefer superintendents whose leader behavior tends towards *initiating structure*. The superintendent's subordinates, however, prefer leaders who rank high in consideration. Similarly, superintendents prefer principals who rank high on *initiating* structure while teachers prefer principals who rank high on *consideration*. Superiors, in other words, prefer subordinates who exhibit *initiating structure* while subordinates prefer superiors who exhibit *consideration*. Faced with conflicting expectations, how should school administrators behave?

DIAGNOSING EDUCATIONAL LEADERSHIP PROBLEMS: A SITUATIONAL APPROACH

By
Philip E. Gates, Kenneth H. Blanchard, Paul Hersey

Before describing situational leadership theory, three basic concepts are defined and discussed: task behavior, relationship behavior, and maturity. A situational leadership theory model is then presented and explained.

Situational leadership theory is applied to two school situations, one involving a principal and department head and the other a student and teacher.

The theory is presented as a means by which educational leaders can improve their probability of success in working with and through others to accomplish goals.

Over the past few decades, practitioners and writers in the field of leadership and management have been involved in a search for a "best" style of leadership which would be successful in most situations. Yet, the evidence from research clearly indicates that there is no single all-purpose leadership style.[1] Successful leaders are those who can adapt their behavior to meet the demands of their own unique environment. This conclusion that leadership "all depends on the situation" is not very helpful to the practicing educational leader who may be personally interested in how he or she can find some practical value in theory.

Unless one can help this leader determine when it is appropriate to behave in what way, all theory and research have done is set the practitioner up for frustration. As a result, one of the major concerns of the work of Paul Hersey and Kenneth H. Blanchard has been the development of a conceptual framework which can help practicing managers make effective day-to-day decisions on how various situations should be handled. Situational

---

[1] A. K. Korman. " 'Consideration,' 'Initiating Structure,' and 'Organizational Criteria' — A Review." *Personnel Psychology: A Journal of Applied Research* 19 (4): 349-61; Winter 1966. See also: Fred E. Fiedler. *A Theory of Leadership Effectiveness.* New York: McGraw-Hill Book Company, 1967.

"Diagnosing Educational Leadership Problem," by Philip E. Gates, Kenneth W. Blanchard and Paul Hersey, in *Educational Leadership,* Volume 33, No. 5. Copyright © 1976 by the Association for Supervision and Curriculum Development, and reprinted by their permission.

Leadership Theory[2] (sometimes referred to as "Life Cycle Theory of Leadership") will be presented in this article by Hersey and Blanchard, the theorists, and applied to educational leadership situations by Philip E. Gates, the practitioner.

SITUATIONAL LEADERSHIP THEORY

This theory grew out of earlier leadership models that were based on two kinds of behavior central to the concept of leadership style: task behavior and relationship behavior. *Task behavior* is the extent to which a leader engages in one-way communication by explaining what each subordinate is to do as well as when, where, and how tasks are to be accomplished. *Relationship behavior* is the extent to which a leader engages in two-way communication by providing socio-emotional support, "psychological strokes," and facilitating behaviors. The two dimensions of leader behavior, plotted on two separate axes, are shown in Figure 1.

Since research in the past several decades has clearly supported the contention that there is no "best" style of leadership, any of the four basic styles shown in Figure 1 may be effective or ineffective depending on the situation.

Situational Leadership Theory is based upon an interplay among (1) the amount of direction (task behavior) a leader gives, (2) the amount of socio-emotional support (relationship behavior) a leader provides, and (3) the "maturity" level that followers exhibit on a specific task.

Level of Maturity

Maturity is defined in Situational Leadership Theory as the capacity to set high but attainable goals (achievement-motivation[3]), willingness and ability to take responsibility, and education and/or experience of an individual or a group. *These variables of maturity should be considered only in relation to a specific task to be performed.* That is to say, an individual or a group is not mature or immature in any *total* sense. People tend to have varying

---

[2] Situational Leadership Theory was first published by Hersey and Blanchard as "Life Cycle Theory of Leadership" in the *Training and Development Journal,* May 1969. The theory has continually been refined until in its present form it is referred to as "Situational Leadership Theory." The most complete presentation of the theory will appear in: Paul Hersey and Kenneth H. Blanchard. *Management of Organizational Behavior.* Third edition. Englewood Cliffs, New Jersey: Prentice-Hall, Inc., 1976.

[3] David C. McClelland, J. W. Atkinson, R. A. Clark, and E. L. Lowell. *The Achievement Motive.* New York: Appleton-Century-Crofts, 1953; and David C. McClelland. *The Achieving Society.* Princeton, New Jersey: D. Van Nostrand Co., Inc., 1961.

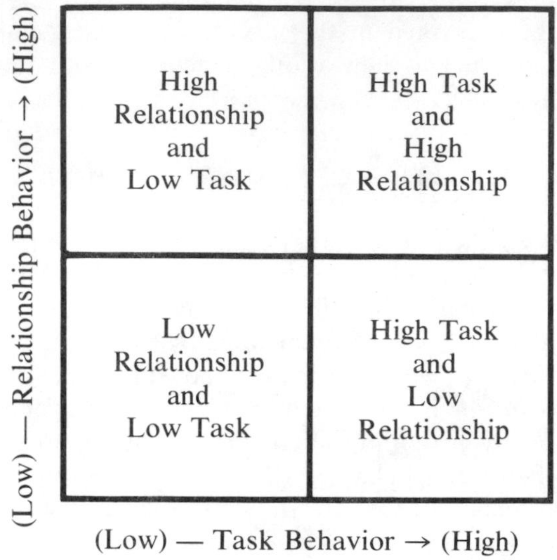

(Low) — Relationship Behavior → (High)		
	High Relationship and Low Task	High Task and High Relationship
	Low Relationship and Low Task	High Task and Low Relationship
	(Low) — Task Behavior → (High)	

Figure 1

BASIC LEADER BEHAVIOR STYLES

degrees of maturity depending on the specific task, function, or objective that a leader is attempting to accomplish through their efforts. Thus, a teacher may be very responsible in organizing lesson plans but very casual about handling discipline in the classroom. As a result, it may be appropriate for a principal to provide little supervision for this teacher when organizing the classroom curriculum, yet to closely supervise when class discipline is the issue.

The Basic Concept

According to Situational Leadership Theory, as the level of maturity of their followers continues to increase in terms of accomplishing a specific task, leaders should begin to *reduce* their task behavior and *increase* their relationship behavior. This should be the case until the individual or group reaches a moderate level of maturity. As the followers begin to move into an above average level of maturity, it becomes appropriate for leaders to decrease not only task behavior but relationship behavior as well. Now the individual or group is not only mature in terms of the performance of the task but also is psychologically mature.

Since the individual or group can provide their own "strokes" and reinforcement, a great deal of socio-emotional support from the leader is no longer necessary. People at this maturity level see a reduction of close supervision and an increase in delegation by the leader as a positive indication of trust and confidence. Thus, Situational Leadership Theory focuses on the appropriateness or effectiveness of leadership styles according to the task relevant maturity of the followers. This cycle can be illustrated by a bell-shaped curve superimposed upon the four leadership quadrants, as shown in Figure 2.

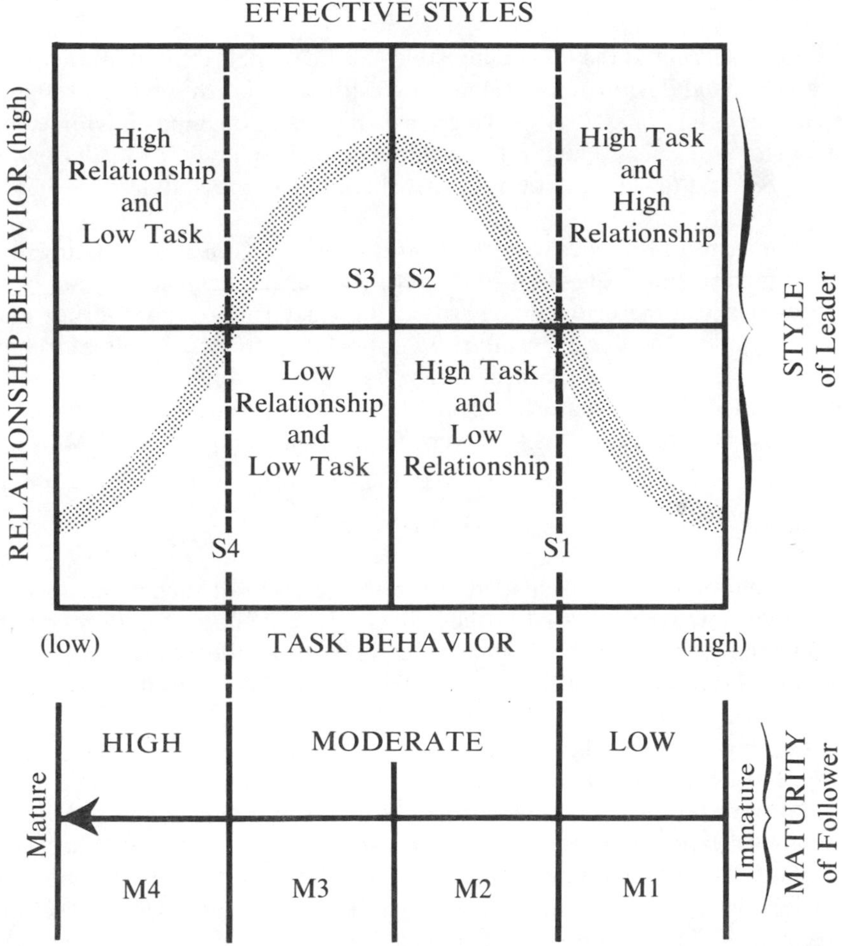

Figure 2

SITUATIONAL LEADERSHIP THEORY

Style of Leader vs. Maturity of Followers

Figure 2 attempts to portray the relation between task relevant maturity and the appropriate leadership styles to be used as followers move from immaturity to maturity. As indicated, the reader should keep in mind that the figure represents two different phenomena. The appropriate leadership style (*style of leader*) for given levels of follower maturity is portrayed by a curvilinear function in the four leadership quadrants. The maturity level of the individual or group being supervised (*maturity of follower*) is depicted below the leadership model as a continuum ranging from immaturity to maturity.

In referring to the leadership styles in the model, we will use the following shorthand designations: (1) high task-low relationship will be referred to as leader behavior style S1; (2) high task-high relationship behavior as leader behavior style S2; (3) high relationship-low task behavior as leader behavior style S3; and (4) low relationship-low task behavior as style S4.

In terms of follower maturity, it is not simply a question of being mature or immature but a question of degree. As can be seen in Figure 2, some benchmarks of maturity can be provided for determining appropriate leadership style by dividing the maturity continuum into four levels of maturity. Low levels of task relevant maturity are referred to as maturity level M1; low to moderate as maturity level M2; moderate to high as maturity level M3; and high levels of task relevant maturity as maturity level M4.

APPLICATION

What does the bell-shaped curve in the style-of-leader portion of the model mean? It means that as the maturity level of one's followers develops along the continuum from immature to mature, the appropriate style of leadership moves accordingly along the curvilinear function.

Determining Appropriate Style

To determine what leadership style is appropriate to use in a given situation, one must first determine the maturity level of the individual or group in relation to a specific task that the leader is attempting to accomplish through their efforts. Once this maturity level is identified, the appropriate leadership style can be determined by constructing a right angle (90° angle) from the point on the continuum that identifies the maturity level of the followers to a point where it intersects on the curvilinear function in the style of leader portion of the model. The quadrant in which that intersection takes place suggests the appropriate style to be used by the leader in that situation with followers of that maturity level. Let us look at an example in Figure 3.

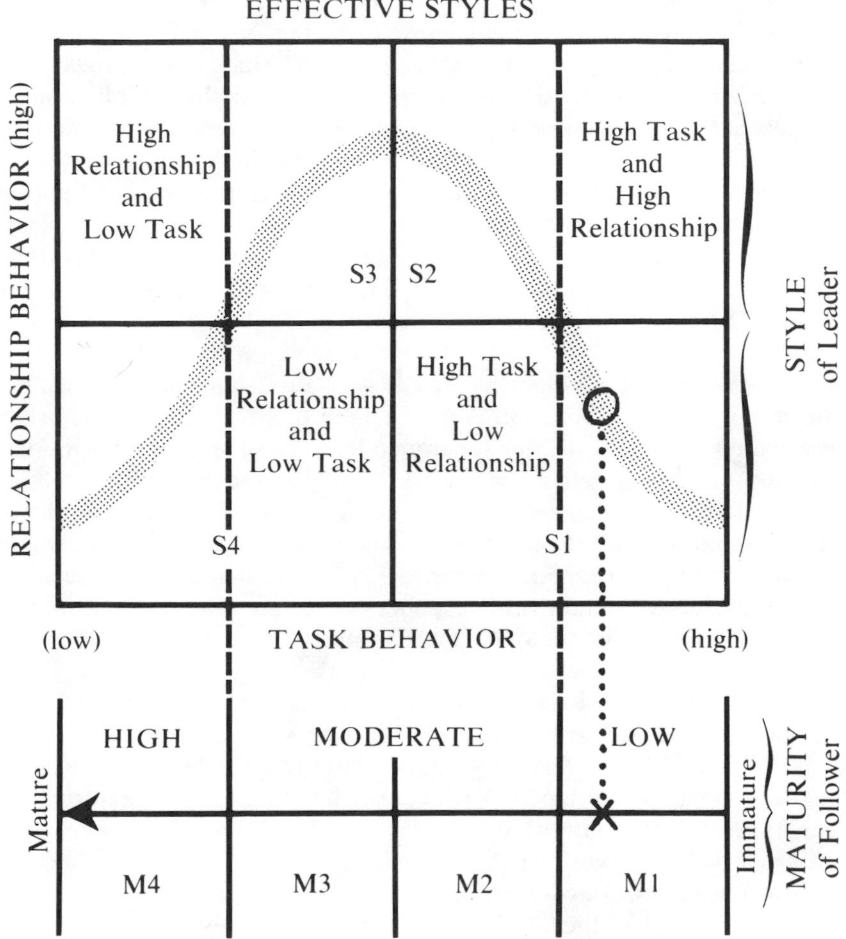

Figure 3

DETERMINING AN APPROPRIATE LEADERSHIP STYLE

Suppose a superintendent has determined that a principal's maturity level in terms of administrative paper work (reports, attendance records) is low. Using Situational Leadership Theory he or she would place an X on the maturity continuum as shown in Figure 3 (above M1). Once the superintendent had decided that he or she wanted to influence the principal's behavior in this area, the superintendent could determine the appropriate initial style to use by constructing a right angle from the X drawn on the maturity continuum to a point where it intersects the bell-shaped curve (designated in Figure 3 by 0). Since the intersection occurs in the S1 quadrant, it is suggested that when working with people who demonstrate M1 maturity on a particular task, a leader should use an S1 style (high task-low relationship behavior). If one follows this technique for determining the appropriate leadership style for all four of the maturity levels, it will become clear that the four maturity designations (M1, M2, M3, M4) correspond to the four leader behavior designations (S1, S2, S3, S4); that is, M1 maturity needs S1 style, M2 maturity needs S2 style, etc.

In this example, when we say low relationship behavior, we do not mean that the superintendent is not friendly or personable to the principal. We merely suggest that the superintendent, in supervising the principal's handling of administrative paper work, should spend more time directing the principal in what to do and how, when, and where to do it, than providing socio-emotional support and reinforcement. The increased relationship behavior should occur when the principal begins to demonstrate the ability to handle necessary administrative paper work. At that point, a movement from Style 1 to Style 2 may be appropriate.

Thus, Situational Leadership Theory contends that in working with people who are low in maturity (M1) in terms of accomplishing a specific task, a high task low relationship style (S1) has the highest probability of success; in dealing with people who are of low to moderate maturity (M2), a moderate structure and socio-emotional style (S2) appears to be most appropriate; while in working with people who are of moderate to high maturity (M3) in terms of accomplishing a specific task, a high relationship/low task style (S3) has the highest probability of success; and finally, a low relationship/low task style (S4) has the highest probability of success in working with people of high task relevant maturity (M4).

Developing Maturity in Followers

In attempting to help an individual or group mature in a particular area, such as getting them to take more and more responsibility for performing a specific task, a leader must be careful not to delegate responsibility and/or provide socio-emotional support too rapidly. If the leader does this, the individual or group may view the leader as a "soft-touch" and take advantage. Observe the teachers whose supervisor presents the staff with the district supply list, and without establishing any parameters, instructs them to go ahead and order from it. Some of the staff may not have any experience in ordering supplies and will order virtually everything available, whether they need it or not. At the opposite extreme, others will order too frugally and end up short. Teachers experienced with this task will select needed items efficiently and economically. Obviously, it is up to the supervisor to determine exactly how much direction should be given to each teacher for ordering supplies. The degree of individual structure the supervisor provides will depend on the maturity of each of the teachers in relation to the task at hand.

A leader must develop the maturity of followers slowly on each task that they perform, using less task behavior and more relationship behavior as they mature and become more willing and able to take responsibility. When an individual's performance is low on a specific task, one must not expect drastic changes overnight. For a desirable behavior to be obtained, a leader must reward as soon as possible the slightest behavior exhibited by the individual in the desired direction and continue this process as the individual's behavior comes closer and closer to the leader's expectations of good performance. This behavior modification concept[4] is called *positively reinforcing successive approximations* of desired behavior.

For example, a principal might want to move a newly appointed department head through the cycle so that she would be assuming significantly more supervisory responsibilities. If this individual has had no experience chairing departmental meetings, the principal might help her plan a written agenda for her first meeting, and then evaluate the results with her. If this responsibility is well handled by the department head, the principal will want to reinforce this behavior with increases in socioemotional support (relationship behavior). This is a two-step process: first, a reduction in structure, and second, if adequate performance follows, an increase in socioemotional support as reinforcement. This process should continue until the department head has reached moderate levels of maturity (M2 and M3) in chairing departmental meetings. This does not mean that her meetings will be less structured; rather it means that the direction provided will be given by the department head rather than being provided by the principal.

As the department head continues to develop in this area, the appropriate leadership style for the principal to use begins to move toward Style 4.

---

[4]The most classic discussions of behavior modification, reinforcement theory, or operant conditioning, have been done by B. F. Skinner. See: B. F. Skinner. *Science and Human Behavior*. New York: The Macmillan Company, 1953. Some excellent applications of this field to education are presented in: Glenna Holsinger. *Motivating the Reluctant Learner*. Lexington, Massachusetts: Motivity, Inc., 1970; Lloyd Homme. *How To Use Contingency Contraction in the Classroom*. Champaign, Illinois: Research Press, Inc., 1970; and Madeline Hunter. *Reinforcement Theory for Teachers*. El Segundo, California: TIP Publications, 1967.

Now the department head is not only able to chair department meetings, but is able to provide her own satisfaction for interpersonal and emotional needs. At this stage of maturity (M4), the department head will tend to be positively reinforced for her accomplishments by the principal not looking over her shoulder at department meetings and leaving her more and more on her own. It is not that there is less mutual trust and friendship between the principal and department head but rather that less interaction time is needed to prove it.

Let us look at another example of how knowledge of the developmental aspect of Situational Leadership Theory could help an individual increase the maturity level of followers in a particular area.

Tom was a bright student who failed ninth grade English. He failed, not because he could not do the work, but because his teacher used an inappropriate teaching style for him in this subject. Since Tom's English class was considered a "bright" group, the teacher assumed that he could make assignments to students with little direction or close supervision. While this approach worked with other students, Tom was an exception. He came from a broken home where he got little support or encouragement in his school work. When he brought home written assignments from English, he was often "side-tracked" and interrupted. As a result, even if he completed an assignment, it was sloppy and disorganized. All his teacher did was *tell* Tom continually that he had to be both more careful with his work and get it in on time. But generally, his teacher left him alone and merely kept score of his "failures" in the grade book. At the end of the semester, Tom failed the course.

The next semester he was asked to repeat the course with the same teacher. This time he earned honor roll grades in English.

How did this dramatic change in behavior occur?

Between the two classes, Tom's teacher was exposed to Situational Leadership Theory. Bothered by Tom's failure, the teacher was continually thinking about Tom while learning about the theory. Analyzing the situation, the teacher realized that Tom's maturity level in terms of the course requirements for English was very low (M1) and yet generally, the teacher was using a "hands off" (S4) teaching style with him.

Armed with these new insights, the teacher developed a strategy for working with Tom this time. Since his maturity level was low in writing and compositional skills, the teacher knew that Tom would need some significant task behavior (S1) from the beginning. As a result, knowing that Tom loved sports, the teacher directed him to start writing some sports stories for the student newspaper. As advisor to the paper, the teacher was able to give Tom specific assignments and work with him closely (S1) as he wrote his articles. After they had worked together on his first article and it was published. Tom really got excited about writing and began to take it more seriously. Since Tom was doing his writing at school, he was in a supportive environment where he could get supervision as he needed it. In the long run, the teacher was able to reduce direction and supervision and provide Tom with more socio-emotional support (S2).

Eventually Tom became responsible enough that he was able to turn out acceptable copy with little help from the teacher. Now the teacher was able to concentrate almost exclusively on commending his efforts (S3). This gradual development paid dividends. Not only did Tom's English grades improve to B's and eventually A's, but he also was able to get a part-time job working with the local community newspaper. He wrote and proofread copy, and learned to set type. This was accomplished with limited teacher involvement (S4). Tom had completely accepted responsibility for the task of writing well. In terms of Situational Leadership Theory, he had fully matured with respect to the desired task as a result of the teacher's adopting appropriate leadership styles.

Intervening When Maturity is Decreasing

Although Situational Leadership Theory suggests a specific style for each different level of task maturity, it is not a one-way street. When an individual begins to regress in maturity for whatever reason, such as a crisis at home or a change of job, it becomes appropriate for the leader to adjust his or her leadership style accordingly. For example, take a teacher who was highly motivated and competent (M4) and therefore could be left on his own (S4). Suppose he is promoted to principal, based on his teaching ability alone. While it may have been appropriate to leave him alone (S4) as a teacher, now that he is principal, a task for which he has little experience, it may be appropriate for his supervisor in the central office to change styles by providing more socio-emotional support and then increasing the direction and supervision of his activities (Style 3 to Style 2). This high task-high relationship style should continue until he is able to grasp his new responsibilities. At that time, a movement back from Style 2 through Style 3 to Style 4 may be appropriate. Starting off using the same leadership style that was successful while he was a teacher may now prove devastating because it may be inappropriate for the needs of this situation.

We have endeavored to present Situational Leadership Theory as a means by which educational leaders at every level can increase their probability of success in working with and through others to accomplish goals.

QUESTIONS

1. Are there any elements common to the trait, situational, contingency, and behavioral theories of leadership? If so, what are they?

2. Describe a school situation, real or imaginary, to which you might apply situational leadership theory.

STYLE OR CIRCUMSTANCE

By
Fred E. Fiedler

Leader behavior refers to specific acts which a leader engages in while directing or coordinating the work of his group. Leadership style refers to the underlying needs of the leader that motivate his behavior.

To classify leadership styles a simple questionnaire was developed which asked the leader to describe the person with whom he could work least well. From the replies a Least-Preferred-Co-worker score (LPC) was obtained.

To classify group situations three factors were identified: position power of the leader, task structure, and leader-member personal relationships. Group situations were ranked according to their favorableness to the leader.

By correlating leadership style against a scale of group situations, the leadership style that works best in each situation was found. The results show that a task-oriented leader performs best in situations in which he has a great deal of influence and power, and also in situations where he has no influence and power over group members.

Relationship-oriented leaders perform best in mixed situations where they have only moderate influence over the group.

The organization for which a leader works is as responsible for his success or failure as is the leader himself.

What is it that makes a person an effective leader?

We take it for granted that good leadership is essential to business, to government and to all the myriad groups and organizations that shape the way we live, work and play.

We spend at least several billions of dollars a year on leadership development and executive recruitment in the United States. Leaders are paid 10, 20 and 30 times the salary of ordinary workers. Thousands of books and

---

"Style and Circumstance: The Leadership Enigma," by Fred F. Fiedler, from *Psychology Today*. Copyright © 1969 by Ziff-Davis Publishing Company. Reprinted by permission of Psychology Today magazine.

articles on leadership have been published. Yet, we still know relatively little about the factors that determine a leader's success or failure.

Psychologists have been concerned with two major questions in their research on leadership: How does a man become a leader? What kind of personality traits or behavior makes a person an *effective* leader? For the past 15 years, my own work at the University of Illinois Group-Effectiveness Research Laboratory has concentrated on the latter question.

Psychologists used to think that special personality traits would distinguish leaders from followers. Several hundred research studies have been conducted to identify these special traits. But the search has been futile.

People who become leaders tend to be somewhat more intelligent, bigger, more assertive, more talkative than other members of their group. But these traits are far less important than most people think. What most frequently distinguishes the leader from his co-workers is that he knows more about the group task or that he can do it better. A bowling team is likely to choose its captain from good rather than poor bowlers, and the foreman of a machine shop is more likely to be a good machinist than a poor one.

In many organizations, one only has to live long in order to gain experience and seniority, and with these a position of leadership.

In business and industry today, the men who attain a leadership position must have the requisite education and talent. Of course, as W. Lloyd Warner and James C. Abegglen of the University of Chicago have shown, it has been most useful to come from or marry into a family that owns a large slice of the company's stock.

Becoming a leader, then, depends on personality only to a limited extent. A person can become a leader by happenstance, simply by being in the right place at the right time, or because of such various factors as age, education, experience, family background and wealth.

Almost any person in a group may be capable of rising to a leadership position if he is rewarded for actively participating in the group discussion, as Alex Bavelas and his colleagues at Stanford University have demonstrated. They used light signals to reward low-status group members for supposedly "doing the right thing." However, unknown to the people being encouraged, the light signal was turned on and off at random. Rewarded in this unspecified, undefined manner, the low-status member came to regard himself as a leader and the rest of the group accepted him in his new position.

It is commonly observed that personality and circumstances interact to determine whether a person will become a leader. While this statement is undoubtedly true, its usefulness is rather limited unless one also can specify how a personality trait will interact with a specific situation. We are as yet unable to make such predictions.

Having become a leader, how does one get to be an effective leader? Given a dozen or more similar groups and tasks, what makes one leader succeed and another fail? The answer to this question is likely to determine the philosophy of leader-training programs and the way in which men are selected for executive positions.

There are a limited number of ways in which one person can influence others to work together toward a common goal. He can coerce them or he can coax them. He can tell people what to do and how to do it, or he can share the decision-making and concentrate on his relationship with his men rather than on the execution of the job.

Of course, these two types of leadership behavior are gross oversimplifications. Most research by psychologists on leadership has focused on two clusters of behavior and attitudes, one labeled autocratic, authoritarian and task-oriented, and the other as democratic, equalitarian, permissive and group-oriented.

The first type of leadership behavior, frequently advocated in conventional supervisory and military systems, has its philosophical roots in Frank W. Taylor's *Principles of Scientific Management* and other early 20th Century industrial engineering studies. The authoritarian, task-oriented leader takes all responsibility for making decisions and directing the group members. His rationale is simple: "I do the thinking and you carry out the orders."

The second type of leadership is typical of the "New Look" method of management advocated by men like Douglas McGregor of M.I.T. and Rensis Likert of the University of Michigan. The democratic, group-oriented leader provides general rather than close supervision and his concern is the effective use of human resources through participation. In the late 1940s, a related method of leadership training was developed based on confrontation in unstructured group situations where each participant can explore his own motivations and reactions. Some excellent studies on this method, call T-group, sensitivity or laboratory training, have been made by Chris Argyris of Yale, Warren Bennis of State University of New York at Buffalo and Edgar Schein of M.I.T.

Experiments comparing the performance of both types of leaders have shown that each is successful in some situations and not in others. No one has been able to show that one kind of leader is always superior or more effective.

A number of researchers point out that different tasks require different kinds of leadership. But what kind of situation requires what kind of leader? To answer this question, I shall present a theory of leadership effectiveness that spells out the specific circumstances under which various leadership styles are most effective.

We must first of all distinguish between leadership style and leader behavior. Leader behavior refers to the specific acts in which a leader engages while directing or coordinating the work of his group. For example, the leader can praise or criticize, make helpful suggestions, show consideration for the welfare and feelings of members of his group.

Leadership style refers to the underlying needs of the leader that motivate his behavior. In other words, in addition to performing the task, what personal needs is the leader attempting to satisfy? We have found that a leader's actions or behavior sometimes does change as the situation or group changes, but his basic needs appear to remain constant.

To classify leadership styles, my colleagues and I have developed a simple questionnaire that asks the leader to describe the person with whom he can work least well:

LPC — Least-Preferred Co-worker

Think of the person with whom you can work least well. He may be someone you work with now, or he may be someone you knew in the past. Use an X to describe this person as he appears to you.

helpful	: 8 :	7 :	6 :	5 :	4 :	3 :	2 :	1 :	frustrating
unen-thusiastic	: 1 :	2 :	3 :	4 :	5 :	6 :	7 :	8 :	enthusiastic
efficient	: 8 :	7 :	6 :	5 :	4 :	3 :	2 :	1 :	inefficient

From the replies, a Least-Preferred-Co-worker (LPC) score is obtained by simply summing the item scores. The LPC score does not measure perceptual accuracy, but rather reveals a person's emotional reaction to the people with whom he cannot work well.

In general, the high-scoring leader describes his least-preferred co-worker in favorable terms. The high-LPC leader tends to be "relationship-oriented." He gets his major satisfaction from establishing close personal relations with his group members. He uses the group task to gain the position of prominence he seeks.

The leader with a low score describes his least-preferred co-worker in unfavorable terms. The low-LPC leader is primarily "task-oriented." He obtains his major satisfaction by successfully completing the task, even at the risk of poor interpersonal relations with his workers.

Since a leader cannot function without a group, we must also know something about the group that the leader directs. There are many types of groups, for example, social groups which promote the enjoyment of individuals and "counteracting" groups such as labor and management at the negotiating table. But here we shall concentrate on groups that exist for the purpose of performing a task.

From our research, my associates and I have identified three major factors that can be used to classify group situations: (1) position power of the leader, (2) task structure, and (3) leader-member personal relationships. Basically, these classifications measure the kind of power and influence the group gives its leader.

We ranked group situations according to their favorableness for the leader. Favorableness here is defined as the degree to which the situation enables the leader to exert influence over the group.

Based on several studies, leader-member relations emerged as the most important factor in determining the leader's influence over the group. Task structure is rated as second in importance and position power as third. *(See Figure 1.)*

Under most circumstances, the leader who is liked by his group and has a clear-cut task and high position power obviously has everything in his favor. The leader who has poor relationships with his group members, an unstructured task and weak position power likely will be unable to exert much influence over the group.

The personal relationships that the leader establishes with his group

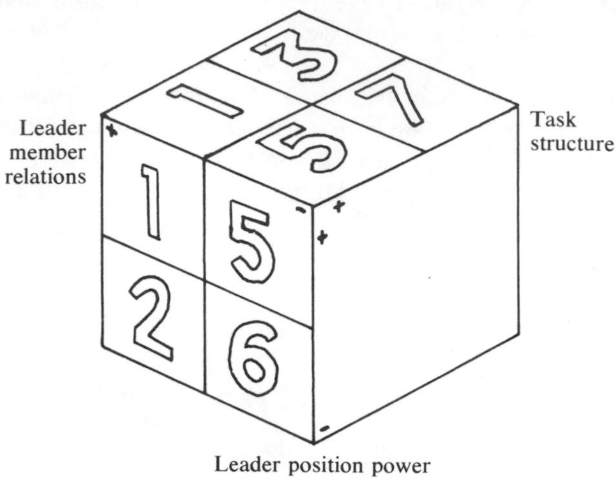

Figure 1

GROUP SITUATION MODEL. Task-oriented groups are classified in a three-dimensional model *(top)* using the three major factors affecting group performance.

members depend at least in part upon the leader's personality. The leader who is loved, admired and trusted can influence the group regardless of his position power. The leader who is not liked or trusted cannot influence the group except through his vested authority. It should be noted that a leader's assessment of how much he is liked often differs markedly from the group's evaluation.

Task structure refers to the degree the group's assignment can be programmed and specified in a step-by-step fashion. A highly structured task does not need a leader with much position power because the leader's role is detailed by the job specifications. With a highly structured task, the leader clearly knows what to do and how to do it, and the organization can back him up at each step. Unstructured tasks tend to have more than one correct solution that may be reached by any of a variety of methods. Since there is no step-by-step method that can be programmed in advance, the leader cannot influence the group's success by ordering them to vote "right" or be creative. Tasks of committees, creative groups and policy-making groups are typically unstructured.

Position power is the authority vested in the leader's position. It can be readily measured in most situations. An army general obviously has more power than a lieutenant, just as a department head has more power than an office manager. But our concern here is the effect this position power has on group performance. Although one would think that a leader with great power will get better performance from his group, our studies do not bear out this assumption.

However, it must be emphasized that in some situations position power may supersede task structure (the military). Or a very highly structured task (launching a moon probe) may outweigh the effects of interpersonal relations. The organization determines both the task structure and the position power of the leader.

In our search for the most effective leadership style, we went back to the studies that we had been conducting for more than a decade. These studies investigated a wide variety of groups and leadership situations, including basketball teams, business management, military units, boards of directors, creative groups and scientists engaged in pure research. In all of these studies, we could determine the groups that had performed their tasks successfully or unsuccessfully and then correlated the effectiveness of group performance with leadership style.

Now by plotting these correlations of leadership style against our scale of group situations, we could, for the first time, find what leadership style works best in each situation. When we connected the median points on each column, the result was a bell-shaped curve. *(See Figure 2.)*

The results show that a task-oriented leader performs best in situations at both extremes — those in which he has a great deal of influence and power, and also in situations where he has no influence and power over the group members.

Relationship-oriented leaders tend to perform best in mixed situations where they have only moderate influence over the group. A number of subsequent studies by us and others have confirmed these findings.

The results show that we cannot talk about simply good leaders or poor leaders. A leader who is effective in one situation may or may not be effective in another. Therefore, we must specify the situations in which a leader performs well or badly.

This theory of leadership effectiveness by and large fits our everyday experience. Group situations in which the leader is liked, where he has a clearly defined task and a powerful position, may make attempts at non-directive, democratic leadership detrimental or superfluous. For example, the captain of an airliner can hardly call a committee meeting of the crew to share in the decision-making during a difficult landing approach. On the other hand, the chairman of a voluntary committee cannot ask with impunity that the group members vote or act according to his instructions.

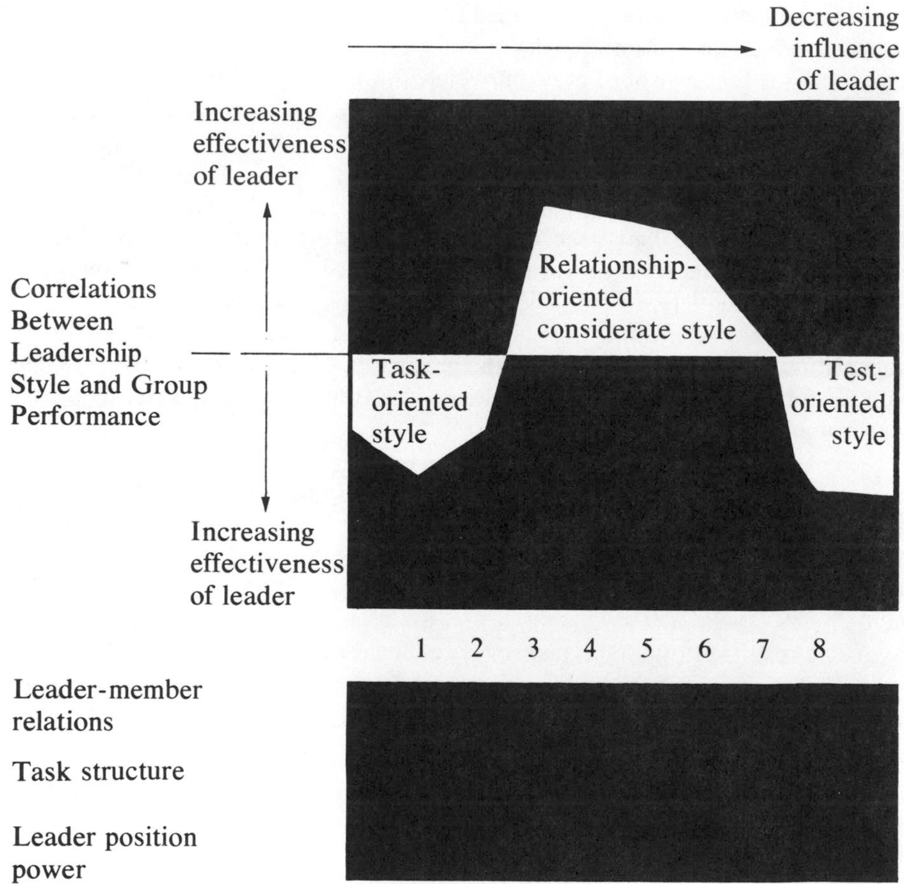

Figure 2

GROUP SITUATION

THE EFFECTIVE LEADER. Directive leaders perform best in very favorable or in unfavorable situations. Permissive leaders are best in mixed situations. Graph is based on studies of over 800 groups.

Our studies also have shown that factors such as group-member abilities, cultural heterogeneity and stressfulness of the task affect the degree to which the leader can influence members of the group. But the important finding and the consistent finding in these studies has been that mixed situations require relationship-oriented leadership while very favorable and very unfavorable job situations require task-oriented leaders.

Perhaps the most important implication of this theory of leadership is that the organization for which the leader works is as responsible for his success or failure as is the leader himself.

The chances are that *anyone* who wants to become a leader can become one if he carefully chooses the situations that are favorable to his leadership style.

The notion that a man is a "born" leader, capable of leading in all circumstances, appears to be nothing more than a myth. If there are leaders who excel under all conditions, I have not found them in my 18 years of research.

When we think of improving leadership performance, we tend to think first of training the leader. Personnel psychologists and managers typically view the executive's position as fixed and unchangeable and the applicant as highly plastic and trainable. A man's basic style of leadership depends upon his personality. Changing a man's leadership style means trying to change his personality. As we know from experiences in psychotherapy, it may take from one to several years to effect lasting changes in a personality structure. A leader's personality is not likely to change because of a few lectures or even a few weeks of intensive training.

It is doubtful that intensive training techniques can change an individual's style of leadership. However, training programs could be designed to provide the opportunity for a leader to learn in which situations he can perform well and in which he is likely to fail. Laboratory training also may provide the leader with some insights into his personal relationships with group members.

Our theory of leadership effectiveness predicts that a leader's performance can be improved by engineering or fitting the job to the leader. This is based, at least in part, on the belief that it is almost always easier to change a leader's work environment than to change his personality. The leader's authority, his task and even his interpersonal relations within his group members can be altered, sometimes without making the leader aware that this has been done.

For example, we can change the leader's position power in either direction. He can be given a higher rank if this seems necessary. Or he can be given subordinates who are equal or nearly equal to him in rank. His assistants can be two or three ranks below him, or we can assign him men who are expert in their specialties. The leader can have sole authority for a job, or he may be required to consult with his group. All communications to group members may be channeled through the leader, making him the source of all the inside information, or all members of the group can be given the information directly, thus reducing the leader's influence.

The task structure also can be changed to suit the leader's style. Depending upon the group situation, we can give the leader explicit instructions or we can deliberately give him a vague and nebulous goal.

Finally, we can change the leader-member relations. In some situations it may be desirable to improve leader-member relations by making the group homogeneous in culture and language or in technical and educational background. Interdisciplinary groups are notoriously difficult to handle, and it is even more difficult to lead a group that is racially or culturally mixed. Likewise, we can affect leader-member relations by giving a leader subordinates who get along well with their supervisor or assign a leader to a group with a history of trouble or conflict.

It may seem that often we are proposing the sabotaging of the leader's influence over his group. Although common sense might make it seem that weakening the leader's influence will lower performance, in actuality our studies show that this rarely happens. The average group performance (in other words, the leader's effectiveness) correlates poorly with the degree of the leader's influence over the group.

In fact, the findings from several studies suggest that a particular leader's effectiveness may be improved even though the situation is made less favorable for him.

The leader himself can be taught to recognize the situations that best fit his style. A man who is able to avoid situations in which he is likely to fail, and seek out situations that fit his leadership style, will probably become a highly successful and effective leader. Also, if he is aware of his strengths and weaknesses, the leader can try to change his group situation to match his leadership style.

However, we must remember that good leadership performance depends as much upon the organization as it does upon the leader. This means that we must learn not only how to train men to be leaders, but how to build organizations in which specific types of leaders can perform well.

In view of the increasing scarcity of competent executives, it is to an organization's advantage to design jobs to fit leaders instead of attempting merely to fit a leader to the job.

QUESTIONS

1. Is Fiedler's contingency theory applicable to educational situations? Explain and illustrate.

2. If you had an opportunity to question Mr. Fiedler about his theory, what questions would you ask?

HOW TO CHOOSE A LEADERSHIP PATTERN

By
Robert Tannenbaum and Warren H. Schmidt

Many discussions on leadership give the impression that there are only two ways of running an enterprise: the democratic, participatory approach and the authoritarian, one-man method. No such conflict should exist. There is a whole spectrum of leadership attitudes, and different approaches are appropriate to different situations. In working with his organization on problems that come up day by day, a manager should consider three factors in deciding his choice of leadership pattern. But as he looks ahead months or even years, he need not be fettered by these forces, for he can view many of them as variables over which he has some control. A successful manager is neither a strong or permissive leader. He is one who maintains a high batting average in accurately assessing the forces that determine what his most appropriate behavior at any time should be.

- "I put most problems into my group's hands and leave it to them to carry the ball from there. I serve merely as a catalyst, mirroring back the people's thoughts and feelings so that they can better understand them."
- "It's foolish to make decisions oneself on matters that affect people. I always talk things over with my subordinates, but I make it clear to them that I'm the one who has to have the final say."
- "Once I have decided on a course of action, I do my best to sell my ideas to my employees."
- "I'm being paid to lead. If I let a lot of other people make the decisions I should be making, then I'm not worth my salt."
- "I believe in getting things done. I can't waste time calling meetings. Someone has to call the shots around here, and I think it should be me."

Each of these statements represents a point of view about "good leadership." Considerable experience, factual data, and theoretical principles could be cited to support each statement, even though they seem to be inconsistent when placed together. Such contradictions point up the dilemma in which the modern manager frequently finds himself.

"How to Choose a Leadership Pattern," by Robert Tannenbaum and Warren H. Schmidt, March-April 1958, *Harvard Business Review*. Copyright © 1958 by the President and Fellows of Harvard College; all rights reserved. Reprinted by permission of Harvard Business Review.

NEW PROBLEM

The problem of how the modern manager can be "democratic" in his relations with subordinates and at the same time maintain the necessary authority and control in the organization for which he is responsible has come into focus increasingly in recent years.

Earlier in the century this problem was not so acutely felt. The successful executive was generally pictured as possessing intelligence, imagination, initiative, the capacity to make rapid (and generally wise) decisions, and the ability to inspire subordinates. People tended to think of the world as being divided into "leaders" and "followers."

New Focus

Gradually, however, from the social sciences emerged the concept of "group dynamics" with its focus on *members* of the group rather than solely on the leader. Research efforts of social scientists underscored the importance of employee involvement and participation in decision making. Evidence began to challenge the efficiency of highly directive leadership, and increasing attention was paid to problems of motivation and human relations.

Through training laboratories in group development that sprang up across the country, many of the newer notions of leadership began to exert an impact. These training laboratories were carefully designed to give people a firsthand experience in full participation and decision making. The designated "leaders" deliberately attempted to reduce their own power and to make group members as responsible as possible for setting their own goals and methods within the laboratory experience.

It was perhaps inevitable that some of the people who attended the training laboratories regarded this kind of leadership as being truly "democratic" and went home with the determination to build fully participative decision making into their own organizations. Whenever their bosses made a decision without convening a staff meeting, they tended to perceive this as authoritarian behavior. The true symbol of democratic leadership to some was the meeting — and the less directed from the top, the more democratic it was.

Some of the more enthusiastic alumni of these training laboratories began to get the habit of categorizing leader behavior as "democratic" *or* "authoritarian." The boss who made too many decisions himself was thought of as an authoritarian, and his directive behavior was often attributed solely to his personality.

New Need

The net result of the research findings and of the human relations training based upon them has been to call into question the stereotype of an effective leader. Consequently, the modern manager often finds himself in an uncomfortable state of mind.

Often he is not quite sure how to behave; there are times when he is torn between exerting "strong" leadership and "permissive" leadership. Sometimes new knowledge pushes him in one direction ("I should really get the group to help make this decision"), but at the same time his experience pushes him in another direction ("I really understand the problem better than the group and therefore I should make the decision"). He is not sure when a group decision is really appropriate or when holding a staff meeting serves merely as a device for avoiding his own decision-making responsibility.

The purpose of our article is to suggest a framework which managers may find useful in grappling with this dilemma. First we shall look at the different patterns of leadership behavior that the manager can choose from in relating himself to his subordinates. Then we shall turn to some of the questions suggested by this range of patterns. For instance, how important is it for a manager's subordinates to know what type of leadership he is using in a situation? What factors should he consider in deciding on a leadership pattern? What difference do his long-run objectives make as compared to his immediate objectives?

RANGE OF BEHAVIOR

Exhibit I presents the continuum or range of possible leadership behavior available to a manager. Each type of action is related to the degree of authority used by the boss and to the amount of freedom available to his subordinates in reaching decisions. The actions seen on the extreme left characterize the manager who maintains a high degree of control while those seen on the extreme right characterize the manager who releases a high degree of control. Neither extreme is absolute; authority and freedom are never without their limitations.

Now let us look more closely at each of the behavior points occurring along this continuum:

a. The manager makes the decision and announces it.

In this case the boss identifies a problem, considers alternative solutions, chooses one of them, and then reports this decision to his subordinates

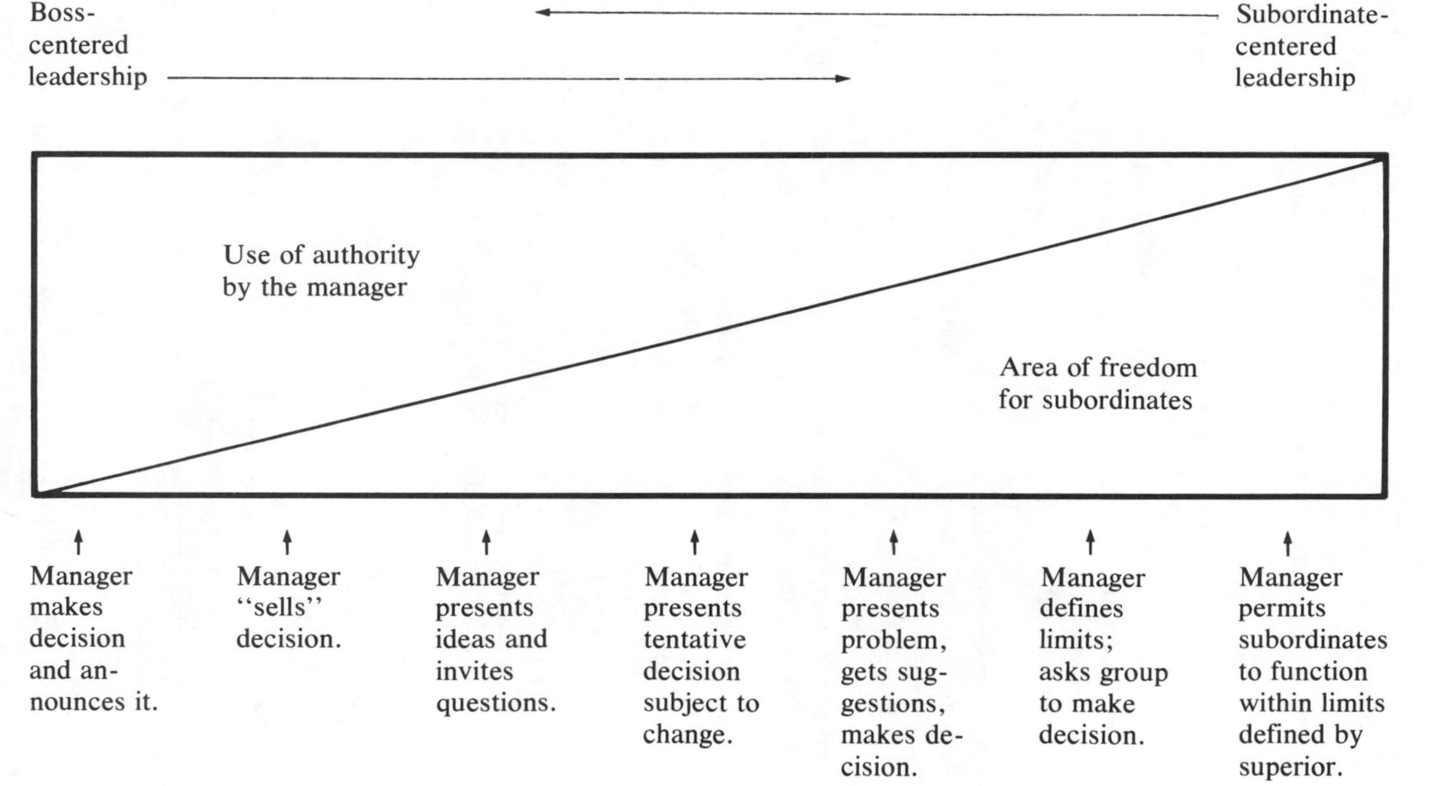

Exhibit I

CONTINUUM OF LEADERSHIP BEHAVIOR

for implementation. He may or may not give consideration to what he believes his subordinates will think or feel about his decision; in any case, he provides no opportunity for them to participate directly in the decision-making process. Coercion may or may not be used or implied.

b. The manager "sells" his decision.

Here the manager, as before, takes responsibility for identifying the problem and arriving at a decision. However, rather than simply announcing it, he takes the additional step of persuading his subordinates to accept it. In doing so, he recognizes the possibility of some resistance among those who will be faced with the decision, and seeks to reduce this resistance by indicating, for example, what the employees have to gain from his decision.

c. The manager presents his ideas, invites questions.

Here the boss who has arrived at a decision and who seeks acceptance of his ideas provides an opportunity for his subordinates to get a fuller explanation of his thinking and his intentions. After presenting the ideas, he invites questions so that his associates can better understand what he is trying to accomplish. This "give and take" also enables the manager and the subordinates to explore more fully the implications of the decision.

d. The manager presents a tentative decision subject to change.

This kind of behavior permits the subordinates to exert some influence on the decision. The initiative for identifying and diagnosing the problem remains with the boss. Before meeting with his staff, he has thought the problem through and arrived at a decision — but only a tentative one. Before finalizing it, he presents his proposed solution for the reaction of those who will be affected by it. He says in effect, "I'd like to hear what you have to say about this plan that I have developed. I'll appreciate your frank reactions, but will reserve for myself the final decision."

e. The manager presents the problem, gets suggestions, and then makes his decision.

Up to this point the boss has come before the group with a solution of his own. Not so in this case. The subordinates now get the first chance to suggest solutions. The manager's initial role involves identifying the problem. He might, for example, say something of this sort: "We are faced with a number of complaints from newspapers and the general public on our service policy. What is wrong here? What ideas do you have for coming to grips with this problem?"

The function of the group becomes one of increasing the manager's repertory of possible solutions to the problem. The purpose is to capitalize on the knowledge and experience of those who are on the "firing line." From the expanded list of alternatives developed by the manager and his subordinates, the manager then selects the solution that he regards as most promising.[1]

f. The manager defines the limits and requests the group to make a decision. At this point the manager passes to the group (possibly including himself as a member) the right to make decisions. Before doing so, however, he defines the problem to be solved and the boundaries within which the decision must be made.

An example might be the handling of a parking problem at a plant. The boss decides that this is something that should be worked on by the people involved, so he calls them together and points up the existence of the problem. Then he tells them:

> "There is the open field just north of the main plant which has been designated for additional employee parking. We can build underground or surface multilevel facilities as long as the cost does not exceed $100,000. Within these limits we are free to work out whatever solution makes sense to us. After we decide on a specific plan, the company will spend the available money in whatever way we indicate."

g. The manager permits the group to make decisions within prescribed limits. This represents an extreme degree of group freedom only occasionally encountered in formal organizations, as, for instance, in many research groups. Here the team of managers or engineers undertakes the identification and diagnosis of the problem, develops alternative procedures for solving it, and decides on one or more of these alternative solutions. The only limits directly imposed on the group by the organization are those specified by the superior of the team's boss. If the boss participates in the decision-making process, he attempts to do so with no more authority than any other member of the group. He commits himself in advance to assist in implementing whatever decision the group makes.

KEY QUESTIONS

As the continuum in Exhibit I demonstrates, there are a number of alternative ways in which a manager can relate himself to the group or

[1] For a fuller explanation of this approach, see Leo Moore, "Too Much Management, Too Little Change," HBR January-February 1956, p. 41.

individuals he is supervising. At the extreme left of the range, the emphasis is on the manager — on what *he* is interested in, how *he* sees things, how *he* feels about them. As we move toward the subordinate-centered end of the continuum, however, the focus is increasingly on the subordinates — on what *they* are interested in, how *they* look at things, how *they* feel about them.

When business leadership is regarded in this way, a number of questions arise. Let us take four of especial importance:

Can a boss ever relinquish his responsibility by delegating it to someone else?

Our view is that the manager must expect to be held responsible by his superior for the quality of the decisions made, even though operationally these decisions may have been made on a group basis. He should, therefore, be ready to accept whatever risk is involved whenever he delegates decision-making power to his subordinates. Delegation is not a way of "passing the buck." Also, it should be emphasized that the amount of freedom the boss gives to his subordinates cannot be greater than the freedom which he himself has been given by his own superior.

Should the manager participate with his subordinates once he has delegated responsibility to them?

The manager should carefully think over this question and decide on his role prior to involving the subordinate group. He should ask if his presence will inhibit or facilitate the problem-solving process. There may be some instances when he should leave the group to let it solve the problem for itself. Typically, however, the boss has useful ideas to contribute, and should function as an additional member of the group. In the latter instance, it is important that he indicate clearly to the group that he sees himself in a *member* role rather than in an authority role.

How important is it for the group to recognize what kind of leadership behavior the boss is using?

It makes a great deal of difference. Many relationship problems between boss and subordinate occur because the boss fails to make clear how he plans to use his authority. If, for example, he actually intends to make a certain decision himself, but the subordinate group gets the impression that he has delegated this authority, considerable confusion and resentment are likely to follow. Problems may also occur when the boss uses a "democratic" façade to conceal the fact that he has already made a decision which he hopes the group will accept as its own. The attempt to "make them think it was their idea in the first place'' is a risky one. We believe that it is highly important for the manager to be honest and clear in describing what authority he is keeping and what role he is asking his subordinates to assume in solving a particular problem.

Can you tell how ''democratic'' a manager is by the number of decisions his subordinates make?

The sheer *number* of decisions is not an accurate index of the amount of freedom that a subordinate group enjoys. More important is the *significance* of the decisions which the boss entrusts to his subordinates. Obviously a decision on how to arrange desks is of an entirely different order from a decision involving the introduction of new electronic data-processing equipment. Even though the widest possible limits are given in dealing with the first issue, the group will sense no particular degree of responsibility. For a boss to permit the group to decide equipment policy, even within rather narrow limits, would reflect a greater degree of confidence in them on his part.

DECIDING HOW TO LEAD

Now let us turn from the types of leadership that are possible in a company situation to the question of what types are *practical* and *desirable*. What factors or forces should a manager consider in deciding how to manage? Three are of particular importance:

- Forces in the manager.
- Forces in the subordinates.
- Forces in the situation.

We should like briefly to describe these elements and indicate how they might influence a manager's action in a decision-making situation.[2] The strength of each of them will, of course, vary from instance to instance, but the manager who is sensitive to them can better assess the problems which face him and determine which mode of leadership behavior is most appropriate for him.

Forces in the Manager

The manager's behavior in any given instance will be influenced greatly

[2] See also Robert Tannenbaum and Fred Massarik, ''Participation by Subordinates in the Managerial Decision-Making Process,'' *Canadian Journal of Economics and Political Science*, August 1950, pp. 413-418.

by the many forces operating within his own personality. He will, of course, perceive his leadership problems in a unique way on the basis of his background, knowledge, and experience. Among the important internal forces affecting him will be the following:

(1) ***His value system.*** How strongly does he feel that individuals should have a share in making the decisions which affect them? Or, how convinced is he that the official who is paid to assume responsibility should personally carry the burden of decision making? The strength of his convictions on questions like these will tend to move the manager to one end or the other of the continuum shown in Exhibit I. His behavior will also be influenced by the relative importance that he attaches to organizational efficiency, personal growth of subordinates, and company profits.[3]

(2) ***His confidence in his subordinates.*** Managers differ greatly in the amount of trust they have in other people generally, and this carries over to the particular employees they supervise at a given time. In viewing his particular group of subordinates, the manager is likely to consider their knowledge and competence with respect to the problem. A central question he might ask himself is: "Who is best qualified to deal with this problem?" Often he may, justifiably or not, have more confidence in his own capabilities than in those of his subordinates.

(3) ***His own leadership inclinations.*** There are some managers who seem to function more comfortably and naturally as highly directive leaders. Resolving problems and issuing orders come easily to them. Other managers seem to operate more comfortably in a team role, where they are continually sharing many of their functions with their subordinates.

(4) ***His feelings of security in an uncertain situation.*** The manager who releases control over the decision-making process thereby reduces the predictability of the outcome. Some managers have a greater need than others for predictability and stability in their environment. This "tolerance for ambiguity" is being viewed increasingly by psychologists as a key variable in a person's manner of dealing with problems.

The manager brings these and other highly personal variables to each situation he faces. If he can see them as forces which, consciously or unconsciously, influence his behavior, he can better understand what makes him

---

[3]See Chris Argyris, "Top Management Dilemma: Company Needs vs. Individual Development," *Personnel,* September 1955, pp. 123-134.

prefer to act in a given way. And understanding this, he can often make himself more effective.

Forces in the Subordinate

Before deciding how to lead a certain group, the manager will also want to consider a number of forces affecting his subordinates' behavior. He will want to remember that each employee, like himself, is influenced by many personality variables. In addition, each subordinate has a set of expectations about how the boss should act in relation to him (the phrase "expected behavior" is one we hear more and more often these days at discussions of leadership and teaching). The better the manager understands these factors, the more accurately he can determine what kind of behavior on his part will enable his subordinates to act most effectively.

Generally speaking, the manager can permit his subordinates greater freedom if the following essential conditions exist:

- If the subordinates have relatively high needs for independence. (As we all know, people differ greatly in the amount of direction that they desire.)
- If the subordinates have a readiness to assume responsibility for decision making. (Some see additional responsibility as a tribute to their ability; others see it as "passing the buck.")
- If they have a relatively high tolerance for ambiguity. (Some employees prefer to have clear-cut directives given to them; others prefer a wider area of freedom.)
- If they are interested in the problem and feel that it is important.
- If they understand and identify with the goals of the organization.
- If they have the necessary knowledge and experience to deal with the problem.
- If they have learned to expect to share in decision making. (Persons who have come to expect strong leadership and are then suddenly confronted with the request to share more fully in decision making are often upset by this new experience. On the other hand, persons who have enjoyed a considerable amount of freedom resent the boss who begins to make all the decisions himself.)

The manager will probably tend to make fuller use of his own authority if the above conditions do *not* exist; at times there may be no realistic alternative to running a "one-man show."

The restrictive effect of many of the forces will, of course, be greatly modified by the general feeling of confidence which subordinates have in the boss. Where they have learned to respect and trust him, he is free to vary his behavior. He will feel certain that he will not be perceived as an authoritarian boss on those occasions when he makes decisions by himself. Similarly, he will not be seen as using staff meetings to avoid his decision-making responsibility. In a climate of mutual confidence and respect, people tend to feel less threatened by deviations from normal practice, which in turn makes possible a higher degree of flexibility in the whole relationship.

Forces in the Situation

In addition to the forces which exist in the manager himself and in his subordinates, certain characteristics of the general situation will also affect the manager's behavior. Among the more critical environmental pressures that surround him are those which stem from the organization, the work group, the nature of the problem, and the pressures of time. Let us look briefly at each of these:

Type of Organization. Like individuals, organizations have values and traditions which inevitably influence the behavior of the people who work in them. The manager who is a newcomer to a company quickly discovers that certain kinds of behavior are approved while others are not. He also discovers that to deviate radically from what is generally accepted is likely to create problems for him.

These values and traditions are communicated in many ways — through job descriptions, policy pronouncements, and public statements by top executives. Some organizations, for example, hold to the notion that the desirable executive is one who is dynamic, imaginative, decisive, and persuasive. Other organizations put more emphasis upon the importance of the executive's ability to work effectively with people — his human relations skills. The fact that his superiors have a defined concept of what the good executive should be will very likely push the manager toward one end or the other of the behavioral range.

In addition to the above, the amount of employee participation is influenced by such variables as the size of the working units, their geographical distribution, and the degree of inter- and intra-organizational security required to attain company goals. For example, the wide geographical dispersion of an organization may preclude a practical system of participative decision making, even though this would otherwise be desirable. Similarly, the size of the working units or the need for keeping plans confidential may make it necessary for the boss to exercise more control than would otherwise be the case. Factors like these may limit considerably the manager's ability to function flexibly on the continuum.

Group Effectiveness. Before turning decision-making responsibility over to a subordinate group, the boss should consider how effectively its members work together as a unit.

One of the relevant factors here is the experience the group has had in working together. It can generally be expected that a group which has functioned for some time will have developed habits of cooperation and thus be able to tackle a problem more effectively than a new group. It can also be expected that a group of people with similar backgrounds and interests will work more quickly and easily than people with dissimilar backgrounds, because the communication problems are likely to be less complex.

The degree of confidence that the members have in their ability to solve problems as a group is also a key consideration. Finally, such group variables as cohesiveness, permissiveness, mutual acceptance, and commonality of purpose will exert subtle but powerful influence on the group's functioning.

The Problem Itself. The nature of the problem may determine what degree of authority should be delegated by the manager to his subordinates. Obviously he will ask himself whether they have the kind of knowledge which is needed. It is possible to do them a real disservice by assigning a problem that their experience does not equip them to handle.

Since the problems faced in large or growing industries increasingly require knowledge of specialists from many different fields, it might be inferred that the more complex a problem, the more anxious a manager will be to get some assistance in solving it. However, this is not always the case. There will be times when the very complexity of the problem calls for one person to work it out. For example, if the manager has most of the background and factual data relevant to a given issue, it may be easier for him to think it through himself than to take the time to fill in his staff on all the pertinent background information.

The key question to ask, of course, is: "Have I heard the ideas of everyone who has the necessary knowledge to make a significant contribution to the solution of this problem?"

The Pressure of Time. This is perhaps the most clearly felt pressure on the manager (in spite of the fact that it may sometimes be imagined). The more that he feels the need for an immediate decision, the more difficult it is to involve other people. In organizations which are in a constant state of "crisis" and "crash programming" one is likely to find managers personally using a high degree of authority with relatively little delegation to subordinates. When the time pressure is less intense, however, it becomes much more possible to bring subordinates in on the decision-making process.

These, then, are the principal forces that impinge on the manager in any given instance and that tend to determine his tactical behavior in relation to his subordinates. In each case his behavior ideally will be that which makes possible the most effective attainment of his immediate goal within the limits facing him.

LONG-RUN STRATEGY

As the manager works with his organization on the problems that come up day by day, his choice of a leadership pattern is usually limited. He must take account of the forces just described and, within the restrictions they impose on him, do the best that he can. But as he looks ahead months or even years, he can shift his thinking from tactics to large-scale strategy. No longer need he be fettered by all of the forces mentioned, for he can view many of them as variables over which he has some control. He can, for example, gain new insights or skills for himself, supply training for individual subordinates, and provide participative experiences for his employee group.

In trying to bring about a change in these variables, however, he is faced with a challenging question: At which point along the continuum *should* he act?

Attaining Objectives

The answer depends largely on what he wants to accomplish. Let us suppose that he is interested in the same objectives that most modern managers seek to attain when they can shift their attention from the pressure of immediate assignments:

1. To raise the level of employee motivation.
2. To increase the readiness of subordinates to accept change.
3. To improve the quality of all managerial decisions.
4. To develop teamwork and morale.
5. To further the individual development of employees.

In recent years the manager has been deluged with a flow of advice on how best to achieve these longer-run objectives. It is little wonder that he is often both bewildered and annoyed. However, there are some guidelines which he can usefully follow in making a decision.

Most research and much of the experience of recent years give a strong factual basis to the theory that a fairly high degree of subordinate-centered behavior is associated with the accomplishment of the five purposes mentioned.[4] This does not mean that a manager should always leave all decisions to his assistants. To provide the individual or the group with greater freedom than they are ready for at any given time may very well tend to generate anxieties and therefore inhibit rather than facilitate the attainment of desired objectives. But this should not keep the manager from making a continuing effort to confront his subordinates with the challenge of freedom.

CONCLUSION

In summary, there are two implications in the basic thesis that we have been developing. The first is that the successful leader is one who is keenly aware of those forces which are most relevant to his behavior at any given time. He accurately understands himself, the individuals and group he is dealing with, and the company and broader social environment in which he operates. And certainly he is able to assess the present readiness for growth of his subordinates.

But this sensitivity or understanding is not enough, which brings us to the second implication. The successful leader is one who is able to behave appropriately in the light of these perceptions. If direction is in order, he is able to direct; if considerable participative freedom is called for, he is able to provide such freedom.

Thus, the successful manager of men can be primarily characterized neither as a strong leader nor as a permissive one. Rather, he is one who maintains a high batting average in accurately assessing the forces that determine what his most appropriate behavior at any given time should be and in actually being able to behave accordingly. Being both insightful and flexible, he is less likely to see the problems of leadership as a dilemma.

---

[4] For example, see Warren H. Schmidt and Paul C. Buchanan, *Techniques that Produce Teamwork* (New London, Arthur C. Croft Publications, 1954); and Morris S. Viteles, *Motivation and Morale in Industry* (New York, W. W. Norton & Company, Inc., 1953).

QUESTIONS

1. This article, which originally appeared in the Harvard Business Review, was intended for an audience of businessmen. Can it be applied to education without substantive modification? For example, is the continuum of leadership behavior (Exhibit 1) applicable to a school situation if "principal" or "superintendent" is substituted for "manager?"
   Apply the four questions listed on pp. 172-173 to the practices of a school administrator whom you know. Does his behavior correspond to the views expressed by the authors in their answers to these questions?

2. The authors state that a successful leader is flexible. "The successful leader is one who is able to behave appropriately in the light of these perceptions. If direction is in order, he is able to direct; if considerable participative freedom is called for, he is able to provide such freedom. Thus the successful manager of men can be primarily characterized neither as a strong leader nor as a permissive one."
   In the light of the foregoing, comment on the leadership of a school administrator under whom you have worked, citing specific instances to illustrate your points.

MISCONCEPTIONS ABOUT LEADERSHIP

By
William W. Wayson

Six misconceptions about leadership are identified and refuted: leadership comes with positions; leadership should be exercised exclusively by people in titled positions; no one can perform a leadership act without permission; leaders never get opposition; leadership always has to be democratic; a democratic leader never leads.

Freeing principals of misconceptions about leadership may enable them to act more freely as human beings and to substitute personal meaning and action for the abstraction of leadership.

Perhaps we should stop talking about leadership. Remaking the principalship, as it has been discussed in the Chautauqua series and at the 1975 NAESP Convention, centers on a theme of leadership. After reading the articles, listening to the discussions, reviewing the presentations, and conversing with principals on the job and about the job, I find much confusion about what leadership is, whether it is possible, how it is expressed and by whom, and whether the principal can or even should exercise it. It is certain that principals will never remake the principalship into something that is meaningless. It is even more certain that principals won't engage in more constructive, more effective functions if their tutors have only vague phrases to guide them. Leadership has no usefulness for the principal unless it conveys images of actions that are possible and feasible. The word merely conjures up guilt — and few positive actions have ever been undertaken in guilt.

Yet leadership is what we need from principals. We need it from teachers, from students, from whoever happens to be around when the situation calls for facilitative action. If leadership is so important for everyone, it must be something everyone is capable of. Then why does it occur so infrequently? I think it is because we seldom take time to develop its meaning. When the word has no clear meaning, the processes to which it is applied may be occurring more frequently than we think, but we do not recognize them. Furthermore, if there is no clear meaning, we may never learn to carry out those processes.

"Misconceptions about Leadership," by William W. Wayson, from *The National Elementary Principal,* Nov-Dec 1975.
Copyright © 1975 by NAESP. Reprinted by permission of NAESP and the author.

To illustrate, let's suppose that a parent writes to the newspaper and complains that there is a lack of frottage in the school. One principal may fire off a response that there is too a lot of frottage in the school because the school believes in giving each child what that particular child needs and can profit from. A second principal will assure the PTA (whose members will nod approval) that fraternities are against the state law and, besides, they violate the American democratic ethic. A third will stew all weekend about how he goofed by not providing enough frottage to keep that parent from complaining in public. Another will call downtown to requisition some. Another will ask the superintendent to appoint a study commission to report on the whole matter (hoping that the consultants will know what it means). Another, who is taking evening courses, will call a professor and ask about frottage. One professor will pronounce it a fad, nothing to worry about. A second will say that it is what frotteurs produce, and that maybe an inservice program will calm the waters until the university can launch a full-scale preservice program to fill the obvious need. The principals' association might debate whether they need to denounce the denouncer, condemn either school district penuriousness or training programs, or initiate a series of articles on the need for frottage in the elementary school.

Absurd? Perhaps, but if the parent's letter had condemned the lack of leadership, we would have seen each of those responses and more. There is no more meaning for the term *leadership* in the minds and viscera of most practitioners and professors (or parents) than there is for the term *frottage* in the minds of most people reading this article.*

* * *

Leadership is always expressed in groups or organizations. It is a social function and cannot be carried out by oneself. Although leadership can be defined in any way one wishes, the definition that seems best to express what I mean when I speak of leadership in the principalship is that *leadership is the process by which a member helps a group to meet its goals.* In an organization, those goals include some of the purposes for which the group gets support from the rest of society. Therefore, leadership is any act that helps an organization or group solve one or more of the problems that every group must solve.

All organizations or groups continually have to solve at least six problems in order to be productive and to survive. They must:

---

*To save readers a trip to the dictionary, frottage is the technique of creating a design by rubbing a pencil or crayon over an object that is placed underneath a piece of paper.

- keep the people in the organization together long enough to accomplish their purposes. For most groups and organizations, that means for a long time, through thick times and thin.
- preserve and enforce the basic values and rules of operation that have been developed in the organization. In most organizations, there is a tendency to let those rules become more important than whatever the organization was intended to achieve.
- produce whatever the rest of society expects them to produce. The stated purposes are not always those that everyone expects, or they may not be the only or even the most important goals that are expected.
- secure resources that are necessary for functioning. Those include people, time, materials, and public approval.
- interpret and integrate goals that are expressed as expectations from a wide assortment of people and other groups, meeting as many as possible and rejecting others in some manner that doesn't produce too many enemies, either inside or outside the organization.
- adapt to meet changing conditions in the outside world. Though the first reaction is to ignore those changes or pretend they are not occurring, eventually the rest of society demands a change in the organization.

Most principals are prepared to do the first two things very well. These two tasks have been relatively easy ones, because teacher training has prepared teachers to be docile if not obedient and because the central office has done all of the selection and, in many districts, provided day-to-day supervision. Nevertheless, if principals are prepared through training and selection at all, they are prepared to perform well enough to ensure that these tasks are carried out. They are the tasks for maintaining the organization, and, traditionally, they are the ones for which principals have been rewarded or sanctioned.

The other four tasks have either been performed by other people or have not been considered important. For example, neighborhood schools have been in relatively homogeneous areas, at least for the white middle classes, and the principal has had few pressures to seek contact with diverse clients or to integrate differing demands into the school program. Superintendents have handled all of that for the total district. Not so long ago, even superintendents didn't have to worry about what certain groups wanted. Similarly, principals seldom had to worry about securing resources, because it was taken for granted that they took whatever the school district supplied and there was no place to go for more.

Times have changed. Principals (or someone in or around the school building) need to be more concerned with producing results that were not expected ten years ago; with securing resources from many sources in addition to the district office; with "politicking" (in the highest sense) with a diverse school population, some of whom were not vocal or expressive ten years ago; and with persuading school people to do things that they traditionally did not have to do. That is why there is a crisis of leadership in schools today: the times require former leaders to do things they never had to do before and for which they are poorly prepared. The same things that made principals seem like instructional leaders in 1955 make them appear recalcitrant today.

Perhaps a few examples can help to make the point. In the summer of 1975, I met principals who saw *both* teachers' associations and top administration as "them," and believed that "they" must be resisted. That attitude not only works against the achievement of the first task, but it was all but unheard of ten years ago. In another place, I met a principal who had been very successful for a decade as the principal of a school serving a Chicano population. Now black residents are moving into the attendance area, and he is beginning to feel inadequate. In a southern state, a group of principals expressed concern about state mandated evaluation procedures that require them to evaluate every teacher in a manner certain to drive a wedge between them and faculty members. All of these examples show that principals are now required to perform tasks for which neither training nor experience nor tradition has prepared them. These new demands require more from principals than the maintenance activities for which they were selected and for which they were rewarded only a short time ago.

The new demands for leadership are coming from points both inside and outside the school system and from both above and below the principalship in the educational hierarchy. The demands are diffuse and contradictory; many are incompatible. The principal might have been able to respond effectively to a single demand from a single source to move in some specified direction, but the first act of leadership that is required now is to make discriminating judgments and to respond diplomatically under conditions where the demands of one group seem to oppose the best interests of another.

* * *

After talking with dozens of principals and many experts on the principalship over the past two years, I have identified six common misconceptions about leadership that seem to blind many to the leadership they do exhibit as well as preventing them from exhibiting more. A better understanding of those misconceptions should foster more leadership in our schools.

The first misconception is that *leadership comes with positions.* This belief is widespread among educational personnel, but it is most highly pronounced in those who practice or preach educational administration. There is some tradition to support the belief. The military and the Catholic Church both adhered to the principle that the right to give orders comes with rank and title. American schools have always closely followed the model of organization presented by those two institutions. The principalship was developed when America worshipped scientific management and Weberian bureaucracy, when teachers were considered poorly trained and workers were commonly felt to be in need of control from superiors, and when schools were faced with the task of forcing thousands of "undisciplined" immigrants to conform to the way of life that local leading citizens deemed acceptable. Consequently, tradition imposes a deep reverence for hierarchical leadership on both principals and those with whom they work. Traditions sometimes continue their grasp on performance in institutions long after their practical value has been disproved.

Much of what we know about leadership has been learned from studies conducted within military units, and these studies clearly show that the authority that comes with an appointment is only half of what an officer needs if he is to exercise leadership — even in the narrow sense of giving orders that will be obeyed. Since Vatican II, the Catholic Church has instituted reforms born of the recognition that titled leadership can do only a fraction of what can be accomplished with the involvement of greater numbers of people in the exercise of leadership.

Leadership vested in positions of authority tends to stagnate. It is useful for only a limited set of functions, and those functions are not the ones needed to help complex organizations produce and survive in dynamic societies.

The principalship suffers because too many principals have assumed that they have become, or should have become, leaders the day they were named principal. It also suffers when the same misconception leads to the belief that higher orders of leadership must come from somewhere higher in the organization. Principals often wait for the superintendent to indicate what he or she wants them to do, what the priorities are, and what the support will be, but they wait in vain. No one at any level is prepared to take the lead. The superintendent may finally reply to demands with some general term or with some faddish and flashy program, but the stuff of which leadership is made is seldom forthcoming. Everyone is sitting and eyeing someone else, like two cats staking out territory, waiting for the other to make a move that will dictate how he himself must move. The crisis in educational leadership is evident throughout the system, but the finger is pointed at principals because they are in a key position in the school building, and it is at the individual building level that leadership must occur if American schools are to successfully educate today's children.

The second misconception — that *leadership should be exercised exclusively by persons in titled positions* — follows from the first misconception, but does more harm to principals. Principals sometimes feel that they must do everything. When they feel pressure, they do not develop the ability to delegate or they refuse to take help from other people. They may even be threatened if someone else does something to lead the school toward its purposes, wondering if "he is out to get my job." This misconception causes principals to compound the errors of the accountability movement by trying to do it all themselves rather than seizing the opportunity to enlist their faculties to develop goals and procedures that will have greater educational outcomes. It also causes leadership to fail because principals cannot distinguish the belief that they must do everything themselves, from the obligation to see that policies are carried out in a manner that will promote better educational practices, more faculty satisfaction, and greater involvement and commitment in the total school enterprise. Outside pressures become an onerous burden rather than a great opportunity.

Of course, the realities of leadership are quite the opposite. It is impossible for one person to do all of the things that must be done to make a group effective. It is even more difficult for a titled person to do some of them because the title and the authority set people apart from one another and inhibit the easy flow of ideas that are essential for the group's operation. When the word *leadership* is applied to official positions, it means that *the official is responsible for creating conditions under which any other members can and will exercise leadership when circumstances call for them to do so*. That responsibility usually requires the official to structure communications and decision making in the building to make it easier for leadership to emerge and to be recognized and accepted, regardless of what person it comes from. It is quite possible that a principal can gain recognition as a great educational leader and never do anything that we commonly call leadership, simply because other members of the school can easily act as leaders and solve their own problems.

The third misconception is that *no one can perform a leadership act unless it is expressly permitted by higher authority*. For example, principals explain that they cannot run inservice meetings or involve their teachers in decision making because the negotiated contract limits the number and duration of meetings they can call. When it is suggested that no contract or no policy — indeed no law — could be enforced that would prohibit their inviting friends to breakfast, lunch, dinner, or to weekend parties, some principals even state that the contract won't permit it. If one adheres to the traditional military definition of leadership, and if one sees educating children as conducting a war, then there must be distance between the officers and the troops. No principal can have a friend on the staff. But from any other point of view, there can be no leadership without frequent communication and a degree of friendly respect among participants.

The principal who waits for formal rules to permit leadership or who thinks that all leadership occurs during school hours will not act until the time for leadership has long passed. Leadership occurs before policies have ever been contemplated. By the time an action has become policy or accepted practice, conditions may require some entirely new action. The best rule for effective leadership is that a person is free to take any action not specifically prohibited by policy or law. The four steps for making the system work for you can help to assure greater effectiveness when that rule is followed. The four steps are:

- Never ask permission.
- Write three reasons why you think the action will be effective.
- When things go wrong, take responsibility for cleaning up.
- Be honest throughout the process.*

These steps were taught to me by dozens of principals who were recognized as educational leaders. They are essential for anyone who wants to be a leader; they make the job easier, and they ensure that you will be around to lead again.

A fourth misconception about leadership is that *leaders never get opposition and never have to answer any questions about what they are doing.* Principals who hold this misconception wait until all conditions are right and all signs are "go" before they make a move. They would be great leaders if only everyone else in the world signed a pledge to follow them and if the gods promised that everything would go all right. Principals who are exercising leadership sometimes aren't satisfied simply because they haven't silenced *all* opposition or haven't eliminated *all* questions.

*See William W. Wayson, "A New Kind of Principal," *National Elementary Principal* 50 (February 1971): 12.

Last spring, I observed a group of teachers berate a principal because he had violated the school policy that a child who broke rules in the school cafeteria would be sent home for lunch periods. He explained that the child's mother, with whom he had talked personally, worked all day and could not be at home to supervise, so he had given the child lunch in his office. Both actions were indicative of educational leadership, I thought. However, the teachers were not satisfied. After a discussion of the legality of suspending the child for the lunch period only, the principal finally lost all chance to lead by agreeing that perhaps it would be better to suspend the child for the whole day instead because there were policies permitting it. I am sure that the principal thought he had little chance to lead, but he missed a chance to engage the staff in problem solving, in examining rules to see what educational value they had, in establishing better contact with parents, or in setting up the cafeteria so it would be an instructional and not just a nuisance activity. He lost the chance to lead because he did not stick to his guns against opposition and because he had not prepared himself to explain the educational, consequences of his and the teachers' actions.

On another occasion, a principal came to me with a letter from the central office. He explained that he had tried to be a leader by planning an inservice program with his staff and sending the plan to the curriculum director to get the released time that district policy made available for such activities. "I told you they wouldn't let me do it!" he exclaimed as he threw the letter down in front of me. The letter said, "We do not completely understand what you plan to do during the hour from 1:00 to 2:00. Please clarify."

When they were graduate students, these principals said, "I have to conform here, but when I get into the job, I will be in charge and I will really make some changes." They are deterred from important actions because they always need assurance that their actions will have no unfortunate consequences. One question can dissuade them from a chosen course; one dissident group can send them into retreat.

Of course, there is no need for leadership, no opportunity to lead, if a situation has only one possible solution and if everyone is agreed to carry it out. No leader can act without stirring up some reaction, and some of that will be opposition. Opposition itself is frequently an indication that leadership is occurring. Also, opposition often indicates that people are involved in the situation and are motivated to invest some energy in it — two vital signs that leadership is possible. Questions also give the decision maker clues about how well his decisions are going, and they often provide alternatives that had not occurred to him. Both help to make for more effective leadership.

A fifth misconception is that *leadership always has to be democratic*. Many of the actions that must be taken to help a group move forward cannot be taken democratically because of the conditions of the moment. Perhaps people won't attend meetings, or if they do, they won't make any decisions. Perhaps traditions in a school building are such that all problems outside the classroom belong to someone else. Perhaps teachers have been working under a dictatorial administration and believe that they should not make any decisions themselves. Whatever the cause, principals will often face situations in which they cannot get anyone else to take action or in which the actions of a majority of one group would be detrimental to another. In such instances, the leader will not act democratically. Moreover, some things in a school should not be decided by a vote any more than we should vote on the sex of a cat.

A sixth misconception is that a *democratic leader never leads*. This misconception is partially related to the previous one, but it is even more limiting. Many amateurs in group process learn that no one should impose his will on the group, and they interpret that to mean that everyone sits back to wait for the others in some magical way to arrive at a conclusion. The official leader who operates under this misconception takes no action, creates no structure, makes no suggestions for fear he is not behaving as a good group member.

Of course, that is not democracy; it is laissez-faire administration. If everyone holds back, then no decision can get made. Effective democracy depends on every member's doing all that he can to make the group successful. The effective principal participates in the group just as he would want any other member to contribute vital information or ideas. Leadership requires that the principal be no more or no less committed to the purposes of the group than any other member.

* * *

The principalship will never be remade without the willing collaboration and active participation of principals themselves. In an important sense, each principal must do the remaking for himself. No policies, no laws, no training programs can effect the change unless principals take control of their own lives to gain more control over what they do. Remaking any role is much more a task of overcoming one's own views that obscure available opportunities and abilities than it is a challenge to eliminate constraints and demands that come from elsewhere. Remaking the principalship, then, depends on how well we can facilitate each principal's personal renewal and reinvigoration. Freeing principals of misconceptions about leadership may enable them to act more freely as human beings and to substitute personal meaning and action for the abstraction of leadership.

QUESTIONS

1. Besides the six misconceptions mentioned by the author, are there any others you know of?
2. Does the principalship need to be remade? If so, by what means?

UNIT IV

CHANGE

CHANGE

OVERVIEW

Change is the only constant. Nothing remains the same from one moment to another.

Change is inevitable but desirable change is not. Desirable change may occur by chance but the likelihood of its occurrence is increased if it is planned for.

How is planned change different from other forms of change? Bennis identifies eight kinds of change to help answer this question.[1] *Planned change* involves mutual and deliberate goal setting with a fairly equal distribution of power on both sides. *Indoctrination change* involves mutual and deliberate goal setting with one side more powerful than the other. *Coercive*

[1] Bennis, Warren G., "A Typology of Change Processes," in Warren G. Bennis, Kenneth D. Benne, and Robert Chin, *The Planning of Change,* New York: Holt, Rinehart, and Wilson, 1961, pp. 154-156.

change involves unilateral goal setting with power and deliberateness on one side only; for example, the change brought about by the communist tactic of brainwashing. *Technocratic change* involves unilateral goal setting but shared power; for example, a client acts upon data gathered and interpreted by a technocrat. *Interactional change* is non-deliberative, mutual goal setting with fairly equal distribution of power; for example, when friends help each other. *Socialization change* involves unilateral power but collaborative goal implementation; for example, a child develops under parents who set the goals. *Emulative change* occurs in formal organizations when a subordinate consciously or unconsciously identifies with a superior and emulates him. *Natural change* results from accidents and unintended events; for example, change resulting from storms and earthquakes.

Fallacies in attempting to change institutions. The *psychological* fallacy consists of selecting individuals, giving them special training, and returning them to the organization in the belief that they will then materially affect the behavior of their associates. This method fails because it ignores interpersonal relationships, role expectations, and organizational norms.

The *sociological* fallacy consists of making changes in an organization's structure in the belief that they will affect individual behavior. Organizational changes do not necessarily bring about changes in individual attitudes, values, and actions.

The *rationalistic* fallacy consists of trying to bring about change by explaining its desirability. It assumes that people always act rationally and that if a proposed change is shown to be advantageous to them they will adopt it. Admittedly, reasoned arguments may sway opinions, especially when listeners are doubtful, uncommitted, or ready for change. But individuals do not always view information objectively. They distort it to fit their prejudices or they do not hear accurately or remember communications with which they disagree. Information of itself does not generate change. It is useful chiefly to reinforce other methods and is most effective when people are receptive to change.[2]

Each of the aforementioned approaches is simplistic. Members of an rganization do not necessarily change their behavior when they change their attitudes, when their roles are redefined, or when they acquire information about the desirability of change. The reasons for resisting change are com-

---

[2] Adapted from David W. Johnson, *The Social Psychology of Education,* New York: Holt, Rinehart, and Wilson, 1970, pp. 254-255.

plex and the methods of effecting it are dependent upon many interacting variables.

Change agent. Changes are brought about by a change agent, that is, an individual or group seeking to alter goals, methods, or outcomes. A change agent acts as an intermediary between an innovation and an eventual acceptor. He advocates innovations he deems desirable and tries to bring about their acceptance.

Change agents are usually cosmopolitans. They are oriented not to a particular school or district but to a profession or field. They read widely in the literature of their discipline, attend educational conventions, participate actively in professional organizations, and effectively communicate their beliefs to their associates. They tend to be young and gregarious individuals who travel beyond the local scene and have social relationships extending over a wide geographical area. To be most effective a change agent should have a theory base for his proposals and a background of knowledge to guide their implementation. According to some researchers, the influence of those who first propose an innovation is transitory and shifts to more conservative individuals who hold influential positions.

Barriers to change. The absence of a change agent hinders innovation. Superintendents and principals do not usually conceive of themselves as advocates of change. They are content to maintain the status quo and keep things running smoothly, making ad hoc adjustments when necessary but avoiding any action which may rock the boat. Since the advocacy of change is a confession that current practices are unsatisfactory, school administrators are understandably loath to admit that what they are doing falls short of being desirable.

Another barrier is the lack of extensive practical research to justify the introduction of innovations. Research findings are frequently contradictory or are based on limited experimentation, often under controlled conditions which are not easily duplicated in school situations. Current educational practices are often not evaluated and there is no experimental comparison of different practices.

Moreover, the school is a domesticated organization. Its continued existence is guaranteed no matter how outdated its methods or unsatisfactory its results. Unlike private organizations, which fight for survival in a competitive market and whose continuance is based on quality of service and product, schools are assured of public support. Tax dollars are not distributed on the basis of performance, and there is always a supply of pupils asking for admission. Stability is looked upon as desirable and deviation from past practice as undesirable. In such an environment change is not stimulated.

Lay control of schools also inhibits change. Boards of education are composed of individuals who are not professional educators and who generally have little knowledge of educational practices beyond their local district boundary.

Suspicion is another "widespread and serious inhibitor of change," according to Henry M. Brickell, author of a study of the dynamics of educational change in New York State.[3] Teachers and administrators are suspicious about the effectiveness of innovations in other school systems, particularly when they are described by representatives of those districts. They suspect they are of little educational consequence and were designed to obtain outside recognition. Yet departures from conventional practice, while accompanied by a normal desire for recognition, are seldom motivated by such a desire. To dispel the suspicions of their listeners, advocates should honestly state the limitations of new programs and cite objective evidence of their merits.

Finally, size is a barrier. Large complex organizations adapt less readily to changing conditions than small, simply-structured organizations. Metropolitan school districts respond ponderously to pressures for change while the small suburban districts which surround them introduce innovations more readily. Innovative ideas are stifled in multi-layered organizations because of communication difficulties and centralized decision-making. Ideas generated at the lower levels fail to percolate to the top. Minor bureaucrats evade responsibility for deciding touchy problems by passing them upward.

Organizations which readily adapt to change are usually decentralized. They hire "idea men," are ready to take risks, and are not run as a "tight ship." They maintain open channels of communication and encourage discussion of ideas, particularly novel ideas, which they judge by their merits rather than on the status of those who originate them. They employ diverse types of personnel and assign both specialists and nonspecialists to problems in need of a solution.

Methods of change. A common means of effecting change is by the

---

[3] Brickell, Henry M., *Preparing for Education Change in New York State,* Albany, N.Y.: State Department of Education, 1961

issuance of a directive by a high authority. A directive is impersonal and formal, compliance is expected, and the results may be beneficial. For example, racially segregated school districts have been forced to integrate by court rulings and, as a result, prejudice against Blacks has been mitigated. However, an attempt to bring about change by fiat may cause resentment and resistance. Individuals may subvert the intent of the order by subtle means which are often difficult to discern and counteract. A formal order may change structures and processes but not attitudes or beliefs. An old adage runs: "A man convinced against his will is of the same opinion still."

Another way of effecting change is by the replacement of personnel. Individuals who are unwilling or unable to change are replaced by others more complacent or adaptable. As in the case of change by directive, this approach is formal and concerned with task accomplishment.

A third method is by the in-service training of individuals in certain skills to improve their performance. Of itself in-service training will not bring changes in organizational role behavior but used in conjunction with other methods it may be helpful.

Sensitivity training is still another method, although its popularity has declined in recent years, perhaps because of misuse. It is a group experience in which an individual through feedback is helped to analyze himself and become aware of others' reactions to his behavior. It develops a sensitivity to others' feelings and provides an opportunity to experiment with new behavior. It can modify the behavior of individuals in work situations, change attitudes, and alter interpersonal behavior, but unless it involves many members of an organization, lasting organizational changes are not likely to result.

Surveys are sometimes used to promote change. School districts conduct surveys, either by themselves or with the help of an outside agency, to discover facts or opinions. The information gathered in the survey is collated, published, and distributed to concerned individuals and groups for study and recommendations. For maximal effectiveness, individuals and groups at all levels must have an opportunity to consider and report on survey findings. Although this approach sounds promising, it is not widely used and the limited research upon it is only partially supportive.

First-hand observation of a new program in action is perhaps the most effective way of convincing people. Speeches and published reports by partisan supporters are not regarded as trustworthy even though they may be accurate. Listeners are not disposed to take them at their face value. But a visit to a school in which an innovation is being tried out has a powerful effect, particulary if the school is similar to the one from which the observer comes. If the setting is markedly different from his home school, the demonstration loses much of its effect.

Resistance to change. Some resistance to change is healthy. It is unfair to label all resisters as reactionaries. If their opposition is based on reasoned argument, they serve an important purpose because they force the advocates of change to re-examine their proposals and spell out all foreseeable consequences. They apply a brake to the headlong adoption of innovative practices unsupported by a conceptual framework or research findings; they protect the organization against random and potentially harmful innovation; and they show that they care enough about an institution to resist altering its character and traditions.

Individuals resist change for both altruistic and personal reasons. They should be listened to because they have something valuable to say about the nature of the organization. Some may sincerely believe that a proposed change is unsound and less effective than the current practice. Others resist because the proposed change may lower their status in an organization, adversely affect their job security, increase their volume of work, or disrupt the informal group to which they belong. Those who are confident in their present roles might feel insecure if they were obliged to learn new ones. They are unwilling to exchange certainty for uncertainty. Some who are insufficiently informed about a proposed change may oppose it because of ignorance.[4]

Resistance is lessened when change results from a collaborative relationship between the change agent and those affected. If the introduction of change is not a cooperative effort, it is likely to meet resistance. As many as possible of those affected by the change should have a voice in its planning and implementation. Those who feel threatened should have ample opportunity to express their fears and concerns in small informal groups and in face-to-face meetings with administrators. Change initiated in an atmosphere of antagonism is not likely to be very successful.

Complexity of change. Behavioral change is a complex and slow process. It cannot be brought about by bringing in an outside speaker, setting up a few workshops, and delivering a pep talk to the staff. A proposed change requires careful study, open discussion, and wide participation of individuals

---

[4]Based upon William W. Savage, *Interpersonal and Group Relations in Educational Administration,* New York: Scott, Foresman, and Company, 1968, pp. 190-192.

at every organizational level before its adoption, and a realistic appraisal of its effectiveness as it progresses and after it has been completed.

Structural change — the rearrangement of subordinate-superordinate relationships and channels of communication — is also slow but relatively easier to effect. An administrator must keep in mind that a change in one organizational component ineluctably affects other components and may cause conflict unless carefully planned.

Evaluation. Many educational innovations are not evaluated objectively. Judgments of their effectiveness are based on subjective and personal criteria rather than on hard data. School districts initiate innovations, sometimes at considerable expense, without establishing evaluative criteria beforehand and, consequently, it is difficult to assess the results of change accurately and to compare one educational practice with another. A 1964 survey of the nationally-financed experiments in one large state showed that less than one-half of one percent were systematically evaluated.[5] The federal government now requires that criteria for evaluation be built into a grant proposal before it can be approved.

It is good sense to formulate the means of assessing the results of change before launching an experiment and to spell out the expected benefits in specific terms instead of stating them abstractly and globally. The experiment itself should be conducted under controlled conditions because control is essential for evaluation. When control is impossible, impartial observers should keep the experimental conditions under close surveillance and accurately report on them. The necessity for control and the cost of evaluation in time and money may partly explain why educational change is infrequently evaluated.

Between 1960 and 1970 the Ford Foundation authorized grants of $30.6 million for 25 projects in 22 states and Puerto Rico to demonstrate that certain traditional aspects of school systems could profitably be changed, for example, the self-contained classroom taught by a single teacher, uniform time schedules, and conventional textbooks. At the end of the decade an independent evaluation showed that only a few of the projects succeeded in changing professional practice. Mechanical aids such as tape recorders and dial retrieval systems were effective only until the novelty wore off. Nonuniform time schedules ran into serious difficulties: discipline got out of hand and parents rebelled against "the perceived erosion of academic stand-

[5] Miles, M. B. *Innovation in Education,* New York: Teachers College Press, Columbia University, 1964, pp. 1-49 (b).

ards." Team teaching seldom accomplished much. Interest quickly waned when conventional textbooks were supplanted by programmed instruction and other sophisticated devices. The report, "A Foundation Goes to School," is unflinchingly honest — and dismaying.[6] Most of the failures were rooted in human problems, notably a lack of leadership, professional jealousy, and resistance to change.

The human side of change. An administrator must be aware that change always involves people. "You write on paper," Catherine of Russia once said to a group of philosophers, "but I write on the sensitive skin of human beings." When change is introduced those affected by it should be helped so that they may continue to be productive under different circumstances.

SELECTED READINGS

Argyris, Chris, *Organization and Innovation,* Homewood, Illinois: Richard D. Irwin Inc., 1965.

A scholarly, readable study of organizational characteristics and adaptability to change.

Bennis, Warren G., Benne, Kenneth D., and Chin, Robert, *The Planning of Change,* New York: Holt, Rinehart, and Wilson, 2nd ed., 1969.

Perhaps the most comprehensive discussion of change available. A compilation of 43 articles by various authors dealing with such topics as the evolution of planned change, changing human systems, utilization of scientific knowledge, collaboration and conflict, relevant theories of change, Lewin's force-field theory, and programs and technologies.

Hillson, Maurie and Hyman, Ronald T., *Change and Innovation in Elementary and Secondary Education,* New York: Holt, Rinehart, and Wilson, 2nd ed., 1971.

An anthology of readings on current innovations in education, among them the continuous progress education movement, team

[6] Ford Foundation, *A Foundation Goes to School,* New York: Ford Foundation, 1972.

teaching, ability grouping, individualized instruction, flexible scheduling, programmed instruction, and schools without walls.

Woodring, Paul, *Investment in Education,* Boston: Little, Brown, 1970.
An historical appraisal of the activities of the Fund for the Advancement of Education from 1951 to 1967. Describes its efforts to bring about change and its influence on teacher education, curriculum reform, educational tv, and other areas.

Havelock, Ronald G., *The Change Agent's Guide to Innovation in Education,* Englewood Cliffs, N.J.: Educational Technology Publications, 1974.
A guide to the process of innovation, written for educators at all levels. It does not tell what changes should be made or recommend specific innovations, but it does provide information on how successful innovation takes place and how change agents can organize their work so that successful innovation will take place.

TOPICS FOR DISCUSSION

1. Describe a change in educational practice recently introduced into your school or district. How was the change prepared for? Implemented? How was resistance, if any, handled? Were methods of evaluation decided upon in advance? Was the change advantageous? To whom? How do you know? What conclusions, if any, can you draw from this experience?

2. "Staff dissatisfaction with existing practices is a sine qua non if change is to take place." Do you agree? Why? If you agree, explain how, as an administrator, you might capitalize on discontent among teachers about what they are doing.

3. Explain and illustrate the following statement:
   "All organizations exhibit some form of progressive segregation or hierarchical order. The order makes it possible for change to occur from the top down but practically impossible for it to occur from the bottom up." Daniel E. Griffiths

4. According to Dr. Carl R. Rogers, psychologist, organizational change inevitably brings turbulence into the organization. Yet, he continues, "the only real avenue to real change is through such turbulence." Is it possible to have change without turbulence? Defend your point of view.

5. If you were a member of a board of education interested in changing existing practices and introducing educational innovations in your school district, would you give preference to candidates for the superintendency who come from outside your district? Why?

6. Justify the following statements:

   "Resistance will be less if administrators, teachers, board members and community leaders feel that the project is their own — not one devised and operated by outsiders.

   Resistance will be less if the project clearly has wholehearted support from top officials of the system."

   Goodwin Watson

7. Besides the barriers to change listed on pages 195 and 196, name at least one other.

8. Report on one research project dealing with opinion change.

9. David C. McClelland has developed principles on how the need for achievement is taught and internalized. An abridged version of his theory appears in Warren G. Bennis, Kenneth D. Benne, And Robert Chin, *The Planning of Change* (Holt, Rinehart, and Wilson, 1969) under the title "Toward a Theory of Motive Acquisition." The influence process which he describes is conceived in terms of input, intervening, and output variables. As a teacher or administrator, what can you put to use from this article?

10. Describe someone who acts as a change agent in your school or district. To what extent does he conform to the description of a change agent on p. 195?

11. This paradox occurs in *The Leopard,* a novel by G. Lampedusa: "If you want things to stay as they are, things will have to change." Apply this statement to a school situation.

EDUCATIONAL CHANGE: ITS ORIGINS AND CHARACTERISTICS

By
Donald Orlosky and B. Othanel Smith

Broad educational changes introduced during the past 75 years are classified according to their degree of success, focus of change, origin, and recency. More changes originated within the school system than from external sources although external ideas had a larger success percentage than internal ideas. The public school is more responsive to change than is generally conceded. Within education, four factors influential in determining educational practice are: research, personnel, commissions and committees, and professional and extra-professional organizations. Outside of education, three factors bearing on change are: state and federal constitution requirements, court decisions, and pressure groups. Planned change should be based on past experiences, current theories, and analysis of all aspects of the field of education. Guidelines are offered for those who promote educational change.

The purpose of this essay is to report a study of educational changes attempted during the past 75 years, examine the efforts to put these ideas into practice, rate the efforts to install them as successful or unsuccessful, attribute that success or failure to particular factors, and make recommendations to those who promote educational change. The changes selected are broad, macrochanges rather than narrow and specific changes. Also, many changes have been attempted during this period for which there is no record, but on the whole it may be assumed that the changes which are included in this account are of general significance.

Four categories were used to classify changes according to their degree of success or failure.* The symbols used and the descriptions for degrees of success were:

*The authors independently classified the changes, then compared the results of their work. Agreement on the inside-outside dichotomy was 88%, for the post-pre 98%, for the success-failure categories 68% (no differences exceeded one scale point), and for the focus of the change, 72%. Differences were resolved on the basis of evidence that supported the rating.

"Educational Change: Its Origins and Characteristics," by Donald Orlosky and B. Othanel Smith, from *Phi Delta Kappan*, March 1972. Copyright © 1972 by Phi Delta Kappan, Inc. and reprinted by their permission.

4 — A change that has successfully been installed and has permeated the educational system.

3 — A change that has successfully been installed and is sufficiently present that instances of the change are obvious.

2 — A change that has not been accepted as a frequent characteristic of schools but has left a residue that influences educational practice.

1 — A change that has not been implemented in the schools and would be difficult to locate in any school system.

Changes that were rated 3 and 4 were regarded as successes and changes rated 1 and 2 were regarded as failures. The changes were also classified according to the aspect of the educational system that was the focus of change. The symbols employed in this classification were: A — instruction, B — curriculum, and C — organization and administration.

Each idea for change was classified according to its origin. Some changes originated outside of the school setting and others arose within the field of education. The changes were classified as internal or external, using these symbols: I — internal origin, within the education field; and EX — external origin, outside the education field.

The fourth distinction made was between changes proposed recently and those proposed some time ago. Changes initiated after 1950 were regarded as recent; all others were listed in the pre-1950 era.

Table 1 provides an alphabetical listing by categories of the changes included in this report.

It is important to observe in Table 1 that a large number of changes (49) originated within the school system, compared with a small number (14) originating from external sources. The schools initiated changes at a ratio of 3½ to 1, compared with individuals or agencies outside the schools. External changes were invariably in the areas of curriculum (eight instances) or organization and administration (six instances). The external ideas had a higher success percentage (93%) than the internal ideas (64%). These data suggest that when an idea has both outside group and school support, success probability is high.

It should not be inferred from the lower success rate of ideas originating within the field of education that ideas are likely to fail because of their origin. For instance, all efforts to alter instructional behavior originated within the education field, but it is notoriously difficult to change teaching habits. Also, the lower percentage of success is quite likely due to the fact

Table 1

CHANGES LISTED ACCORDING TO DATE OF ORIGIN, SOURCE, RATING OF SUCCESS, AND FOCUS OF CHANGE

Change	Post-1950	Source	Rating	Focus
Ability Grouping		I	3	A
Activity Curriculum		I	2	B
Adult Education		EX	4	C
British Infant School	X	I	3	B
Carnegie Unit		I	4	C
Community School		I	2	B
Compensatory Education	X	EX	3	B
Compulsory Attendance		EX	4	C
Conservation Education		EX	3	B
Consolidation of Schools		I	4	C
Core Curriculum		I	1	B
Creative Education	X	I	1	B
Dalton Plan		I	1	A
Desegregation	X	EX	3	C
Driver Education		EX	4	B
Elective System		I	4	B
Environmental Education	X	EX	3	B
Equalization Procedures		I	4	C
Extra-class Activities		I	4	B
Flexible Scheduling	X	I	2	C
Guidance		I	4	A
Head Start	X	EX	3	C
Home Economics		EX	3	B
Individually Prescribed Instruction	X	I	3	A
International Education		I	3	B
Junior College		I	4	C
Junior High School		I	4	C
Kindergarten		I	4	C
Linguistics	X	I	3	A
Look-and-Say Method		I	3	A

(Continued on next page)

Change	Post-1950	Source	Rating	Focus
Media and Technology		I	4	A
Microteaching	X	I	3	A
Middle School	X	I	3	C
Mid-year Promotion		I	1	C
New Leadership Roles		I	4	C
Nongraded Schools	X	I	3	C
Nursery Schools		EX	3	C
Open Classroom	X	I	3	A
Phonics Method		I	3	A
Physical Education		EX	4	B
Platoon System		I	1	C
Programmed Instruction		I	3	A
Project Method		I	2	A
Safety Education		I	4	B
School Psychologist	X	I	3	C
Self-contained Classroom		I	3	C
Sensitivity Training	X	I	2	A
Sex Education	X	EX	2	B
Silent Reading		I	4	A
Social Promotion		I	4	C
Special Education	X	I	4	B
Store Front Schools	X	EX	3	C
Student Teaching		I	4	A
Team Teaching	X	I	2	C
Testing Movement		I	4	C
Tests and Measurements		I	4	A
Thirty-School Experiment		I	1	B
Unit Method		I	2	B
Unit Plan		I	2	A
Updating Curriculum Content		I	3	B
Visiting Teacher		I	2	A
Vocational and Technical Education		EX	4	B
Winnetka Plan		I	1	A

that the professional literature reports a larger number of internal change attempts. Failures that originate outside of education are less likely to remain long enough to be recorded as an effort to change at the macro-level studied.

Changes were successfully implanted in instruction, curriculum, and organization and administration. None of these three categories was immune. Likewise, failures in all three areas suggest that each area had resisted changes or was unable to accommodate some of them. All of the successful changes in instruction came from within the education field, two-thirds of the changes in organization and administration originated within education, and half of the curricular changes came from within the field. Thus it appears that the public school is more responsive to change than is generally conceded.

Government influence was evident in such programs as Head Start, which required heavy financial support, and in compulsory attendance, where the legislative branch produced change through law.

The successful pre-1950 ideas usually involved school organization and administration. It appears to be easy to try and discard changes in curriculum and instruction, but when the machinery of organization and administration is modified the change is relatively permanent.

It should be noted that there are factors and agencies not categorized in this analysis that bear on change and are influential in the determination of educational practice. They cannot be regarded as the basis for any particular change but affect the entire spectrum of educational practice. Four such factors within education are 1) educational research, 2) school personnel (teachers, administrators, state departments, and university personnel), 3) educational commissions and committees, and 4) professional and extra-legal organizations. The elements outside of the field of education that should be taken into account include 1) state and federal constitutional requirements, 2) court decisions that rule on educational practice, and 3) pressure groups in society.

Planned change should be based on a combination of past experiences, current theories, and analysis of all aspects of the field of education. The conclusions that follow encourage such an approach and can serve as guides to those who promote educational change.

1. Changes in methods of instruction are apparently more difficult to make successfully than changes in curriculum or administration.

2. Changes in instruction are most likely to originate within the education profession. In no case in the past did a successful change in instruction come from outside of education. Changes in ways of teaching and organizing instruction are neither the result of legislation nor of social pressure, but rather are the outcome of professional wisdom and research. This is attributable partly to the fact that the teacher's behavior in the classroom is shaped by factors considerably removed from social concerns, partly to the stability of teaching patterns, and partly to the intellectual character of teaching about which the public has little information.

3. A change that requires the teacher to abandon an existing practice and to displace it with a new practice risks defeat. If teachers must be retrained in order for a change to be made, as in team teaching, the chances for success are reduced unless strong incentives to be retrained are provided.

4. Specific curricular changes such as the establishment of the elective system are often initiated from within the field of education. Successful changes in curriculum can orginate either within the profession or from the outside. Neither point of origin monopolizes ideas for curricular change.

5. Curricular changes involving the addition of subjects or the updating of content are more permanent than changes in the organization and structure of the curriculum. Efforts to change the curriculum by integrating or correlating the content, or by creating new category systems into which to organize the content, are made at great risk. Complete or considerable displacement of an existing curriculum pattern is not likely to be permanent even if the faculty initially supports the change. This can be attributed partly to cognitive strain on the faculty, partly to upsetting the expectations of pupils and consequent parental distrust, and partly to faculty mores which tend to become stronger when threatened by change.

6. Changes in the curriculum that represent additions such as new subjects or changes in the substance of subjects can be made most securely with support from legislation or organized interest groups. The failure of curricular changes to be permanent may be attributed either to lack of social support or to resistance to displacement of the existing curriculum pattern. If school authorities are successful in finding social backing for the addition of a subject to a curriculum, the change can be made with little risk of failure. On the other hand, if social opposition is pro-

nounced, the probability of the change not being made is very high, or if it is made it is likely not to persist.

7. Efforts to alter the total administrative structure, or any considerable part of it, are likely to be unsuccessful.

8. Changes that represent additions or extensions of the educational ladder, such as junior college, are more likely to be lasting than changes that entail general modifications of the administrative organization, such as flexible scheduling.

9. The lack of a diffusion system will lead to abortive change. A change initiated in a particular school, in the absence of a plan for diffusion, no matter how loudly it may be acclaimed, is not likely to become widespread or to be permanently entrenched.

10. Changes that have the support of more than one critical element are more likely to succeed. Compulsory education, with legal, social, and educational support, did not have to overcome as much resistance as it would have if only educators had supported it.

11. Changes will be resisted if they require educational personnel to relinquish power or if they cast doubt on educator roles. Accompanying legislative, legal, and financial impetus increases the probability of success in such changes.

12. The weight of the cognitive burden is one of the significant factors that determine the permanence of a change. If the cognitive load is light, i.e., if not many people are required to learn many new facts and procedures, a change is more likely to persist than if the burden is heavy. The weight of the burden is proportional to the number of factors entailed in the change. For example, if the total administrative structure is the object of change, the chances for successful innovation will be low. The same observation can be made about changes in methods of instruction or curricular changes.

13. The initiation of change may come from a number of sources — professionals, social groups, government, and so on — and changes may arise from research, as in the case of ability grouping, or from ideologies, as in the case of the core curriculum, or from professional wisdom, as in the platoon system. The source of the change appears to have far less to do with its staying power than the support the change receives and the strain it places upon the school personnel. The core curriculum and

creative education are constant drains on the time and energy of a faculty and they consequently tend to disappear even though each may enjoy faculty support. On the other hand, international understanding tends to be more persistent as a curricular change. It requires far less time and energy of the teacher and has enjoyed no greater support from the faculty then either the core curriculum or creative education.

14. The federal government, as a change agent, will have optimum success if it takes certain facts into account. In the first place, the government acts in two ways. It passes enabling legislation empowering various federal agencies to do specified things to attain certain goals. In the second place, it acts through the courts to interpret laws, to establish norms, and to order certain actions by school officials. Programs of the U.S. Office of Education are based largely upon enabling legislation. In the development of its programs the USOE is subject to the same conditions of success as any other change agent. For example, its efforts to induce changes in methods of teaching are likely to be less successful than efforts to change curriculum content or to extend or modify the educational ladder; its efforts are likely to be more successful if it has the support of commission recommendation, organized groups, and professional personnel.

The data set forth in this report are too broad to provide insight into the sort of situational analysis that successful change entails. More refined data can be secured by intensive case studies. A few well-chosen case studies can be made to explore the underlying variables whose manipulation and control can give a change agent greater assurance of success.

The educational system in a dynamic society cannot remain stagnant. We should expect changes to be proposed that will alter the school system, since the United States is undergoing rapid change. The idiosyncracies of a particular situation may not always conform to the patterns revealed in this study, but it is likely that an understanding of the characteristics of the changes proposed over the last three-quarters of a century will be helpful in the development of successful procedures in the installation of educational changes.

QUESTIONS

1. According to the authors, changes in methods of instruction are more difficult to make successfully than changes in curriculum and administration.
   a. Why?
   b. If you were a school administrator, what steps would you follow to bring about changes in instructional methods?

2. Research has had little influence on the introduction of educational change. Why?

THE MICROPOLITICS OF INNOVATION: NINE PROPOSITIONS

By
Ernest R. House

The diffusion of innovation depends on direct personal contacts which in turn depend on transportation routes and organizational structure. The smallest units will be the last to adopt and the first to discontinue innovation.

Superintendents, advocacy groups, and central office politics also influence the adoption of innovative practices.

Teachers have little incentive to engage in innovation. Administrators, whose positions are dependent upon satisfying a pluralistic public, settle for a combination of innovative and traditional programs.

Innovation can be enhanced by increasing interpersonal contact and restructuring incentives.

Consider the teacher or administrator who is interested in an educational innovation. Before he will seriously consider implementing it, he must engage in extensive dialogue with someone who knows a good deal about the innovation. Say he is considering computer-assisted learning. There are scores of doubts that must be resolved. Will teachers really like it? Is it any better than a dozen other gimmicks? What are the hidden costs, the ones not mentioned in the brochure, the ones he knows are there? For his own conviction, for his own conscience, he must have answers to these questions from a probing dialogue, preferably with someone who has had extensive experience with the innovation, someone whom he knows or whose credibility he can intuitively assess.

1. ***Innovation diffusion depends on face-to-face personal contact.*** Direct personal contact is so important in innovation because of the uncertainty connected with implementing a new idea. Indirect contact, like the written word, suffices to spread simple, well structured, routine information. But

---

"The Micropolitics of Innovation: Nine Propositions," by Ernest R. House, from *Phi Delta Kappan*, January 1976. Copyright © 1976 by Phi Delta Kappan, Inc., and reprinted by their permission.

when results are unpredictable, the potential innovator needs to engage in extended dialogue, to ask questions, to have his doubts resolved. Direct personal contact is essential in problem solving, in well-considered planning, and in negotiations.

So one way of studying innovation is to trace the flow of personal contact. And one way to control innovation is to control the flow of personal contact. Who knows whom and who talks to whom are powerful indicators of whether, where, and when an innovation will be accepted.

2. ***Two of the major determinants of face-to-face personal contact — and hence of innovation diffusion — are transportation routes and organizational structure.*** Of the two, the influence of transportation routes is most underappreciated in education. Modern geographers have done most in tracing the diffusion of innovations in space. "Contagious" diffusion occurs in homogeneous populations. In farming, for example, one farmer spreads the word to another, and the innovation diffuses from its point of origin outward as in ripples on a pond.

But urbanization changes that completely. In urban centers the population becomes highly concentrated and specialized. A man does not necessarily talk much to his next-door neighbor. Furthermore, many personal contacts are with other urban centers. The villages communicate with the towns, the towns with the cities, the cities with the big cities, and the big cities communicate most with each other. The so-called "urban hierarchy" develops, in which an innovation (or an epidemic, for that matter) diffuses from larger population centers to smaller ones down a scale of size. The more urbanized and "developed" an area, the more pronounced this effect.

One geographer, Poul Pedersen,[1] has combined contagious diffusion and the urban hierarchy into a model which demonstrates that diffusion is dependent on exposure to the innovation, a willingness to adopt, the economic and technical feasibility of the innovation, and the presence of the entrepreneur.

Innovation in a region will be introduced first through the largest city or the city with the highest exchange of people — in other words, the major metropolitan area — and will follow a combination of two routes. One route

[1] Poul Ove Pedersea, "Innovation Diffusion in Urban Systems," in Torsten Hagerstrand and Antoni R. Kuklinski, eds., *Information Systems for Regional Development — A Seminar*, Lund Studies in Geography, Series B, No. 37 (Lund, Sweden: Royal University of Lund, 1971).

leads from town to nearest town over the transportation network. The other leads from larger to smaller towns down the urban hierarchy.

Information flow is not the only factor, however. Some innovations can be adopted only by units of a certain size. There is a threshold of unit size below which the innovation cannot be adopted or maintained. The smallest units will often be the last to adopt and the first to discontinue the innovation. The threshold also rises with the degree of regional development and degree of technical sophistication of the innovation.

One more requirement is that there be an entrepreneur to engineer local implementation of the innovation. Someone must organize the people, secure necessary funds, take care of problems, etc. The social organizer is critical.

How do these ideas apply to education? I mapped the diffusion of programs for the gifted in Illinois between 1963 and 1968.[2] If one looks at a map of the *completed* diffusion, there is no apparent pattern. But maps showing diffusion year by year are quite another story. The first programs appeared in major metropolitan areas with populations over 40,000. The second year the programs diffused along the major highways (Route 66, 40, and 20 in Illinois) like pearls on a string.

In the third year, concentric rings of programs moved outward from the major metropolitan areas into the surrounding countryside — contagious diffusion. In the fourth year, dozens of programs appeared within just a few counties in the east central part of the state. Actually, an entrepreneur operating in one of the first Title III projects organized dozens of smaller districts into a consortium and applied for funds. This is an example of both an entrepureneur at work and the threshold effect — districts must exceed a certain minimum size before they will adopt particular types of innovation.

In the fifth and final year, there was more such entrepreneurial organizing in the north and more contagious diffusion in the rural areas. Overall, the parts of the state slowest to adapt were those with no urban centers and no major highways. I would expect this same pattern to prevail for almost any innovation.

Since then, two major forces have reshaped the face of innovation in

---

[2]Ernest R. House, *The Politics of Educational Innovation* (Berkeley, Calif.: McCutchan, 1974).

Illinois schools: school consolidation, which will make new programs possible by adjusting the threshold; and the interstate highway system which links major cities cities even closer together and opens up new areas that were not innovative before. Sleepy towns will become diffusion centers for innovation. Administrators in those towns will have new problems.

3. ***The superintendent (and his top staff) play a key role in the introducing innovations into their districts, since they have the most outside contact.*** Organizational structures are such that direct external contacts are confined to the highest decision-making levels. In nonschool organizations, high-level administrators spend 40 to 50 hours per week in face-to-face information exchange, while lower-level administrators spend only 20 hours per week in this way.[3] Further down in the organization, there are few external contacts at all. Information has a hierarchic flow up and down the organization.

The people superintendents find most credible as sources of information about innovation are other superintendents. Richard Carlson has demonstrated that district adoption of new math materials in Allegheny County, Pennsylvania, paralleled precisely the friendship network existing among superintendents there.[4] He also distinguished between two types of superintendents. Those who stay in one place most of their lives and work their way up through the ranks into the superintendency he calls "place-bound." Those brought in from the outside he calls "career-bound."

The career-bound superintendents look forward to their next job and feel that they must innovate to build a reputation. They also have a freer hand inside the district, as opposed to the place-bound person, who has made many friends and enemies in his rise to the top. The place-bound man is more constrained by the social structure, whereas the career-bound man does not mind stirring the waters. The man coming in from the outside does indeed introduce many more innovations than the man promoted from within. The outside man also cultivates many more external sources of information. The superintendent acts as a carrier, a catalyst, and a gatekeeper for new ideas — within the framework of advancing his career.

4. ***The politics of the central office staff play a key role in promoting or inhibiting an innovation within the district.*** The members of the central office

---

[3] Peter Gould and Gunnar Tornquist, "Information, Innovation, and Acceptance," in Hagerstrand and Kuklinski, op. cit.

[4] Richard O. Carlson, *Adoption of Educational Innovations* (Eugene, Ore.: Center for the Advanced Study of Educational Administration, Univeristy of Oregon, 1965); see also, Carlson's *School Superintendents: Careers and Performance* (Columbus, O.: Charles F. Merrill, 1972).

staff interact frequently with the superintendents and the school board and, in a sense, control much information flowing to them. The way the staff is divided into small groups and the way these groups interact greatly influence school policy. For example, in one district the staff was divided into several small informal groups of two or three people. Before an idea could be presented to the school board, it had to gain the support of a small group, then advance to a major group and achieve a consensus there, and so up the hierarchy until it was presented to the adminstrative council and finally to the school board.[5]

Any new idea had to run this gantlet. Proposals to the school board by outside groups were intercepted by the staff or, if not, were routed back to the central office staff for consideration. If outside groups presented ideas contrary to those of the staff, their information base and credibility were called into question. In short, for any new idea to reach the stage of policy action, it had to go through the central office staff, whether it was originated by people inside or outside the district. When one understands this form of information control, and recognizes that the staff also controls internal resources, one can see why the sponsorship of a central office staff member is absolutely vital to an innovation within the school district. A new superintendent coming into a district will upset the informal patterns of the central office staff, thus allowing different ideas to enter.

5. ***The successful implementation of an innovation ultimately depends on whether an internal advocacy group is formed around it.*** The advocacy group consists of a small group of people who enthusiastically protect and propagate the innovation. The advocates see the development of the innovation as being in the interests of both the school district and themselves. They cohere around the innovation, competing with other programs for scarce resources, recruiting new members into their group, and aggressively advancing the interests of the innovation. If the innovation is to survive, the advocacy group must thrive and flourish.

At the center of the advocacy group is usually one person, often a charismatic leader, at least on a small scale. He initiates, organizes, and directs. He is the entrepreneur who orchestrates goals, resources, and people. Sometimes he may be an administrator. But often he is a teacher who informally leads the group. The advocacy group provides the real work energy on which the innovation lives. While outside ideas and money may

---

[5]Joseph H. McGivney and James M. Haught, "The Politics of Education: A View from the Perspective of the Central Office Staff," *Educational Administration Quarterly*, Autumn 1972, pp. 18-38.

act as a trigger, the energy must be provided with the organization. Even the high-level administrator is reduced to a support role.

Whether it is provided by a powerful administrator or an external agency, the support role is critical. All innovations fail at one time or another, and it seems that all require heavier investments of resources than anyone anticipates. Strong sponsorship is essential to rejuvenating the innovation when it encounters inevitable problems. The weakly supported innovation bobs and goes under without help. If the innovation is powerfully sponsored, more resources can always be found. Like the son of a rich man, the well-endowed innovation gets many chances. Its deficiencies can be remedied.

If the advocacy group is successful in competing for resources, others in the district are naturally opposed. To the extent that the advocates absorb money and promotions, there is less available for everyone else. A counter group almost always forms, comprised of those who are excluded from the innovation. Their resistance is often intensified by the missionary zeal of the advocates. They concentrate on the bad aspects of the innovation, and it is consistent with their interests to resist the innovation. Contrary to the dreams of reformers, most innovations are contained within the school structure like an encapsulated bacillus.

When the main advocate is promoted or leaves to take a new job, the innovation usually withers on the vine. There are some exceptions to this. In one situation where the innovation thrived, the chief advocate refused to make any decisions for the group for a long time, thus forcing them to make their own. Ordinarily, though, advocacy fades when stripped of its leader, thus giving innovation a "now-you-see-it, now-you-don't" quality, like fireflies in the night.

6. ***The teacher has very limited access to new ideas and innovations.*** First, the teacher's professional information field is surprisingly restricted. Being lower in the organizational hierarchy, the teacher has fewer external contacts with other professionals. Even within the school itself, he seldom has face-to-face contacts with other professionals, or even with other adults, mainly because of time constraints. One survey found that the main sources of new ideas for teachers are other teachers, periodicals and college courses.[6] Fully 54% of their sources of new ideas are their closest friends or

[6] Martyn O. Hotvedt, "Communication Patterns Within the Gifted Program," mimeographed (Urbana, Ill.: Center for Instructional Research and Curriculum Evaluation, Univeristy of Illinois, July, 1973).

those with whom they work most closely. This is not a situation conducive to gaining new ideas.

In addition, having *information* about new innovations is not the same as having *access* to them. For example, if I know about a new-model car, I cannot think seriously about buying it until a dealer near me has it. I must have access to it. Even then, I won't consider it prudent to buy unless the dealer is close enough to service the car. Likewise, even if the teacher should hear about a successful innovation, he must wait until he has access to it, normally through the school district.

7. ***There are few tangible incentives for a teacher to engage in innovation.*** The reward structure of the public school is rather flat. Salary and tenure are tied to years of service, and there are few opportunities for professional advancement. One of the few tangible rewards for working on innovations is the increased opportunity for promotion to an adminstration position. But there are few promotions available relative to the number of people employed. The only other rewards are released time, better classes, more classroom materials, and so on.

Of course, some people expect teachers to innovate without any obvious incentives. And indeed some teachers do. In one of our studies, many teachers listed "student enthusiasm" and other less material rewards as reasons for engaging in an innovative project. But mostly, teachers are like everyone else: They try to do what is right but are much more likely to do something that is not only right but benefits them directly.

The personal costs of trying something new are greatly underestimated. The teacher has acquired his teaching skills laboriously over a long period of time. These skills may not be superb, but he knows how to operate with them — how to get by. Someone comes along and says, "Try this." The new skills make the old ones obsolete.

Costs of acquiring the new skills are high. The amount of time and energy for relearning can be tremendous, depending on how radical the innovation is. In a computer-assisted learning project we recently studied, the teacher had to learn a new programming language and how to use a terminal before he could begin devising lessons. What's more, the teacher is expected to do this at his own expense — to learn new skills on his own time. Furthermore — the crowning disincentive — there is seldom any conclusive evidence that the innovation is really worth much in the classroom.

Thus the teacher finds himself faced with learning a new mode of behavior at high personal costs with no expectation of tangible reward and with no assurance that the innovation will work any better than what he has been doing. No wonder teachers regard many new programs with some cynicism; too many such programs are not worth the personal investment. Few corporations would invest under similar circumstances.

Yet some teachers do invest time in implementing innovations. In the CAI project mentioned above, the most enthusiastic advocates were young, ambitious teachers who saw their career many years hence as lying outside the classroom. However, most of them would invest energy only when they were given substantial released time by the district.

There is one other way in which the teacher can be substantially rewarded: through less tangible rewards available in the peer group. The advocacy group shares the pain and problem of working through an innovation. The group provides informal rewards, and bargains for more formal rewards, within the political structure.

8. ***What is rational for the teacher may not be rational for the administrator or reformer, and vice versa.*** We have noted how it may not be rational for the teacher to implement an innovation. Consider the administrator. He has a very limited set of resources with which to encourage innovation. Furthermore, he has a pluralistic public in his district, some of whom want innovation and some of whom want a traditional program. What to do?

The rational thing to do is to have some innovation and some traditional instruction to make his publics happy. So he disperses his limited resources to a few teachers to encourage their innovation — a differential disbursement of rewards. The others remain traditional. The rational administrator settles on a combination of innovative and traditional programs. He also needs externally supplied funds, for if he takes the necessary funds for innovation from traditional programs, he will demoralize the rest of his faculty. Few innovations are "floated" without externally supplied funds.

Naturally the reformer, the man pushing the innovation from the outside, thinks the innovation should sweep through the schools like a brush fire; he is often puzzled and frustrated when this does not happen.

9. ***Innovation can be enhanced by increasing interpersonal contact and by restructuring incentives within the school district. (Or it can be decreased by the opposite.)*** Educators can do little to determine where major highways will run, but they can take advantage of and build on the communication networks that already exist, keeping in mind that change ultimately comes

about through face-to-face contact. Within geographic networks one can increase diffusion best by promoting adoption in the larger regional centers. Reducing the threshold level by district consolidation or cooperatives will both increase the speed of diffusion and make larger innovations more feasible.

Perhaps the most dramatic step for increased contact would be to give teachers access to outside personal contacts that they do not now have. This would greatly increase idea flow. The disadvantages are that it would be costly and that it would decrease administrator control of innovation.

Increasing superintendent turnover and mobility will also increase innovation — irrespective of what it does to the superintendents. There are also various ways of increasing the permeability of the central office staff to new ideas. Encouraging the formation of advocacy groups and entrepreneurial behavior will increase innovation. Deformalization, decentralization, less rigorous role definition, and loose organizational structure enhance the formation of advocacy groups.

It is also essential to establish relationships with strong external organizations that can serve as sponsors and supply resources and legitimacy at critical times. A reward structure that offers upward mobility and encourages individual entrepreneurial behavior is facilitative. Note that many of these factors — centrality of communication networks, size, looseness of structure, ambition, wealth, proximity to external support organizations, high administrator and teacher turnover come together in rapidly growing suburban districts. These districts often have a surfeit of innovation.

Restructuring the entire incentive system of the school is a much trickier problem. Generally it is better to decrease personal costs by providing released time, consultant help, etc., than it is to increase rewards. I see two generic strategies for restructuring incentives. One would be increased differentiation among the faculty for rank and pay. People would be personally rewarded for being innovative. The other strategy is to increase the power of the teachers to bargain collectively for innovation. The advocacy group does this informally now. The differentiation strategy would result in more frequent but shallower innovation, while the distributive strategy would result in less frequent but more deeply implemented innovation. Both would require more money than the current system.

Nowhere in this article have I talked about the quality of innovation. For the most part, the factors I have enumerated work independently of innovation quality. Although we usually assume that innovation is good. I think that quite often it is bad. Faddism is the bane of education.* But that is a topic for another article.

---

* As my colleague Harry Broudy has observed, "Ignorance of history is often the mother of educational innovation."

QUESTIONS

1. Why do suburban districts often have a surfeit of innovation?
   What retards the introduction of innovative practices in large city districts?

2. "Faddism is the bane of education." Cite innovations which were quickly adopted because they were a current fad and dropped when they failed to meet expectations. How can a school administrator guard against educational fads?

CORE MANAGERIAL STRATEGIES CULLED FROM BEHAVIORAL RESEARCH

By
George F. Truell

This article was written for business executives but school administrators will find that most of it is pertinent to the field of educational administration.

It summarizes ten key themes of behavioral research: motivation, the individual's perception of himself and his environment, the self-fulfilling prophecy, the under-utilization of employees' capabilities, obstacles to teamwork, participation of employees in goal setting, feedback, organizational reward systems, conflict, and organizational change. Managerial strategies suggested by each of these themes are discussed.

Theory X and Theory Y; achievement motivation; the hierarchy of needs; participative management; hygiene factors; MBO; Systems 1 through 4; teambuilding; 9,1 and 1,9. What are they *really* all about?

Most men and women in managerial positions have been exposed to the findings of behavioral research and the strategies of professional management. The mass of data, concepts, strategies, and principles is often overpowering and confusing. After days, months, even years of study, managers frequently ask: "What are the really central themes from all of these courses and books and *how do I apply them in my managerial job?*" In sorting through the tremendous amount and variety of materials contained in management books and presented in development courses, ten key themes emerge that serve as helpful guidelines for managers. Following are the central principles and some of the managerial strategies they suggest:

1. People are self-motivated; you cannot motivate another person.

Central principle. As long as a person is alive, he or she is motivated. What motivates each person is something called "needs." (Other terms, such as desires, drives, and wants are often used.) Many different ap-

---

"Core Managerial Strategies Culled from Behavioral Research," by George F. Truell, *Supervisory Management*, January 1977. Copyright © 1977 by AMACOM, a division of American Management Associations. Reprinted by permission of the publisher from Supervisory Management.

proaches are used to classify these human needs and to explain how they are met or satisfied. However, most researchers do agree that some needs are more basic than others, involve external or environmental factors, and are fairly readily satisfied in our society today. Other needs appear to be much more complex; these are most often internal, mental, and personal in nature. Because of the individual nature of these needs, they are much more difficult to satisfy. Regardless of the classification system used, needs are at work all the time. They cause a person to behave in certain ways — that is, they cause a person to be "motivated."

Managerial strategy. When someone does not appear to be motivated, the question is often asked, "How can we motivate this person?" Managers devote a lot of attention and energy in a search for new and better ways to motivate their employees. This search is often fruitless. Perhaps the wrong question is being asked. Perhaps we should ask, "What is *demotivating* them? What is turning them off?" These questions open up an entirely different area of exploration to management. Managers must seek answers for such questions as: "Is our organizational structure causing our employees to act as they do?" "Is it our managerial style — the way we supervise them?"

In examining these areas, managers frequently find that the real cause of the problem rests with *themselves*. The solution may lie in a revision of their managerial policies, practices, and organizational structure. Many of the items that follow are examples of changes managers are making to reduce the "demotivators" in the work situation.

2. What people do makes sense to them.

Central principle. One of the fundamental principles gleaned from behavioral research is that as each person attempts to satisfy his needs, he behaves in a way that is perfectly sensible and justifiable to him. Those who watch this person's actions may call his behavior "nonsensical, ridiculous, or stupid." But that person has selected a course of action consistent with his perception of himself (what sort of person he believes he is) and his perception of the environment he is in. Those perceptions are individual; no one else sees the situation exactly the same way. His actions, at that moment, make good sense to him.

Managerial strategy. Many managers are quick to brand an employee's actions as good or bad, right or wrong. They often are perplexed when they see an employee doing something they consider dumb. Unfortunately, these managers don't spend much time finding out why the individual acted that way. Instead, they react to the employee's behavior without knowing what caused it.

If a manager is to understand someone else's behavior, he or she has to try to see things the way that person does. He must try to put himself in the other person's shoes and view the world from that person's perspective. This requires more face-to-face dialogue with the other person. It necessitates more listening and less talking. It suggests asking a person how he sees things, rather than telling him how he ought to see things. It means understanding the other person's viewpoint. Successful managers are those who have acquired skills in sharing perceptions, drawing out the other person, listening without preconceived ideas, and viewing the world from someone else's perspective.

3. People tend to behave as others expect them to behave.

Central principle. All managers have personal views about the sort of people they believe their employees to be. As managers work with their employees, they "telegraph" these notions or expectations to them through word choice, gestures, facial expressions, and other personal actions, and their employees react accordingly. Negative managerial expectations frequently result in negative actions by employees. Similarly, employees frequently react positively to a manager's positive expectations. This tendency for people to live up to someone else's expectations about them has been identified by Douglas McGregor as the "self-fulfilling prophecy." Some call it the "Pygmalion effect."

Managerial strategy. If a manager's ideas about another person tend to create the very behavior he anticipates, he may be able to change that behavior by changing his own set of assumptions or expectations. Instead of criticizing the way others are behaving, the manager might find it more helpful to first examine his own ideas to see if he is, through his expectations, causing the very behavior he dislikes. A change in his own set of assumptions or expectations about others may help to create a change in their behavior.

Douglas McGregor's Theory X and Theory Y helped to highlight the importance of "people expectations" on a person's approach to managing. His work provides a useful framework for a careful examination of the underlying managerial assumptions or expectations that permeate an organization. These beliefs, and the way they are often unconsciously expressed by managers on the job, help to explain employee attitudes and behavior. A conscientious change in managerial beliefs is often a critical first step in changing the behavior of others.

4. Many employees are underutilized on the job.

Central principle. Rapid communication and extensive educational systems enable people to acquire information, knowledge, and skills relatively easily. In addition to this rising level of information and education is a general increase in the level of aspirations of people throughout society. People know more, can do more, and expect more. Yet, at the same time, many organizations are designing jobs that require less use of an employee's abilities and capabilities. Many employees are asked to do only a fraction of what they are capable of doing. Not only does this condition have a negative impact on the motivation of employees, it also represents a poor use by organizations of an expensive asset.

Managerial strategy. In the past, much effort was devoted to the "best design" of jobs. An employee placed in a job was expected to conform to the parameters and specific requirements of that job. But the new trend is to approach job design from the opposite direction. Starting with the knowledge, skills, and aspirations of the individual, managers try to design jobs that will best utilize the individual's total capabilities. They are trying to fit the job to the person; to build wholeness back into the job. These enriched jobs require more of an employee's repertoire of skills and provide greater opportunities for personal achievement, recognition, and growth. In many cases, these efforts are paying off in increased productivity, higher quality work, and greater employee satisfaction.

5. Many organizations have unknowingly created obstacles to employee teamwork.

Central principle. Many management theories can be traced back to notions that evolved during the early years of the Industrial Revolution. These are reflected today in organizational structure and work distribution among employees. Distinctive employee groups are established and separate sets of policies and practices are formulated for each group. Some employee groups, for example, (frequently identified as "salaried") are given more leeway in deciding what they will do and how, when, and where they will do it. They are often viewed as the organization's most trustworthy, conscientious, and committed employees. Other employees (frequently identified as "hourly") are viewed as much less reliable. They need to be checked and watched more closely, and they can be given only limited freedom in carrying out their work activities. These differences are reflected in such practices as time clocks for some and not for others, reserved parking places for selected employees, separate dining and washroom facilities, rigid versus flexible starting times, and variations in pay policies and benefit programs. Often these delineations and the disparities in treatment are perceived by employees as implying that some people are "first-class" members of the organization and others are "second-class" members. The result is that one group of employees is frequently pitted against another at the very time when managers are pleading for better cooperation and more teamwork among *all* employees.

Managerial strategy. If the existence of differences among employee groups creates obstacles to employee teamwork, the best solution may be to eliminate all such "differences." Many managers are re-examining their traditional ways of organizing and operating in terms of whether these practices help — or inadvertently hinder — employee cooperation and teamwork. In some cases, differences in the way employees are treated correlate with the nature of the work performed. Where this is true, most employees understand and accept the differences. But where variations in personnel practices have little or no actual relationship to the contributions of a person, or where employees perceive these practices as indicators of distrust, unfair treatment, or downgrading of personal worth, managers would do well to eliminate disparities in treatment to close gaps between employee groups. Removing time clocks, placing all employees on salary, eliminating reserved parking places, and establishing common dining and washroom facilities are all examples of specific steps organizations are taking to close ranks and improve employee teamwork.

6. People support what they help to create.

Central principle. People tend to work harder in attaining their own goals and objectives than they do in attaining someone else's. They like to have some say in what they are doing — to feel that "this is my idea" or "my work." Yet many managers set goals and objectives for their employees, tell them what to do and how to do it, and expect a high degree of loyalty in return. In many organizations, it is not unusual to find employees who know *what* they are supposed to do but have no idea *why*. This frequently forces employees into positions of conflict as they try to choose between what they want to do and what the organization expects them to do. The result is often reluctant conformance or open rebellion by employees.

Managerial strategy. Many managerial strategies are now designed to provide an opportunity for employees to have some say in what they're going to do on the job. Management by objectives is a well-known example of this approach. In the MBO process, employees are given information about the overall goals and objectives for their organizational unit. They also have a clear-cut idea of the roles they are to play. They know not only *what* they do, but *why* they do it; they know how their jobs tie in with the overall activity of their unit. Within this framework, they are given the opportunity to sit down with their managers and set targets for their own areas of responsibility. Managers find that employees are more committed and will exercise greater effort in the attainment of goals and objectives that they have helped to establish. And because employees understand the purpose of their activities, they are able to exercise more ingenuity and creativity in developing better ways to perform their jobs.

7. Operating information given to employees is often too little and too late.

Central principle. When people set out to accomplish a task, they like to get some feedback on how they're doing. Frequently, they don't get sufficient information on the results of their efforts to enable them to keep score on their own performance. Or, if they do receive information on their performance, it comes at sporadic intervals in a format that is not usable, and/or it is too late to be of any value. In addition, the information is frequently processed by and filtered through a manager who decides "what they ought to know." It's very difficult for employees to improve their performance or to get very excited about playing the game when they don't known how well they are doing.

Managerial strategy. Performance appraisal programs, standards of performance, and related managerial strategies are giving employees better feedback sooner and in more usable form. Many managers, instead of deciding what their employees need to know, are asking their employees, "*What* information do you need, *when* do you need it, and *in what format* would it be most helpful to you?" Employees are also being given the opportunity to develop their own criteria for use in measuring their performance. When employees know the measurement criteria, they can keep their own score. They don't have to wait around for any indications from their boss.

8. Many organizational reward systems actually undermine the desired employee behavior.

Central principle. Organizations are too often inconsistent in the kind of behavior they say they want and the kind they actually reward. Many organizations, for example, place high value on creativity, initiative, imagination, resourcefulness, and so forth. Yet in actual practice, they give the greatest rewards to those who follow established guidelines, perpetuate the system, and don't rock the boat. Pay and promotional systems reward employees who are the most "housebroken" — those who conform. Other organizations promise their employees the opportunity for growth and advancement commensurate with their individual contributions and performance. Yet in actual practice, pay systems are geared to longevity and increasing seniority *on the job*. A common inconsistency is for managers to be urged to devote time and attention to their human resources but actually to be rewarded and praised for the effective utilization of physical resources. Is it any wonder, then, that many managers give only lip service to certain management principles when they find that there is no payoff for actually following them?

Managerial strategy. Desired behavior should result in a positive payoff for the employee. Performance appraisal procedures, wage and salary programs, status symbols, and related reward systems should have an actual tie-in with the way employees are expected to act on the job. Not only should these reward systems be designed to reinforce desired behavior, but employees themselves should perceive that the systems are consistent with what's being asked of them. The way employees see the reward system is what really counts. Where inconsistencies appear to exist between words and actions, managers should ask employees how they view the organization's reward system. The reward system should be revised, where necessary, to make certain that it actually supports, rather than undermines, desired employee behavior.

9. Conflict in organizations is natural; it can be managed so that everyone wins.

Central principle. Conflict exists, to some degree in every organization. In some circumstances, conflict or competition can have a beneficial effect in an organization. It increases creativity, innovation, the ability to think clearly, and motivation. However, when employees spend a significant amount of their time in a tense atmosphere where the main concern is coping with others, conflict can dilute the overall effectiveness of the total enterprise. Consequently, whenever managers encounter conflict, they tend to spend a great deal of time and energy devising ways to squash it, neutralize it, or sweep it under the rug. Unfortunately, none of these approaches really solves the problem. The causes of the conflict are not eliminated and the differences of opinion are merely submerged for a period of time — only to arise again at a later date.

Managerial strategy. Behavioral research suggests that there is great value in admitting that conflict exists and bringing it out into the open. Conflict *can* be managed. Sometimes just getting the differences up on the table for all to see helps clarify and resolve the issue. Where the issues are more complex, managers must acquire skills in helping subordinates move from a win/lose position (where one person wins and the other person loses), to a win/win position (where both parties can win). This can be done by identifying the possible cause of conflict, clarifying and understanding the other person's position, focusing on where people are in agreement, isolating those areas where they still disagree, and finding alternative approaches to solving those remaining problems. The objective is to find a positive solution that all parties can support — one that is mutually acceptable to all. Conflict can dilute the effectiveness of a group but it can be managed. It *is* possible for all parties to win. Solving conflicts is a task every manager must perform.

10. Organizational change requires a total systems approach.

Central principle. An organization consists of many interrelated parts. A change in one part of an organization will have an effect on the other parts. Unfortunately, this systemic concept has not been fully recognized and appreciated by managers. When changes are being implemented in their organizations, it is not unusual to see a group of managers focus on one particular aspect of their operations and completely overlook the ramifications of that change on other parts of the organization. Often, an improvement in one area will create unexpected problems and repercussions in other areas. Because there are so many interlocking parts in an organization — similar to the interrelationships found among organs and systems in the human body — change in one part will affect other parts.

Managerial strategy. Organizational change must be planned by considering many different factors: philosophical, environmental, structural, and procedural. One approach many managers use is to identify forces in the organization that tend to resist change and those that are continually pushing for change. Once these have been isolated, managers can then determine whether it is easier to reduce the strength of the resisting forces or to increase the strength of the forces favoring change. The level at which change is desired should also be considered. Do you want a change in *knowledge, application of knowledge,* and/or a change in *attitude?* In many cases, all three must be involved if true change is to occur.

A key aspect of the change process is to find answers to the question, "Who and what will be affected by this change?" In order to identify the various areas that may be impacted by a proposed change, many managers make a conscientious effort to involve in the actual planning of the implementation all employees who may be personally affected by the change. Not only are the possible ramifications of the change explored, but measuring devices are designed and built into the change program so that an ongoing evaluation of the effects can be monitored throughout the change process. By taking this total systems approach, managers can reduce the number of unexpected consequences they encounter and increase the chances for a successful change.

It would be wonderful if there was an easy "cookbook" approach to motivation — one style of leadership that always worked and and a whole series of foolproof strategies for managing that would guarantee success. But there are no simple formulas. People are much to complex to be managed in a "by the numbers" approach. The shifting nature of individual and group needs necessitates a wide repertoire of approaches for working with people. What seems to work one day many not work another day. What seems to turn one employee on will leave another employee cold. Some employees respond to one approach, some to another. The competent manager must remain flexible, adaptive, and responsive to the changing scene. Awareness of the ten key principles outlined above, and application of the management strategies these principles suggest, will help managers make more correct choices and improve their chances for success.

QUESTIONS

1. Choose any one of the key themes and show how you might apply it to your school or district if you were a superintendent or principal.

2. Discuss a central theme of behavioral research not mentioned in this article and show its implications for school administration.

UNIT V

DECISION THEORY

DECISION THEORY

OVERVIEW

An administrator is a decision-maker. In the process of planning, organizing, staffing, directing, coordinating, reporting, and budgeting, he makes decisions. Decision-making and administering are inextricably commingled.

Barnard called decision-making "the central process of adaptation in organizations."[1] Simon, going a step beyond Barnard, equates decision-making with managing, but whether this view is valid need not concern us here.[2] It is sufficient to say that decision-making pervades the administrative process and includes not only the steps leading to the decision but also those necessary to put it into effect.

---

[1] Barnard, Chester I., *The Functions of the Executive,* Cambridge, Mass.: Harvard University Press, 1938, p. 286.

[2] Simon, Herbert A., *The New Science of Management Decision,* New York: Harper and Row, 1960, p. 2.

The nature of decision-making. Decision-making is problem-solving. A problem is an obstacle blocking the achievement of a goal. For example, the principal of a comprehensive high school, discovering that the number of students who drop out of school is increasing year by year, infers that his school is steadily falling behind its goal of preparing young people to enter college or gainful employment upon graduation. He asks himself what can be done about the steadily increasing number of drop-outs.

People differ in their ability to perceive problems. Some fail to see them. Some see them but ignore them as if they didn't exist. Others see them but do not recognize their gravity, Like people, organizations can also be blind to problems, even those that pose serious threats. Many a top executive has been fired for failing to discern a problem in time and many a school principal has said regretfully, "I should have foreseen this." The ability to perceive problems is related to one's knowledge of the area. The more one knows about it, the greater the likelihood that he will recognize problems when they arise.

Decision-making is the reduction of alternatives. According to Barnard, "the processes of decision . . . are largely techniques for narrowing choice."[3] But reaching a decision is not as simple as these statements might suggest. It is a complex series of steps beginning with the recognition of a problem through the consideration of proposed solutions and the final acceptance of a mode of action.

Types of decisions. Decisions may be classified in several ways:

1. Individual and group decisions. One-man decisions, if they occur at all, are made only in small organizations. In large, multi-level organizations a one-man decision is a rarity, indeed almost an impossibility given the complexity of the organizational structure. Nearly all levels participate in some degree in reaching decisions.

   Because they need information and advice from several sources to act rationally, school principals no longer make decisions on their own, especially decisions involving large numbers of pupils and teachers. The dictatorial principal who made all decisions unaided may have functioned in the past but he almost certainly does not exist in the present.
2. Personal and organizational decisions. A personal decision is aimed at a personal goal and an organizational decision at an organizational

[3] Barnard, op. cit., p. 14.

goal. Barnard makes the distinction sharper: ". . . personal decisions cannot be delegated to others whereas organizational decisions can often if not always be delegated."[4] Sometimes the two cannot be separated because the same decision may facilitate the attainment of personal as well as organizational goals.

3. Programmed and non-programmed decisions. Programmed decisions are routine, repetitive, and made in accordance with established rules. They follow standard operating procedures and do not have to be considered each time they occur.

   Non-programmed decisions are discretionary. They are made to resolve problems which are new or unique and for which there is no prescribed method of solution.

   Programmed decisions are not necessarily unimportant nor are programmed decisions necessarily important. Both may have significant consequences.

4. Intermediary, appellate, and creative decisions. The difference among these three lies in their place of origin. When a superior delegates decision-making authority to a subordinate, the resulting decision is called intermediary. When a subordinate refers a case to a superior for decision, the resulting decison is classified as appellate. A creative decision is one which originates on the initiative of the decision-maker.

   Problems involving intermediary and appellate decisions are brought to the attention of the decision-maker who may or may not have been aware of them beforehand. They are likely to be decided because they originate outside and involve the delegation of authority. Creative decisions on the other hand involve an awareness on the part of the decision-maker of a problem requiring a solution. They may imply a change in procedures, policies, and objectives and may require considerable imagination, courage, and interpersonal skill in their implementation. Creative decisions are relatively infrequent. They cannot be delegated although they may sometimes be shared.

5. Rational and non-rational decisions. Rational decisions are those made after deliberation; they are purposive and discretionary. Non-rational decisions are guesses or hunches; they are haphazard and made without serious intellectual activity.

[4] Barnard, op. cit., p. 188.

HOW ARE DECISIONS MADE?

To describe the decision-making process, scholars have studied and described the activities of individuals, groups, and organizations and presented their findings in the form of models. Some models involve the use of quantitative techniques from such fields as applied mathematics, operations research, and computer technology. With the exception of those from computer technology, quantitative techniques are applicable only to programmed decisions. Nowadays computers play an important part in determining both programmed and non-programmed decisions in industrial organizations but less frequently in educational organizations because the necessary equipment is expensive and hence not available to school executives.

Figure 1 is a non-quantitative model. Its various elements are discussed in the paragraphs which follow.

Time. Decisions are made in a time framework. Problems have their roots in the past; alternative solutions are developed and a choice made in the present; and decisions are carried out and evaluated in the future. Present problems result from previous decisions and current decisions change situations so that new problems arise requiring future decisions.

Although decisions are made in the present, the process of choosing among alternatives is not always linear. Alternatives are not always set forth first, their outcomes then delineated, and a decision made. Rather there is a searching and weighing behavior so that a given choice may or may not be eliminated before another choice is considered, and outcomes of one choice will come to mind during the consideration of outcomes of another. This shuttling or back-and-forth movement continues until a decision is reached.

In education, unlike industry, there is rarely any urgency in the decision-making process. Most problems do not have to be settled immediately or even quickly. There is usually time for gathering data, discussion, and reflection before a decision is reached. If a decision has to be reached under time pressure, the participation of personnel in the process may be restricted.

Time is a process variable which influences the number of choices and the process of choice. Other process variables include the resources and information available, the number of persons involved, and procedures for determining effects.

Goal orientation. In his search for a course of action an administrator

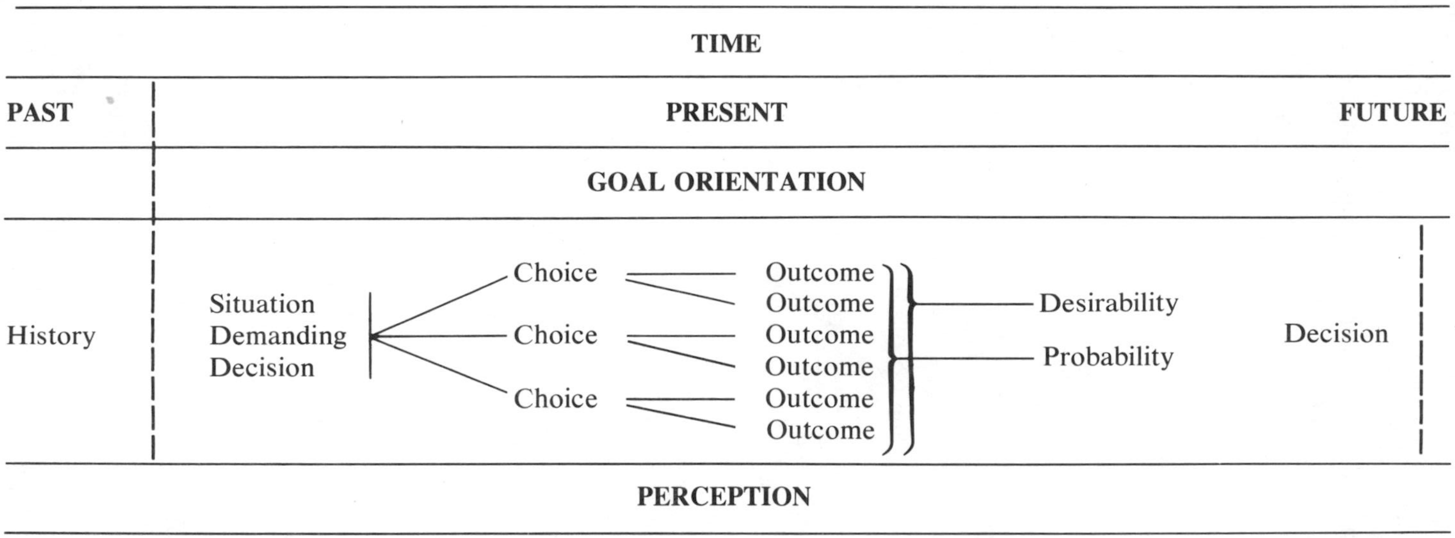

Each decision, a part of an ongoing process, is made from among the perceived choices on the basis of the foreseen probability and desirability of the outcomes of the choices.

Figure 1

A FRAMEWORK FOR DECISION-MAKING

By William Strand, University of Arizona. Used by permission.

takes into consideration the organization's goals as he perceives them and as they are perceived by others. In addition he keeps in mind his own goals which may or may not be identical with the organization's.

History and present situation. An administrator does not come upon a problem neatly packaged and waiting for solution. If he discovers it himself, he may at first experience nothing more than a vague uneasiness, a feeling that something is wrong. If it is brought to his attention by someone else, its dimensions are often not clear. Before he can take any remedial steps, he must "size up" the difficulty, that is, define it more precisely by determining its origin, extent, and urgency.

To define the problem he needs information sufficient in quantity and arranged in logical order. Incomplete or random information is not helpful. He gathers this information from sources within the formal organization and if he is a wise executive, from the informal organization as well.

He verbalizes the problem so that it is unmistakably clear to himself and to all the participants in the decision-making process. The form in which he puts the question affects the solution. "Why are the reading scores of School A below those of School B?" will produce one set of answers, while "What can we do to improve reading skills in our district?" will produce another.

Every problem has a history. It may be an outgrowth of previous decisions or related to an organization's traditions or relationships with external groups. The administrator must consider these in his attempts to solve the difficulty. He asks himself whether his proposed solution accords with established precedents and customary ways of doing things and what effect it will have on other organizations and the community.

Choice. A choice is a course of action which is perceived as possible. In the early stages of decision-making, alternative choices are usually matters of substance, related to needs and opportunities, but in the latter stages they are procedural, related to methods of implementation. Since alternative choices are in competition with one another, decision-making may be viewed as a process of conflict resolution.

Outcome. An outcome is a present judgment of what will result from implementing a given choice. No one can predict with certainty all the consequences of a particular choice. At best, predictions are probabilities. The probability of an outcome rests upon such imponderables as the nature of the individuals or groups affected by the decision, the intensity of their feelings, and their views about its reasonableness.

It is almost impossible to predict the outcomes of all the alternatives because so many varied and complex factors are involved. For example, the choice of a school site involves such factors as population trends and transportation facilities. Since schools are built to last 50 years or more, who can predict such factors with accuracy for a half-century?

Desirability. Desirability is a judgment of the decision-maker which involves his own values but also takes into consideration the anticipated behavior of others. The decision-maker asks himself such questions as:

What are the goals of the organization? Which decision best moves the organization toward those goals or is in accord with them?
Which set of outcomes serves my personal needs?
I have a set of values. Which decision is in accord with them?
What do others expect me to do in my role? What does my role require?
Which outcomes are most likely to keep the group stable?
What relation does this decision have to previous decisions?
What relation does it have to future action?
What effect will it have on relations with other organizations?

Probability. Probability is a judgment of the decision-maker which depends on how others will judge the desirability of each outcome. The decision-maker asks himself such questions as:

How do others perceive the organization's goals?
What do others expect me to do?
What are their value systems?
What power do I have?
What power do others have?
How willing am I to use my power? How effective is the communications network?
What personnel or financial resources are available?
Are there any legal barriers?

Perception. Individuals see situations differently. Each assumes that what he sees is real and acts in accordance with his perception.

What we see is a function of our experience, values, beliefs, attitudes, and expectations. Since no two people have the same frame of reference, perceptions differ from person to person. What we see is not necessarily actuality but rather an externalization of portions of our experience. In a sense we create our own unique worlds.

An administrator views every part of the decisional process through his own perceptual screen. He acts as if what he sees is the "real" world.

Decision. The final decision, which results from many subdecisions, is a choice from among several alternatives and is based on the decision-maker's judgment of the desirability and probability of the anticipated outcomes. It is not always the logical choice.

A decision is often not based on logic as the model might suggest. An administrator functions in an organizational environment in which he is subjected to pressures from within and without. Consequently he finds it difficult to be completely logical and often arrives at a decision not because it is intellectually justified but because it is expedient and less disruptive of personal relationships. He yields to pressures and tries to reach a compromise which, while it completely satisfies nobody, arouses less resentment than a completely logical solution.

This is not to say that logic does not enter into decisions. It does — but decisions are probably based as much on the exigencies of the environment as on logical validity.

Simon refers to this process as satisficing or making decisions for the time being which can be re-made at a later date if necessary.[5] Satisficing is the opposite of optimizing or seeking the best solution. A satisficer temporarily settles a problem, sets it aside, and goes on to handle others. This does not mean that he does not seek the best solutions. In the long run he does. It simply means that he is a pragmatist looking for a way out and trying to rock the organizational boat as little as possible.

Multiple decisions are possible or an administrator may decide to do nothing — which is in itself a decision. Barnard suggests that he may not decide because he does not consider the issue pertinent or not pertinent now; or, if it is pertinent, he may delay action until he has more information; or he may believe he is not capable of deciding or lacks the authority to decide.[6]

The decision environment. The decision environment is characterized by ambiguity, factorability, and heterogeneity.[7] Ambiguity refers to the vague dimensions of a problem when it is first encountered; it may or may not be

---

[5] Simon, Herbert A., *Administrative Behavior, 2nd ed., New York:* Macmillan, 1961, pp. XXV-XXVI.

[6] Barnard, op. cit., pp. 195-199.

defined or it may be erroneously defined. Factorability means that all the variables in the environment need not be considered simultaneously. A relatively simple description may serve as a basis for prediction in much the same way as simplified models are used in physics and chemistry laboratories to approximate actual conditions. Heterogeneity means that the environment is a complex of overlapping perceptions, each perceived by different individuals and groups. It is in this disturbed environment that decision-makers function.

Implementing the decision. The final step in the decision-making process is putting the decision into effect. When a decision is carried out, it may need to be modified because of feedback. Thus the implementation of a decision requires the making of additional decisions. The process is cyclical.

Critique. It goes without saying that decision-making does not invariably follow the mechanistic procedure suggested in the model. The process is involved and may vary with the situation and the participants. Even if the steps of the model are followed carefully, the final decision may still be of dubious quality.

WHO MAKES DECISIONS?

Individuals. The belief that decisions in organizations are made by executives on their own initiative and without participation by others is a myth. Executives do not issue arbitrary directives even though they may be legally empowered to do so. They rely on subordinates to provide specialized information and advice, and they review and approve decisions made at lower echelons. An organizational chart may show that the locus of decision-making is the chief executive but organizations tend to be decentralized informally and decision-making more often occurs at lower echelons than at the top.

In public administration an executive cannot abdicate the responsibility for making decisions imposed on him by law. A school superintendent, for example, may appoint a teachers' committee and may act on its recommendations but legally he alone is responsible. The committee's function is advisory; it has no power to decide or enforce. Student government organizations are largely ineffectual because they cannot control or usurp the decision-making authority of school officials.

---

[7] Dill, William R., "Decision-Making" in *Behavioral Science and Educational Administration*, the Sixty-third Yearbook of the National Society for the Study of Education, Chicago, Ill.: University of Chicago Press, 1964, p. 207.

An executive is "accurately viewed as an arbitrator of interest groups that are seeking to dominate the issues and perhaps to circumscribe the power of his office."[8] His hope is to encourage employee participation but to prevent employee control.

Groups. Some groups such as social clubs and civic organizations make decisions about purposes and activities which affect their members only. Since membership is voluntary and the decisions arrived at by democratic processes, compliance is expected.

Groups created by legal mandate such as boards of education, juries, and legislative bodies make decisions which affect non-members and are enforceable by law.

Staff participation. The rationale for participation is fourfold. First, everyone should have a say in determining policies which affect his welfare. Secondly, policies which are cooperatively developed are easier to implement. Thirdly, participation results in better decisions. Finally, when employees share in decision-making their morale is raised.

Participation has a significant influence on productivity and helps reduce resistance to change, but to be effective it must be planned for. It cannot be haphazard. If it is imposed from above, it will be regarded with suspicion, yet structures and procedures must be established so that participation may be orderly and purposive. Organized, participative patterns of decision-making are more efficient and result in greater satisfaction.

Surveys show that teachers want to participate in determining school policies and that the majority of school superintendents and school boards want them to participate.[9] Teachers especially want more autonomy for individual schools and a voice in decisions relating to instruction and curriculum.[10] Their involvement, however, is sometimes limited to routine matters such as scheduling, school lunch, and discipline problems rather than major policy matters and they regard this kind of participation as bogus.[11]

---

[8] Lane, Willard R., Corwin, Ronald G., and Monahan, William G., *Foundations of School Administration,* New York: Macmillan, 1967, p. 139.

[9] Hoppock, R., "What Teachers Think of School Administrators," *School Executive,* Vol. 69, 1949, pp. 40-42.

[10] Sharma, C. L., "Who Should Make Decisions?," *Administrator's Notebook,* Vol. 3, 1955, pp. 1-4.

[11] Godfrey, Margaret P., "Staff Participation in Decision-Making Procedures in Elementary Schools," unpublished doctoral dissertation, University of Connecticut, 1968.

In recent years some evidence has been offered that teachers do not want to involve themselves in organizational decision-making because of the work and time such participation requires. Participation is time-consuming and prevents them from engaging in activities which they find more pleasant or important. "Many studies show employees quite willing to let superiors make decisions for them."[12] While they do not want to be "bossed," they prefer that someone else make the decisions.[13]

Barnard points out that most decisions fall within a "zone of indifference," an area in which an executive's decisions will be accepted without question.[14] Teachers do not want to become involved with decisions falling within the zone but they will question those which fall outside it.

SELECTED READINGS

Griffiths, Daniel E., *Administrative Theory,* New York: Appleton-Century-Crofts, 1959.
Chapter 5 of this brief book is a synthesis of a large number of studies of how decisions are made. Griffiths emphasizes that decisioning in an organization is not a personal matter and that the effectiveness of decisions is not a product of the quality of the decisions of any one person.

Lipham, James M. and Hoeh, Jr., James A., *The Principalship: Foundations and Functions,* New York: Harper and Row, 1974.
In Chapter 7, "Decision Theory," the authors discuss approaches to decision-making, a model of the decision-making process, the principal's decision-making role, involvement in decision-making, and the decision-making competencies of the principal.

Luthans, Fred, *Organizational Behavior,* New York, McGraw-Hill, 1973.
Presents a blend of management and behavioral science concepts, techniques, and research. Chapters 9 and 10 deal with decision-making, including modern quantitative decision techniques.

---

[12] Dill, op. cit., p. 215.

[13] Seeman, M., *Social Status and Leadership: The Case of the School Executive,* Columbus, Ohio: Bureau of Educational Research, Ohio State University, 1960.

[14] Barnard, op. cit., p. 73.

Monahan, William G., *Theoretical Dimensions of Educational Administration,* New York: Macmillan, 1975.

The contributors to this anthology are nationally known authorities. Monahan's article, "Some Limitations and Cautions in the Use of Quantitative Techniques in Decision-Making," characterizes some of the limitations that impinge upon the use of quantitative techniques and stresses that only men are accountable for decisions regardless of how they are reached.

National Education Association, Department of Elementary School Principals, *Decision Making and the Elementary School Principal,* Washington, D.C., 1975.

A kit of nine simulated problems designed to help elementary school principals learn the art of executive decision. The problems are related to school organization, curriculum, school-community relations, professional organizations, supervision of instruction, and student-parent relations.

National Society for the Study of Education, Chicago, Ill.: *Behavioral Science and Educational Administration,* the Sixty-Third Yearbook, University of Chicago Press, 1964.

A collection of articles on various aspects of school administration. William R. Dill's article on decision-making is a succinct treatise from the behavioral standpoint.

Simon, Herbert A., *The New Science of Management Decision,* New York: Harper and Row, 1960.

Generally acknowledged to be an important contribution to the study of decision-making. Analyzes how decisions are made and how they might be made more effectively.

TOPICS FOR DISCUSSION

1. Cite an example for each of the following types of decisions:
   a. Group decision
   b. Personal decision
   c. Programmed decision
   d. Creative decision
   e. Rational decision
   f. Organizational decision

2. Interview your school principal or superintendent to discover what steps he followed in reaching a decision on some major policy recently. What considerations impelled him to reach his final decision? Was his final decision based on several sub-decisions? Was it an instance of satisficing? Explain. Compare his decision-making procedure with that pictured in Figure 1.

3. Draw your own model of the decision-making process. It may be humorous, if you wish, but it should be as accurate as you can make it.

4. "Individuals see situations differently." Explain and illustrate from your own experience.

5. By referring to your school or college, show that organizations tend to be decentralized informally.

6. To what extent do the teachers in your school participate in decision-making? What kinds of decisions do they help make? What kinds of decisions do they prefer to leave to administrators? Do your school administrators welcome teacher participation in decision-making? Do teachers want to participate to a greater extent than they now do? Why?

7. Report on the quantitative decision-making techniques used in some industrial concern with which you are acquainted. Can these techniques be used to settle educational problems? Explain.

8. There are many models of the decision-making process. Select one from any text you choose and compare it with Figure 1.

DECISION MAKING BY MANAGEMENT

By
The Royal Bank of Canada

Management is a decision-making process. Decision-making is difficult, even for highly trained men.

A decision must be adequate to the solution of the problem. Decisions on important matters are not within the reach of men and women whose knowledge of facts and the forces working on them is small.

Excuses for postponing a decision are not hard to find and while there are justifiable reasons for postponement we must guard against unwise or frivolous putting off.

The manager of today must know the limitations of using mechanical aids and committee procedures to arrive at a decision.

Seven steps in decision-making are described. The implementation of a decision involves both mechanical and human problems. No decision can be better than the people who have to carry it out.

MANAGEMENT is a decision-making process. Its special function is to choose between alternative means of moving toward an objective.

None of the many changes brought about by technology appears likely to diminish the opportunities open to men who are gifted with skill in making decisions and trained in administration.

Doing business in an economy like ours demands foresight and judgment besides resourcefulness and courage. Only the person who applies all these qualities in making decisions advances his company's business.

The management principle is readily stated: the business manager is paid to find and define the problem, analyse it, develop alternate solutions, decide upon the best solution, and convert his decision into effective action.

The world is full of people who shun this sort of responsibility. Only a

---

"Decision Making By Management," by The Royal Bank of Canada, *Monthly Newsletter*, Vol. 44, No. 1, January 1963.
Copyright © 1963 by The Royal Bank of Canada. Reprinted by permission of The Royal Bank of Canada.

few seek it, and they become leaders. They know that there is a possibility that a decision they reach may be wrong, but they know that this chance may be minimized by following some simple rules and procedures.

Many business decisions made from day to day are routine and repetitive to the manager, but he must bear patiently in mind that the problems are new to his staff and it is part of his duty to give guidance.

This is part of the leadership function of the business manager. Everyone has a stake of the most concrete kind in leadership, because the manager is accountable for the success of his business or his department and for the continued employment of all those associated with it and the satisfaction of those holding stock in it.

On a wall of the Engineering Societies' Library in New York we read this inscription: "Management is the art and science of preparing, organizing and directing human effort applied to control the forces and utilize the materials of nature for the benefit of man." In carrying out this mandate, the manager has to weigh the risks of every course of action against the expected gains. Then, having decided, he must issue clear orders and put forth the drive to get things done.

Administration of a business is a network, in which every decision is connected in some way with other decisions which have preceded it, and will have a bearing upon decisions to be made in the future.

Decision making has never been easy, even for the highly trained man, but history is made up of the stories of men and women who were good at it. Business is complex, not only within its own walls but because of outside influences and pressures. A manager needs the qualities of a statesman, so as to see his business in all its relationships. He has to know his firm's objectives and policies, what resources he can call upon, the capabilities of those who will make his decisions effective, and then produce plans that take all these into account.

A cardinal rule is that his decision must be adequate to the solution of the problem. There is no use in attacking a tank with a bow and arrow, and it is wasteful to shoot sparrows with a big game rifle.

Wide knowledge

Decisions on important matters are not within the reach of men and women whose knowledge of facts and the forces acting upon them is small. There must be on hand a large store of memories of previous experiences and things learned which can be linked with the current problem.

No reasoning can be done by our minds unless we have units of comparison gathered through experience and study. When we have many objects in our minds, our imagination ranges over them, assesses them, takes a little of this and a little of that, relates them significantly, and produces a decision. What is the faculty we praise so highly as "good judgment" except this: the ability to bring together a fact which we have just unearthed and a general judgment suitable to the purpose long since deposited in the archives of our memory, and unite them effectively.

The business man must never stop adding to his stock of knowledge and understanding, but this need not be a burdensome task. If he is under pressure all day long he will find it relaxing as well as useful to spend his leisure hours at something in which he must be deliberative: such as reading one of the classics (like the *Thoughts* of Marcus Aurelius or the *Teachings* of Epictetus, which have many ideas useful in thinking through to decisions) or watching documentary films which broaden his horizons.

It is altogether foolish to think of the capable decision maker in terms of a cartoon stereotype — as a table pounder, a window gazer, a pacer of the office, an aspirin user or a man with a wet towel around his head. One general belief may be given credence in some measure: the person who makes important decisions may not be sweet tempered. He is under pressure, he takes risks, he wrestles with the task of getting his ideas carried out, he has little patience with incompetency.

Some firms make no provisions for the stress of management. Their managers are loaded with detail instead of being relieved of all trivia so that they may devote their special talents to important things.

The man who has to swim hard in muddy waters to get his head out where he can make an important decision may be plagued with "doubting folly." This is a state of mind in which a man cannot remember whether he did this or decided that or whether he did it in the best way. He is forever returning to see if he has turned off the gas, locked the door, and the like. He calls back decisions for review.

When to be careful

It is necessary in the convulsive scene of business life to assign proportions to our problems and to set up priorities. Clearing up mechanical difficulties is different from reaching a decision on a course of action which involves people, budgets, and markets.

You need to give patience, time and thought to decision making when you are on unfamiliar ground or dealing with a strange subject. Decisions come easily to the sales manager who has been twenty years on the job so long as they involve only the factors to which he is accustomed. When a new factor is introduced, or the manager moves into an area where he is a stranger, he must take time for orientation.

The power of deciding involves the danger of going astray — that is the essence of deciding. And going astray involves some kind of penalty — that is the essence of error. The consequences of a decision are part of the total problem, and should be considered as factors in it. We must balance risk against gain, and be neither deterred by the one nor dazzled by the other.

This involves forethought. The manager is subject to one trial not common to the worker: he has the continual feeling of incompletion. His job is never done. His energy drives him to consideration of the next job while this one is still in the works, and he needs to keep his balance in both.

There is no necessary virtue in "planning" itself. Its value depends upon what the plan is for, what ends it will serve, what difficulties it is designed to overcome — difficulties arising from the caprices of fate, the actions of competitors and the quirks of human nature. Without a plan, fluid though it may be, we cannot reach decisions intelligently.

An umpire must call the strikes and balls as he sees them, instantly. But mere speed in coming to decisions may have small relevance at the top business management level where a man's contribution to the enterprise may be the making of two or three significant decisions a month.

This is not to say that we should debate and stew over every problem. We are probably too much given to sending out a man with a red flag in front of every new idea as they used to do with steam locomotives. On the whole, it is wiser to make a decision promptly and crisply after giving the matter adequate thought than to linger over it and lose momentum and drive.

To make a sound decision it is not necessary to have all the facts, but it is necessary to know what facts are missing so that we may make allowance for the gap and decide the degree of rigidity to give our orders.

Some managers, in trying to avoid off-the-cuff masterminding, make it a practice to take time to sleep on a problem. This can be useful if a tentative decision has been reached or workable alternative outlined so that the subconscious has something tangible to push around.

Very little that is good can be said about procrastinating. Any business will become paralyzed if there are persistently long delays in the making of managerial decisions. They cause waste of time among personnel, loss of team-work, and forfeiture of faith in management.

Excuses for postponing a decision are not hard to find. Recall the hesitancy of Hamlet. One moment he pretended that he was too cowardly to perform the deed; at another he questioned the truthfulness of the ghost; at another he thought the time was unsuitable, that it would be better to wait until the King was at some evil act and then to kill him, and so on. Every reason had a certain plausibility, but it would not stand serious consideration.

There are, of course, times for postponement, when a resolute determination to take no action until more facts are available is a constructive contribution to wise decision. The warning is against unwise or frivolous putting off. We must keep in mind that to make no decision is itself a decision, and must be justified.

Effective use of postponement was made by Penelope in Homer's *Odyssey*. During the protracted absence of her husband, Ulysses, Penelope was besieged by suitors for her hand in marriage. She put them off for several years by telling them that she would give her decision when the burial cloth on which she was working was complete. Then she undid by night what she had woven by day, and so staved off decision. Ulysses returned and drove out the suitors.

Computers and committees

The manager of today and the future will have to make decisions involving an infinite number of considerations. While he will make all possible use of electronic equipment and committees, the final choice between alternatives is his alone.

Mechanical aids are widely in use. They make the assembly of data and the calculation of quantities easy. But, in a competitive market, the firm whose managers best handle the qualitative factors which are indigestible to machines will have the edge in business success.

The results of massive computations depend upon the knowledge, discrimination and intelligence of the men who feed in the raw data and assess the resulting report. The machines cannot define the problem, determine the right questions to ask, set objectives or lay down rules. They do help in analyzing the problem and presenting alternatives. They give facts instead of guesses and generalities. They are tools for decision making.

We recall *The Sorcerer's Apprentice,* the great symphonic composition of Paul Lukas. The apprentice learned his master's secret for turning a broom handle into a servant, and ordered the automaton to take a pail and fetch water. Then he couldn't stop the creature, which kept splashing water all over the room. The apprentice, who hadn't learned the magic words to bring the automaton to a standstill, seized an axe and split it in two: now there were two creatures busily carrying water. Not until the magician returned were the robots stopped.

Unless the manager of today knows the limitations of machines, when and how to cut them off, and the fact that he himself must define, analyze, judge and decide, he will be like the Sorcerer's Apprentice, a victim of his own bag of tricks.

Decision by committee holds perils of another sort. There is no virtue in reaching a decision by yourself when there is time and opportunity to consult others who have special knowledge. To do so would be to waste available talent. But no business can prosper under a debating society.

The function of a committee is to talk around a subject so that all its facets are revealed, to bring out the facts and to spark thought. Then the manager must judge the relative value of what has been said, assess the alternatives presented, and make the decision.

Making a decision

The manager who wishes to build up the habit of making decisions with wisdom and effectiveness might do well to consider these steps: (1) look at the situation generally and from it extract the problem; (2) put the problem into words; (3) tidy up the problem; (4) do the preparatory research thoroughly; (5) brush aside preconceived ideas; (6) consider the facts; (7) think through to a solution.

The first job is to find the real problem, divesting the situation of all irrelevant details. Masses of data may look impressive, but only those facts which apply to the problem in hand are worth considering.

It is quite right to see the pattern of the total situation and how the parts hang together, but successful managers have the capacity to reduce the whole picture to simple terms. Mendel, to whom we are indebted for the first effective work on hybridization, did not follow his predecessors' lead in taking only a summary view, but examined every plant separately.

A problem only becomes intelligible when it is put into words. There simply is no magic formula for decision making, but the man who approaches the point of decision by setting out his problem in an orderly way stands a better chance of reaching the right outcome than one who relies on snap judgments.

In laying out an approach to decision making we need to differentiate between tasks which demand only the application of known techniques and those which have unusual conditions that require clarification and directed action. For example, the mail despatching staff faced with an unusual spate of envelopes knows that extra effort and perhaps extra time will see them through; but if there is an unusual number of complaints about wrong addresses, accompanied by a mounting pile of uncompleted orders, then there is a real problem.

It can be solved if the person responsible grasps its nature, gauges its true dimension, decides what to do about it, and takes immediate steps to cope with it. He breaks a big problem down into small, easily-tackled units, changing a vague difficulty into a specific concrete form. He may go so far as to answer one "yes or no" question and then ask others until the major problem is solved.

One method advocated by some teachers is "take it apart." You write down the problem about which you must make a decision. In two columns underneath write down the points "for" and "against". When this is done seriously and honestly you have a good accounting, and your decision will be based upon the balance.

Tidy up problems

Managers may smooth their way by having all proposals and problems tidied up before moving toward decisions. Almost every problem needs to be explored through such questions as these: Why is this necessary or desirable? What can it be expected to accomplish? How can it be worked out? Who will do it? Who will be affected by it? What harmful situations might result?

Superiority in decision making rests on a solid basis of preparation, with a grasp of all the possibilities. When you reach a tentative conclusion, try to knock it down with dispassionate energy. Ask: "What will happen if . . . ? Does this decision take care of A, B and C possibilities?" By proceeding in this way the business executive will borrow a bit of the value of the scientific method and spirit: the resolute asking of the questions: "What else?" . . . "What if?"

You need to pay attention to detail in the preliminary stages, while keeping in mind the end purpose. Toscanini, the great orchestra leader, is quoted as saying: "In rehearsing a musical work, the important passages can frequently take care of themselves; it is the supposedly unimportant phrase or line that demands careful consideration."

The manager needs suppleness of mind. He will display enthusiasm, but not the sort of zeal which blinds him to facts. He recognizes that his opinion about a thing is only something that comes between ignorance and understanding. It is knowledge in the making. To change an opinion in the face of new facts is a sign of vitality and progress.

In the course of his deliberation he will have taken advantage of subconscious thought. All creative thinking, including scientific research, emerges from the subconscious. The "passed to you for action" memo which consciousness receives may be couched in vague terms, and may have to be worked into shape. But this is no mystical process: it goes on hour after hour throughout our lives. It is, however, an advantage to recognize it so that fullest use may be made of it.

Last in this group of seven suggestions is the thinking through of the proposed decision to its conclusion. This involves testing every step leading to the decision as well as anticipating what may follow upon it.

When you have reached the point where you have gathered the facts and tested them, thought about them and weighed the consequences, then make your decision. Here are two illustrations of the folly of hesitating. Buridan, a French philosopher of the twelfth century, told us about the ass which was placed midway between two equally attractive bales of hay, and died of starvation because he couldn't choose which one to eat. Robert Browning's poem reminds us that Saul, crowned king at a time when one swift blow would have scattered his foes and united his friends, stood midway between his duty and his task, and indecision slew him.

The end result

We have located and defined our problem, collected facts, weighed the favourable against the unfavourable; we have listened to what can be said by experts, friends and enemies; we have checked the accuracy of our information and of our thinking; we have analysed the causes of our problem and the effects of various solutions; and we have arrived at a decision. What do we do next?

The fatal thing to do is pigeon-hole it. The only place to put a good decision is into execution. An idea has been born, it has evolved, and has been transformed into a decision. Now the manager must participate in carrying the decision into execution.

It would be a mistake at this point to spend time looking back to see if you are too far from shore. You are obligated, having made the decision, to develop a certain amount of blindness to the possibility of failure. By that act you give confidence to those who must do the work of implementing the decision: your junior managers, foremen and workers.

It would be wrong to cling to a course if some vital new facts in its disfavour become known, but don't change your mind merely because you are running into obstacles. The road may be strewn with rocks, but that merely means that it is a rough road, not that it is going in the wrong direction.

Be sure that your decision is promulgated clearly. Unless you make order and relation for your people out of the unrelated ideas and facts with which you have wrestled, they cannot be expected to respond with effective action. They must know what change in behaviour is expected of them, what change to expect in the behaviour of others with whom they work, and what change will be made in the working conditions.

This is the manager's directional guidance. He establishes goals and shows how to reach them. Children reciting Longfellow's poem ''Excelsior'' have wondered where the ambitious, sad, self-denying and daring boy carrying his banner with the strange device was climbing to. Let's not leave workers in the dark about our purposes and paths.

Mechanical problems associated with your decision are relatively simple compared with the human problems.

For example, your decision may change the apparent status of workers, and it is astonishing how infallibly a man will be annoyed and deeply pained by any seeming wrong done to his feeling of self-importance.

This is one reason for careful advance consultation of all those who are to be affected by the decision. It will give you the benefit of their experience and their ideas, and make them participants in whatever comes to pass.

Being a decisive manager doesn't mean being truculent or living apart. To be part of the working force was emphasized as a necessity of management by speakers at the Duke of Edinburgh's Study Conference in Oxford. The manager must make the time to keep in touch with juniors and to visit the production line frequently. Only thus can he appraise the spirit of his people, tap their interest, and assure their co-operation in carrying out plans upon which he decides. Human motivations and human emotions are involved as factors in the solution of every problem.

Of this be sure: no decision can be better than the people who have to carry it out. Their enthusiasm, competence and understanding determine what they can and will do.

QUESTIONS

1. Under what circumstances is indecision justified?

2. "The only place to put a good decision is into execution." What human problems might prevent you from carrying it out? Can these be minimized or avoided by advance consultation with those who are to be affected by the decision? Explain.

DECISION-MAKING AND ADMINISTRATIVE ORGANIZATION

By
Herbert A. Simon

Simon analyzes the manner in which the organization influences the behavior of its operative employees.

Organization involves a horizontal specialization of work and a vertical specialization in decision-making. Vertical specialization is essential for coordination, expertise, and control.

The organization's influence is a matter of degree. There is a progressive particularization of influence from the top to the bottom of the administrative hierarchy. Toward the top, discretion is limited by the assignment of broad objectives and the specification of very general methods; lower in the hierarchy, more specific objectives are set and procedures determined in greater detail.

Each member of an organization retains a certain sphere of discretion but even within this sphere he is held responsible for the correctness of his decisions.

The organization influences an individual by authority, identification, the criterion of efficiency, advice and information, and training. These are interchangeable to a large extent and a major task of administration is to determine the degree to which each will be employed.

The structure of influence and lines of communication are more complex than the structure of authority. Planning and review are two organizational processes of particular importance to decision-making.

It is clear that the actual physical task of carrying out an organization's objectives falls to the persons at the lowest level of the administrative hierarchy. The automobile, as a physical object, is built not by the engineer or the executive, but by the mechanic on the assembly line. The fire is extinguished, not by the fire chief or the captain, but by the team of firemen who play a hose on the blaze.

"Decision Making and Administrative Organization," by Herbert A. Simon, *Public Administration Review*, Winter, 1944, Vol. IV. Copyright © 1944 by Public Administration Review; all rights reserved. Reprinted by permission of Public Administration Review and Herbert A. Simon.

It is equally clear that the persons above this lowest or operative level in the administrative hierarchy are not mere surplus baggage, and that they too must have an essential role to play in the accomplishment of the agency's objectives. Even though, as far as physical cause and effect are concerned, it is the machine-gunner, and not the major, who fights battles, the major will likely have a greater influence upon the outcome of a battle than will any single machine-gunner.

How, then, do the administrative and supervisory staff of an organization affect that organization's work? The nonoperative staff of an administrative organization participate in the accomplishment of the objectives of that organization to the extent that they influence the decisions of the operatives — the persons at the lowest level of the administrative hierarchy. The major can influence the battle to the extent that his head is able to direct the machine-gunner's hand. By deploying his forces in the battle area and assigning specific tasks to subordinate units, he determines for the machine-gunner where he will take his stand and what his objective will be. In very small organizations the influence of all supervisory employees upon the operative employees may be direct, but in units of any size there are interposed between the top supervisors and the operative employees several levels of intermediate supervisors who are themselves subject to influences from above and who transmit, elaborate, and modify these influences before they reach the operatives.

If this is a correct description of the administrative process, then the construction of an efficient administrative organization is a problem in social psychology. It is a task of setting up an operative staff and superimposing on that staff a supervisory staff capable of influencing the operative group toward a pattern of coordinated and effective behavior. I have deliberately used the term "influencing" rather than "directing," for direction — that is, the use of administrative authority — is only one of several ways in which the administrative staff may affect the decisions of the operative staff; and, consequently, the construction of an administrative organization involves more than a mere assignment of functions and allocation of authority.

It is the operative employee who must be at the focus of attention in studying an organization, for the success of the structure will be judged by the way in which he performs within it. In this paper administrative theory will be approached from this standpoint: by analyzing the manner in which the decisions and behavior of operative employees are influenced by the organization.

NECESSITY FOR "VERTICAL" SPECIALIZATION

Most analyses of organization have emphasized "horizontal" specialization — the division of work — as the basic characteristic of organized activity. Luther Gulick, for example, in his "Notes on the Theory of Organization," says: "Work division is the foundation of organization; indeed, the reason for organization."[1]

In this paper we shall be primarily concerned with "vertical" specialization — the division of decision-making duties between operative and supervisory personnel. Our first inquiry will be into the reasons why the operative employees are deprived of a portion of their autonomy in the making of decisions and subjected to the authority and influence of supervisors.

There would seem to be at least three reasons for vertical specialization in organization. First, if there is any horizontal specialization, vertical specialization is absolutely essential to achieve coordination among the operative employees. Second, just as horizontal specialization permits greater skill and expertise to be developed by the operative group in the performance of their tasks, so vertical specialization permits greater expertise in the making of decisions. Third, vertical specialization permits the operative personnel to be held accountable for their decisions: to the board of directors in the case of a business organization; to the legislative body in the case of a public agency.

Coordination. Group behavior requires not only the adoption of *correct* decisions, but also the adoption by all members of the group of the *same* decisions. Suppose ten persons decide to cooperate in building a boat. If each has his own plan, and they don't bother to communicate their plans, the resulting craft is not apt to be very seaworthy; they would probably have met with better success if they had adopted even a very mediocre design, and if then all had followed this same design.

By the exercise of authority or other forms of influence, it is possible to centralize the function of deciding so that a general plan of operations will govern the activities of all members of the organization. This coordination may be either procedural or substantive in nature: by procedural coordination is meant the specification of the organization itself — that is, the generalized description of the behaviors and relationships of the members of the organization. Procedural coordination establishes the lines of authority and

[1]Luther Gulick and L. Urwick (eds.), *Papers on the Science of Administration,* p. 3.

outlines the spheres of activity of each organization member, while substantive coordination specifies the content of his work. In an automobile factory, an organization chart is an aspect of procedural coordination; blueprints for the engine-block of the car being manufactured are an aspect of substantive coordination.

Expertise. To gain the advantages of specialized skill at the operative level, the work of an organization must be so subdivided that all processes requiring a particular skill can be performed by persons possessing that skill. Likewise, to gain the advantages of expertise in decision-making, the responsibility for decisions must be so allocated that all decisions requiring a particular skill can be made by persons possessing that skill.

To subdivide decisions is rather more complicated than to subdivide performance; for while it is not usually possible to combine the sharp eye of one workman with the steady hand of another to secure greater precision in a particular operation, it *is* often possible to add the knowledge of a lawyer to that of an engineer in order to improve the quality of a particular decision.

Frederick Taylor's theories of shop organization were primarily concerned with this aspect of the decision-making process. The purpose of his scheme of functional foremanship was to make certain that the decisions respecting every aspect of the workman's job would be reached by a highly specialized and expert technician.

Responsibility. Writers on the political and legal aspects of authority have emphasized that a primary function of organization is to enforce the conformity of the individual to norms laid down by the group, or by its authority-wielding members. The discretion of subordinate personnel is limited by policies determined near the top of the administrative hierarchy. When the maintenance of responsibility is a central concern, the purpose of vertical specialization is to assure legislative control over the administrator, leaving to the administrative staff adequate discretion to deal with technical matters which a legislative body composed of laymen would not be competent to decide.

In designing an organization all three factors — expertise, coordination, and responsibility — must be given weight. Taylor's theory, for example, has been deservedly criticized for ignoring the factors of coordination and responsibility, while some of his critics can perhaps be accused of undervaluing the importance of expertise in decision-making. The real question is one of how much each of these aims is to be sacrificed to the others, and our present knowledge of administrative theory does not permit us to give any *a priori* answer to this question.

THE RANGE OF DISCRETION

The term "influence" covers a wide range, both in the degree to which one person affects the behavior of another and in the method whereby that influence is exercised. Without an analysis of these differences of degree and kind no realistic picture can be drawn of an administrative organization. It is because of its failure to account for variations in influence that the usual organization chart, with its oversimplified representation of the "lines of authority," fails to record the complexity of actual organizations. The organization chart does not reveal the fact that the actual exercise of authority may, and often does, cut across formal organizational lines, and that forms of influence other than authority — information, training, identification — may be far more important than the former in securing coordination throughout the organization.

Influence is exercised in its most complete form when a decision promulgated by one person governs every aspect of the behavior of another. On the parade ground, the marching soldier is permitted no discretion whatsoever. His every step, his bearing, the length of his pace are all governed by authority. Frederick the Great is reported to have found the parade-ground deportment of his Guards perfect — with one flaw. "They breathe," he complained. Few examples could be cited, however, from any other realm of practical affairs where influence is exercised in such complete and unlimited form.

Most often, organizational influences place only partial limits upon the exercise of discretion. A subordinate may be told what to do, but given considerable leeway as to how he will carry out the task. The "what" is, of course, a matter of degree also and may be specified within narrower or broader limits. The commands of a captain at the scene of a fire place much narrower limits on the discretion of the firemen than those placed on a fire chief by the city charter which states in general terms the function of the fire department.

Since influence can be exercised with all degrees of specificity, in order to determine the scope of influence or authority which is exercised in any concrete case, it is necessary to dissect the decisions of the subordinate into their component parts and then determine which of these parts are controlled by the superior and which are left to the subordinate's discretion.

Influence over Value and Fact. Any rational decision may be viewed as a conclusion reached from certain premises. These premises are of two different kinds: value premises and factual premises — roughly equivalent to ends and means, respectively. Given a complete set of value and factual premises, there remains only one unique decision which is consistent with rationality. That is, with a given system of values and a specified set of possible alternatives, there is one alternative of the set which is preferable to the others.

The behavior of a rational person can be controlled, therefore, if the value and factual premises upon which he bases his decisions are specified for him. This control can be complete or partial — all the premises can be specified, or some can be left to his discretion. The scope of influence, and conversely the scope of discretion, are determined by the number and importance of the premises which are specified and the number and importance of those which are left unspecified.

There is one important difference between permitting a subordinate discretion over value premises and permitting him discretion over factual premises. The latter can always be evaluated as correct or incorrect in an objective, empirical sense (of course, we do not always have the evidence we would need to decide whether a premise is correct or incorrect, but at least the terms "correct" and "incorrect" are applicable to a factual premise). To a value premise, on the other hand, the terms "correct" and "incorrect" do not apply. To say that a means is correct is to say that it is appropriate to its end; but to say that an end is correct is meaningless unless we redefine the end as a means to some more final end — in which case its correctness as means ceases to be a value question and becomes a factual question.

Hence, if only factual premises are left to the subordinate's discretion, there is, under the given circumstances, only one decision which he can correctly reach. On the other hand, if value premises are left to the subordinate's discretion, the "correctness" of his decision will depend upon the value premises he selects, and there is no universally accepted criterion of right or wrong which can be applied to his selection.[2]

This distinction between factual and value premises has an obvious bearing on the question of how discretion is to be reconciled with responsibility and accountability, and what the line of division is to be between "policy" and "administration." To pursue this subject further would take

[2] In a sense, the discretion over factual questions which is left the operative is illusory, for he will be held accountable for reaching correct conclusions even with respect to those premises which are not specified in his orders. But it is a question of salient importance for the organization whether the subordinate is guided by orders *in making his decision* or whether he makes it on his own responsibility, subject to subsequent review. Hence, by "discretion" we mean only that standing orders and "on-the-spot" orders do not completely determine the decision.

us beyond the bounds of the present analysis, and we leave it with a reference to two recent contributions to the problem.[3]

Implications for Unity of Command. When it is admitted that influence need extend to only a few of the premises of decision, it follows that more than one order can govern a given decision, provided that no two orders extend to the same premise. An analysis of almost any decision of a member of a formal organization would reveal that the decision was responsive to a very complex structure of influences.

Military organization affords an excellent illustration of this. In ancient warfare, the battlefield was not unlike the parade ground. An entire army was often commanded by a single man, and his authority extended in a very complete and direct form to the lowest man in the ranks. This was possible because the entire battlefield was within range of a man's voice and vision and because tactics were for the most part executed by the entire army in unison.

The modern battlefield presents a very different picture. Authority is exercised through a complex hierarchy of command. Each level of the hierarchy leaves an extensive area of discretion to the level below, and even the private soldier, under combat conditions, exercises a considerable measure of discretion.

Under these circumstances, how does the authority of the commander extend to the soldiers in the ranks? How does he limit and guide their behavior? He does this by specifying the general mission and objective of each unit on the next level below and by determining such elements of time and place as will assure a proper coordination among the units. The colonel assigns to each battalion in his regiment its task; the lieutenant colonel to each company; the captain to each platoon. Beyond this the officer ordinarily does not go. The internal deployment of each unit is left to the officer in command of that unit. The United States Army Field Service Regulations specify that "an order should not trespass upon the province of a subordinate. It should contain everything that the subordinate must know to carry out his mission, but nothing more."[4]

So far as field orders go, then, the discretion of a subordinate officer is

---

[3] Wayne A. R. Leys, "Ethics and Administrative Discretion," 3 *Public Administration Review* 10-23 (Winter, 1943); and Herman Finer, "Administrative Responsibility in Democratic Government," 1 *Public Administration Review* 335-50 (Summer, 1941).

[4] *U. S. Army Field Service Regulations (1941)*, p. 31.

limited only by the specification of the objective of his unit and its general schedule. He proceeds to narrow further the discretion of his own subordinates so far as is necessary to specify what part each sub-unit is to play in accomplishing the task of the whole.

Does this mean that the decision of the officer is limited only by his objective or mission? Not at all. To be sure, the field order does not go beyond this point, for it specifies only the "what" of his action. But the officer is also governed by the tactical doctrine and general orders of the army which specify in some detail the "how." When the captain receives field orders to deploy his company for an attack, he is expected to carry out the deployment in accordance with the accepted tactical principles in the army. In leading his unit, he will be held accountable for the "how" as well as the "what."

The same kind of analysis could be carried out for the man who actually does the army's "work" — the private soldier; and we would see that the mass of influences that bear upon his decisions include both direct commands and tactical training and indoctrination.

We find, then, that to understand the process of decision in an organization it is necessary to go far beyond the on-the-spot orders which are given by superior to subordinate. It is necessary to discover how the subordinate is influenced by standing orders, by training, and by review of his actions. It is necessary to study the channels of communication in the organization in order to determine what information reaches him which may be relevant to his decisions. The broader the sphere of discretion left to the subordinate by the orders given him, the more important become those types of influence which do not depend upon the exercise of formal authority.

Once this complex network of decisional influences comes into view it becomes difficult to defend either the sufficiency or the necessity of the doctrine of "unity of command." Its sufficiency must be questioned on the same grounds that the sufficiency of the organization chart is questioned: at best it tells only a half-truth, for formal authority is only one aspect — and that probably not the most important — of organizational structure.

The necessity of "unity of command" must be questioned because there do not appear to be any *a priori* grounds why a decision should not be subject to several organizational influences. Indeed, a number of serious students of administration have advocated this very thing — we have already mentioned Taylor's theory of functional supervision — and their arguments cannot be waved aside with the biblical quotation that "no man can serve two masters."[5] It remains to be demonstrated that "unity of command" rather than "plurality of command" either is, or should be, the prevalent form of administrative structure.

ORGANIZATIONAL INFLUENCES ON THE SUBORDINATE

Thus far we have been talking about the extent of the organization's influence over its employees. Next we must consider the ways in which this influence is exerted. The subordinate is influenced not only by command but also by his organizational loyalties, by his strivings toward "efficient" courses of action, by the information and advice which is transmitted to him through the organization's lines of communication, and by his training. Each of these items deserves brief discussion.

Authority. The concept of authority has been analyzed at length by students of administration. We shall employ here a definition substantially equivalent to that put forth by C. I. Barnard.[6] A subordinate is said to accept authority whenever he permits his behavior to be guided by a decision reached by another, without independently examining the merits of that decision. When exercising authority, the superior does not seek to convince the subordinate, but only to obtain his acquiescence. In actual practice, of course, authority is usually liberally admixed with suggestion and persuasion.

An important function of authority is to permit a decision to be made and carried out even when agreement cannot be reached, but perhaps this arbitrary aspect of authority has been overemphasized. In any event, if it is attempted to carry authority beyond a certain point, which may be described as the subordinate's "zone of acquiescence," disobedience will follow.[7] The magnitude of the zone of acquiescence depends upon the sanctions which authority has available to enforce its commands. The term "sanctions" must be interpreted broadly in this connection, for positive and neutral stimuli — such as community of purpose, habit, and leadership — are at least as important in securing acceptance of authority as are the threat of physical or economic punishment.

---

[5] For a recent advocacy of plural supervision, see Macmahon, Millet, and Ogden, *The Administration of Federal Work Relief* (Chicago: Public Administration Service, 1941), pp. 265-68.

[6] Chester I. Barnard, *The Functions of the Executive* (Cambridge: Harvard University Press, 1940), pp. 163ff.

[7] Barnard calls this the "zone of indifference" *(op.cit.,* p. 169), but I prefer the term "acquiescence."

It follows that authority, in the sense here defined, can operate "upward" and "sidewise" as well as "downward" in the organization. If an executive delegates to his secretary a decision about file cabinets and accepts her recommendation without re-examination of its merits, he is accepting her authority. The "lines of authority" represented on organization charts do have a special significance, however, for they are commonly resorted to in order to terminate debate when it proves impossible to reach a consensus on a particular decision. Since this appellate use of authority generally requires sanctions to be effective, the structure of formal authority in an organization usually is related to the appointment, disciplining, and dismissal of personnel. These formal lines of authority are commonly supplemented by informal authority relations in the day-to-day work of the organization, while the formal hierarchy is largely reserved for the settlement of disputes.

Organizational Loyalties. It is a prevalent characteristic of human behavior that members of an organized group tend to identify with that group. In making decisions their organizational loyalty leads them to evaluate alternative courses of action in terms of the consequences of their action for the group. When a person prefers a particular course of action because it is "good for America," he identifies with Americans; when he prefers it because it will "boost business in Berkeley," he identifies with Berkeleyans. National and class loyalties are examples of identifications which are of fundamental importance in the structure of modern society.

The loyalties which are of particular interest in the study of administration are those which attach to administrative organizations or segments of such organizations. The regimental battle-flag is the traditional symbol of this identification in military administration; in civil administration, a frequently encountered evidence of identification is the cry: "Our Bureau needs more funds!"

The psychological bases of identification are obscure, but seem to involve at least three elements. First, personal success often depends upon organizational success — the administrator who can build up his unit expects (with good reason) promotion and salary increases. Second, loyalty seems based partly on a transfer to the field of public management of the spirit of competition which is characteristic of private enterprise. Third, the human mind is limited in the number of diverse considerations which can occupy the area of attention at one time, and there is a consequent tendency to over-emphasize the importance of those elements which happen to be within that area. To the fireman, fires are the most serious human problem; to the health officer, disease, and so forth.

This phenomenon of identification, or institutional loyalty, performs one very important function in administration. If an administrator, each time he is faced with a decision, must perforce evaluate that decision in terms of the whole range of human values, rationality in administration is impossible. If he need consider the decision only in the light of limited organizational aims, his task is more nearly within the range of human powers. The fireman can concentrate on the problem of fires, the health officer on problems of disease, without irrelevant considerations entering in.

Furthermore, this concentration on a limited range of values is almost essential if the administrator is to be held accountable for his decisions. When the organization's objectives are specified by some higher authority, the major value-premise of the administrator's decisions is thereby given him, leaving to him only the implementation of these objectives. If the fire chief were permitted to roam over the whole field of human values — to decide that parks were more important than fire trucks, and consequently to remake his fire department into a recreation department — chaos would displace organization, and responsibility would disappear.

Organizational loyalties lead also, however, to certain difficulties which should not be underestimated. The principal undesirable effect of identification is that it prevents the institutionalized individual from making correct decisions in cases where the restricted area of values with which he identifies must be weighed against other values outside that area. This is a principal cause of the interbureau competition and wrangling which characterizes any large administrative organization. The organization members, identifying with the bureau instead of with the over-all organization, believe the bureau's welfare more important than the general welfare when the two conflict. This problem is frequently evident in the case of "housekeeping" agencies, where the facilitative and auxiliary nature of the agency is lost sight of in the effort to force the line agencies to follow standard procedures.

Institutional loyalties also result in incapacitating almost any department head for the task of balancing the financial needs of his department against the financial needs of other departments — whence the need for a centrally located budget agency which is free from these psychological biases. The higher we go in the administrative hierarchy, the broader becomes the range of social values which must come within the administrator's purview, the more harmful is the effect of valuational bias, and the more important is it that the administrator be freed from his narrower identifications.

The Criterion of Efficiency. We have seen that the exercise of authority and the development of organizational identifications are two principle means whereby the individual's value premises are influenced by the organization. What about the issues of fact which underly his decisions? These are largely determined by a principle which underlies all rational behavior: the criterion of efficiency. In its broadest sense, to be efficient simply means to take the shortest path, the cheapest means, toward the attainment of the desired goals. The efficiency criterion is completely neutral as to what goals are to be attained.

The concept of efficiency has been discussed at length by economists and writers on administration, and there is little that can be added to that discussion within the scope of the present paper. Suffice it to say that the commandment. "Be efficient!" is a major organizational influence over the decisions of the members of any administrative agency; and a determination whether this commandment has been obeyed is a major function of the review process.[8]

Advice and Information. Many of the influences the organization exercises over its members are of a less formal nature than those we have been discussing. These influences are perhaps most realistically viewed as a form of internal public relations, for there is nothing to guarantee that advice produced at one point in an organization will have any effect at another point in the organization unless the lines of communication are adequate to its transmission and unless it is transmitted in such form as to be persuasive. It is a prevalent misconception in headquarters offices that the internal advisory function consists in preparing precisely-worded explanatory bulletins and making certain that the proper number of these are prepared and that they are placed in the proper compartment of the "router." No plague has produced a rate of mortality higher than the rate which customarily afflicts central-office communications between the time they leave the issuing office and the moment when they are assumed to be effected in the revised practice of the operative employees.

These difficulties of communication apply, of course, to commands as well as to advice and information. As a matter of fact, the administrator who is serving in an advisory capacity is apt to be at some advantage in solving problems of communication, because he is likely to be conscious of the necessity of transmitting and "selling" his ideas, while the administrator who possesses authority may be oblivious of his public-relations function.

---

[8] For further discussion of the efficiency concept, see Clarence E. Ridley and Herbert A. Simon, *Measuring Municipal Activities* (Chicago: International City Managers' Association, 1943).

Information and advice flow in all directions through the organization — not merely from the top downward. Many of the facts which are relevant to decision are of a rapidly changing nature, ascertainable only at the moment of decision, and often ascertainable only by operative employees. For instance, in military operations knowledge of the disposition of the enemy's forces is of crucial importance, and military organization has developed elaborate procedures for transmitting to a person who is to make a decision all relevant facts which he is not in a position to ascertain personally.

Information and advice may be used as alternatives to the actual exercise of authority, and vice versa. Where promptness and discipline are not primary considerations, the former have several very impressive advantages. Chief among these is that they preserve morale and initiative on the part of the subordinate — qualities which may disappear if excessively harassed by authority. Again, when the influences are advisory in nature, the formal organization structure loses its unique position as the sole channel of influence. The relation between the adviser and the person advised is essentially no different when they are members of the same organization than when the adviser is outside the organization. The extent of the influence of the adviser will depend on the desire of the decision-maker for advice and on the persuasiveness with which it is offered.

Training. Like institutional loyalties, and unlike the other modes of influence we have been discussing, training influences decisions "from the inside out." That is, training prepares the organization member to reach satisfactory decisions himself, without the need for the constant exercise of authority or advice. In this sense, training procedures are alternatives to the exercise of authority or advice as means of control over the subordinate's decisions.

Training may be of an in-service or a pre-service nature. When persons with particular educational qualifications are recruited for certain jobs, the organization is depending upon this pre-training as a principal means of assuring correct decisions in their work. The mutual relation between training and the range of discretion which may be permitted an employee is an important factor to be taken into consideration in designing the administrative organization. That is, it may often be possible to minimize, or even dispense with, certain review processes by giving the subordinates training which enables them to perform their work with less supervision. Similarly, in drafting the qualifications required of applicants for particular positions, the possibility should be considered of lowering personnel costs by drafting semi-skilled employees and training them for particular jobs.

Training is applicable to the process of decision whenever the same elements are involved in a large number of decisions. Training may supply the trainee with the facts necessary in dealing with these decisions, it may provide him a frame of reference for his thinking, it may teach him "approved" solutions, or it may indoctrinate him with the values in terms of which his decisions are to be made.

Training, as a mode of influence upon decisions, has its greatest value in those situations where the exercise of formal authority through commands proves difficult. The difficulty may lie in the need for prompt action, in the spatial dispersion of the organization, or in the complexity of the subject matter of decision which defies summarization in rules and regulations. Training permits a higher degree of decentralization of the decision-making process by bringing the necessary competence into the very lowest levels of the organizational hierarchy.

Implications for Organization. It can be seen that there are at least five distinct ways in which the decisions of operative employees may be influenced: authority, identification, the efficiency criterion, advice, and training. It is the fundamental problem of organization to determine the extent and the manner in which each of these forms of influence is to be employed. To a very great extent, these various forms are interchangeable — a fact which is far more often appreciated in small than in large organizations.

The simplest example of this is the gradual increase in discretion which can be permitted an employee as he becomes familiar with his job. A secretary learns to draft routine correspondence; a statistical clerk learns to lay out his own calculations. In each case, training has taken the place of authority in guiding the employee's decisions.

Another illustration is the process of functional supervision whereby technical experts are given advisory, but not usually authoritative, relations with subordinate employees. This substitution of advice for authority may prove necessary in many situations in order to prevent conflicts of authority between line officers, organized on a geographical basis, and functional experts, organized along subject-matter lines. To the extent that these forms of influence supplement, or are substituted for, authority, the problem of influence becomes one of education and public relations, as has already been explained.

Administrators have increasingly recognized in recent years that authority, unless buttressed by other forms of influence, is relatively impotent to control decision in any but a negative way. The elements entering into all but the most routine decisions are so numerous and so complex that it is impossible to control positively more than a few. Unless the subordinate is himself able to supply most of the premises of decision, and to synthesize them adequately, the task of supervision becomes hopelessly burdensome. To cite an extreme illustration: no amount of supervision or direction, and no quantity of orders, directives, or commands, would be sufficient to enable a completely untrained person to prepare a legal brief for a law suit. In such a case, the problem is definitely not one of direction, but one of education or training.

Viewed from this standpoint, the problem of organization becomes inextricably interwoven with the problem or recruitment. For the system of influence which can effectively be used in the organization will depend directly upon the training and competence of employees at the various levels of the hierarchy. If a welfare agency can secure trained social workers as interviewers and case workers, broad discretion can be permitted them in determining eligibility, subject only to a sampling review and a review of particularly difficult cases. If trained workers can be obtained only for supervisory positions, then the supervisors will need to exercise a much more complete supervision over their subordinates, perhaps reviewing each decision and issuing frequent instruction. The supervisory problem will be correspondingly more burdensome than in the first example, and the effective span of control of supervisors correspondingly narrower.

Likewise, when an organization unit is large enough so that it can retain within its own boundaries the specialized expertise that is required for some of its decisions, the need for functional supervision from other portions of the organization becomes correspondingly less. When a department can secure its own legal, medical, or other expert assistance, the problems of functional organization become correspondingly simpler, and the lines of direct authority over the department need less supplementation by advisory and informational services.

Hence, problems of organization cannot be considered apart from the specifications and actual qualifications of the employees who are to fill the positions established by the organization. The whole subject of job classification must be brought into close coordination with the theory of organization. The optimum organizational structure is a variable, depending for its form upon the staffing of the agency. Conversely, the classification of a position is a variable, depending upon the degree of centralization or decentralization which is desired or anticipated in the operation of the organizational form.

THE COMMUNICATION OF INFLUENCE

It has already been pointed out that if it is wished to bring orders or advice to bear on the decisions of a subordinate, the orders or advice must be communicated to the subordinate; and that this communication is not merely a matter of physical transmission, but a process of actually inducing changes in the subordinate's behavior. The costs of the communication process are comparable to, and as real as, a manufacturer's advertising costs.

A manufacturer determines his advertising budget by the amount by which additional advertising will increase sales. When the additional receipts he expects are no longer sufficient to cover the additional advertising and manufacturing costs, he stops the expansion of his advertising program. An approach of a very similar kind needs to be introduced in the designing of administrative organizations. The cost of "producing" decisions in the supervisory staff and the cost of communicating these decisions to the operating personnel must be weighed against the expected increase in effectiveness of the latter.

The different forms of organizational influence must be balanced against each other in the same way. A training program involves a large initial investment in each operative employee, but low "maintenance" costs; orders and commands require no initial investment, but high and continuous costs of "production" and communication; if pre-trained employees are recruited, salaries may be higher, but a less elaborate supervisory structure will be required; and so forth. Again, we have reached a question of *how much,* and theory, without data, cannot give us an answer.

ADMINISTRATIVE PROCESSES FOR INSURING CORRECT DECISIONS

Having analyzed the various kinds of influence which condition the decisions of members of administrative organizations, we turn next to some concrete administrative processes to see how they fit into our scheme of analysis. The first of these is planning — the process whereby a whole scheme is worked out in advance before any part of it is carried out through specific decisions. The second of these is review — the process whereby subordinates are held to an accounting for the quality of their decisions and of the premises from which these decisions were reached.

Planning. Plans and schedules are ordinarily carried into effect by the exercise of authority, but of greater importance than this final act of approving or authorizing a plan are the decisional processes which go into the making of the plan. Planning is an extremely important decision-making process because of the vast amount of detail that can be embodied in the plan for a complex project and because of the broad participation that can be secured, when desirable, in its formulation.

As a good illustration of this we may summarize the procedure a navy department goes through in designing a battleship, as described by Sir Oswyn A. R. Murray. First, the general objectives are set out — the speed, radius of action, armor, and armament it is desired to attain in the finished design. Next, several provisional designs are developed by a staff of "generalists" who are familiar with all aspects of battleship design. On the basis of these alternative provisional designs, a final decision is reached on the general lines of the new ship. At this point the specialists are brought in to make recommendations for the detailed plan. Their recommendations will often require modification of the original design, and they will often recommend mutually conflicting requirements. To continue with Sir Oswyn's description:

> In this way the scheme goes on growing in a tentative manner, its progress always being dependent upon the cooperation of numbers of separate departments, all intent upon ensuring the efficiency of different parts, until ultimately a more or less complete whole is arrived at in the shape of drawings and specifications provisionally embodying all the agreements. This really is the most difficult and interesting stage, for generally it becomes apparent at this point that requirements overlap, and that the best possible cannot be achieved in regard to numbers of points within the limits set to the contractors. These difficulties are cleared up by discussion at round-table conferences, where the compromises which will least impair the value of the ship are agreed upon, and the completed design is then finally submitted for the Board's approval. Some fourteen departments are concerned in the settlement of the final detailed arrangements.[9]

The point which is so clearly illustrated here is that the planning procedure permits expertise of every kind to be drawn into the decision without any difficulties being imposed by the lines of authority in the organization. The final design undoubtedly received authoritative approval, but, during the entire process of formulation, suggestions and recommendations flowed freely from all parts of the organization without raising the problem of "unity of command." It follows from this that to the extent to which planning procedures are used in reaching decisions, the formal organization has relevance only in the final stages of the whole process. So long as the appropri-

---

[9] "The Administration of a Fighting Service," 1 *Journal of Public Administration* 216-17 (July, 1923).

ate experts are consulted, their exact location in the hierarchy of authority need not much affect the decision.

This statement must be qualified by one important reservation. Organizational factors are apt to take on considerable importance if the decision requires a compromise among a number of competing values which are somewhat incompatible with each other. In such a case, the focus of attention and the identifications of the person who actually makes the decision are apt to affect the degree to which advice offered him by persons elsewhere in the organization actually influences him.

Our illustration of the warship throws into relief the other aspect of the planning process which was mentioned above: that the plan may control, down to minute detail, a whole complex pattern of behavior — in this case, the construction of the battleship down to the last rivet. The task of the construction crew is minutely specified by this design.

Review. Review enables those who are in a position of authority in the administrative hierarchy to determine what actually is being done by their subordinates.

Review may extend to the results of the subordinate's activities measured in terms of their objectives; to the tangible products, if there are such, of his activities; or to the method of their performance.

When authority is exercised through the specification of the objective of the organizational unit, then a primary method of review is to ascertain the degree to which the organizational objective is attained — the results of the activity. A city manager, for instance, may evaluate the fire department in terms of fire losses, the police department in terms of crime and accident rates, the public works department in terms of the condition of streets and the frequency of refuse collection.

A second very important method of review is one which examines each piece of completed work to see whether it meets set requirements of quantity and quality. This method assumes that the reviewing officer is able to judge the quality and quantity of the completed work with a certain degree of competence. Thus, a superior may review all outgoing letters written by his subordinates, or the work of typists may be checked by a chief clerk, or the work of a street repair crew may be examined by a superintendent.

It has not often enough been recognized that in many cases the review of work can just as well be confined to a randomly selected sample of the work as extended to all that is produced. A highly developed example of such a sampling procedure is found in the personnel administration of the Farm Credit Administration. This organization carries out its personnel functions on an almost completely decentralized basis, except for a small central staff which lays down standards and procedures. As a means of assuring that local practices follow these standards, field supervisors inspect the work of the local agencies and, in the case of certain personnel procedures such as classification, the setting of compensation scales, and the development of testing materials, assure themselves of the quality of the work by an actual inspection of a sample of it.

The third, and perhaps simplest, method of review is to watch the employee at work, either to see that he puts in the required number of hours, or to see that he is engaging in certain movements which if continued will result in the completion of the work. In this case, the review extends to procedures and techniques, rather than to the product or results. It is the prevalent form of review at the foremanship level.

To determine what kind of a review method should be employed in any concrete administrative situation, it is necessary to be quite clear as to what this particular review process is to accomplish. There are at least four different functions which a review process may perform: diagnosis of the quality of decisions being made by subordinates, modification through influence on subsequent decisions, the correction of incorrect decisions which have already been made, the enforcement of sanctions against subordinates so that they will accept authority in making their decisions.[10]

In the first place, review is the means whereby the administrative hierarchy learns whether decisions are being made correctly or incorrectly, whether work is being done well or badly at the lower levels of the hierarchy. It is a fundamental source of information upon which the higher levels of the hierarchy must rely heavily for their own decisions. With the help of this information, improvements can be introduced into the decision-making process.

This leads to the second function of review — to influence subsequent decisions. This is achieved in a variety of ways. Orders may be issued covering particular points on which incorrect decisions have been made or laying down new policies to govern decisions; employees may be given

---

[10] A somewhat similar, but not identical, analysis of the function of review can be found in Sir H. N. Bunbury's paper, "Efficiency as an Alternative to Control," 6 *Public Administration* 97-98 (April, 1928).

training or retraining with regard to those aspects of their work which review has proved faulty; information may be supplied them, the lack of which has led to incorrect decisions. In brief, change may be brought about in any of the several ways in which decisions can be influenced.

Third, review may perform an appellate function. If the individual decision has grave consequences, it may be reviewed by a higher authority, to make certain that it is correct. This review may be a matter of course, or it may occur only on appeal by a party at interest. The justification of such a process of review is that (1) it permits the decision to be weighed twice, and (2) the appellate review requires less time per decision than the original decision, and hence conserves the time of better-trained personnel for the more difficult decisions. The appellate review may, to use the language of administrative law, consist in a consideration *de novo,* or may merely review the original decision for substantial conformity to important rules of policy.

Fourth, review is often essential to the effective exercise of authority. Authority depends to a certain extent on the availability of sanctions to give it force. Sanctions can be applied only if there is some means of ascertaining when authority has been respected, and when it has been disobeyed. Review supplies the person in authority with this information.

Decision making is said to be centralized when only a very narrow range of discretion is left to subordinates; decentralized when a very broad range of discretion is left. Decision making can be centralized either by using general rules to limit the discretion of the subordinate or by taking out of the hands of the subordinate the actual decision-making function. Both of these processes fit our definition of centralization because their result is to take out of the hands of the subordinate the actual weighing of competing considerations and to require that he accept the conclusions reached by other members of the organization.

There is a very close relationship between the manner in which the function of review is exercised and the degree of centralization or decentralization. Review influences decisions by evaluating them and thereby subjecting the subordinate to discipline and control. Review is sometimes conceived as a means of detecting wrong decisions and correcting them. This concept may be very useful as applied to those very important decisions where an appellate procedure is necessary to conserve individual rights or democratic responsibility; but, under ordinary circumstances, the function of correcting the decisional processes of the subordinate which lead to wrong decisions is more important than the function of correcting wrong decisions.

Hence, review can have three consequences: (1) if it is used to correct individual decisions, it leads to centralization and an actual transfer of the decision-making functions; (2) if it is used to discover where the subordinate needs additional guidance, it leads to centralization through the promulgation of more and more complete rules and regulations limiting the subordinate's discretion; (3) if it is used to discover where the subordinate's own resources need to be strengthened, it leads to decentralization. All three elements can be, and usually are, combined in varying proportions in any review process.

SUMMARY

We may now briefly retrace the path we have traveled in the preceding pages. We have seen that a decision is analogous to a conclusion drawn from a number of premises — some of them factual and some ethical. Organization involves a "horizontal" specialization of work and a "vertical" specialization in decision making — the function of the latter being to secure coordination of the operative employees, expertness in decision making, and responsibility to policy-making agencies.

The influence of an organization, and its supervisory employees, upon the decisions of the operative employees can be studied by noting how the organization determines for the operative employee the premises — factual and ethical — of his decisions. The organization's influence is a matter of degree. As we travel from top to bottom of the administrative hierarchy, we note a progressive particularization of influence. Toward the top, discretion is limited by the assignment of broad objectives and the specification of very general methods; lower in the hierarchy, more specific objectives are set, and procedures are determined in greater detail.

Within the limits fixed by his superiors, each member of the organization retains a certain sphere of discretion, a sphere within which he is responsible for the selection of premises for decision. For the most part, this sphere of discretion lies within the factual area of the decisional process rather than within the area of values; but the individual's decision is not "free" even within the area of discretion, in the sense that his superiors are indifferent what decision he will make. On the contrary, he will be held for the correctness of his decision even within that area.

There are at least five ways in which influence is exerted over the individual: (1) authority, (2) identification, (3) the criterion of efficiency, (4) advice and information, and (5) training. To a large extent, these are interchangeable, and a major task of administration is to determine to what extent each will be employed. The structure of influence in an organization and the lines of communication are far more complex than the structure of authority. In designing an organization, it is not enough to establish lines of authority; it is equally important to determine the ways in which all forms of influence are to be exercised.

Two organizational processes are of particular importance to decision making: planning and review. Planning permits the control of decisions in very great detail and permits all the available expertise to be brought to bear on a particular decision with little concern for the lines of formal authority. Review is a source of information to the administrative hierarchy, a means of influencing subsequent decisions of subordinates, a means for correcting decisions on important individual matters, and a means for enforcing authority by determining when sanctions need to be applied. Depending upon the way in which they are employed, review processes may lead either to the centralization or to the decentralization of decision making.

QUESTIONS

1. Apply Simon's analysis to your school or school district. Touch on the following points:
   a. Horizontal specialization of work and vertical specialization in decision-making.
   b. Progressive particularization of influence from top to bottom.
   c. The sphere of discretion allowed teachers, supervisors, principals, assistant superintendents, and the superintendent of schools.
   d. The influence exerted by the organization over the individual by authority, identification, the criterion of efficiency, advice and information, and training.
   e. The effects of planning and review on decision-making.

2. Are there any aspects of Simon's analysis which you question or which you accept only with qualification?

A MEANS OF MEASURING TEACHER PARTICIPATION IN DECISION-MAKING

By
John K. Best

Teachers in a selected district responded to a questionnaire that asked the extent to which each was involved in 12 decisional situations. They were also asked whether they wanted to be involved in each of the decisions.

The results showed that no less than 50% of the staff was participating to the degree that it preferred. Very few participated more than they desired. Relatively large numbers indicated that current participation was less than desired.

A procedure is described for administrators interested in measuring the level of teacher participation in decision-making in their school or district.

The school administrator, as a student of organizational theory, knows that individuals want to be involved in making decisions that affect them. Whether his teachers are participating as much as each prefers (known as being at *decisional equilibrium*), more than each prefers (being *decisionally saturated*), or less than each prefers (being decisionally deprived) is an important organizational variable, moreover, for there is evidence that suggests that these levels of decisional condition significantly affect other organizational variables such as morale, organizational commitment, and interpersonal trust.[1]

Among the means the administrator can use to encourage a measure of teacher participation in decisions made in his unit (building, district, level) equivalent to that which each teacher prefers is the following device. It was developed as an incidental result of a study whose purpose was to test for correlations between these decisional conditions and teacher morale.[2]

---

[1]The concept of decisional condition and significant differences among the conditions was first proposed by Joseph A. Alutto and James A. Belasco in "A Typology for Participation in Organizational Decision Making," *Administrative Science Quarterly,* 17:117-125.

[2]See John K. Best, *Decisional Status and Teacher Morale: A Study of the Relationship Between Decisional Condition/Decisional Deviation and Teacher Morale,* unpublished doctoral dissertation, State University of New York at Buffalo, 1973.

"A Means of Measuring Teacher Participation in Decision Making," by John K. Best, *The Clearing House,* September 1975, Vol. 49, pp. 26-27. Copyright © 1975 by The Clearing House. Reprinted by permission of Heldref Publications.

The teachers of a public school district in western New York responded to a questionnaire that asked the extent to which each was involved in 12 decisional situations (listed in Table 1).

1. Hiring new faculty members
2. Preparing school or departmental budgets
3. Making textbook selections
4. Resolving students' academic or personal problems
5. Making faculty assignments
6. Resolving grievances
7. Adopting new instructional methods
8. Deciding on new building facilities
9. Resolving difficulties with community groups
10. Resolving problems with administrative services (e.g., clerks, typists)
11. Deciding faculty members' salaries
12. Establishing general instructional policy

Table 1

DECISIONAL SITUATIONS

They were also asked if they wanted to be involved in each of the above decisions. The data for each decisional situation were then analyzed. Those who were presently involved in the specific situation to the degree that was preferred (whether actively — participating and wanting to be, or passively — not participating and not wanting to participate) were said to be at *decisional equilibrium*. Those who were presently involved in the specific situation but would have preferred *not* to be participating were said to be *decisionally saturated*. Finally, those who were not involved in the given situation and wanted to participate were said to be *decisionally deprived*. Table 2 gives a breakdown of the frequency of faculty participation in each of the decisional situations.

No less than 50% of the staff was participating to the degree that it preferred in each of the decisional situations. Total decisional equilibrium

DECISIONAL SITUATION	DEPRIVED	ACTIVE EQUILIBRIUM	SATURATED	PASSIVE EQUILIBRIUM	TOTAL EQUILIBRIUM	PERCENTAGE OF TOTAL EQUILIBRIUM
1. Faculty Hiring	74	49	0	59	108	59.34
2. Budgets	50	107	4	21	128	70.32
3. Textbooks	15	160	1	6	166	91.20
4. Student Problems	24	144	4	10	154	84.61
5. Faculty Assignments	85	52	0	45	97	53.29
6. Grievances	58	27	1	96	123	67.58
7. Instructional Methods	77	97	2	6	103	56.59
8. Building Facilities	89	59	2	32	91	50.00
9. Community Problems	51	42	4	85	127	69.78
10. Administrative Services	42	15	1	124	139	76.37
11. Salaries	62	49	4	67	116	63.73
12. General Instructional Policies	61	104	2	15	119	65.38

Table 2

FREQUENCY OF PARTICIPATION IN EACH DECISIONAL SITUATION

RANK		PERCENTAGE
1.	Making textbook selection	91.20
2.	Resolving students' academic or personal problems	84.61
3.	Resolving problems with administrative services (e.g., clerks, typists)	76.37
4.	Preparing school or departmental budgets	70.32
5.	Resolving difficulties with community groups	69.78
6.	Resolving grievances	67.58
7.	Establishing general instructional policy	65.38
8.	Deciding faculty members' salaries	63.73
9.	Hiring new faculty members	59.34
10.	Adopting new instructional methods	56.59
11.	Making faculty assignments	53.29
12.	Deciding on new building facilities	50.00

Table 3

RANK AND PERCENTAGE OF TEACHER EQUILIBRIUM

ranged from 91 teachers participating as preferred in decisions concerning new building facilities to 166 teachers (91.2%) participating as they preferred in making textbook selections. Very few teachers participated more than they desired, while there were relatively large numbers who indicated current participation that was less than desired.

The response of the teachers to the questionnaire, therefore, provided a profile of their decisional condition to the administrators of the district employed in the survey. The interpretation of the above data, however, and the implications that might be contained for school practice depended, however, on the criteria for involvement that had been established by those administrators. Should they have desired full teacher participation to the degree that each preferred, they fell short of achieving that goal. Yet, in selecting textbooks, 91.2% of the teachers participated as they desired. They also discovered, as they looked at the rankings on Table 3, that only 50% of the staff was involved as it desired in decisions relating to new buildings. Therefore, they could substantiate the need for greater efforts to increase, decrease, or maintain the opportunities for participation by their staff members in each of the specific decisional situations.

Implications For Administrative Practice

Having in mind the findings reported above, the school administrator interested in ascertaining the level of teacher participation in decisions in his organizational unit might take the following steps:

1. Establish the criteria of teacher involvement in decision-making that he wishes to employ.
2. List any number of significant decisional situations that existed during the past year (or some specified period of time.)
3. Substitute each of those decisional situations into the questionnaire framework described above.
4. Ask the teachers to respond to the questionnaire.
5. Collect the data and display the frequencies on tables similar to those employed above.
6. In the light of the criteria established in step number one, evaluate the levels of decisional condition in the unit and take the appropriate administrative actions to continue or change the results.

QUESTIONS

1. Using the procedure described by Dr. Best, find the level of teacher participation in decision-making in your school or district.

2. Find evidence that the level of teacher participation in decision-making affects morale, organizational commitment, and interpersonal trust.

THE PRINCIPAL AS A COUNTERPUNCHER

By
Ray Cross

Principals function in an environment in which they are constantly countering the initiatives of others. They respond to requests, appeals, demands, and complaints of many people and become so enmeshed in day-to-day problems that they are unable to perform the critical tasks of leadership.

The Barnard classification of problems in terms of their origin as intermediary, appellate, and creative was used by two studies of the decision-making activities of principals. These studies, which explored the nature of principals' problems and their variability with the school's socioeconomic setting, showed that principals in low socioeconomic communities were particularly burdened with appellate problems.

Suggestions are offered for reducing the number of intermediary and appellate problems so that principals may free themselves for leadership tasks.

As a raw youth, I decided that my appropriate field of athletic endeavor was boxing. A few bouts, however, persuaded me that this ambition had been ill conceived and that my true forte lay in games requiring less bodily contact, say, table tennis or shuffleboard. Nevertheless, during my brief tenure as an ineffective gladiator, I acquired a concept that I have since concluded has application to the elementary school principal's world — the concept of counterpunching.

Counterpunching, as a pugilistic strategy, consists of taking advantage of the openings afforded by the opponent's attack. The counterpuncher lets the opponent take the initiative, parries his thrusts, and clobbers him while he is exposed. Although many boxers have enjoyed considerable success with this kind of strategy, I am convinced that elementary school principals who consistently use this approach will eventually find themselves flat on the canvas, metaphorically speaking.

"The Principal As Counter-Puncher," by Ray Cross, from *The National Elementary Principal,* October 1971, pp. 43-45.
Copyright © 1971 by NAESP. Reprinted by permission of NAESP and the author.

Although it is to be hoped that principals do not engage in counterpunching in the literal sense, they often function in an environment in which they are constantly countering the initiatives of others.

Counterpunching for the elementary school principal consists of responding to requests, appeals, demands, and complaints of the many people who look to him as the school's ultimate decision maker. Counterpunching suggests reaction rather than action, and struggle for survival rather than growth.

I realize that a certain amount of counterpunching is inherent in the principal's role. He cannot retreat to an ivory tower, refusing to deal with the less glamorous problems of everyday school life. I am concerned, however, that too many principals have the opposite problem: They become so enmeshed in the day-to-day problems that they are unable to perform the critical tasks of leadership. A principal severely afflicted by the counterpunching syndrome is dealing almost entirely with issues raised by others, each of whom is concerned with only a part of the school operation or with his own personal interests. When a principal responds only to issues raised by others, his actions become random movements in terms of the direction of the school program as a whole.

All principals, I think, are aware that they are counterpunching some of the time. The results of two recent studies on the problems of elementary school principals suggest that many principals may be counterpunching most of the time.[1,2] Both studies viewed elementary school principals within a problem/decision framework. Observers shadowed elementary school principals, recording and classifying the problems that came up for decision. These studies have several focuses, but each documented the origins of principals' problems according to the three categories for executive decision discussed by Chester I. Barnard in his classic book on administration.[3] Barnard suggests that administrative problems can be classified in terms of three distinct origins.

One occasion for administrative decision is upon receipt of instructions from, or general requirements of, superior authority. For example: *A princi-*

---

[1] Cross, Ray, and Bennet, Vernon. "Problem Situations Encountered by School Principals in Different Socio-Economic Settings." A paper presented at the American Educational Research Association, February 8, 1969, Los Angeles, Calif.

[2] Cross, Ray. "A Description of Decision-Making Patterns of Elementary School Principals." (in process.)

[3] Barnard, Chester I. *The Functions of the Executive*. Cambridge, Mass.: Harvard University Press, 1938.

pal receives notice from the state education authority that at least three fire drills must be held annually. A number of decisions by the principal might stem from this one order, such as when to hold drills and which children should leave by which exit. Administrative problems of this type are classified as *intermediary problems.*

A second occasion for decision is when a case is referred to the administrator by subordinates in the organization. Such occasions may arise from the inability or unwillingness of the subordinate to make a decision, from novel conditions, conflict of jurisdiction, or lack of clarity in policy. Examples of this kind of decision are all too plentiful:

The first-grade teacher reports that Ralph has brought his dog to school again and asks the principal what to do about it.

or

The school counselor and social worker sharply disagree about their respective roles and request that the principal arbitrate the matter.

Such issues, referred to principals by teachers, pupils, and parents, are classified as *appellate problems.*

The third and final occasion for decision originates with the administrator. His own understanding of a situation leads him to decide whether something ought to be done or corrected. According to Barnard, such occasions are the most significant indicators of administrative effectiveness, since it is the administrator's most important obligation to raise those issues that no one else can or will. Examples:

The principal notes that reading achievement scores in the primary unit have slipped and calls the primary teachers together to discuss causes and possible remedies.

or

The principal believes that the involvement of a team of teachers in hiring new staff will result in greater collegial support of new teachers, and he initiates a structure for such involvement.

When such activities are initiated by the principal, they are classified as *creative problems.*

In one of the two studies mentioned earlier,[4] Cross and Bennett explored the nature of elementary school principals' problems and their variability with the school's socioeconomic setting:

Origins of Principals' Problems
In High and Low Socioeconomic Settings

Problem Origin	High Socioeconomic Setting % of Problems	Low Socioeconomic Setting % of Problems
Appellate	41	61
Intermediary	6	7
Creative	53	32

These data indicate that, taken as a whole, principals of schools in low socioeconomic communities are particularly burdened with appellate problems. As one might expect, it appears that appellate problems "drive out" creative problems, since principals in "high" settings had 53 percent creative problems and principals in "low" settings had only 32 percent creative problems. Neither group was often confronted with intermediary problems — 6 percent for principals in "high" settings and 7 percent for principals in "low" settings. Thus, if we accept intermediary and appellate problems as instances of counterpunching, principals of schools in low socioeconomic settings were counterpunching on 68 percent of their problems, and principals of schools in high socioeconomic settings on only 47 percent of theirs.

An interesting sidelight of this study is the large volume of problems that confronted the principals each day. Principals in both high and low socioeconomic settings worked with an average of approximately 100 problems a day. Thus, the percentages mentioned above are fairly accurate indicators of problem frequencies in raw numbers.

A study still in progress has reinforced the above findings.[5] In this study, it was found that a group of principals in inner-city elementary schools had a problem origin distribution of 68 percent appellate, 12 percent intermediary, and 20 percent creative. This very closely parallels the percentage distribution for principals in "low" settings in the first study mentioned.

It should not be assumed that the socioeconomic level of the school's community completely controls the origins of the principal's problems. Within each of the groups of principals in the Cross and Bennett study, there were variations in problem origin distributions. In some of the schools in high socioeconomic settings, the principals dealt with a high percentage of counterpunching problems.

---

[4] See footnote 1.

[5] See footnote 2.

As I have said, I think that it is neither possible nor desirable for principals to avoid appellate and intermediary problems completely. I do think, however, that if principals intend to exercise educational leadership, they should reduce appellate and intermediary problems to 40 percent of the total number.

For principals of schools in the inner city, additional administrative assistance is probably necessary to relieve them from the press of appellate problems. Many large school systems have moved in this direction during the past few years. This Minneapolis public schools, for example, now staff their inner-city elementary schools with assistant principals and administrative interns.

Additional administrative staff is not, however, the only possible solution for the principal who would like to trade some of his appellate problems for leadership opportunities. The power to do this is at the disposal of every principal. To some extent, each principal must prescribe his own antidote for the counterpunching syndrome. I would, however, like to offer the following suggestions to principals who are interested in reducing an overload of appellate and intermediary problems:

1. *Assess your own pattern of problems.* A useful starting point is to acquire some assessment of the problems with which you are now dealing. Who originates them? What is their nature? Are they the types of problems you would like to work with? A log kept over a week's period should provide a reliable assessment.
2. *Avoid solving problems that can best be handled by others.* Daniel E. Griffiths has set forth the proposition that an administrator's effectiveness is inversely proportional to the number of decisions he personally makes concerning the affairs of the organization.[6] Even though teachers in general are seeking wider responsibilities, many individual faculty members have been conditioned to seek the principal's judgment on every matter of significance. Although playing the role of Mr. Wonderful Decision Maker may do a great deal for a principal's ego, usually such a role leads to overly dependent teachers and overwhelmed principals. I am *not* suggesting that principals turn a deaf ear to teachers who are seeking help. I am suggesting that principals may sometimes need to provide a different form of help from that of making a teacher's decision for him. If Miss Newcomer is sending all of her discipline problems to the principal for his

[6]Griffiths, Daniel E., *Administrative Theory*. New York: Appleton-Century-Crofts, 1959. p. 89.

decision, perhaps the best course of action for the principal is to see that Miss Newcomer acquires the skills needed to make her own discipline decisions.

3. *Set up structures that will provide bases for decisions to be made without your attention.* I once observed a principal who, during a period of minutes, was asked by four teachers whether it was too cold to take children outside for physical education. Apparently, it had not occurred to him to establish guidelines that would permit teachers themselves to make this kind of decision.
4. *Delegate.* Many of the tasks for which a principal is directly responsible do not really require a high level of professional competence. The willingness of a principal to assign tasks, such as routine reports to secretaries, clerks, and aids, can lighten the minutia load considerably. Although he may be ultimately responsible for such reports, it does not follow that the principal must perform the simple clerical tasks necessary to complete them.
5. *Seek opportunities to turn appellate and intermediary problems into creative ones.* Such a strategy is available to a principal who looks beyond the immediate problem to its larger possibilities and implications. For instance, in the previously cited example of a principal who was called on to arbitrate the role conflict between a counselor and a social worker, the principal might choose to form a pupil personnel team that would include the two parties to the conflict. Such a move could not only remove the conflict but could also enhance pupil personnel services through a more coordinated effort.

Relieving the overburden of appellate and intermediary problems is not, of course, an end in itself. It offers the principal only a means of freeing himself for leadership tasks. There is no doubt, however, that for many principals amelioration of the counterpunching malady is a prerequisite that has remained too long ignored.

QUESTIONS

1. Why should principals of schools in low socioeconomic settings be particularly burdened with appellate problems?

2. Discuss the merits of the five suggestions offered by the author.

UNIT VI

COMMUNICATION THEORY

COMMUNICATION THEORY

OVERVIEW

If an organization is to accomplish its goals, cooperation and coordination are essential. But there can be no cooperation and coordination without communication. Communication is the heartbeat of an organization. No matter how small an organization, communication is essential for its existence.

Communication is the transfer of meaning from one person to another. When we succeed in making another person believe as we want him to believe, feel as we want him to feel, or act as we want him to act, we have communicated. Etymologically the word derives from *communis*, common, which suggests that it is a process of sharing.

The average person spends 70 percent of his waking day in communication. Nine percent of that time is spent in writing, 16 percent in reading, 30 percent in talking, and 45 percent in listening.[1]

[1] Taylor, Stanford E., *Listening,* Washington, D.C.: NEA, 1964, p. 3.

An administrator probably spends more time than the average man in communication. He issues directives, offers suggestions, telephones, dictates letters, reads reports and correspondence, listens to complaints, inquiries, and recommendations — in short, he lives in a verbal environment. He interacts with others by means of spoken or written symbols and, whether he is aware of it or not, communicates his attitudes by non-symbolic means as well. Non-symbolic, non-verbal communication is an ever-present influence in the communication process.

NON-SYMBOLIC COMMUNICATION

Only in recent years has the influence of non-symbolic or non-verbal behavior been recognized and systematically studied. Communication may occur without intent. Our inadvertent postures, gestures, facial expressions, and other bodily movements silently convey our feelings and attitudes, often more powerfully than the words we use. School administrators need to be aware of the effect of unintentional non-verbal behavior in their interpersonal relationships since so much of their time is spent in face-to-face communication.

According to Mehrabian, the basic dimensions of human feelings that are conveyed non-verbally are like-dislike, domination, and responsiveness, each of which he states in the form of a principle.[2]

The immediacy principle asserts that people approach the persons and things they like and avoid those they dislike. At social and business gatherings we sit near people we regard highly. When we are part of a group, we address our remarks to those we prefer or are attempting to please. A host sits himself at the head of the table so that he can distribute his attention more evenly among his guests and places the guest of honor at his right so that he may give him special attention. We prefer to sit alone in a restaurant rather than with a stranger.[3]

Sometimes we cannot physically draw near the things we like or move away from those we dislike. In such instances we use abbreviated forms of approach or avoidance; for example, we lean forward or establish eye contact with a speaker to show our interest, or we lean back and look away from him to show a negative reaction. The lift of a hand in greeting is an abbreviated form of reaching to touch. When an executive slightly pushes back

---

[2] Mehrabian, Albert, *Silent Messages,* Belmont, Cal.: Wadsworth Publishing Co., 1971, p. v.
[3] Ibid., pp. 1-5.

his chair or glances away from the person before him, he is giving unconscious signals that an interview is at an end. We form impressions of a person's social style and draw inferences about his attitudes from such abbreviated movements.[4]

The power principle asserts that "people behave in a more formal and ritualized fashion in situations involving status differences than they do when interacting with their peers."[5] Lower status persons are more tense and speak more guardedly in the presence of a superior. They do not enter his office without knocking and receiving permission, do not sit down unless invited, and do not act in a familiar manner unless encouraged to do so.

The responsiveness principle states that we react emotionally to our environment in negative and positive ways. Anger, for example, is a negative reaction and praise is a positive. "Responsiveness is probably the most basic way in which humans convey their feelings."[6] We stop our walk from one office to another to exchange greetings with a friend. We quicken our pace and direct our gaze at the sight of an unusual occurrence and we smile, frown, scowl, or shrug our shoulders in response to the comments of our associates.

In sum, we are continuously sending silent messages about ourselves and those around us, and these silent signals are observed and interpreted by our listeners, often to our disadvantage. When there is a conflict between the words we utter and the silent language of our body, our listeners give greater credence to the latter.

Silence is also a form of non-symbolic communication, as Fabun has eloquently shown:

> When someone says "Good morning," and we fail to respond, we communicate something. When someone asks us a question and we fail to answer, we also communicate. We are social creatures and our society is made up of responses to each other. For one thing, we are in constant need of reassurance; not only that we are, indeed, alive (because we evoke responses from others) but also reassurance that those other creatures around us are friendly and not hostile. The stroked cat purrs; the petted dog wags his tail. We talk. When we fail to do so, a little bit of our word crumbles away. The world of silence may be a cold

---

[4] Ibid.
[5] Ibid., p. 24.
[6] Ibid., p. 117.

and bitter one like the deep wastes of the Arctic regions, it is fit for neither man nor beast. Holding one's tongue may be prudent, but it is an act of rejection; silence builds walls — and walls are the symbols of failure.[7]

Time is a form of non-symbolic language which different cultures regard in various ways. In our society, punctuality is a form of courtesy. When an appointment is made for a particular hour, those concerned are expected to be on time or at least to give notification well in advance that they will be late or that they cannot be present. Lateness which is the result of carelessness is looked upon as discourtesy and may create a situation in which communication is difficult. On the other hand an early arrival is interpreted as a sign of interest and respect.

In some cultures time does not have the importance that our society attaches to it. Some Indian tribes have no word for waiting. South American peasants use mañana not in the literal sense of tomorrow but as an indefinite time period. A peasant who promises to do something manana is saying that it will be done in the indefinite future if it ever gets done at all. Even in our own society the meaning of *awhile* varies with the context in which it is used. A mechanic who says that a repair will take awhile may mean a period of a few minutes or a few days, depending on the extent of the damage.

Color and dress are non-symbolic language forms which say something about ourselves and the way we regard our associates. A business man does not wear flamboyant clothes because garish colors and outré dress would convey disturbing messages about him, his attitude toward his job, and his feelings about his colleagues. If a school principal were to come to school wearing a gaudy sports shirt and faded jeans, his teachers and students would regard his dress not only as inappropriate but as an expression of his opinion about himself, faculty, and students. "The apparel oft proclaims the man," said Polonius.

Space is also a non-symbolic language form. The offices of executives are located at or near the top of buildings. The more important the executive, the higher and larger his office. The arrangement of furniture in a room can inhibit or promote communication and have detrimental effects on professional relationships.[8]

---

[7] Fabun, Don, *Communications: The Transfer of Meaning*, Beverly Hills, Cal.: Glencoe Press, 1965, p. 20.

[8] Mehrabian, op. cit., p. 17.

Some non-verbal language may be intentional. Our society attaches meanings to certain gestures and head movements just as it attaches meanings to certain combinations of sounds called words. We use gestures to point, beckon, and defy, and we show approval or disapproval by nodding or shaking our head. A driver obeys the arm movements of a traffic policeman, a crane operator follows the hand signals of a foreman, a mother places her finger on her lips to admonish a child to be quiet. The range of meanings conveyed by gestures is narrower than that conveyed by oral or written language but it is extensive nonetheless.

It has been observed that teachers who habitually gesture are more effective than those who gesture very little. Their effectiveness, however, derives from their affiliative or out-going style which uses gestures and other bodily movements to convey positive feelings and evoke affirmative responses. Their inner concern is manifested in bodily action.[9]

SYMBOLIC COMMUNICATION

Language is an audible and visible code. It consists of combinations of sounds called words. Words, which can be spoken or written, are symbols; they stand for something else and there is no necessary connection between them and the things they stand for. This seems obvious but confusion between symbol and thing has caused enmities and wars throughout history.

Language is based on this distinction between symbol and reality. It is a symbolic process, a systems of sounds which can be arranged in various ways to represent objects, ideas, and emotions. By agreement, men can make anything stand for anything. In one culture they might agree that certain sounds should stand for certain things while in another culture they agree that a different set of sounds should stand for the same things. *Cat* in English is *chat* in French and *gatto* in Italian. Communication breakdowns occur because of misunderstandings about the symbolic nature of language and because of inadequacies in creating, using, and perceiving the audible and written symbols of which it is composed.

Our English language is constantly changing. Words become obsolete or they signify different things as times change. New words are created to represent new experiences. The number of words in English is estimated to be 600,000 but only about 2000 occur in the daily conversation of the average educated person. Most words have multiple definitions. The 500 most com-

---

[9] Mehrabian, op. cit., p. 120.

monly used have 14,000 definitions; *run* for example, has 250 and *round* has 73.[10]

Strictly speaking, words do not have meaning. Only people do. Meaning results from experience and, since no two people have the same experiences, no two people have the same meanings for even the most commonplace things. A boy whose family has always owned a dog and whose experiences with a dog have always been happy attaches a different meaning to *dog* from that of a boy whose family has never owned one and who has been taught to fear all animals. Meanings are developed in us and differ from individual to individual and from situation to situation. Dictionaries do not give meanings; they give equivalent verbalizations. Cognition, for instance, is defined as an act of knowing, and knowing is defined as cognition.

THE COMMUNICATION CYCLE

Although mathematical models of the communication cycle are undoubtedly the most advanced, they are not useful to school administrators because of their technical complexity.

Physical models are based on an analogy with electrical transmitters and receivers. Shannon's model, developed for use in information theory, has been adapted for interpersonal and organizational approaches to communication. (Figure 1)

The source is the originator of the message. The message may consist of spoken or written words, pictures, music, or other modes of expression. The transmitter converts the message into a signal which is sent over the communication channel from the transmitter to the receiver. The receiver changes the transmitted signal back into a message and sends it on to its destination.

In oral communication the source is the brain, the transmitter is the larynx and articulatory organs which produce varying sound pressures (signal) which are transmitted through the air (channel) to the ear and eighth nerve (receiver) and then to the brain (destination) of the listener.

Noise is any interference occurring between transmission and reception. It may be physical as, for example, static (radio), distortion of sound (telephony), distortion of picture (TV), or errors in transmission. It may also

[10] Fabun, op. cit., p. 19.

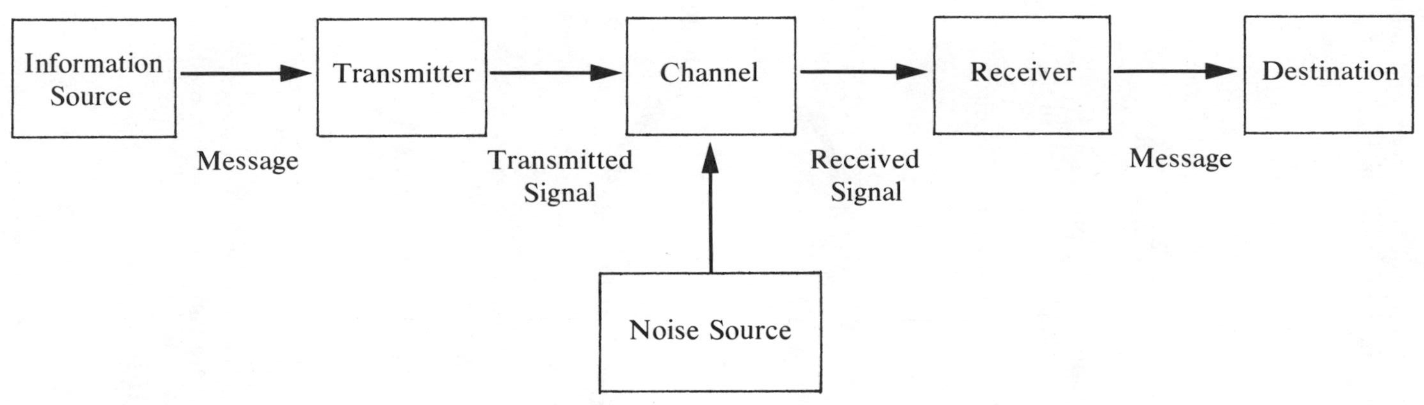

Figure 1

A MODEL OF THE COMMUNICATION PROCESS

Adapted from Claude E. Shannon and Warren Weaver, *The Mathematical Theory of Communication*, Urbana, Ill.: University of Illinois Press, 1949, p. 98.

be psychological as, for example inattention, emotional upset, and failure to comprehend. In physical models, any communication problem that cannot be explained is classified as noise.

A social model is probably more helpful to school administrators because it is oriented to social interaction without the aid of electronic devices. It may take the form of

SENDER → MESSAGE → MEDIUM → RECEIVER

as, for example, a newspaper, book, radio, or TV program. In these examples the receiver's response is internal and does not go back to the sender.

A social model may also take the form of a loop or circuit:

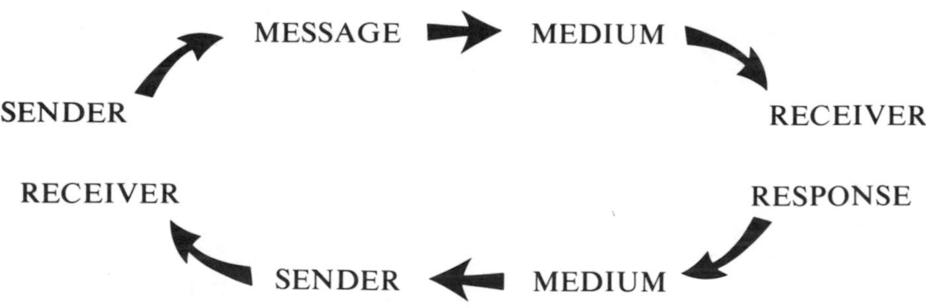

Figure 2

A MODEL OF THE COMMUNICATION CYCLE

In Figure 2 a sender encodes a message in words, gestures, pictures, Morse code, or some other form, and transmits it through a medium (airwaves, printed materials, etc.) to a receiver who decodes the message as received. After decoding, the receiver responds to the sender. When the response is sent and received, the roles are reversed, the original receiver becoming a sender and the original sender becoming a receiver. The response or feedback completes the loop.

Feedback or the reactions of listeners is an important element in communication because it enables a speaker to check upon the accuracy with which his message has been received. If he perceives that he is not getting through, he can adapt his content and method.

Feedback need not be immediate. It can come later in the form of letters, printed statements, public opinion polls, and the like. Teachers administer tests to determine the effectiveness of their teaching and administrators encourage questions and discussion to find out whether their proposals have been understood and accepted.

COMMUNICATION BREAKDOWNS

A breakdown may occur at any point in the communication cycle. The cause may be ascribed to the speaker, the message, the medium, or the receiver.

The speaker. Aristotle said that the effectiveness of a speaker depends on his character or ethos, which he identified as the most powerful of all means of persuasion. Three variables contribute to a speaker's ethos: expertness, credibility, and forcefulness. If a speaker is knowledgeable in his subject field, honest and objective in his arguments, and dynamic in his presentation, his listeners will regard his ethos as favorable and will more readily be persuaded by his reasoning. On the other hand, if his knowledge of his topic is shallow or his delivery lacklustre or his credibility uncertain he cannot communicate efficaciously with his audience.

A speaker must have a clear understanding of what he wants to say. He cannot encode a message clearly unless he has a definite picture in his mind that he wants to transfer to others. If he has no image or only a vague one, his listeners can form at best only a vague image of what he is talking about or, more likely, none at all. If he has a definite, thorough understanding, there is a greater likelihood, though no assurance, that he will be able to transfer this understanding to his hearers. The image formed in their mind will not be precisely the same as his because words do not evoke exactly the same meanings as a result of differences in experiential backgrounds. It may, however, be a close approximation.

The range of a speaker's vocabulary and the precision with which he uses words affects the comprehension of his listeners. An extensive vocabulary is typical of executives and all successful persons, even those with limited schooling. A study of 100 major executives who were presidents or vice-presidents of successful companies shows that they scored higher on a

150-item college vocabulary test with a mean score of 143 than engineering college graduates (120), academic college graduates (129), and college professors (142).[11] Large vocabularies characterize outstanding men and women in every field because words are the instruments by which people grasp the thoughts of others and with which they do much of their own thinking. There appears to be a positive relationship between verbal and intellectual ability.

The medium. The medium or channel is the means through which a sender transmits a message. It includes spoken words (which are actually disturbances in the air caused by vibration of the vocal cords), gestures, facial expressions, printed messages, and so on. Breakdowns may occur because of mechanical deficiencies resulting in noise, distortion, or indistinctness, or the medium may be inappropriate for the message or audience. Face-to-face communication is more effective than written communication. A speaker who is physically present or seen on TV is more effective than an unseen speaker on radio. Radio has a dulling effect on mental processes.

Although the relative merits of group discussion and lecture as communication channels have been the subject of considerable research, the findings are inconclusive. There is some evidence that both group discussion and lecture are equally effective in disseminating information and concepts but that group discussion is more effective in transmitting attitudes and values.

In the past, organizations operating on classical principles stressed the importance of the downward flow of orders through formal channels, minimized lateral communication, and ignored upward communication. Nowadays organizations recognize the importance of establishing communication channels for the downward, lateral, and upward flow of information. Upward communication is essential because it gives an administrator an understanding of conditions faced by operatives at every level. Moreover, it reveals employee needs, provides information for decision-making, and shows whether orders have been understood and carried out. For these reasons an alert administrator is not satisfied with creating channels for the upward flow of information; he actively encourages their use.

The message. School administrators sometimes employ so much jargon and abstract language in speaking to lay audiences that their listeners have difficulty understanding what they are saying.

---

[11] O'Connor, Johnson, *Psychometrics,* Cambridge, Mass.: Harvard University Press, 1934, pp. xvii-xxii.

Jargon is the specialized vocabulary of an occupation. All occupations and professions use terms not familiar to the general population. Journalists speak of datelines, which have nothing to do with dates. Yachtsmen refer to mainsheets, which have nothing to do with sails. Computer technicians refer to bits, which have nothing to do with fragments. The use of such terminology is legitimate when communicating with specialists in the same field but not with persons who do not have the same specialized background.

The term "pedaguese" has been coined to refer humorously to the specialized vocabulary of education. The meaning of such terms as *motivation, frame of reference, norms, reference groups, values clarification,* and *differentiated staffing* may be clear to teachers and administrators but not to parents and other citizens.

Abstract terms may also impede communication. Some words refer to specific objects or referents which can be perceived by the senses; for example, pencil, typewriter, telephone, desk, radio, stapler. These naming words are the first dimension of language. Others cannot be sensed because they are abstractions; for instance, justice, patriotism, goodness, democracy. These constitute the second dimension of language.

To put it differently: some words stand for things, and some words stand for other words. Boots, the name you give your cat, stands for a specific cat; its referent may be seen and felt. *Principle* stands for other words; its referent is not perceivable by the senses.

An abstraction is a statement of common qualities in a number of discrete events or objects. It is a verbal shortcut, a convenience. Much of our oral and written language is abstract. Without abstract language we could not generalize or show relationships.

Abstractions can be classified on several levels depending on their closeness to the sense data they symbolize. Boots, your cat, is at a lower level of abstraction than *feline*, which refers to a class of animals of which Boots is a member. *Animal* is a still higher level of abstraction and *living thing* is higher still.

Hayakawa's abstraction ladder, based on a diagram by Alfred Korzybski, illustrates the different levels of abstraction. (Figure 3)

At the lowest level Bessie is a whirling mass of electrons whose number is uncountable. She cannot be known in her totality even by the most modern scientific instruments, but even if, at a particular moment, all the elec-

ABSTRACTION LADDER

Start reading from the bottom UP

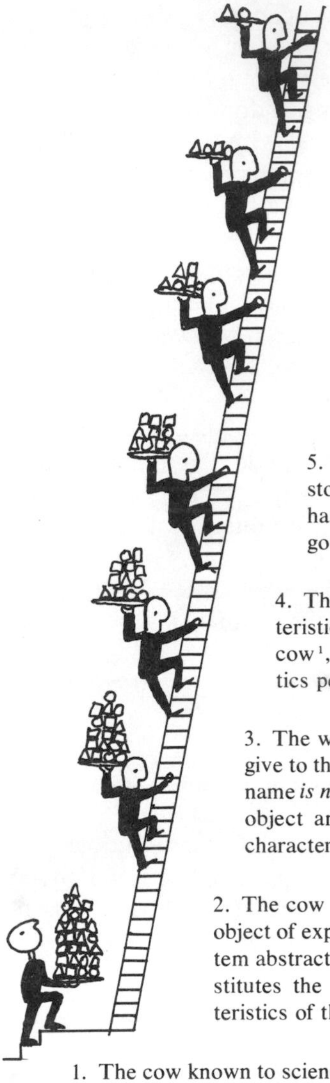

8. "wealth"

8. The word "wealth" is at an extremely high level of abstraction, omitting *almost* all reference to the characteristics of Bessie.

7. "asset"

7. When Bessie is referred to as an "asset," still more of her characteristics are left out.

6. "farm assets"

6. When Bessie is included among "farm assets," reference is made only to what she has in common with all other salable items on the farm.

5. "livestock"

5. When Bessie is referred to as "livestock," only those characteristics she has in common with pigs, chickens, goats, etc., are referred to.

4. "cow"

4. The word "cow" stands for the characteristics we have abstracted as common to cow^{1}, cow^{2}, cow^{3} . . . cow$_{n}$. Characteristics peculiar to specific cows are left out.

3. "Bessie"

3. The word "Bessie"(cow^{1}) is the *name* we give to the object of perception of level 2. The name *is not* the object; it merely *stands for* the object and omits reference to many of the characteristics of the object.

2.

2. The cow we perceive is not the word, but the object of experience, that which our nervous system abstracts (selects) from the totality that constitutes the process-cow. Many of the characteristics of the process-cow are left out.

1. The cow known to science ultimately consists of atoms, electrons, etc., according to present-day scientific inference. Characteristics (represented by circles) are infinite at this level and everchanging. This is the *process level*.

Figure 3

THE ABSTRACTION LADDER

Adapted from S. I. Hayakawa, *Language in Thought and Action*, New York: Harcourt Brace Jovanovich, 1972, p. 153.

trons could be counted and their movements precisely described, at the next moment Bessie would have changed so that the description would no longer be exact.

The Bessie that presents herself to our senses is only a part of the totality. We observe her shape, size, color, and other external features, and because of her resemblance to other similar objects we have known, we label this object of our experience *cow*. At the lowest level of abstraction Bessie's characteristics were infinite; at the second level we omitted some of these characteristics. At the third level we omit still more, and so on as we go up the ladder. In other words, we progressively abstract differences and select only similarities. At the topmost rung of the ladder, "wealth", nearly all of Bessie's characteristics have been omitted.

We cannot avoid using abstractions but we must be aware that we are using them and we must make their referents unmistakably clear to our listeners so that they know what we are talking about. *Progressive education* may mean one thing to a speaker and another to his audience so that in effect they are not considering the same thing. A speaker can reduce the possibility of misunderstanding by citing specific instances, drawing comparisons, and — when possible — by actual demonstrations. Perhaps the best way to define *open classroom* would be to show one in action and to compare it with a traditional self-contained classroom in action.

Feedback or the reactions and responses of listeners is an invaluable means of checking upon listeners' comprehension. By feedback a speaker can determine whether he is communicating accurately and whether he needs to adapt his content and delivery to secure better understanding. By encouraging questions and discussion he can discover whether he has communicated what he intended to.

The listener. Successful oral communication depends on the listener as much as the speaker.

Until about 25 years ago it was generally assumed that everyone knew how to listen but research has since shown that poor listening habits are common. The average person listening to a ten-minute talk listens at a 25 percent efficiency level. Fortunately, this level can be substantially improved by training.[12] Since the training of school teachers and administrators and other oververbalized professionals is mainly in speaking and only rarely

[12] Nichols, Ralph, "Unto You That Hear," New York State Education, March 1969, pp. 16-44.

in listening, a serious effort to improve listening habits may be professionally and personally advantageous.

Listening is not hearing. Nor is it remaining silent while rehearsing in your mind what you are going to say when you get a conversational opening, or looking for errors in the other fellow's arguments so that you can demolish him when he stops talking. Hearing is a passive act. Listening is an active process, a strenuous intellectual exercise. It means putting yourself in another person's place, seeing a situation from his point of view, and grasping his opinions and reasons for them. It entails differentiating between fact and opinion, separating examples from the points they illustrate, perceiving the evidence offered in support of a contention, seeing relationships between ideas, and summarizing from time to time in your own words to check on your understanding of what has been said.

Concentration in listening is difficult because of the differential in speed between thinking and speaking. The usual conversational rate of speaking is about 125 words a minute. A public speaker in front of an audience slows down to 100 words a minute. But research shows that we can think at a rate of more than 400 words a minute. The lag between speech and thought invites daydreaming, woolgathering, and tangential thinking. Listeners attend in spurts to what a speaker is saying because they can think four to seven times faster than he speaks.

A speaker can use several techniques to help listeners understand him easily. He keeps his speeches brief because he is aware of the short attention span of most audiences. He does not try to deal with more than three or four main ideas in any talk. He clarifies his points with specific examples, summarizes from time to time, and reads the facial expressions and postures of his audience to determine whether he is getting his message across. Most important of all, he encourages feedback, particularly in the form of questions and objections, to find out whether he needs to clarify what he has said.

An authority on listening, Ralph G. Nichols, has enumerated what he considers to be the ten worst listening habits of the American people.[13]

1. ***Calling the subject uninteresting.*** A poor listener tunes out a speaker because the subject is dull. A good listener tunes in to find out what he can use.
2. ***Criticizing a speaker's delivery.*** A good listener recognizes that the message is ten times as important as its delivery.

[13] Ibid. (Adapted.)

3. ***Getting over-stimulated.*** A good listener is not a snap-judgment maker. He wants to fully understand a proposition before deciding to accept or reject it.
4. ***Listening only for the facts.*** A good listener listens for the central ideas which give sense and system to a discourse. The central ideas limit and control facts.
5. ***Trying to make an outline out of everything.*** A good listener outlines a speech only if the speaker is carefully organized. He adjusts his note-taking pattern to the pattern the speaker is following.
6. ***Faking attention to the speaker.*** A good listener is not relaxed and passive. He has tensions within him that can only be resolved by getting the ideas the speaker is trying to convey.
7. ***Tolerating or creating distractions in the audience.*** A good listener is intolerant of noise created by those around him. He shows his disapproval of distracting conversation.
8. ***Evading difficult material.*** A good listener subjects himself to uncomfortably tough listening.
9. ***Letting emotion-laden words get between the listener and speaker.*** A good listener does not black out because a speaker uses words with unpleasant connotations.
10. ***Wasting the differential between speech speed and thought speed.*** A good listener anticipates a speaker's next point — he runs ahead of him mentally. He identifies what he has for evidence and he recapitulates periodically as he listens.

SELECTED READINGS

Condon Jr., John C., *Semantics and Communication,* 2nd ed., New York: Macmillan, 1975.

A brief introduction to the study of semantics, including such topics as signs and symbols, symbolic transformation, abstracting, instrumental and affective communication, catharsis, magic, and ritual, all discussed in a lively style with up-to-the-minute examples.

Fabun, Don, *Communications: The Transfer of Meaning,* Beverly Hills, Cal.: Glencoe Press, 1968.

A brief, profusely illustrated pamphlet which introduces readers to the meaning of communication and some of the problems of transferring ideas and feelings from one person to another. The author wears his scholarship lightly.

Hayakawa, S. I., *Language and Thought in Action,* New York: Harcourt Brace Jovanovich, 1972.

A justifiably popular introduction to semantics aiming to help people "to think more clearly, to speak and write more effectively, and to listen and read with greater understanding." Combines sound scholarship with an engaging style.

Leavitt, Harold J., *Managerial Psychology,* rev. ed., Chicago: University of Chicago Press, 1964.

Three chapters discuss communication in an organizational setting. Chapter 15: Communication networks, which affect the way groups solve problems. Chapter 16: What information ought to be transmitted over a particular network. Chapter 17: The operating problems of committees and small groups.

Mehrabian, Albert, *Silent Messages,* Belmont, Cal.: Wadsworth Publishing Co., 1971.

A novel approach to the profound and often overlooked contribution of nonverbal behavior to the process of communication. Discusses the conventions that underlie nonverbal communication and convey varying degrees of like-dislike, dominance or status, and responsiveness.

Nichols, Ralph G. and Stevens, Leonard, *Are You Listening?,* New York: McGraw-Hill, 1957.

The authors first show how we listen and how inefficient listening is usually the result of poor habits of concentration. Then they apply their findings to methods of improving listening and communication efficiency. The text includes exercises to develop good listening habits.

TOPICS FOR DISCUSSION

1. By describing one or more situations, show that when there is a conflict between spoken words and body language, we give greater credence to the latter.

2. By citing examples, show that time, color, dress, and space may convey meaning.

3. There is no necessary connection between symbol and thing, yet confusion between the two is not uncommon. Give evidence in support of this statement.

4. Why is feedback important in teaching? In administration?

5. A speaker may be a cause of a communication breakdown because his ethos is viewed as unfavorable by his audience, or because he has no clear picture in his mind of what he wants to say, or because his vocabulary is too limited. These are only three ways. Can you mention others?

6. Marshall McLuhan has said that the medium is the message. Explain. (cf. Marshall McLuhan, *Understanding Media,* New York: Signet Books, 1964, Chapter 1.)

7. List several examples of educational jargon.

8. From an article on education written for a lay audience, point out high level abstractions which might adversely affect comprehension.

9. Arrange the following words in order of increasing abstraction, starting at the bottom of the abstraction ladder.
   a. Human being, capitalist, creature, Henry Ford, man, inventor.
   b. Motion picture, Gone With The Wind, production, entertainment, business enterprise.

10. Administer one or more listening exercises from *Are You Listening* by Nichols and Stevens to the class and discuss the results.

11. Observe the nonverbal communicative aspects of a conversation between a school administrator or supervisor and a teacher. Orally report on your observations.

12. Try to explain orally any communication model without using nonverbal communication. Is it possible to perform this exercise?

DEALING WITH BREAKDOWNS IN COMMUNICATION — INTERPERSONAL AND INTERGROUP

By
Carl R. Rogers

It is hypothesized that the major barrier to mutual interpersonal communication is a natural tendency to approve or disapprove the statements of others. The tendency is heightened in emotional situations.

Real communication occurs when we listen with understanding — when we see an idea or attitude from the other person's point of view. This approach has been found extremely potent in the field of psychotherapy.

The chances are great that our listening has not been of the type described. An experiment is suggested to test the quality of understanding.

If this approach were widely practiced, it would have far-reaching results.

I would like to propose, as an hypothesis for consideration, that the major barrier to mutual interpersonal communication is our very natural tendency to judge, to evaluate, to approve or disapprove, the statement of the other person, or the other group. Let me illustrate my meaning with some very simple examples. As you leave the meeting tonight, one of the statements you are likely to hear is, "I didn't like that man's talk." Now what do you respond? Almost invariably your reply will be either approval or disapproval of the attitude expressed. Either you respond, "I didn't either. I thought it was terrible," or else you tend to reply, "Oh, I thought it was really good." In other words, your primary reaction is to evaluate what has just been said to you, to evaluate it from *your* point of view, your own frame of reference.

Or take another example. Suppose I say with some feeling, "I think the Republicans are behaving in ways that show a lot of good sound sense these days," what is the response that arises in your mind as you listen? The overwhelming likelihood is that it will be evaluative. You will find yourself agreeing, or disagreeing, or making some judgment about me such as "He

---

"Dealing With Breakdowns in Communication — Interpersonal and Intergroup," reprinted from "On Becoming a Person", by Carl R. Rogers. Copyright © 1961 by Carl R. Rogers. Used by permission of Houghton Mifflin Company.

must be a conservative,'' or ''He seems solid in his thinking.'' Or let us take an illustration from the international scene. Russia says vehemently, ''The treaty with Japan is a war plot on the part of the United States.'' We rise as one person to say ''That's a lie!''

This last illustration brings in another element connected with my hypothesis. Although the tendency to make evaluations is common in almost all interchange of language, it is very much heightened in those situations where feelings and emotions are deeply involved. So the stronger our feelings the more likely it is that there will be no mutual element in the communication. There will be just two ideas, two feelings, two judgments, missing each other in psychological space. I'm sure you recognize this from your own experience. When you have not been emotionally involved yourself, and have listened to a heated discussion, you often go away thinking, ''Well, they actually weren't talking about the same thing.'' And they were not. Each was making a judgment, an evaluation, from his own frame of reference. There was really nothing which could be called communication in any genuine sense. This tendency to react to any emotionally meaningful statement by forming an evaluation of it from our own point of view, is I repeat, the major barrier to interpersonal communication.

But is there any way of solving this problem, of avoiding this barrier? I feel that we are making exciting progress toward this goal and I would like to present it as simply as I can. Real communication occurs, and this evaluative tendency is avoided, when we listen with understanding. What does this mean? It means to see the expressed idea and attitude from the other person's point of view, to sense how it feels to him, to achieve his frame of reference in regard to the thing he is talking about.

Stated so briefly, this may sound absurdly simple, but it is not. It is an approach which we have found extremely potent in the field of psychotherapy. It is the most effective agent we know, for altering the basic personality structure of an individual, and improving his relationships and his communications with others. If I can listen to what he can tell me, if I can understand how it seems to him, if I can see its personal meaning for him, if I can sense the emotional flavor which it has for him, then I will be releasing potent forces of change in him. If I can really understand how he hates his father, or hates the university, or hates communists — if I can catch the flavor of his fear of insanity, or his fear of atom bombs, or of Russia — it will be of the greatest help to him in altering those very hatreds and fears, and in establishing realistic and harmonious relationships with the very people and situations toward which he has felt hatred and fear. We know from our research that such empathic understanding — understanding *with* a person, not *about* him — is such an effective approach that it can bring about major changes in personality.

Some of you may be feeling that you listen well to people, and that you have never seen such results. The chances are very great indeed that your listening has not been of the type I have described. Fortunately I can suggest a little laboratory experiment which you can try to test the quality of your understanding. The next time you get into an argument with your wife, or your friend, or with a small group of friends, just stop the discussion for a moment and for an experiment, institute this rule. "Each person can speak up for himself only *after* he has first restated the ideas and feelings of the previous speaker accurately, and to that speaker's satisfaction." You see what this would mean. It would simply mean that before presenting your own point of view, it would be necessary for you to really achieve the other speaker's frame of reference — to understand his thoughts and feelings so well that you could summarize them for him. Sounds simple, doesn't it? But if you try it you will discover it is one of the most difficult things you have ever tried to do. However, once you have been able to see the other's point of view, your own comments will have to be drastically revised. You will also find the emotion going out of the discussion, the differences being reduced, and those differences which remain being of a rational and understandable sort.

Can you imagine what this kind of an approach would mean if it were projected into larger areas? What would happen to a labor-management dispute if it was conducted in such a way that labor, without necessarily agreeing, could accurately state management's point of view in a way that management could accept; and management, without approving labor's stand, could state labor's case in a way that labor agreed was accurate? It would mean that real communication was established, and one could practically guarantee that some reasonable solution would be reached.

QUESTIONS

1. Cite an instance from your own experience to illustrate the natural tendency to approve or disapprove the statements of other individuals or groups. How was communication affected?

2. In the midst of a class discussion, your instructor will stop the exchange of opinions for a moment and institute the rule that no one may speak until he has first restated the ideas and feelings of the previous speaker accurately and to his satisfaction. Observe the consequences.

SERIAL COMMUNICATION OF INFORMATION IN ORGANIZATIONS

By
William V. Haney

Much of the communication that occurs in organizations consists of serial transmissions — that is, messages which flow up or down the organizational chain or along informal organizational lines. Serial transmissions are especially susceptible to distortion and disruption.

The motives of communicators which influence a serial transmission include the desire to simplify the message, to convey a sensible message, and to make the conveyance of the message pleasant.

The assumptions of communicators which influence a serial transmission include the assumption that words are used in only one way and that inferences are always distinguishable from observations.

As a consequence of these motives and assumptions, details are omitted, altered, or added.

Ten suggestions are offered for improving serial transmissions.

An appreciable amount of the communication which occurs in business, industry, hospitals, military units, government agencies — in short, in chain-of-command organizations — consists of serial transmissions. *A* communicates a message to *B*; *B* then communicates *A*'s message (or rather his *interpretation* of *A*'s message) to *C*; *C* then communicates his interpretation of *B*'s interpretation of *A*'s message to *D*; and so on. The originator and the ultimate recipient of the message[1] are separated by "middle men."

"The message" may often be passed down (but not necessarily all the way down) the organization chain, as when in business the chairman acting on behalf of the board of directors may express a desire to the president.

[1] "The message," as already suggested, is a misnomer in that what is being conveyed is not static, unchanging, and fixed. I shall retain the term for convenience, however, and use quotation marks to signify that its dynamic nature is subject to cumulative change.

"Serial Communication of Information in Organizations," by William V. Haney, reprinted from "Concepts and Issues in Administrative Behavior", by Sidney Mailick and Edward H. Van Ness. Copyright © 1962, pp. 150-165. Reprinted by permission of Prentice-Hall, Inc., Englewood Cliffs, New Jersey.

"The message" begins to fan out as the president, in turn, relays "it" to his vice presidents; they convey "it" to their respective subordinates; and so forth. Frequently "a message" goes up (but seldom all the way up) the chain. Sometimes "it" travels laterally. Sometimes, as with rumors, "it" disregards the formal organization and flows more closely along informal organizational lines.

Regardless of its direction, the number of "conveyors" involved, and the degree of its conformance with the formal structure, serial transmission is clearly an essential, inevitable form of communication in organizations. It is equally apparent that serial transmission is especially susceptible to distortion and disruption. Not only is it subject to the shortcomings and maladies of "simple" person-to-person communication but, since it consists of a series of such communications, the anomalies are often *compounded*.

This is not to say, however, that serial transmissions in organizations should be abolished or even decreased. We wish to show that such communications *can be improved* if communicators are able (1) to recognize some of the patterns of miscommunication which occur in serial transmissions; (2) to understand some of the factors contributing to these patterns; (3) to take measures and practice techniques for preventing the recurrence of these patterns and for ameliorating their consequences.

I shall begin by cataloguing some of the factors which seemingly influence a serial transmission.[2]

MOTIVES OF THE COMMUNICATORS

When *B* conveys *A*'s message to *C* he may be influenced by at least

[2] During the past three years I have conducted scores of informal experiments with groups of university undergraduate and graduate students, business and government executives, military officers, professionals, and so on. I would read the "message" (below) to the first "conveyor." He would then relay his interpretation to the second conveyor who, in turn, would pass along his interpretation to the third, etc. The sixth (and final member of the "team") would listen to "the message" and then write down his version of it. These final versions were collected and compared with the original.

Every year at State University, the eagles in front of the Psi Gamma fraternity house were mysteriously sprayed during the night. Whenever this happened, it cost the Psi Gams from $75 to $100 to have the eagles cleaned. The Psi Gams complained to officials and were promised by the president that if ever any students were caught painting the eagles, they would be expelled from school.*

*Adapted from "Chuck Jackson" by Diana Conzett, which appears in Irving J. Lee's *Customs and Crises in Communication* (New York: Harper & Bros., 1954), p. 245. Reprinted by permission.

three motives of which he may be largely unaware.

The desire to simplify the message

We evidently dislike conveying detailed messages. The responsibility of passing along complex information is burdensome and taxing. Often, therefore, we unconsciously simplify the message before passing it along to the next person.[3] It is very probable that among the details most susceptible to omission are those we already knew or in some way presume our recipients will know without our telling them.

The desire to convey a "sensible" message

Apparently we are reluctant to relay a message that is somehow incoherent, illogical, or incomplete. It may be embarrassing to admit that one does not fully understand the message he is conveying. When he receives a message that does not quite make sense to him he is prone to "make sense out of it" before passing it along to the next person.[4]

The desire to make the conveyance of the message as pleasant and/or painless as possible for the conveyor

We evidently do not like to have to tell the boss unpleasant things. Even when not directly responsible, one does not relish the reaction of his superior to a disagreeable message. This motive probably accounts for a considerable share of the tendency for a "message" to lose its harshness as it moves up the organizational ladder. The first line supervisor may tell his foreman, "I'm telling you, Mike, the men say that if this pay cut goes through they'll strike — and they mean it!" By the time "this message" has been relayed through six or eight or more echelons (if indeed it goes that far) the executive vice president might express it to the president as, "Well, sir, the men seem a little concerned over the projected wage reduction but I am confident that they will take it in stride."

---

[3] On an arbitrary count basis the stimulus message used in the serial transmission demonstrations described in footnote 2 contained 24 "significant details." The final versions contained a mean count of approximately 8 "significant details" — a "detail loss" of 65%.

[4] The great majority (approximately 93%) of the final versions (from the serial transmission demonstrations) made "sense." Even those which were the most bizarre and bore the least resemblance to the original stimulus were in and of themselves internally consistent and coherent.

For example,

"At a State University there was an argument between two teams — the Eagles and the Fire Gems in which their clothing was torn."

"The Eagles in front of the university had parasites and were sprayed with insecticide."

"At State U. they have many birds which desecrate the buildings. To remedy the situation they expelled the students who fed the birds."

One of the dangers plaguing some upper managements is that they are effectively shielded from incipient problems until they become serious and costly ones.

ASSUMPTIONS OF THE COMMUNICATORS

In addition to the serial transmitter's motives we must consider his assumptions — particularly those he makes about his communications. If some of these assumptions are fallacious and if one is unaware that he holds them, his communication can be adversely affected. The following are, in this writer's judgment, two of the most pervasive and dangerous of the current myths about communication:

The assumption that words are used in only one way

A study[5] indicates that for the 500 most commonly used words in our language there are 14,070 different dictionary definitions — over 28 usages per word, on the average. Take the word *run*, for example:

Babe Ruth scored a *run*.
Did you ever see Jesse Owens *run*?
I have a *run* in my stocking.
There is a fine *run* of salmon this year.
Are you going to *run* this company or am I?
You have the *run* of the place.
Don't give me the *run* around.
What headline do you want to *run*?
There was a *run* on the bank today.
Did he *run* the ship aground?
I have to *run* (drive the car) downtown.
Who will *run* for President this year?
Joe flies the New York-Chicago *run* twice a week.
You know the kind of people they *run* around with.
The apples *run* large this year.
Please *run* my bath-water.

We could go on at some length — my small abridged dictionary gives eighty-seven distinct usages for *run*. I have chosen an extreme example, of course, but there must be relatively few words (excepting some technical terms) used in one and in only one sense.

---

[5]Lydia Strong, "Do You Know How to Listen?" *Effective Communication on the Job*, Dooher and Marquis, eds. (New York: American Management Association, 1956), p. 28.

Yet communicators often have a curious notion about words *when they are using them*, i.e., when they are speaking, writing, listening, or reading. It is immensely easy for a "sender" of a communication to assume that words are used in only one way — the way he intends them. It is just as enticing for the "receiver" to assume that the sender intended his words as he, the receiver, happens to interpret them at the moment. When communicators are unconsciously burdened by the assumption of the mono-usage of words they are prone to become involved in the pattern of miscommunication known as *bypassing*.

> A foreman told a machine operator he was passing: "Better clean up around here." It was ten minutes later when the foreman's assistant phoned: "Say, boss, isn't that bearing Sipert is working on due up in engineering pronto?"
>
> "You bet your sweet life it is. Why?"
>
> "He says you told him to drop it and sweep the place up. I thought I'd better make sure."
>
> "Listen," the foreman flared into thephone, "get him right back on that job. It's got to be ready in twenty minutes."
>
> . . . What the foreman had in mind was for Sipert to gather up the oily waste, which was a fire and accident hazard. This would not have taken more than a couple of minutes, and there would have been plenty of time to finish the bearing.[6]

Bypassing: Denotative and Connotative. Since we use words to express at least two kinds of meanings there can be two kinds of bypassings. Suppose you say to me, "Your neighbor's grass is certainly green and healthy looking, isn't it?" You could be intending your words merely to *denote*, i.e., to point to or to call my attention, to the appearance of my neighbor's lawn. On the other hand, you could have intended your words to *connote*, i.e., to imply something beyond or something other than what you were ostensibly denoting. You might have meant any number of things: that my own lawn needed more care; that my neighbor was inordinately meticulous about his lawn; that my neighbor's lawn is tended by a professional, a service you do not have and for which you envy or despise my neighbor; or even that his grass was not green at all but, on the contrary, parched and diseased; and so forth.

---

[6] Reprinted from *The Foreman's Letter* with permission of National Foremen's Institute, New London, Conn.

Taking these two kinds of meanings into account it is clear that bypassing occurs or can occur under anyof four conditions:

1. *When the sender intends one denotation while the receiver interprets another*. (As in the case of Sipert and his foreman.)
2. *When the sender intends one connotation while the receiver interprets another*.

   A friend once told me of an experience she had had years ago when as a teenager she was spending the week with a maiden aunt. Joan had gone to the movies with a young man who brought her home at a respectable hour. However, the couple lingered on the front porch somewhat longer than Aunt Mildred thought necessary. The little old lady was rather proud of her ability to deal with younger people so she slipped out of bed, raised her bedroom window, and called down sweetly, "If you two knew how pleasant it is in bed, you wouldn't be standing out there in the cold."
3. *When the sender intends only a denotation while the receiver interprets a connotation*.

   For a brief period the following memorandum appeared on the bulletin boards of a government agency in Washington:

   > *Those department and section heads who do not have secretaries assigned to them may take advantage of the stenographers in the secretarial pool*.
4. *When the sender intends a connotation while the receiver interprets a denotation only*.

   Before making his final decision on a proposal to move to new offices, the head of a large company called his top executives for a last discussion of the idea. All were enthusiastic except the company treasurer who insisted that he had not had time to calculate all the costs with accuracy sufficient to satisfy himself that the move was advantageous. Annoyed by his persistence, the chief finally burst out:

   "All right, Jim, all right! Figure it out to the last cent. A penny saved is a penny earned, right?"

   The intention was ironic. He meant not what the words denoted but the opposite — forget this and stop being petty. For him this was what his words connoted.

   For the treasurer "penny saved, penny earned" meant exactly what it said. He put several members on his staff to work on the problem and, to test the firmness of the price, had one of them interview the agent renting the proposed new quarters without explaining whom he represented. This indication of additional interest in the premises led the agent to raise the rent. Not until the lease was signed, did the agency discover that one of its own employes had, in effect, bid up its price.[7]

The assumption that inferences are always distinguishable from observations

It is incredibly difficult, at times, for a communicator (or anyone) to discriminate between what he "knows" (i.e., what he has actually observed — seen, heard, read, etc.) and what he is only inferring or guessing. One of the key reasons for this lies in the character of the language used to express observations and inferences.

Suppose you look at a man and observe that he is wearing a white shirt and then say, "That man is wearing a white shirt." Assuming your vision and the illumination were "normal" you would have made a statement of *observation* — a statement which directly corresponded to and was corroborated by your observation. But suppose you now say, "That man bought the white shirt he is wearing." Assuming you were not present when and if the man bought the shirt that statement would be *for you a statement of inference*. Your statement went *beyond* what you observed. You inferred that the man bought the shirt; you did not observe it. Of course, your inference may be correct (but it could be false: perhaps he was given the shirt as a gift; perhaps he stole it or borrowed it; etc.).

Nothing in the nature of our language (the grammar, spelling, pronunciation, accentuation, syntax, inflection, etc.) prevents you from speaking or writing (or thinking) a statement of inference *as if* you were making a statement of observation. Our language permits you to say "Of course, he bought the shirt" with certainty and finality, i.e., with as much confidence as you would make a statement of observation. The effect is that it becomes exceedingly easy to confuse the two kinds of statements and also to confuse inference and observation on nonverbal levels. The destructive consequences of acting upon inference as if acting upon observation can range from mild embarrassment to tragedy. One factual illustration may be sufficient to point up the dangers of such behavior.

The case of Jim Blake[8]

Jim Blake, 41, had been with the Hasting Co. for ten years. For the last seven years he had served as an "inside salesman," receiving phone

[7] Robert Froman, "Make Words Fit the Job," *Nation's Business* (July 1959), p. 78. Reprinted by permission.

[8] The names have been changed.

calls from customers and writing out orders. "Salesman," in this case, was somewhat of a euphemism as the customer ordinarily knew what he wanted and was prepared to place an order. The "outside salesmen," on the other hand, visited industrial accounts and enjoyed considerably more status and income. Blake had aspired to an outside position for several years but no openings had occurred. He had, however, been assured by Russ Jenkins, sales manager, that as senior inside man he would be given first chance at the next available outside job.

Finally, it seemed as if Jim's chance had come. Harry Strom, 63, one of the outside men, had decided in January to retire on the first of June. It did not occur to Jenkins to reassure Blake that the new opening was to be his. Moreover, Blake did not question Jenkins because he felt his superior should take the initiative.

As the months went by Blake became increasingly uneasy. Finally, on May 15 he was astonished to see Strom escorting a young man into Jenkins' office. Although the door was closed Blake could hear considerable laughing inside. After an hour the three emerged from the office and Jenkins shook hands with the new man saying, "Joe, I'm certainly glad you're going to be with us. With Harry showing you around his territory you're going to get a good start at the business." Strom and the new man left and Jenkins returned to his office.

Blake was infuriated. He was convinced that the new man was being groomed for Strom's position. Now he understood why Jenkins had said nothing to him. He angrily cleaned out his desk, wrote a bitter letter of resignation and left it on his desk, and stomped out of the office.

Suspecting the worst for several months, Blake was quite unable to distinguish what he had inferred from what he had actually observed. The new man, it turned out, was being hired to work as an inside salesman — an opening which was to be occasioned by Blake's moving into the outside position. Jenkins had wanted the new man to get the "feel" of the clientele and thus had requested Strom to take him along for a few days as Strom made his calls.

TRENDS IN SERIAL TRANSMISSION

These assumptions,[9] the mono-usage of words, and the inference-observation confusion, as well as the aforementioned motives of the com-

[9] For a more detailed analysis of these assumptions and for additional methods for preventing and correcting their consequences, see William V. Haney, *Communication: Patterns and Incidents* (Homewood, Ill.: Irwin, 1960), chs. III, IV, V.

municators, undoubtedly contribute a significant share of the difficulties and dangers which beset a serial transmission. Their effect tends to be manifested by three trends: omission, alteration, and addition.

Details become omitted

It requires less effort to convey a simpler, less complex message. With fewer details to transmit the fear of forgetting or of garbling the message is decreased. In the serial transmissions even those final versions which most closely approximated the original had omitted an appreciable number of details.

> There are Eagles in front of the frat house at the State University.
> It costs $75 to $100 to remove paint each year from the eagles.

The essential question, perhaps, is which details *will be retained?* Judging from interviewing the serial transmitters after the demonstrations these aspects will *not* be dropped out:

1. those details the transmitter wanted or expected to hear.
2. those details which "made sense" to the transmitter.
3. those details which seemed important *to the transmitter*.
4. those details which for various and inexplicable reasons seemed to stick with the transmitter — those aspects which seemed particularly unusual or bizarre; those which had special significance to him; etc.

Details become altered

When changes in detail occurred in the serial transmissions it was often possible to pinpoint the "changers." When asked to explain why they had changed the message most were unaware that they had done so. However, upon retrospection some admitted that they had changed the details in order to simplify the message, "clarify it," "straighten it out," "make it more sensible," and the like. It became evident, too, that among the details most susceptible to change were the qualifications, the indefinite. Inferential statements are prone to become definite and certain. What may start out as "The boss seemed angry this morning" may quickly progress to "The boss was angry."

A well-known psychologist once "planted" a rumor in an enlisted men's mess hall on a certain Air Force base. His statement was: "Is it true that they are building a tunnel big enough to trundle B-52's to — (the town two miles away)?" Twelve hours later the rumor came back to him as: "They are building a tunnel to trundle B-52's to — ." The "Is-it-true" uncertainty had been dropped. So had the indefinite purpose ("big enough to").

It became obvious upon interviewing the serial transmitters that bypassing (denotative and connotative) had also played a role. For example, the "president" in the message about the "eagles" was occasionally bypassed as the "President of the U.S." and sometimes the rest of the message was constructed around this detail.

> The White House was in such a mess that they wanted to renovate it but found that the cost would be $100 to $75 to paint the eagle so they decided not to do it.

Details become added

Not infrequently details are added to the message to "fill in the gaps," "to make better sense," and "because I thought the fellow who told it to me left something out."

The psychologist was eventually told that not only were they building a tunnel for B-52's but that a mile-long underground runway was being constructed at the end of it! The runway was to have a ceiling slanting upward so that a plane could take off, fly up along the ceiling and emerge from an inconspicuous slit at the end of the cavern! This, he admitted, was a much more "sensible" rumor than the one he had started, for the town had no facilities for take-offs and thus there was nothing which could have been done with the B-52's once they reached the end of the tunnel!

PICTORIAL TRANSMISSION

An interesting facet about serial transmission is that the three trends — omission, alteration, and addition — are also present when the "message" is pictorial as opposed to verbal. Our procedure was to permit the "transmitter" to view the stimulus picture (drawing below) for thirty seconds. He then proceeded to reproduce the picture as accurately as possible from memory. When he finished his drawing he showed it to Transmitter² for thirty seconds, who then attempted to reproduce the first transmitter's drawing from memory, etc. Drawings 1 through 5 represented the work of a fairly typical "team" of five transmitters.

STIMULUS PICTURE

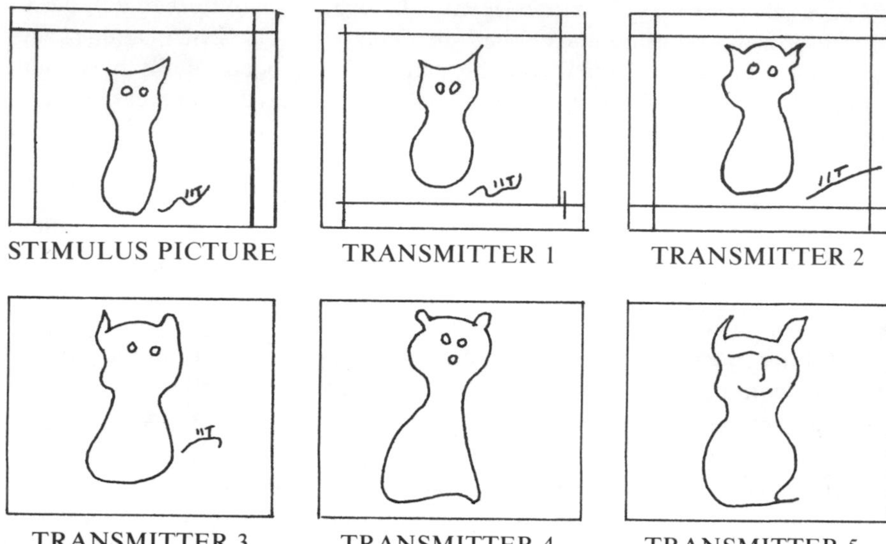

Details Become Omitted. Note the progressive simplification of the configuration in the lower right and the eventual omission of it altogether. Note the omission of the border.

Details Become Altered. The border is an interesting example of alteration. The original border is quite irregular, difficult to remember. Transmitter[1] when interviewed afterward said, "I remembered that the frame was incomplete somehow but couldn't remember just how it was incomplete." Note how indefinitely irregular his border is. So subtle, in fact, that Transmitter[2] said he never recognized it as purposefully asymmetrical. "I thought he was a little careless." Transmitter[2] drew a completely regular border — easy to remember but also easy to fail to notice. Transmitter[3] was surprised afterwards to discover that the drawing he had tried to memorize had had a border. It had apparently seemed so "natural," so much a part of the background, that he had failed to attend to it.

Details Become Added. Transmitter[1] perceived the stimulus picture as a cat and a cat it remained through the series. When shown that he had added a nose Transmitter[4] admitted, "You know, I knew there was something missing from that cat — I knew it had a body, a head, ears, and eyes. I thought it was the mouth that was missing but not the nose." Providing everything *except* a mouth was far too enticing for Transmitter[5]. "I thought the other fellow made a mistake so I corrected it!"

CORRECTIVES[10]

Even serial transmissions, as intricate and as relatively uncontrolled communications as they are, can be improved. The suggestions below are not sensational panaceas. In fact, they are quite commonplace, common sense, but uncommonly used techniques.

1. ***Take notes.*** Less than five percent of the serial transmitters took notes. Some said that they assumed they were not supposed to (no such restriction had been placed upon them) but most admitted that they rarely take notes as a matter of course. In the cases where all transmitters on a team were instructed to take notes the final versions were manifestly more complete and more accurate than those of the non-notetakers.
2. ***Give details in order.*** Organized information is easier to understand and to remember. Choose a sequence (chronological, spatial, deductive, inductive, etc.) appropriate to the content and be consistent with it. For example, it may suit your purpose best to begin with a proposal followed by supporting reasons or to start with the reasons and work toward the proposal. In either case take care to keep proposals and reasons clearly distinguished rather than mixing them together indiscriminately.
3. ***Be wary of bypassing.*** If you are the receiver, query (ask the sender what he meant) and paraphrase (put what you think he said or wrote into your own words and get the sender to check you). These simple techniques are effective yet infrequently practiced, perhaps because we are so positive we *know* what the other fellow means; perhaps because we hesitate to ask or rephrase for fear the other fellow (especially if he is the boss) will think less of us for not understanding the first time. The latter apprehension is usually unfounded, at least if we can accept the remarks of a hundred or more executives questioned on the matter during the last four years. "By all means," they have said almost to a man, "I *want* my people to check with me. The person who wants to be sure he's got it straight has a sense of responsibility and that's the kind of man (or woman) I want on my payroll."

   Although executives, generally, may take this point of view quite sincerely, obviously not all of them practice it. Querying and paraphrasing are *two-way* responsibilities and the sender must be

[10]Most of these suggestions are offered by Irving J. and Laura L. Lee, *Handling Barriers in Communication* (New York: Harper & Bros., 1956), pp. 71-74.

truly approachable by his receivers if the techniques are to be successful.

This check-list may be helpful in avoiding bypassing:

Could he be denoting something other than what I am?
Could he be connoting something other than what I am?
Could he be connoting whereas I am merely denoting?
Could he be merely denoting whereas I am connoting?

4. ***Distinguish between inference and observation.*** Ask yourself sharply: Did I *really* see, hear, or read this — or am I guessing part of it? The essential characteristics of a statement of observation are these:
   1. It can be made only by the observer.
      (What someone tells you as observational is still inferential for you if you did not observe it.)
   2. It can be made only *after* observation.
   3. It stays with what has been observed; does not go beyond it.

   This is not to say that inferential statements are not to be made — we could hardly avoid doing so. But it is important or even vital at times to know *when* we are making them.
5. ***Slow down your oral transmissions.*** By doing so, you give your listener a better opportunity to assimilate complex and detailed information. However, it is possible to speak *too* slowly so as to lose his attention. Since either extreme defeats your purpose, it is generally wise to watch the listener for clues as to the most suitable rate of speech.
6. ***Simplify the message.*** This suggestion is for the *originator* of the message. The "middlemen" often simplify without half trying! Most salesmen realize the inadvisability of attempting to sell too many features at a time. The customer is only confused and is unable to distinguish the key features from those less important. With particular respect to oral transmission, there is impressive evidence to indicate that beyond a point the addition of details leads to disproportionate omission. Evidently, you can add a straw to the camel's back without breaking it, but you run the decided risk of his dropping two straws.
7. ***Use dual media when feasible.*** A message often stands a better chance of getting through if it is reinforced by restatement in another communication medium. Detailed, complex, and unfamiliar information is often transmitted by such combinations as a memo follow-up on a telephone call; a sensory aid (slide, diagram, mockup, picture, etc.) accompanying a written or oral message, etc.
8. ***Highlight the important.*** Presumably the originator of a message knows (or should know) which are its important aspects. But this

does not automatically insure that his serial transmitters will similarly recognize them. There are numerous devices for making salient points stand out as such; e.g., using underscoring, capitals, etc., in writing; using vocal emphasis, attention-drawing phrases ("this is the main point . . .," "here's the crux . . .," "be sure to note this . . ."), etc., in speaking.

9. ***Reduce the number of links in the chain.*** This suggestion has to be followed with discretion. Jumping the chain of command either upward or downward can sometimes have undesirable consequences. However, whenever it is possible to reduce or eliminate the "middlemen," "the message" generally becomes progressively less susceptible to aberrations. Of course, there are methods of skipping links which are commonly accepted and widely practiced. Communication downward can be reduced to person-to-person communication, in a sense, with general memos, letters, bulletins, group meetings, etc. Communication upward can accomplish the same purpose via suggestion boxes, opinion questionnaires, "talk-backs," etc.
10. ***Preview and review.*** A wise speech professor of mine used to say: "Giving a speech is basically very simple if you do it in three steps: First, you tell them what you're going to tell them; then you tell; then, finally, you tell them what you've told them." This three step sequence is often applicable whether the message is transmitted by letter, memo, written or oral report, public address, telephone call, etc.

SUMMARY

After the last suggestion I feel obliged to review this article briefly. We have been concerned with serial transmission — a widespread, essential, and yet susceptible form of communication. Among the factors which vitiate a serial transmission are certain of the communicator's motives and fallacious assumptions. When these and other factors are in play the three processes — omission, alteration, and addition — tend to occur. The suggestions offered for strengthening serial transmission will be more or less applicable, of course, depending upon the communication situation.

An important question remains: What can be done to encourage communicators to practice the techniques? They will probably use them largely to the extent that they think the techniques are needed. But *do* they think them necessary? Apparently many do not. When asked to explain how the final version came to differ so markedly from the original, many of the serial transmitters in my studies were genuinely puzzled. A frequent comment was

"I really can't understand it. All I know is that I passed the message along the same as it came to me." If messages *were* passed along "the same as they came," of course, serial transmission would no longer be a problem. And so long as the illusion of fidelity is with the communicator it is unlikely that he will be prompted to apply some of these simple, prosaic, yet effective techniques to his communicating. Perhaps a first step would be to induce him to question his unwarranted assurance about his communication. The controlled serial transmission experience appears to accomplish this.

QUESTIONS

1. Comment on the ten correctives mentioned in this article. Are any or all of them used in your school or district? Should they be used?

2. Cite an example from your experience in which the final version of a serial communication differed markedly from the original.

INFORMATION, COMMUNICATIONS, AND UNDERSTANDING

By
Peter F. Drucker

Since 1910 much has been learned about information and communications, much of it from seemingly unrelated fields.

Communication is perception, expectations, and involvement. Communication and information are totally different, but information presupposes functioning communications.

Downward communication cannot work because it assumes that the utterer communicates; but communication is the act of the recipient. Listening does not work either because it assumes that subordinates can communicate and because it does not take into account that communications is involvement. Nor does more and better information solve the communications problem.

Communication has to start from the intended recipient rather than from the emitter. Downward communications come after upward communications have been successfully established. The start of communications in organization must be to get the intended recipient himself to try to communicate. Employees or students must share in the responsibility of decisions to the fullest extent.

There will be no communication if it is conceived as going from the "I" to the "Thou." It only works from one member of "us" to the other.

Concern with "information" and "communications" started shortly before World War I. Russell and Whitehead's *Principia Mathematica*, which appeared in 1910, is still one of the foundation books. And a long line of illustrious successors — from Ludwig Wittgenstein through Norbert Wiener and A. N. Chomsky's "mathematical linguistics" today — has continued the work on the *logic* of information. Roughly contemporaneous is

---

Paper read before the Fellows of the International Academy of Management, Tokyo, Japan, October, 1969.

"Information, Communications and Understanding," in *Technology, Management and Society* by Peter F. Drucker. Copyright © 1970 by Peter F. Drucker. Reprinted by permission of Harper & Row, Publishers, Inc.

the interest in the *meaning* of communication; Alfred Korzybski started on the study of "general semantics," i.e., on the meaning of communications, around the turn of the century. It was World War I, however, which made the entire Western world communications-conscious. When the diplomatic documents of 1914 in the German and Russian archives were published, soon after the end of the fighting, it became appallingly clear that the catastrophe had been caused, in large measure, by communications failure despite copious and reliable information. And the war itself — especially the total failure of its one and only strategic concept, Winston Churchill's Gallipoli campaign in 1915-16 — was patently a tragicomedy of noncommunications. At the same time, the period immediately following World War I — a period of industrial strife and of total noncommunication between Westerners and "revolutionary" Communists (and a little later, equally revolutionary Fascists) — showed both the need for, and the lack of, a valid theory or a functioning practice of communications, inside existing institutions, inside existing societies, and between various leadership groups and their various "publics."

As a result, communications suddenly became, forty to fifty years ago, a consuming interest of scholars as well as of practitioners. Above all, communications in management has this last half century been a central concern to students and practitioners in all institutions — business, the military, public administration, hospital administration, university administration, and research administration. In no other area have intelligent men and women worked harder or with greater dedication than psychologists, human relations experts, managers, and management students have worked on improving communications in our major institutions.

We have more attempts at communications today, that is, more attempts to talk to others, and a surfeit of communications media, unimaginable to the men who, around the time of World War I, started to work on the problems of communicating. The trickle of books on communications has become a raging torrent. I recently received a bibliography prepared for a graduate seminar on communications; it ran to ninety-seven pages. A recent anthology (*The Human Dialogue*, edited by Floyd W. Matson and Ashley Montagu, The Free Press of Glencoe, 1967) contains articles by forty-nine different contributors.

Yet communications has proven as elusive as the unicorn. Each of the forty-nine contributors to *The Human Dialogue* has a theory of communications which is incompatible with all the others. The noise level has gone up so fast that no one can really listen any more to all that babble about communications. But there is clearly less and less communicating. The communications gap within institutions and between groups in society has been widening steadily — to the point where it threatens to become an unbridgeable gulf of total misunderstanding.

In the meantime, there is an information explosion. Every professional and every executive — in fact, everyone except the deaf-mute — suddenly has access to data in inexhaustible abundance. All of us feel — and overeat — very much like the little boy who has been left alone in the candy store. But what has to be done to make this cornucopia of data redound to information, let alone to knowledge? We get a great many answers. But the one thing clear so far is that no one really has an answer. Despite "information theory" and "data processing," no one yet has actually seen, let alone used, an "information system," or a "data base." The one thing we do know, though, is that the abundance of information changes the communications problem and makes it both more urgent and even less tractable.

There is a tendency today to give up on communications. In psychology, for instance, the fashion today is the T-group with its "sensitivity training." The avowed aim is not communications, but self-awareness. T-groups focus on the "I" and not on the "thou." Ten or twenty years ago the rhetoric stressed "empathy"; now it stresses "doing one's thing." However needed self-knowledge may be, communication is needed at least as much (if, indeed, self-knowledge is possible without action on others, that is, without communications). Whether the T-groups are sound psychology and effective psychotherapy is well beyond my competence and the scope of this paper. But their popularity attests to the failure of our attempts at communications.

Despite the sorry state of communications in theory and practice, we have, however, learned a good deal about information and communications. Most of it, though, has not come out of the work on communications to which we have devoted so much time and energy. It has been the byproduct of work in a large number of seemingly unrelated fields, from learning theory to genetics and electronic engineering. We equally have a lot of experience — though mostly of failure — in a good many practical situations in all kinds of institutions. Communications we may, indeed, never understand. But communications in organizations — call it *managerial communications* — we do know something about by now. It is a much narrower topic than communications per se — but it is the topic to which this paper shall address itself.

We are, to be sure, still far away from mastery of communications, even in organizations. What knowledge we have about communications is scattered and, as a rule, not accessible, let alone in applicable form. But at least we increasingly know what does not work and, sometimes, why it does not work. Indeed, we can say bluntly that most of today's brave attempts at communication in organizations — whether business, labor unions, government agencies, or universities — is based on assumptions that have been proven to be invalid — and that, therefore, these efforts cannot have results. And perhaps we can even anticipate what might work.

What We Have Learned

We have learned, mostly through doing the wrong things, the following four fundamentals of communications:

(1) Communication is perception,
(2) Communication is expectations,
(3) Communication is involvement,
(4) Communication and information are totally different. But information presupposes functioning communications.

Communication Is Perception

An old riddle asked by the mystics of many religions — the Zen Buddhists, the Sufis of Islam, or the rabbis of the Talmud — asks: "Is there a sound in the forest if a tree crashes down and no one is around to hear it?" We now know that the right answer to this is "no." There are sound waves. But there is no sound unless someone perceives it. Sound is created by perception. Sound is communication.

This may seem trite; after all, the mystics of old already knew this, for they, too, always answered that there is no sound unless someone can hear it. Yet the implications of this rather trite statement are great indeed.

(a) First, it means that it is the recipient who communicates. The so-called communicator, that is, the person who emits the communication, does not communicate. He utters. Unless there is someone who hears, there is no communication. There is only noise. The communicator speaks or writes or sings — but he does not communicate. Indeed he cannot communicate. He can only make it possible, or impossible, for a recipient — or rather percipient — to perceive.

(b) Perception, we know, is not logic. It is experience. This means, in the first place, that one always perceives a configuration. One cannot perceive single specifics. They are always part of a total picture. *The Silent Language* (as Edward T. Hall called it in the title of his pioneering work ten years ago) — that is, the gestures, the tone of voice, the environment all together, not to mention the cultural and social referents — cannot be dissociated from the spoken language. In fact, without them the spoken word has no meaning and cannot communicate. It is not only that the same words, e.g., "I enjoyed meeting you," will be heard as having a wide variety of meanings. Whether they are heard as warm or as icy cold, as endearment or as rejection, depends on their setting in the silent language, such as the tone of voice or the occasion. More important is that by themselves, that is, without being part of the total configuration of occasion, value, silent language, and so on, the phrase has no meaning at all. By itself it cannot make possible communication. It cannot be understood. Indeed, it cannot be heard. To paraphrase an old proverb of the Human Relations school: "One cannot communicate a word; the whole man always comes with it."

(c) But we know about perception also that one can only perceive what one is capable of perceiving. Just as the human ear does not hear sounds above a certain pitch, so does human perception all together not perceive what is beyond its range of perception. It may, of course, hear physically, or see visually, but it cannot accept. The stimulus cannot become communication.

This is a very fancy way of stating something the teachers of rhetoric have known for a very long time — though the practitioners of communications tend to forget it again and again. In Plato's *Phaedrus*, which, among other things, is also the earliest extant treatise on rhetoric, Socrates points out that one has to talk to people in terms of their own experience, that is, that one has to use a carpenter's metaphors when talking to carpenters, and so on. One can only communicate in the recipient's language or altogether in his terms. And the terms have to be experience-based. It, therefore, does very little good to try to explain terms to people. They will not be able to receive them if the terms are not of their own experience. They simply exceed their perception capacity.

The connection between experience, perception, and concept formation, that is, cognition, is, we now know, infinitely subtler and richer than any earlier philosopher imagined. But one fact is proven and comes out strongly in the most disparate work, e.g., that of Piaget in Switzerland, that of B. F. Skinner of Harvard, or that of Jerome Bruner (also of Harvard). Percept and concept in the learner, whether child or adult, are not separate. We cannot perceive unless we also conceive. But we also cannot form concepts unless we can perceive. To communicate a concept is impossible unless the recipient can perceive it, that is, unless it is within his perception.

There is a very old saying among writers: "Difficulties with a sentence always mean confused thinking. It is not the sentence that needs straightening out, it is the thought behind it." In writing we attempt, of course, to communicate with ourselves. An unclear sentence is one that exceeds our own capacity for perception. Working on the sentence, that is, working on what is normally called communications, cannot solve the problem. We have to work on our own concepts first to be able to understand what we are trying to say — and only then can we write the sentence.

In communicating, whatever the medium, the first question has to be, "Is this communication within the recipient's range of perception? Can he receive it?"

The "range of perception" is, of course, physiological and largely (though not entirely) set by physical limitations of man's animal body. When we speak of communications, however, the most important limitations on perception are usually cultural and emotional rather than physical. That fanatics are not being convinced by rational arguments, we have known for thousands of years. Now we are beginning to understand that it is not "argument" that is lacking. Fanatics do not have the ability to perceive a communication which goes beyond their range of emotions. Before this is possible, their emotions would have to be altered. In other words, no one is really "in touch with reality," if by that we mean complete openness to evidence. The distinction between sanity and paranoia is not in the ability to perceive, but in the ability to learn, that is, in the ability to change one's emotions on the basis of experience.

That perception is conditioned by what we are capable of perceiving was realized forty years ago by the most quoted but probably least heeded of all students of organization, Mary Parker Follett, especially in her collected essays, *Dynamic Administration* (New York, Harper's, 1941). Follett taught that a disagreement or a conflict is likely not to be about the answers, or, indeed, about anything ostensible. It is, in most cases, the result of incongruity in perceptions. What A sees so vividly, B does not see at all. And, therefore, what A argues has no pertinence to B's concerns, and vice versa. Both, Follett argued, are likely to see reality. But each is likely to see a different aspect thereof. The world, and not only the material world, is multidimensional. Yet one can only see one dimension at a time. One rarely realizes that there could be other dimensions, and that something that is so obvious to us and so clearly validated by our emotional experience has other dimensions, a back and sides, which are entirely different and which, therefore, lead to entirely different perception. The old story about the blind men and the elephant in which every one of them, upon encountering this strange beast, feels one of the elephant's parts, his leg, his trunk, his hide, and reports an entirely different conclusion, each held tenaciously, is simply a story of the human condition. And there is no possibility of communication until this is understood and until he who has felt the hide of the elephant goes over to him who has felt the leg and feels the leg himself. There is no possibility of communications, in other words, unless we first know what the recipient, the true communicator, can see and why.

Communication Is Expectations

We perceive, as a rule, what we expect to perceive. We see largely what we expect to see, and we hear largely what we expect to hear. That the unexpected may be resented is not the important thing — though most of the writers on communications in business or government think it is. What is truly important is that the unexpected is usually not received at all. It is either not seen or heard but ignored. Or it is misunderstood, that is, misseen as the expected or misheard as the expected.

On this we now have a century or more of experimentation. The results are quite unambiguous. The human mind attempts to fit impressions and stimuli into a frame of expectations. It resists vigorously any attempts to make it "change its mind," that is, to perceive what it does not expect to perceive or not to perceive what it expects to perceive. It is, of course, possible to alert the human mind to the fact that what it perceives is contrary to its expectations. But this first requires that we understand what it expects to perceive. It then requires that there be an unmistakable signal — "this is different," that is, a shock which breaks continuity. A "gradual" change in which the mind is supposedly led by small, incremental steps to realize that what is perceived is not what it expects to perceive will not work. It will rather reinforce the expectations and will make it even more certain that what will be perceived is what the recipient expects to perceive.

Before we can communicate, we must, therefore, know what the recipient expects to see and to hear. Only then can we know whether communication can utilize his expectations — and what they are — or whether there is need for the "shock of alienation," for an "awakening" that breaks through the recipient's expectations and forces him to realize that the unexpected is happening.

Communication Is Involvement

Many years ago psychologists stumbled on a strange phenomenon in their studies of memory, a phenomenon that, at first, upset all their hypotheses. In order to test memory, the psychologists compiled a list of words to be shown to their experimental subjects for varying times as a test of their retention capacity. As control, a list of nonsense words, mere jumbles of letters, were devised to find out to what extent understanding influenced memory. Much to the surprise of these early experimenters almost a century ago or so, their subjects (mostly students, of course,) showed totally uneven memory retention of individual words. More surprising, they showed amazingly high retention of the nonsense words. The explanation of the first phenomenon is fairly obvious. Words are not mere information. They do carry emotional charges. And, therefore, words with unpleasant or threatening associations tend to be suppressed, words with pleasant associations retained. In fact, this selective retention by emotional association has since been used to construct tests for emotional disorders and for personality profiles.

The relatively high retention rate of nonsense words was a greater problem. It was expected, after all, that no one would really remember words that had no meaning at all. But it has become clear over the years that the memory for these words, though limited, exists precisely because these words have no meaning. For this reason, they also make no demand. They are truly neuter. In respect to them, memory could be said to be truly mechanical, showing neither emotional preference nor emotional rejection.

A similar phenomenon, known to every newspaper editor, is the amazingly high readership and retention of the fillers, the little three- or five-line bits of irrelevant incidental information that are being used to balance a page. Why should anybody want to read, let alone remember, that it first became fashionable to wear different-colored hose on each leg at the court of some long-forgotten duke? Why should anybody want to read, let alone remember, when and where baking powder was first used? Yet there is no doubt that these little tidbits of irrelevancy are read and, above all, that they are remembered far better than almost anything in the daily paper except the great screaming headlines of the catastrophes. The answer is that these fillers make no demands. It is precisely their total irrelevancy that accounts for their being remembered.

Communications are always propaganda. The emitter always wants "to get something across." Propaganda, we now know, is both a great deal more powerful than the rationalists with their belief in "open discussion" believe, and a great deal less powerful than the mythmakers of propaganda, e.g., a Dr. Goebbels in the Nazi regime, believed and wanted us to believe. Indeed, the danger of total propaganda is not that the propaganda will be believed. The danger is that nothing will be believed and that every communication becomes suspect. In the end, no communication is being received any more. Everything anyone says is considered a demand and is resisted, resented, and in effect not heard at all. The end results of total propaganda are not fanatics, but cynics — but this, of course, may be even greater and more dangerous corruption.

Communication, in other words, always makes demands. It always demands that the recipient become somebody, do something, believe something. It always appeals to motivation. If, in other words, communication fits in with the aspirations, the values, the purposes of the recipient, it is powerful. If it goes against his aspirations, his values, his motivations, it is likely not to be received at all, or, at best, to be resisted. Of course, at its most powerful, communication brings about conversion, that is, a change of personality, of values, beliefs, aspirations. But this is the rare, existential event, and one against which the basic psychological forces of every human being are strongly organized. Even the Lord, the Bible reports, first had to strike Saul blind before he could raise him as Paul. Communications aiming at conversion demand surrender. By and large, therefore, there is no communication unless the message can key in to the recipient's own values, at least to some degree.

Communication and Information Are Different and Largely Opposite — Yet Interdependent

(a) Where communication is perception, information is logic. As such, information is purely formal and has no meaning. It is impersonal rather than interpersonal. The more it can be freed of the human component, that is, of such things as emotions and values, expectations and perceptions, the more valid and reliable does it become. Indeed, it becomes increasingly informative.

All through history, the problem has been how to glean a little information out of communications, that is, out of relationships between people, based on perception. All through history, the problem has been to isolate the information content from an abundance of perception. Now, all of a sudden, we have the capacity to provide information — both because of the conceptual work of the logicians, especially the symbolic logic of Russell and Whitehead, and because of the technical work on data processing and data storage, that is, of course, especially because of the computer and its tremendous capacity to store, manipulate, and transmit data. Now, in other words, we have the opposite problem from the one mankind has always been struggling with. Now we have the problem of handling information per se, devoid of any communication content.

(b) The requirements for effective information are the opposite of those for effective communication. Information is, for instance, always specific. We perceive a configuration in communications; but we convey specific individual data in the information process. Indeed, information is, above all, a principle of economy. The fewer data needed, the better the information. And an overload of information, that is, anything much beyond what is truly needed, leads to a complete information blackout. It does not enrich, but impoverishes.

(c) At the same time, information presupposes communication. Information is always encoded. To be received, let alone to be used, the code must be known and understood by the recipient. This requires prior agreement, that is, some communication. At the very least, the recipient has to know what the data pertain to. Are the figures on a piece of computer tape the height of mountain tops or the cash balances of Federal Reserve member banks? In either case, the recipient would have to know what mountains are or what banks are to get any information out of the data.

The prototype information system may well have been the peculiar language known as *Armee Deutsch* (Army German), which served as language of command in the Imperial Austrian Army prior to 1918. A polyglot army in which officers, noncommissioned officers, and men often had no language in common, it functioned remarkably well with fewer than two hundred specific words, "fire," for instance, or "at ease," each of which had only one totally unambiguous meaning. The meaning was always an action. And the words were learned in and through actions, i.e., in what behaviorists now call operant conditioning. The tensions in the Austrian army after many decades of nationalist turmoil were very great indeed. Social intercourse between members of different nationalities serving in the same unit became increasingly difficult, if not impossible. But to the very end, the information system functioned. It was completely formal, completely rigid, completely logical in that each word had only one possible meaning; and it rested on completely pre-established communication regarding the specific response to a certain set of sound waves. This example, however, shows also that the effectiveness of an information system depends on the willingness and ability to think through carefully what information is needed by whom for what purposes, and then on the systematic creation of communication between the various parties to the system as to the meaning of each specific input and output. The effectiveness, in other words, depends on the pre-establishment of communication.

(d) Communication communicates better the more levels of meaning it has and the less possible it is, therefore, to quantify it.

Medieval esthetics held that a work of art communicates on a number of levels, at least three if not four: the literal, the metaphorical, the allegorical, and the symbolic. The work of art that most consciously converted this theory into artistic practice was, of course, Dante's *Divina Commedia*. If, by information, we mean something that can be quantified, then the *Divina Commedia* is without any information content whatever. But it is precisely the ambiguity, the multiplicity of levels on which this book can be read, from being a fairy tale to being a grand synthesis of metaphysics, that makes it the overpowering work of art it is, and the immediate communication which it has been to generations of readers.

Communications, in other words, may not be dependent on information. Indeed, the most perfect communications may be purely shared experiences, without any logic whatever. Perception has primacy rather than information.

I fully realize that this summary of what we have learned is gross oversimplification. I fully realize that I have glossed over some of the most hotly contested issues in psychology and perception. Indeed, I may well be accused of brushing aside most of the issues which the students of learning and of perception would themselves consider central and important.

But my aim has, of course, not been to survey these big areas. My concern is not with learning or with perception. It is with communications, and, in particular, with communications in the large organization, be it business enterprise, government agency, university, or armed service.

This summary might also be criticized for being trite, if not obvious. No one, it might be said, could possibly be surprised at its statements. They say what everybody knows. But whether this be so or not, it is not what everybody does. On the contrary, the logical implications of these apparently simple and obvious statements for communications in organizations are at odds with current practice and, indeed, deny validity to the honest and serious efforts to communicate which we have been making for many decades now.

What, then, can our knowledge and our experience teach us about communications in organizations, about the reasons for our failures, and about the prerequisites for success in the future?

(1) For centuries we have attempted communication downward. This, however, cannot work, no matter how hard and how intelligently we try. It cannot work, first, because it focuses on what we want to say. It assumes, in other words, that the utterer communicates. But we know that all he does is utter. Communication is the act of the recipient. What we have been trying to do is to work on the emitter, specifically on the manager, the administrator, the commander, to make him capable of being a better communicator. But all one can communicate downward are commands, that is, prearranged signals. One cannot communicate downward anything connected with understanding, let alone with motivation. This requires communication upward, from those who perceive to those who want to reach their perception.

This does not mean that managers should stop working on clarity in what they say or write. Far from it. But it does mean that how we say something comes only after we have learned what to say. And this cannot be found out by "talking to," no matter how well it is being done. "Letters to the Employees," no matter how well done, will be a waste unless the writer knows what employees can perceive, expect to perceive, and want to do. They are a waste unless they are based on the recipient's rather than the emitter's perception.

(2) But "listening" does not work either. The Human Relations School of Elton Mayo, forty years ago, recognized the failure of the traditional approach to communications. Its answer — especially as developed in Mayo's two famous books, *The Human Problems of an Industrial Civilization* (Boston, Harvard Business School, 1933) and *The Social Problems of an Industrial Civilization* (Boston, Harvard Business School, 1945) — was to enjoin listening. Instead of starting out with what I, this is, the executive, want to get across, the executive should start out by finding out what subordinates want to know, are interested in, are, in other words, receptive to. To this day, the human relations prescription, though rarely practiced, remains the classic formula.

Of course, listening is a prerequisite to communication. But it is not adequate, and it cannot, by itself, work. Perhaps the reason why it is not being used widely, despite the popularity of the slogan, is precisely that, where tried, it has failed to work. Listening first assumes that the superior will understand what he is being told. It assumes, in other words, that the subordinates can communicate. It is hard to see, however, why the subordinate should be able to do what his superior cannot do. In fact, there is no reason for assuming he can. There is no reason, in other words, to believe that listening results any less in misunderstanding and miscommunications than does talking. In addition, the theory of listening does not take into account that communications is involvement. It does not bring out the subordinate's preferences and desires, his values and aspirations. It may explain the reasons for misunderstanding. But it does not lay down a basis for understanding.

This is not to say that listening is wrong, any more than the futility of downward communications furnishes any argument against attempts to write well, to say things clearly and simply, and to speak the language of those whom one addresses rather than one's own jargon. Indeed, the realization that communications have to be upward — or rather that they have to start with the recipient, rather than the emitter, which underlies the concept of listening — is absolutely sound and vital. But listening is only the starting point.

(3) More and better information does not solve the communications problem, does not bridge the communications gap. On the contrary, the more information, the greater is the need for functioning and effective communication. The more information, in other words, the greater is the communications gap likely to be.

The more impersonal and formal the information process in the first place, the more will it depend on prior agreement on meaning and application, that is, on communications. In the second place, the more effective the information process, the more impersonal and formal will it become, the more will it separate human beings and thereby require separate, but also much greater, efforts, to re-establish the human relationship, the relationship of communication. It may be said that the effectiveness of the information process will depend increasingly on our ability to communicate, and that, in the absence of effective communication — that is, in the present situation — the information revolution cannot really produce information. All it can produce is data.

It can also be said — and this may well be more important — that the test of an information system will increasingly be the degree to which it frees human beings from concern with information and allows them to work on communications. The test, in particular, of the computer will be how much time it gives executives and professionals on all levels for direct, personal, face-to-face relationships with other people.

It is fashionable today to measure the utilization of a computer by the number of hours it runs during one day. But this is not even a measurement of the computer's efficiency. It is purely a measurement of input. The only measurement of output is the degree to which availability of information enables human beings not to control, that is, not to spend time trying to get a little information on what happened yesterday. And the only measurement of this, in turn, is the amount of time that becomes available for the job only human beings can do, the job of communication. By this test, of course, almost no computer today is being used properly. Most of them are being misused, that is, are being used to justify spending even more time on control rather than to relieve human beings from controlling by giving them information. The reason for this is quite clearly the lack of prior communication, that is, of agreement and decision on what information is needed, by whom and for what purposes, and what it means operationally. The reason for the misuse of the computer is, so to speak, the lack of anything comparable to the *Armee Deutsch* of yesterday's much-ridiculed Imperial Austrian Army with its two hundred words of command which even the dumbest recruit could learn it two weeks' time.

The Information Explosion, in other words, is the most impelling reason to go to work on communications. Indeed, the frightening communications gap all around us — between management and workers; between business and government; between faculty and students, and between both of them and university administration; between producers and consumers; and so on — may well reflect in some measure the tremendous increase in information without a commensurate increase in communications.

Can we then say anything constructive about communication? Can we do anything? We can say that communication has to start from the intended recipient of communications rather than from the emitter. In terms of traditional organization we have to start upward. Downward communications cannot work and do not work. They come *after* upward communications have successfully been established. They are reaction rather than action, response rather than initiative.

But we can also say that it is not enough to listen. The upward communication must first be focused on something that both recipient and emitter can perceive, focused on something that is common to both of them. And second, it must be focused on the motivation of the intended recipient. It must, from the beginning, be informed by his values, beliefs, and aspirations.

One example — but only an example: There have been promising results with organizational communication that started out with the demand by the superior that the subordinate think through and present to the superior his own conclusions as to what major contribution to the organization — or to the unit within the organization — the subordinate should be expected to perform and should be held accountable for. What the subordinate then comes up with is rarely what the superior expects. Indeed, the first aim of the exercise is precisely to bring out the divergence in perception between superior and subordinate. But the perception is focused, and focused on something that is real to both parties. To realize that they see the same reality differently is in itself already communication.

Second, in this approach, the intended recipient of communication — in this case the subordinate — is given access to experience that enables him to understand. He is given access to the reality of decision making, the problems of priorities, the choice between what one likes to do and what the situation demands, and above all, the responsibility for a decision. He may not see the situation the same way the superior does — in fact, he rarely will or even should. But he may gain an understanding of the complexity of the superior's situation, and above all of the fact that the complexity is not of the superior's making, but is inherent in the situation itself.

Finally, the communication, even if it consists of a "no" to the subordinate's conclusions, is firmly focused on the aspirations, values, and motivation of the intended recipient. In fact, it starts out with the question, "What would you *want* to do?" It may then end up with the command, "This is what I tell you to do." But at least it forces the superior to realize that he is overriding the desires of the subordinate. It forces him to explain, if not to try to persuade. At least he knows that he has a problem — and so does the subordinate.

A similar approach has worked in another organizational situation in which communication has been traditionally absent: the performance appraisal, and especially the appraisal interview. Performance appraisal is today standard in large organizations (except in Japan, where promotion and pay go by seniority so that performance appraisal would serve little purpose). We know that most people want to know where they stand. One of the most common complaints of employees in organizations is, indeed, that they are not being appraised and are not being told whether they do well or poorly.

The appraisal forms may be filled out. But the appraisal interview in which the appraiser is expected to discuss his performance with a man is almost never conducted. The exceptions are a few organizations in which performance appraisals are considered a communications tool rather than a rating device. This means specifically that the performance appraisal starts out with the question, "What has this man done well?" It then asks, "And what, therefore, should he be able to do well?" And then it asks, "And what would he have to learn or to acquire to be able to get the most from his capacities and achievements?" This, first, focuses on specific achievement. It focuses on things the employee himself is likely to perceive clearly and, in fact, gladly. It also focuses on his own aspirations, values, and desires. Weaknesses are then seen as limitations to what the employee himself can do well and wants to do, rather than as defects. Indeed, the proper conclusion from this approach to appraisal is not the question, "What should the employee do?" but "What should the organization and I, his boss, do?" A proper conclusion is not "What does this communicate to the employee?" It is "What does this communicate to both of us, subordinate *and* superior?"

These are only examples, and rather insignificant ones at that. But perhaps they illustrate conclusions to which our experience with communications — largely an experience of failure — and the work in learning, memory, perception, and motivation point.

The start of communications in organization must be to get the intended recipient himself to try to communicate. This requires a focus on

(a) the impersonal but common task, and (b) on the intended recipient's values, achievements, and aspirations. It also requires the experience of responsibility.

Perception is limited by what can be perceived and geared to what one expects to perceive. Perception, in other words, presupposes experience. Communication within organization, therefore, presupposes that the members of the organization have the foundation of experience to receive and perceive. The artist can convey this experience in symbolical form: he can communicate what his readers or viewers have never experienced. But ordinary managers, administrators, and professors are not likely to be artists. The recipients must, therefore, have actual experience themselves and directly rather than through the vicarious symbols.

Communications in organization demands that the masses, whether they be employees or students, share in the responsibility of decisions to the fullest possible extent. They must understand because they have been through it, rather than accept because it is being explained to them.

I shall never forget the German trade union leader, a faithful Socialist, who was shattered by his first exposure to the deliberations of the Board of Overseers of a large company to which he had been elected as an employee member. That the amount of money available was limited and that, indeed, there was very little money available for all the demands that had to be met, was one surprise. But the pain and complexity of the decisions between various investments, e.g., between modernizing the plant to safeguard workers' jobs and building workers' houses to safeguard their health and family life, was a much bigger and totally unexpected experience. But, as he told me with a half-sheepish, half-rueful grin, the greatest shocker was the realization that all the things he considered important turned out to be irrelevant to the decisions in which he found himself taking an active and responsible part. Yet this man was neither stupid nor dogmatic. He was simply inexperienced — and, therefore, inaccessible to communication.

The traditional defense of paternalism has always been "It's a complex world; it needs the expert, the man who knows best." But paternalism, as our work in perception, learning, and motivation is beginning to bring out, really can work only in a simple world. When people can understand what Papa does because they share his experiences and his perception, then Papa can actually make the decisions for them. In a complex world there is need for a shared experience in the decisions, or there is no common perception, no communications, and, therefore, neither acceptance of the decisions, nor ability to carry them out. The ability to understand presupposes prior communication. It presupposes agreement on meaning.

There will be no communication, in sum, if it is conceived as going from the "I" to the "Thou." Communication only works from one member of "us" to another. Communications in organization — and this may be the true lesson of our communications failure and the true measure of our communications need — are not a *means* of organization. They are a *mode* of organization.

QUESTIONS

1. Explain the author's contention that the start of communications in organization must be to get the intended recipient himself to try to communicate. Why? Is this the mode of communication established in your school district? If not, should it be?

2. What does the author mean by saying that communications are a *mode* rather than a *means* of organization?

Johnny, the Grad You Hired Last Week, Can't Write

By
Joseph A. Rice

In this sprightly article Professor Rice offers suggestions to an administrator who wants to improve the writing of a young employee. An administrator can be an effective writing teacher because he knows how written communications work in his organization. Everyone benefits when he shares that knowledge.

Organize writing into a triangle with the conclusion or recommendation at the top. List supporting reasons in descending order of importance.

The biggest error in upward communication is defensiveness, and the biggest errors in downward communication are being too directive and using jargon. The most common mistake in communicating with people outside the organization is failing to say what they should do.

Avoid redundant, extraneous, and irrelevant material. Never write a caustic message. Pay attention to the layout. Communicate willingly and revise before sending.

A sender's thoughts become clearer when he puts them into words.

Johnny, who recently graduated from ________ High School or University, is a functional illiterate — and *you* hired him. And it looks as though you'll have to live with him. That means *you* have to teach him to write.

Here's the situation with Johnny, that fresh-out-of-school youngster you put on the payroll last week: Johnny sees himself as an *accountant* (or *engineer* or *marketer* or whatever). Johnny thinks he doesn't need to write/spell/paragraph letters/memos/reports.

Where did he get such notions? Well . . . maybe from his experiences in our public schools/colleges/universities. Everything Johnny has learned in the educational system has prepared him to expect to earn his living in —

"Johnny, the Grad You Hired Last Week, Can't Write," by Joseph A. Rice, *Supervisory Management*, September 1976. Copyright © 1976 by AMACOM, a division of American Management Associations. Reprinted by permission of the publisher from Supervisory Management.

there's no better term for it — a "multiple-choice world." He thinks he will be able to satisfy every need of the job for which you have hired him by blocking in "A" or "B" or "C" or "None of the above."

Indeed, scratch Johnny and just under the surface you'll find a firm layer of belief that the written language is moribund — about to pass into history like the steam locomotive. Johnny has accepted a position with your progressive company because his sensitive antennae tell his pulsating brain that you will be among the first to do away with written communication. You'll lead the way in replacing the memo, the report, the letter with tapes, cassettes, television sets. Entirely. When will this dramatic switch to totally oral communication take place? "Soon," the vibes tell him, "very soon." Maybe you'll announce the good news Wednesday: *No more writing! Ever!*

Of course, that's not what you'll do Wednesday. What you *will* do Wednesday is spend the morning deciphering one of Johnny's memos. And the afternoon working up your own multiple-choice list:

1. Dribble Johnny down the hall like a basketball.
2. Fire him.
3. Demote him.
4. Transfer him into the department of your worst enemy.

Face the problem squarely

Restrain yourself. Face the problem squarely, like the good manager that you are. Consider the situation realistically:

- You hired Johnny and Johnny can't write. But neither can the other candidates you interviewed.
- Johnny is, if anything, a bit more highly motivated than the others. He's quick. He respects you. He wants to keep his job.
- The buck has been passed right down the line. And you're at the end of it. You'll have to teach Johnny to write because nobody else did and nobody else will.

Now for the good news:

- Since Johnny can't write, he will have less to unlearn. That may be more of a plus than you might think.
- There's something called the "language acquisition mechanism" which gets turned on when a young new-hire goes to work at his first career job. Because of the language acquisition mechanism (L.A.M.), Johnny will absorb a formidably large array of technical and jargon terms over the next few months. He will never again learn so much so

quickly — and that's another plus.

- You're better prepared to teach Johnny than you might think. If Johnny is a hunk of raw granite, you're . . . Michelangelo. And that's the biggest plus of all — as I'm about to show you.

From the top, then. If Johnny had been taught how to write, he would probably have learned writing-through-literature (because that's what 98.7 percent of the teachers in the schools know). By coincidence, writing-through-literature is 98.7 percent oriented to a pretechnology world. It is writing out of the past. It has virtually 0 percent to do with the writing Johnny must produce from now until the day he retires. If Johnny had paid attention, he would have learned writing as a "subjective outpouring of innermost feelings" or some such — a concept that generally results in an outpouring replete with woolly lambs, fleecy clouds, springy grass, and the like.

The door is open for you to introduce Johnny to a new concept: *Writing is the single most effective method for objectively recording and storing and sharing complex information.*

A clean slate

If Johnny doesn't have to unlearn writing-as-imaginative-outpouring, you're miles ahead. The woolly-lamb, fleecy-cloud, springy-grass guys have delivered to you a pure specimen. Not because they wanted to. Because they weren't able to get him to go along for the ride.

Now, about the L.A.M. (not to be confused with woolly lambs). Psycholinguists, scholars of language, note that small children acquire linguistic concepts at a phenomenal rate. Every observant parent has reached a similar conclusion. And parents who have lived abroad note that their children absorb a foreign language much more readily than they, the adults, are able to.

It is possible to show a parallel (though less dramatic) language acquisition ability in the young adult world. The young adult, the recent grad, experiencing the fascinating career-world after years of boredom in school, is as alert as he will ever be. His L.A.M. is turned up full force.

Hit him now and hit him hard.

What follows is a memo you might hand to Johnny — as a subtle reminder that writing is as important as his academically acquired accounting (or other) skills. I would recommend that you place the memo in Johnny's hand at the same time you hand him his gate pass.

You're the expert

And one more thing, before we review that important memo-to-Johnny: There's not a reason in the world why you shouldn't be an effective writing teacher for Johnny. You don't know the difference between a gerund and a present participle? So what? You know the most important thing — how written communications work in your organization. Share that with Johnny and everybody benefits for as long as there's a you or a Johnny or a corporation.

Here's the memo you hand Johnny with his parking sticker:

JOHNNY, THE SUBJECT IS WRITING. REMEMBER:

---

1. You nearly always write for two purposes —
   To communicate.
   To document.
2. Your written message goes in one or more of these directions —
   Up.
   Down.
   Laterally.
   Out.
3. Your most common sin is probably dullness from material that is —
   Redundant.
   Extraneous.
   Irrelevant.
4. The most costly sin you'll ever commit is —
   Taking a caustic tone.
5. Your most overlooked aid to good communication is —
   Layout.
6. Finally, Johnny, I know you can't spell. You should know that I expect you to learn — on your own. English is full of nonphonetic words, variants, exceptions, oddities. You have no choice but to memorize 'em one by one.

Johnny won't read the memo, of course. He may even lose it. So the next move is yours. Start walking Johnny through that memo point by point. A few minutes a day. An hour a week. Whatever is necessary until it's covered. Maybe you can start by drawing him a picture . . . a triangle.

To communicate and document

Johnny (you might begin), organize your writing into a triangle. Know why you do that? Because you're just about always writing for two purposes. Know what those are? To communicate is the first one. To document is the second.

Up at the top of the triangle, at the beginning of your memo, you're making a recommendation or stating a conclusion or answering a boss's question. That's where you are doing your most important communicating. Know the single biggest mistake you can make when you're communicating with a boss? To put something in his way that he doesn't need to read.

As you work down the triangle, as it gets broader, give the reasons behind your recommendation. Itemize these when you can. Know why you do that? So that the reader can refer back quickly. It saves time if he or she can say: "I buy everything except item number three, Johnny," instead of "In the section of your report where you examine imported trichlorethylene over the next five-year period . . ."

The boss will appreciate it if you'll give him some tables, or "pictures," of your data wherever possible — so that he won't have to dig it out of long paragraphs.

Finally, Johnny, you have to keep in mind that the boss who assigned you that report won't always be around. Your main job is to write to him, of course. And in doing so, you must keep in mind how busy he is. But you should also keep in mind that the report goes into the files. In a year or 18 months it may be read by who knows who for who knows what reasons. Keep that mystery-reader in mind as you write. Document everything you can. Provide all the data. Lock it together with the best judgment you've got.

Okay, Johnny, have you got the first lesson? Communicate quickly for the first reader. Document thoroughly for the down-the-line reader.

Upward defensiveness

Now let's go to lesson number two:

Johnny, a message going up has different problems from one going down, laterally, or out. Here's what I mean by that. Suppose you could look at every memo ever written by an employee to his boss — or his boss's boss. What problem would you find over and over? You'd find defensiveness. Overcaution. You'd find hidden recommendations. Evasive language. Why? Because a lot of people have figured out that you don't get fired as quickly for pulling your neck in as you do for sticking it out too far.

I'll make a bargain with you, Johnny. I won't fire you for sticking your neck out. The other side of that bargain is that I'll raise hell every time you hide your recommendation from me in the middle of a fat paragraph or at the bottom of a wordy memo loaded with inflated words.

Now, Johnny, you make a bargain with me. Any time you can collect data, conduct a survey, show hard facts to beef up your recommendation, be sure and do it. In other words, Johnny, don't say:

- "I feel that we should . . ." (Sounds too subjective.)
- "It is recommended that . . ." (Who recommends?)
- "I recommend that . . ." (Did you collect any *data?*)

Say this whenever you can: "After collecting the data and studying it, I recommend that . . ."

What goes wrong with messages going down? Let's draw another picture. (Begin drawing a picture of a STOP sign.) Can you tell me what word goes in that picture? Sure. "*Stop*." That's an example of what semanticists call a "directive" message. A stop sign doesn't ask. It doesn't persuade. It doesn't give options. It doesn't suggest alternatives. It doesn't provide for feedback. The shape of it, the size of it, the color and location all simply shout a command: STOP! The message is about as "directive" as anything could be.

On the other hand, an "affective" message, to continue using the semanticist's terms, uses persuasion to communicate. This kind of message forms part of a "loop" and calls for feedback.

The biggest error

The biggest error in downward communication lies in being too directive. The second biggest error lies in using jargon words or professional terms that won't be understood by the person out in the plant. If you are an accountant, Johnny, and you write a memo to a lathe operator the way you'd write it to another accountant, you insult that lathe operator.

What's that, Johnny? You say that there's *no way* a lathe operator can understand the new federal regulations about profit-sharing benefits? You have no choice but to state the regs as written?

Maybe. But let me tell you what you should also do:

- Give some examples.
- Draw some pictures.
- Set up an oral communication exchange. Speaking is always more persuasive than writing, Johnny. Set up a loop. Give the lathe

operator a number to call. A person to talk to. An office to visit.

In short, Johnny, use a little imagination. Put your back into it. Frankly, a good lathe operator is worth more to us than an accountant, anyway. Exercise a little humility.

Now, what can go wrong laterally, when you communicate with somebody of your own rank in another department? Well, we have these procedures, these standard ways of doing things. Walls, some people call 'em. After a while you'll get a feel for the territory. You'll sense when you'd better go up before you go across. You'll know when you can get away with a "blind carbon." This will come with practice.

What can go wrong when you communicate out? When you're writing a letter to a customer or contractor or subsidiary or anybody else out there in the world who does some kind of business with us?

I think the mistake I notice most often, Johnny, is simply not saying what it is you want the reader to *do*. There's an ancient letter-writing formula called A.I.D.A. — short for *Attention, Interest, Desire, Action*. "Get the reader's Attention in the first paragraph . . ." and so forth.

An accent on action

Okay. You write that formula this way, Johnny: A.I.D.A. But don't think you have to put that big "A-for-Action" last. In a letter, as opposed to a memo, you may not want to put the Action right up front. But *say it*, Johnny — say what you want the reader to do, and don't hide it when you do.

Johnny, you need to know some new words: *redundant, extraneous, irrelevant*. Why did I choose those three words — and how are they different from each other?

Let's use an example, Johnny. Let's say that I could make a million-dollar decision if you'd collect data on a certain subject and give me the information I needed about three factors relating to that subject. Let's call those factors A, B, and C.

You're redundant, Johnny, if you tell me: ABC — ABBCCAB AACB. You're spinning around, digging a hole. You probably do that because you feel you haven't made the point clear the first time you said it. Redundancy is a common mistake in corporate writing.

I said I could make a decision based on factors ABC. If you told me

ABC — DEFGHIJKLMN, you'd be committing the error of loading your communication with extraneous material. This is not quite so common a failing as redundancy, and it is a harder one to pin down. Here's where judgment comes into play. One logical mind might say that the decision could be made on factors AB. Another, equally logical, might say ABC. Another, ABCD. Just to be sure, you might include all the back-up factors that seem the least bit important — in the supporting, or bottom, section of your communication. Like this:

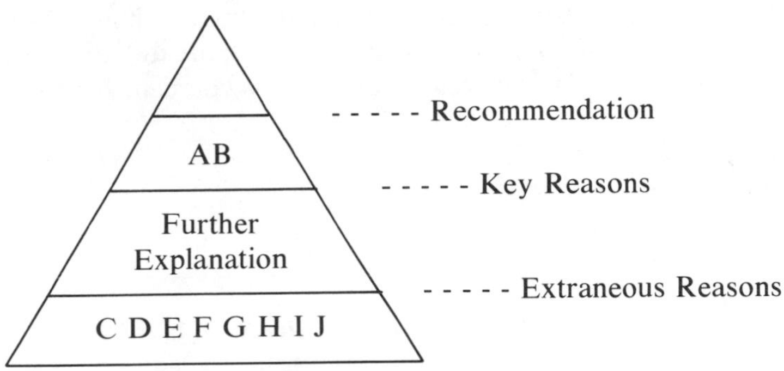

What is irrelevant? If I can make a decision based on factors AB as they relate to a certain product, and if you get into things that don't relate to the problem I've set up for you — things that are completely off the subject — you've gotten irrelevant, Johnny: AB & % + @. It's the second most heinous sin and can get your name on the "bump" list.

The most deadly sin is a caustic tone — and don't forget it! What could cause you to be caustic-cutting-bitter-biting in a written message, Johnny? I can give you a raft of causes:

- Rude customers.
- Unrealistic federal regulations.
- Shutdowns.
- Bad weather.
- Pressure.
- Lack of support.
- Shoddy workmanship.
- Errors.

Sometimes, Johnny, you'll get mad and the anger will come out subconsciously. It will creep between the lines of the message. Know how to prevent this?

- Don't put off writing until the last minute.
- Let it cool and revise it.
- Let a colleague look it over.
- Talk about it.

Don't ever write a caustic message, Johnny. Even though your reader files it away somewhere, it can come back to haunt you years later. Besides, if word gets back to me, it's an automatic bump.

Nobody has ever taught you anything about layout, Johnny? You don't want to get cute. You don't want your memo or report to look like a real-estate promotion. But *help* your reader every way you can, Johnny.

- Set off important information.
- Write in short paragraphs.
- Use white space.
- Don't do this: !!!

Mostly, Johnny, you want to *be conservative* with layout and punctuation. But be conservative in a way that helps your reader.

Johnny, nothing you do here is worth a dime until you communicate it. Do it willingly, not reluctantly. Do it as soon as you can. Don't put it off. Revise it. Show it around. Let me give you one last thought, Johnny, before I send you out into the corporation on your own:

You explain something to somebody because *you* benefit. Every time you put it into words for somebody else — spoken words or written words — it gets just a bit clearer in your own head. There's a reverse spin on communication, Johnny. Take advantage of it. And good luck. We think the company's fortunate to have you with us.

QUESTIONS

1. Re-read this article and observe whether its structure and style reflect the author's recommendations.

2. Although this article is ostensibly directed at Johnny, the author may tactfully be offering some hints to administrators.
   Imagine yourself a school principal. Write a memorandum to your superintendent recommending certain changes in school or district policies or procedures. As you write, keep Professor Rice's suggestions in mind.

IS LISTENING YOUR UNDEVELOPED RESOURCE?

By
Roger Gray

Listening pays off if one reacts to it. There are always opportunities for valuable listening but one must be alert to them and energetic enough to take advantage of them.

Ten skills of public listening and six skills of private listening are described. Some skills apply to both public and private listening.

Because listening gives an administrator a background for making decisions, it pays him to develop "listening posts" around the community.

To make listening valuable an administrator must be selective. Intelligent selection come from discovering what one needs to know.

Awareness and caution are by-products of conscientious listening. Listening can change knowledge into wisdom.

Listening Pays Off

In social work and teaching, patient listening produces wonderfully improved rapport. In business, listening increases the opportunities to produce income. In social life and recreation, listening increases one's fellowship and enjoyment. And as a citizen, listening helps one make intelligent choices among candidates and levies and issues. But, for best results, one doesn't just hear, he must put effort and skill into his listening. If the listening is going to pay off, one must react to it. Without reaction there is little retention! Only what we retain can contribute to our success.

This One Practice Contributed Most to Valuable Listening

From my early teen years on, one practice was significantly helpful: *to be where successful people are gathered, and do more listening than talking.*

Henry J. Kaiser remarked: "I make progress by having people around me who are smarter than I am — and listening to them. And I assume that EVERYONE is smarter about something than I am."

"Is Listening Your Undeveloped Resource?" by Roger Gray, *The Hillsdale Report*, Vol. 12, No. 1. Copyright © 1973 by Hillsdale College, and is reprinted by their permission.

One does not have to be a sleuth or an eavesdropper to be where important and successful people are gathered. Often one is there just by happenstance; but he needs to recognize when this happens. A little initiative can *produce* opportunities. If one develops helpful skills, his or her presence may even be *requested*. For instance, as a youngster, the author was on the scene first as a volunteer custodian's helper and then as a projector operator at school, the Y.M.C.A., and church affairs. Later in high school he was asked to be in on the action as reporter for the paper. Then he was involved in various volunteer capacities . . . sometimes as a participant. Then he was working on committees . . . then on boards and councils . . . even national committees. Next came attendance at conferences and conventions for social agencies, for business, etc., in which the small group informal chats outside the scheduled sessions often produced more valuable listening than the regular conference sessions.

There always were *opportunities* for valuable listening; there are still more today. One just has to be *alert* to the opportunities . . . and *energetic* enough to take advantage of them.

How *valuable* the listening will be will depend upon how skillfully one listens. Let's look at some of the skills.

There Are Skills of Public Listening, Just as There Are Skills of Public Speaking

"Public listening" may require more effort than listening during private conversation. In public listening the communication is listening rather than participatory and responsive. To have *meaning*, the topic, the speaker, and the language may demand considerable effort on the part of the listener. To have value the listener must discover in what he hears, something to which he can react. He may say to himself: "That is useful *new* information." "That man must be the mayor;" "I can't believe that;" etc. It is *reaction* to what one hears which helps one *retain* the thoughts. The conscious and sub-conscious association (of what one retains of his listening) with past and future input to the mind, gives the listener wisdom.

Besides *reacting to what one hears*, there are skills such as these (not necessarily in order of importance; the numbering is only for aiding reference to the skills):

1. Determine to whom you are listening . . . would this person be a source of accurate information or of misinformation?
2. Consider what the speaker is doing at the time: Is he *reporting observations* of his own, or is he quoting someone's observations,

facts, or opinions? Is he expressing *assumptions*, and making *predications* based on those assumptions? Is he stating facts or just telling a story of illustration? Is he talking about a *special situation* or about things in general? Is he rendering a personal judgment or is he making professional recommendations? Is he speaking in seriousness, or casually, or in jest? Is he making statements which he intends to be taken as questions . . . or asking questions which he intends to be considered as statements? The list could go on and on.

3. Discover who the other listeners and responders are (and what positions they hold); it gives more meaning to what is being said.
4. Carefully watch for *qualifiers* in people's statements, such as: I think, It is possible that, One could assume, I wouldn't be a bit surprised that, or Perhaps. The qualifiers often start or end *escape clauses*. They make it easy for the speaker to claim he was misquoted, or reveal that speaker is not sure about what he is saying, or that he is truly indicating that his statement applies only under certain situations. *Understanding the qualifiers* is important to understanding what you are hearing!
5. Do picture-thinking of what you are hearing . . . it quickly puts the thoughts into total *situations*. This brings about stronger *reaction*, more *association* with previous input, and multiplies the ability to recall. ALSO get the actual visual in mind . . . the actual conditions, surroundings, associates, and *gestures* at the time.
6. Become a student of non-verbal communication. It will help you determine when non-verbal communication is strengthening or contradicting what the speaker says (his own non-verbal communication and the non-verbal communication of his listeners).
7. Listen for the names of *people*. Who are the lawyers, accountants, bankers, counsellors, specialists, and authors whom the successful people mention in their conversations? This resource information can be very helpful when you are deciding about whom to seek for professional services.
8. Listen for the name of newspapers, magazines, books, and columnists whom the successful people quote, or cite as sources of their information (or whose judgment they accept and intend to act upon).
9. Remember that *incomplete information can be a dangerous thing*. Be careful about drawing conclusions or making assumptions when your listening gives you only *clues* rather than complete information. But also recognize that clues can *lead* you to complete information.
10. Listen for the problems people have . . . many people like to complain about products and services, government bureaus, new regu-

lations, etc. You can learn a great deal about problems you may soon face . . . and with that knowledge be able to avoid trouble.

One Needs to Be Skillful in Private Listening

Conversation with one or several other people is made meaningful and productive by how well the parties listen to each other. *Listening is what gives meaning to speaking*. But often we are so busy thinking of what we are going to say next that we don't absorb or react to what the other person is saying. Sometimes we decide what we want to say even before the other person is finished speaking . . . and at the earliest pause in his speech we *interrupt* him. This discourtesy not only irritates the speaker, but reveals that we were not really listening to him. Being a patient listener demands a lot of self-discipline.

Many of the skills of public listening apply to private listening, but we can also develop these skills:

1. Avoid distractions. This is more difficult to do than one realizes. During listening you want to *hear* and concentrate on what you hear. But alert eyes will see dozens of things (especially actions) which can take one's mind off listening. One's sense of smell and sense of taste present powerful interference. Any discomfort distracts. Any anxiety distracts. When the listening is going to be extra important, make preparations of time and place so as to eliminate all the distractions one can. When caught unprepared one still can keep his eyes on the eyes of the speaker. By keeping his mind busy analyzing what he is hearing (and preparing careful questions or responses) he can fend off stimuli arriving via his other sense.
2. Be alert for language you don't understand. Every trade and profession has a jargon all its own. When conversing with specialists and professionals outside your own field you may find yourself guessing about the meaning of phrases and words the speaker uses. Let the person know that you are not familiar with the special trade language and that you would appreciate interpretation. If you are paying a doctor or a lawyer or some other professional for his advice or for service you have a right to *demand* answers which YOU can understand . . . not just a lot of language which confuses you.
3. Don't "tune out" what you *don't* like to hear. All of us have a tendency to hear what is pleasing to us — so much so that we sometimes fail to hear the unpleasant qualifiers. For instance, if dad tells the kids, "You may get a raise in your allowance next month if my pay raise comes through." The kids will hear: "You get a raise in your allowance next month." Or, if you are seeking advice on some

matter, your advisor may tell the things in favor and the things unfavorable. One can all to easily remember the favorable and forget the unfavorable. And then there are unpleasant things we should be told; but when people don't bluntly come out and pound them into us (but just mention them in casual conversation), we are likely to feel that "nobody ever told me." Develop an alertness for "negatives hidden in positives."

4. Listen for what is NOT SAID. That which people DON'T say, often is more important than what they do say. Sometimes what they don't say are the real facts or the whole truth. This often is the case in employment interviews, interviews with prospective tenants, etc. You may have to ask for the information in several different questions.
5. Keep the mind open. When a person starts to speak you may make up your mind, "I've heard all this before." Hear the person out; the *deviations* from what you expect may be significantly worthwhile. If not, you have at least improved rapport.
6. Listen objectively. Sometimes we have to deal with individuals whose personalities we don't like. Perhaps they don't like us either. Be able to be thoroughly objective about the subject and the facts. Remember that *opinions* are important . . . they reveal how the individual looks at the facts. Sometimes opinions are expressed in nasty language; ask for clarification. Show that you are above attacking personalities . . . that you are truly interested in *communication*, rather than in swapping insults.

LISTENING Gives You Background for Decisions

One reason top executives don't make many poor decisions is that they have (or get) a thorough background and understanding of a *complete situation* before they make a decision. They spend a tremendous amount of their on-the-job time LISTENING to people. And off the job they listen in community boards and committees. They see things in greater perspective than people who are limited to just department information. All can read the newspapers and listen to TV. But it is the extra listening and extra sources of information that give the executive the edge.

The small business head or the individual professional man also has to make intelligent decisions. That is why it pays him to develop "listening posts" around the community. Since he has work he has to get done, he doesn't have as much listening time as the big executive. So he has to be *selective* in his listening! Some observations follow.

To Make Listening Valuable, Be Selective

The busier a person is the less time that man or woman has for listening and reading; therefore the more careful that person must be in the selection of reading material and of listening opportunities.

Intelligent selection comes from *discovering what one needs to know.* Reviewing one's projects and problems will help one see what he needs to know . . . and determine what he *must yet find out*. Then a review of one's listening opportunities (people, places, affairs, and counsellors) reveals the choices which he or she can select.

For instance: A printer was bothered about two particular problems — (1) should he renew the lease on the building where he had his shop, and (2) what should he do about buying a larger press. Before deciding about renewing his lease he wanted to know what was going to happen where they were tearing down an old mansion just a block down the street. He had a choice of two committee meetings — he decided to attend the one at which he would be in the company of a real estate broker, a builder, a banker, and a newspaper staff man. He would only have to mention about the old mansion . . . the flow of conversation would give him all the information he needed. On the matter of the press, he would chat with some of the paper salesmen who came in . . . find out what they knew about presses in the plants they called on; and he would go to the printers' convention and talk with plant owners and the printers' association officers. He discovered that very few shops, according to paper salesmen, were using the size press he had in mind. At dinner at the convention he mentioned his problem . . . what size press to buy. Everyone had an opinion, but two printing plant accountants were there. They showed that the size press he was considering was not economical. For 50% more money he could have a press that would turn out twice as much production . . . and he would have the *capacity for growth* into larger-size work. It meant borrowing $8000 more than he had anticipated, but there was no longer any question in his mind that such was the correct step. He has often told of how his selective listening had kept him from making a poor investment, and had led him to one of the most profitable investments he had ever made in equipment. And he was glad he didn't talk with a banker first . . . because the banker would have loaned him the money he needed and he would have bought the smaller press before discovering it was the wrong one to buy.

AWARENESS and CAUTION Are By-products of Conscientious Listening

Companies don't buy products or services — some *person* in the company does. A bank or a government bureau doesn't make decisions — *people* within the bank or the bureau make decisions. It has often been said: WHO you know is more important than WHAT you know. People who are not wise think that means you must know the right people to pull strings for you. That may be true in some situations, but, on the whole, business and social life is straight forward. You get business and you get decisions because you know enough to *deal with the people who make the decisions* . . . and your listening gives you an awareness of who those people are.

Listening carefully to the *names* and *connections* of people not only develops awareness . . . it develops *caution*. One learns to be cautious until he fully understands the connections of people. For instance: At one plant an office equipment salesman found that a young "handy-man" was always sticking his nose into what was going on. During demonstration of a new machine this nosy guy showed up again. The irritated salesman sure told him off. THEN he found out that the young "handy-man" was the grandson of the company president and was being broken in to become plant manager. The salesman recalled then that he had heard that a local businessman had no sons, but five daughters, and those daughters all had daughters . . . only one son among all the grandchildren. And that boy was his grandfather's protege. But, he had never bothered to remember names or find out what plant the names were connected with!

Knowing the family connections and connections-through-marriage of people can save a person a lot of wasted time and effort trying to compete against the relatives of purchasing agents and office managers.

Gold is Where You Find It

Often information is worth a lot of gold. And just as there may be gold where you are if you look for it, valuable information is where you are if you listen for it!

There is no room here for all the very interesting true stories of where, when, and how valuable information was there just for the listening. But here are some of the places:

At meetings of the service club; at staff meetings.
At conventions of social agency volunteers.
At business and Chamber of Commerce conventions.
At board and committee meetings of community agencies.
In chats with people I met at the banks and at the post office.
Chats with stenographers and executives in all kinds of places.
Chats with newspaper editors and reporters.
Discussions with salesmen and manufacturers' representatives.
Chats with doormen, elevator operators, and parking lot attendants.
In customers' offices . . . and the waiting room at plants.
In barber shops, restaurants, the dentist's office.
Chatting with used car salesmen, insurance agents, politicians.

Attending lectures, open houses, church, PTA.
At the swimming pool, on the golf course, and in the club house.
In hotel restrooms; in check-out line at the super market.
Wherever I could start a conversation; wherever people were talking.

LISTENING Can Change Knowledge into WISDOM

Someone said: *knowledge is power*. I don't quite agree. I say: knowledge is *potential* power. Knowledge between the covers of a book or dormant within the skull is like a frozen asset. When one learns when, where, and how to *apply* that knowledge to produce progress toward his or her goals, then knowledge can become *wisdom*. Listening to successful people not only gives one a lot of knowledge, it also reveals how successful people *use* their knowledge. One discovers applications for his or her knowledge . . . one becomes wise. And one of the most important bits of wisdom is: don't limit yourself to your own knowledge; *use resources* beyond yourself (gained by listening to others).

QUESTIONS

1. The author's lists of public and private listening skills are not exhaustive. What other skills are necessary for intelligent public and private listening?

2. Should a superintendent of school develop "listening posts" around the community? Why? How?

SPEECH PATTERNS OF ADMINISTRATORS

By
Lena L. Lucietto

Until recently, research in administration has ignored the relationship between administrative performance and the speech patterns of administrators. This article addresses this intriguing question and reports the provocative finding that differences in the speech patterns of elementary school principals are directly related to facets of administrative leadership.

The original idea to study the linguistic behavior of school principals was prompted by a nagging belief that language contains the key to many questions concerning interactions in the school situation. While there are many ways in which principals can communicate with their teachers, the spoken word is often used by principals in day-to-day situations. This paper reports the findings of a study[1] which analyzed the language usage of a group of administrators to determine whether or not a relationship exists between spoken language and administrative performance.

The Problem

The basic assumption is that there is a relationship between the language usage of school administrators and the intensity of certain characteristics in their nonverbal behavior. This assumption prompts the following question:

> whether (and if so, the degree to which) the administrator's language is related to staff perceptions of his administrative behavior.

Halpin's[2] work on administrative leadership provides a useful conceptualization of teacher perceptions of administrative behavior. Halpin identified

[1] Lena L. Lucietto, "The Verbal Behavior of Educational Administrators: An Analysis of the Language of School Principals" (unpublished Ph. D. dissertation, Department of Education, University of Chicago, 1969). This research also inquired into possible relationships between language and Schutz' FIRO dimensions of Inclusion, Control, and Affection. Detailed findings of this inquiry will be reported in a forthcoming monograph to be published by the Midwest Administration Center. This research was funded under the U. S. Office of Education, Small Research Project #8-E-081.

"Speech Patterns of Administrators," by Lena L. Lucietto, *Administrator's Notebook,* Vol. XVIII, No. 5, 1970. The *Administrator's Notebook* is published by the Midwest Administration Center of The University of Chicago, and is reprinted by their permission.

two dimensions of administrative leadership behavior: Initiating Structure and Consideration.

> ***Initiating Structure*** is that aspect of the leader's behavior which delineates the relationship between himself and the members of the group and establishes well-defined patterns of organization, channels of communication, and methods of procedure.
> ***Consideration*** refers to behavior indicative of friendship, mutual trust, and warmth in the relationship between the leader and the members of his staff.

In Halpin's conceptualization, superior leadership is associated with above-average performance in both dimensions. The administrator must be skilled in dealing with impersonal goals as well as with personal goals.

The guiding hypothesis in this inquiry was that differences in the subjects' scores on Halpin's LBDQ instrument would be related to differences in their linguistic behavior.[3]

Design and Methodology

The original sample consisted of thirty-seven male elementary school principals selected from schools in the suburbs of a large midwestern city. Of these, twenty participated in all phases of the research.

Preliminary identification of the principals was accomplished by administering the LBDQ to the full-time staffs of the schools in the original sample. Twenty principals who rated extreme scores on the LBDQ were asked to participate in the verbal segment of the research.

The verbal data consisted of spontaneous conversations between these twenty principals and their teachers. Three five-minute random segments of conversations, recorded with a different teacher, were transcribed for each of the twenty principals. The verbal data base included a total of 55,569 words used in 4,203 statements.

Statistical analyses[4] determined the relative emphasis which subgroups of principals gave to different elements of spoken language. The General

---

[2] Andrew W. Halpin, *The Leadership Behavior of School Superintendents. Their Perceptions of Board Members, Staff Members, and Superintendents.* (Chicago: Midwest Administration Center, University of Chicago, 1959); see also Andrew W. Halpin, "A Paradigm for Research on Administrative Behavior," and "How Leaders Behave," in *Theory and Research in Administration*, (New York: Macmillan, 1966), Chapters 2 & 3.

[3] For details of the Leadership Behavior Description Questionnaire see Halpin, *Ibid.*

Inquirer System[5] was then used to identify language differences among the principals as classified along the LBDQ dimensions. Sentences retrieved along the two dimensions were organized into composite dialogues reflecting the total speech output of the sample. The object of the verbal analysis[6] was to search for meaningful differences between composite dialogues and to see if these differences provided insights consistent with the nonverbal behavior patterns of the subjects. A careful analysis was made of contextual usage and level of meaning within composite dialogues. As a result, certain consistent language patterns emerged which substantiated the conclusions reached during the statistical phase of the study.

Summary Findings

Initiating Structure Dimension. Two major contrasts distinguished principals perceived as high in Initiating Structure from those perceived as low on this dimension. First, high Initiating Structure principals use fewer "self" words.[7] But when they do use words like *I* or *me*, they employ them in direct, specific, and forceful contexts:

> "*I* want to know why you would reject it."
> "Now this is *my* responsibility."
> "Let's get your reaction to some of the statements *I've* made."
> "Remember what *I* said to you though."

Such usage confirms Halpin's notion of the High Initiating Structure principal as one who maintains a structured organization and who delineates the relationship between himself and members of his staff. On the other hand, principals perceived by their teachers as low in Initiating Structure use more "self" words and use them in contexts of cooperation and agreement:

---

[4] Analyses of variance (using the MESA 97 program) were performed on the basis of percentage scores on language categories and scores obtained on Halpin's LBDQ. Both the Initiating Structure and Consideration dimensions yielded statistically significant results. The analyses of variance were also effective in determining which language categories were significant discriminators of the speech patterns of subgroups of principals.

[5] Philip J. Stone, *et al.*, *The General Inquirer: A Computer Approach to Content Analysis* (Cambridge, Mass.: The M.I.T. Press, 1966). The General Inquirer System was developed at Harvard in 1961 for content analysis research problems in the behavioral sciences.

[6] The researcher's verbal analyses of the composite dialogues were subjected to the scrutiny of two language professors with backgrounds in linguistics and an elementary school principal. The results of the researcher's analyses were substantiated by this panel of judges on 95.5 per cent of the composite dialogues developed from the retrieved language categories.

[7] For the category referring to the personal self the square root of the mean for principals perceived as being high in Initiating Structure is 4.99; for the principals perceived as being low in Initiating Structure the square root of the mean is 5.54.

"*I* kind of thought you were."
"It's all right with *me*, in a way."
"*I* agree with you that the other would be top priority."
"I'm not trying to be, I don't want to be dictatorial here."
"And *I* do too, you know."
"No, *I'd* agree with you."

Principals high in Initiating Structure are distinguished from those perceived as low by their use of "attempt" words, like *try, pursue*, and *effort*. Operationalizing Halpin's concept that high initiators are intent upon getting the job done, the principals perceived as being high in Initiating Structure use "attempt" words in positive, direct, action-oriented contexts and in sppecific statements concerning what they want themselves or their teachers to do, as the following examples show:

"The problem is there and we're going to take action to *try* to eliminate the problem."

"Especially mention that you know that he is scheduled for testing and that the teacher should *pursue* that, should see that it gets accomplished."

"*Try* and do it that way."

"And then let me know what happens there and then I'll *try* to set up an appointment for early next week and I will have her come in, and I will go over the achievement scores with her and then let her decide."

Principals perceived as low in Initiating Structure use similar words but in a less direct way. The sense of strength which might have been conveyed by "attempt" words is attenuated by the word *think* before it:

"I *think* that if you *try* something like that, I think along those lines, you may get some success with John . . . ."

"I *think* that I'd *try* to get the kindergarten througgh three using the same door."

Consideration Dimension. Several points of contrast were revealed between the language patterns of principals perceived by their teachers as being high in Consideration and those perceived by their teachers as being low.

High Consideration principals use a great deal of language which demonstrates a concern for helping the individual child, whom they view as a many-faceted person, not just as a pupil having relationships to the school. They understand the child's needs, as the following examples show:

> "These are the emotional problems and I think this is one of the things I indicated to you and to the mother when we talked about it, when I said we had some reservations about piling one more thing on this child."
>
> "And of course, we go along with this because this is the case I'm thinking of, that we just mentioned earlier, the father felt this boy was learning slowly, but he thought it was a pattern that would always be with him, just as it had always been with him."
>
> "Sure, and this is why I thought it was so important that we did not keep this kid back, because, if you know, academically, you know, it could have been a good case, but I think it would have just wiped him out completely."
>
> "This kid needs somebody strong."
>
> "This boy is very bright, and he has a lot of potential as far as leadership, but he is extremely impatient and intolerant of people."
>
> "Right now we have something that probably you can handle and which you are handling, and I don't think we will have to go into the homebound situation," and ". . . at the same time you are reinforcing what the first grade teachers are going to be doing."
>
> "This is true and he isn't home as often as a normal father, you know, and you can even see this in the boy."

Low Consideration principals, on the other hand, generally restrict themselves to viewing the child as a pupil, talking about the child in the context of the school setting, judging him only by what goes on in school. The general impression is that of an overriding concern with structure, an absolute tone, and a prevailing impersonality. The following statements exemplify these interpretations:

> "We're going to have this special education program in the township going, and we'll have a place to put emotionally disturbed children and the culturally deprived and all the other classifications."
>
> "They will just either sit there or they will get themselves involved in another breaking of your rules in the room and then become a discipline problem."
>
> "I think it's my figure, the figure and the office that I represent here in the school, and my relationship to the students."
>
> "You'd better have Mrs. ________ order that report and if not you'll have to write up a new one and get all the pertinent information on it."
>
> "Well, now, this point of taking tests is a very pertinent point because if it is obvious that he just is not going to be able to take tests and we have to discount this and evaluate him in some other way or we are going to obviously be in trouble."

According to Halpin, leaders who are perceived by their subordinates as being high in Consideration are easy to understand, accept suggestions made by staff members and find time to listen to staff members. The word usage of the sample of High Consideration principals makes the point obvious. Example after example of clarifying and supportive words occur in the High Consideration dialogues. High Consideration principals support teachers against parental pressures or interference, and sometimes even against pressures from the child. The words used are quite ordinary, such as *say, saying, talk,* and *tell,* but it is the context surrounding them which is revealing.

In these examples the principal is most often speaking to the teacher and reiterating or clarifying something which that same teacher has previously said. For example, "Are you saying, . . . ," "I know what you are going to say," "And as you said," "Of course, I know from what you have already said . . . ," and "Yes, that is what I was going to suggest." In all cases the impression is conveyed of a man who cares about what his teachers have to say, who values and takes into consideration their feelings and opinions. Perhaps the most striking finding of the entire analysis is just this: that High Consideration principals listen a great deal and let their teachers know that they are listening through verbal cues.

Rather than clarifying and supporting the teacher being addressed, Low Consideration principals typically indicate a concern for students, although often in a negative context. For example, "I talked with him about having friends and he did not seem to have any." At times negative comments are inspired by interactions with parents: "I think in most cases where I've talked to the parents they have not followed up." Instead of finding the considerate tone which is so obvious in the language of the High Consideration principals, the statements are terse: "You are a teacher and you could say it;" "Telling the teacher specifically what?" and "All right, he is educationally retarded, I'm not denying that, and I'm not talking about promoting him." Indeed, it is not surprising that these principals are perceived as being low in Consideration by their teachers.

In summary, Low Consideration principals do not appear to use clarifying language. The High Consideration principals do a great deal of clarifying and listening, and in a sense, are more open while Low Consideration principals seem defensive.

Implications

This study has succeeded in extending knowledge concerning the relationships between the language usage of principals and teacher perceptions of their behavior. The findings support the prediction that subgroups of principals, as indentified by the LBDQ, do have characteristic language patterns. The verbal instrument correlates highly with the Halpin dimensions of Initiating Structure and Consideration. These findings have important practical implications for the inservice and preservice training of administrators.

The administrator could be sensitized to the effects of his speech on others through a seminar devoted to increasing awareness of the impact of verbal behavior in interpersonal relationships. Using this strategy, the administrator's sensitivity to the facilitation of desired behaviors in teachers, students and other reference groups through appropriate verbal cues could be increased.

As an example, consider the finding that High Consideration principals use a great deal of clarifying language. Halpin's research demonstrated that certain aspects of a principal's behavior lead teachers to make the inference that he is high in Consideration. The study reported here concentrated on the verbal component of a principal's behavior and found that the use of clarifying language leads teachers to make the same inference — that the principal is high in Consideration. One way of identifying a principal likely to be perceived as high in Consideration is to administer the LBDQ to staff members. A simpler method, however, is to study a principal's language usage directly in terms of a set of specific language criteria.

Thus, it is possible that the use of clarifying language can provide a means of distinguishing groups of potenial administrators. This is reasonable because clarifying language is a behavior which lends itself readily to identification and training. Moreover, clarifying language has been the object of considerable emphasis in the psychological literature.[8] Patterns of behavior which create a non-threatening, accepting atmosphere manifest themselves in speech.[9] Seemingly, the principal who is perceived as being high in Consideration has mastered the task of responding to his teachers, of really listening to them, of conveying respect for their contributions. When the principal reflects back the teachers' comments he furnishes proof that he has been paying attention to them and that he welcomes their contributions. Such response on the part of the principal is rewarding to the teacher who in

---

[8] In this connection see Thomas Gordon, "Group-Centered Leadership and Administration," in *Client-Centered Therapy,* ed. by Carl R. Rogers (New York: Houghton-Mifflin Co., 1958). See also "The Clarifying Response," in Louis E. Raths, Merrill Harmin, and Sidney Simon, *Values and Teaching* (Columbus, O.: Charles E. Merrill Books, Inc., 1966), and Edgar H. Schein and Warren G. Bennis, *Personal and Organizational Change through Group Methods: The Laboratory Approach* (New York: John Wiley and Sons, Inc., 1965).

[9] Thomas Gordon, in *Client-Centered Therapy, op. cit.,* p. 349.

turn feels more accepted and more secure. This feeling of acceptance and security encourages more spontaneity in the teacher's speech.[10]

[10] *Ibid.*, pp. 350-55.

QUESTIONS

1. Listen to your principal or superintendent of schools over a period of several weeks, paying particular attention to his use of "self" and "attempt" words and the context in which he uses them. Listen also for language which demonstrates a concern for helping the individual child or judges him only by what goes on in school.
   Does your informal observation support the findings of Dr. Lucietto's investigation?

2. What question about this investigation would you like to ask Dr. Lucietto if you had the opportunity of meeting her?

UNIT VII

JOB MOTIVATION AND MORALE THEORIES

JOB MOTIVATION AND MORALE THEORIES

OVERVIEW

Job Motivation

What are the factors that cause workers to be satisfied and motivated or dissatisfied and unmotivated?

The "common sense" answer to this question used to be a listing of such items as salary, working conditions, tenure, fringe benefits, and the like, which were said to create dissatisfaction if they were poor and satisfaction if they were good. These factors were arranged in a conceptual continuum ranging from dissatisfaction at one end to satisfaction at the other.

The continuum assumes that dissatisfaction and satisfaction are polar opposites and that the same factors which cause dissatisfaction can cause satisfaction if they are eliminated or improved. Thus, if teachers are unhappy because of a low salary scale or board of education policies, the way to make them happy is to improve the salary scale or eliminate the policies which cause disgruntlement.

Dissatisfaction ←——→	**Satisfaction**
Low salary	Good salary
Inadequate fringe benefits	Adequate fringe benefits
Poor working conditions	Pleasant working conditions
Etc.	Etc.

Figure 1

CONTINUUM ASSUMPTION OF FACTORS CAUSING SATISFACTION AND DISSATISFACTION

Representative of this approach is a study by Chase who sampled 2000 teachers in 43 states and found that their job satisfaction was related to the quality of professional leadership and supervision of their school administrators and supervisors.[1] Other variables which affected their satisfaction included freedom to plan their own work, opportunity to participate in policy making, salary and adequate physical facilities. It is interesting to note that all but the last two relate to teachers' control over their own work.

Herzberg's motivation-hygiene theory. Frederick Herzberg challenged the continuum assumption by his bold and imaginative theory that the events which lead to dissatisfaction are of a different kind from those that lead to satisfaction.

Dissatisfaction and satisfaction are not polar opposites but instead are related to different ranges of needs. Maslow had theorized that men's needs could be arranged in a hierarchy of importance with life preservation needs at the bottom, security needs at the next higher level, and social, ego, and self-actualization needs following in that order. (See p. 71) The lowest three levels of needs — food and water, security, and belonging — are related to man's animal nature and man strives to satisfy them by earning money. The upper two levels stem from man's need to achieve and to grow in psychological maturity through achievement. The characteristically human needs are powerful incentives.

The animal needs, which are concerned with the avoidance of dissatis-

[1]Chase, F. S., "Factors for Satisfaction in Teaching," Phi Delta Kappan, Vol. 33, 1951, pp. 127 ff.

faction, are affected by inadequacies in salary, working conditions, tenure, and other aspects of the job environment. Because they are extrinsic to the job itself, Herzberg calls them hygienic factors. The absence of proper hygiene may bring on disease but the presence of hygienic conditions does not necessarily produce health. Similarly, the absence of hygienic factors in the working environment causes dissatisfaction but their presence does not of itself cause satisfaction.

Satisfaction and dissatisfaction in work are concerned with different factors serving the animal and human nature of man. The opposite of job dissatisfaction is not satisfaction but *no dissatisfaction*. The opposite of satisfaction is not dissatisfaction but *no satisfaction*. The difference is not semantic; it is substantive.

With this theory as a base, Herzberg surveyed 200 engineers and accountants in a Pittsburg industry, using a critical incident technique. Each of the men was asked to tell about a time when he felt exceptionally good about his job and another time when he felt quite unhappy about it. The sequences were repeated so that for each individual there were two favorable and two unfavorable events recorded. The investigators probed for the underlying causes of the feelings in each instance and by a process of content analysis classified the responses by topic to discover the types of events that led to job dissatisfaction or satisfaction.[2]

The findings of the study supported Herzberg's theoretical formulation that factors causing satisfaction are different in kind from those causing dissatisfaction. Herzberg discovered that the determinants of job satisfaction were achievement, recognition, the attraction of the work itself, responsibility, and advancement. The determinants of dissatisfaction were a different set of factors: company policy and administration, technical supervision, salary, interpersonal relations, and working conditions — all related to the work environment rather than to the nature of the work. The discovery that two distinctly different sets of factors were associated with satisfaction and dissatisfaction supported Herzberg's contention that these feelings are not opposites of one another but concerned with two different ranges of needs.

The satisfying factors are not operative until the hygienic factors are removed or improved. The removal or improvement of the job hygiene elements

[2] For a more detailed description of the procedure and its statistical treatment, see Sergiovanni's article, "Factors Which Affect Satisfaction and Dissatisfaction of Teachers," which is included in this text, pp. 402-420.

will reduce dissatisfaction but will not automatically bring about satisfaction or release motivational potential. The reason for this is that employees now look upon adequate salaries, good working conditions, acceptable fringe benefits, and helpful supervision as rights to be expected and not as satisfiers or incentives to increased achievement. Only accomplishment, recognition, responsibility, the opportunity for advancement, and the attraction of the work itself cause satisfaction and motivate toward greater achievement and psychological growth.

This is not to say that adequate salaries are not important. They are, but of themselves they do not motivate to increased effort. An increase in salary over and above the prescribed annual increment may be interpreted as a form of recognition and hence act as a satisfier and motivator but only if it is substantial. Small salary increases may allay dissatisfaction but fail to motivate. The incentive value of money is usually short-lived. Employees always feel underpaid and constantly seek for wage increases.

So, too, with other aspects of the work environment. Employees regard favorable conditions of work as a right. The rectification of unsatisfactory conditions removes causes of dissatisfaction but does not satisfy the human needs of man for psychological growth and maturity.

Satisfied workers are more productive workers only if their satisfaction stems from the work itself rather than the conditions of work. A feeling of achievement, the opportunity to exercise responsibility, recognition of their ability by their superiors and fellow workers, opportunity for advancement — these are potent incentives to increased effort.

Herzberg's experiment has been replicated many times with different populations — agricultural administrators, professional women, hospital maintenance personnel, nurses, manufacturing supervisors, food handlers, scientists, engineers, assemblers, accountants, military officers, and managers about to retire. It has been repeated in Finland and in the Iron Curtain countries of Yugoslavia, Hungary, and the Soviet Union. All the replications have confirmed the original findings.

Sergiovanni replicated it, with some modifications and additions, with 71 teachers selected randomly from a total population of 3682. His results once more demonstrated that many of the factors which accounted for satisfaction and many which accounted for dissatisfaction were mutually exclusive. He found that achievement, recognition, and responsibility were factors which contributed to satisfaction among teachers but, unlike the Herzberg study, that advancement and the work itself did not.

The findings of all the replications are consistent with Maslow's hierarchy of needs and McGregor's Theory Y.

Herzberg's motivator-hygiene theory has generated considerable controversy despite the large amount of empirical evidence supporting it and the extent to which its findings are consonant with other studies of job satisfaction. Evidence is offered by several investigators in support of a uni-scalar explanation of job satisfaction in opposition to Herzberg's duality theory. The differences in results may arise from the use of different research techniques or from a disagreement about the nature of job satisfaction. Is job satisfaction a single unitary attitude of an individual towards his employment or is it composed of varied and often conflicting evaluations of various aspects of it? The problem is still unresolved.

Implications of Herzberg's theory for educational administration. If Herzberg's motivator-hygiene theory is valid, school administrators should be aware that motivation and job satisfaction cannot be increased by attention to job hygiene factors only. Job hygiene factors should be modified to reduce job dissatisfaction and to permit the powerful satisfaction and motivating factors to operate.

It is doubtful that satisfaction can be attained by job rotation and job enlargement as practiced in some industries. The rotation of teachers to different grades or subjects of instruction has limited practicality and adding more tasks to a teacher's burden is self-defeating.

Job enrichment, which allows a teacher a larger degree of autonomy and freedom to innovate and experiment, and the substitution of supportive and clinical supervision for close or punitive supervision, are promising approaches. It is important that teachers have a large measure of control over their work and that administrators respect their opinions especially when offering them criticism or advice.

Recognition of achievement by praise or other means can create satisfaction providing it is recognized by others as truly merited.

Advancement to supervisory and administrative positions within the school system on the basis of demonstrated fitness and merit rather than seniority or favoritism contributes to the satisfaction of those fortunate enough to be promoted and also to the satisfaction of the members of the entire system who recognize the fairness of the procedure.

Vroom's motivational theory. Arguing that Herzberg's and Maslow's motivational theories are simplistic, Victor H. Vroom has proposed an alternative theory based on the assumption that an individual's course of action is related to the psychological events occurring at the same time as his behavior.[3]

Vroom's theory involves the concepts of valence, expectancy, instrumentality, and force. Valence is the strength of an individual's preference for a particular outcome. It is positive when he prefers the attaining of the outcome to not attaining it and negative when he prefers not attaining it to attaining it. It is neutral or zero when he is indifferent about the outcome.

Outcomes are classified as first-level and second-level. First-level outcomes are organizational objectives and are means of achieving second-level objectives or worker goals. For example, a teacher who seeks promotion decides that superior teaching performance rather than unsatisfactory or mediocre performance is the best means to that end. His first-level outcome, then, is superior performance and its valence is positive because of its relationship to the second-level outcome of promotion.

Expectancy is the perceived relationship between effort and first-level outcomes. It is the probability, ranging from 0 to 1, that a particular effort will result in a first-level outcome.

Instrumentality is the relationship between first-level and second-level outcomes. It refers to the probability that a first-level outcome will lead to a second-level outcome.

Force is synonymous with motivation. In algebraic terms it is the product of valences for the outcomes multiplied by the expectancies, $F = V \cdot E$.

Implications of Vroom's theory for educational administration. Vroom stresses the individualistic nature of motivation. Since every individual's combination of valences and expectancies is unique, specific suggestions for motivating individual behavior in organizations cannot be offered. Vroom offers no specifics for motivating individuals but he does identify some relevant variables. His theory needs further research and explication before it can be of practical value to school administrators. However, it does help us understand the relationship between individual and organizational goals, as Hunt and Hill point out:

Thus instead of assuming that satisfaction of a specific need is likely to

[3] Vroom, Victor H., *Work and Motivation,* New York: John Wiley & Sons, Inc., 1964.

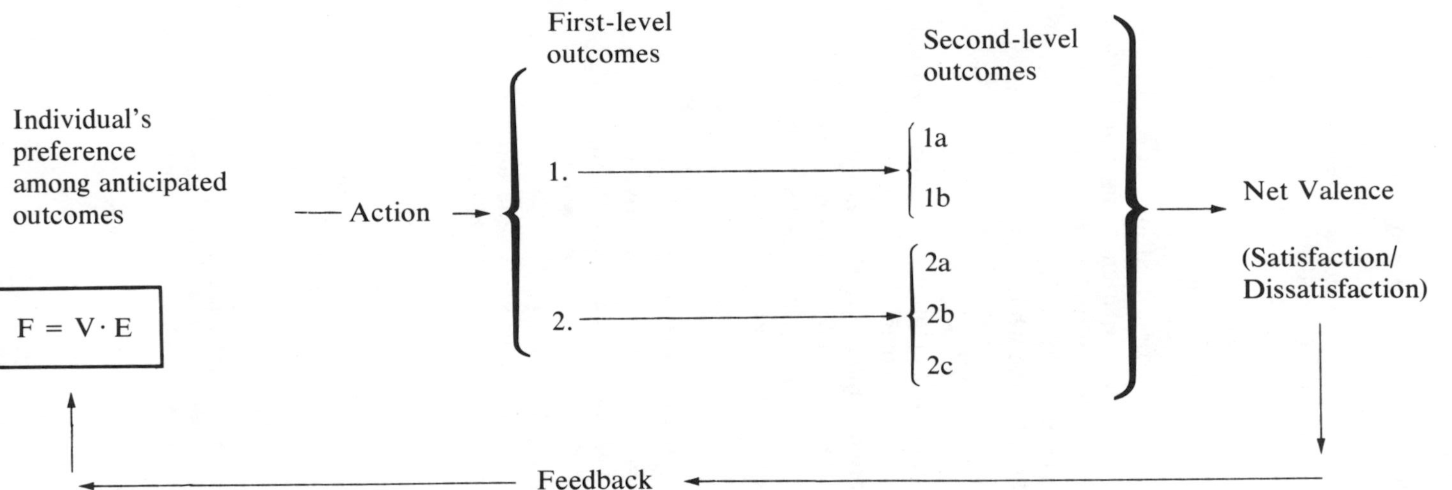

Figure 2

VROOM'S MOTIVATION MODEL

Adapted from Marvin D. Dunnette, "The Motives of Industrial Managers," *Organizational Behavior and Human Performance*, New York: John Wiley & Sons, Inc., 1964.

An individual's motivation is the product of the strength of his preference for a particular outcome and the probability that his actions will achieve a first-level outcome or organizational objective which in turn will lead to his second-level outcome or desired personal goal.

influence organizational objectives in a certain way, we can find out how important to the employees are the various second-level outcomes (worker goals), the instrumentality of various first-level outcomes (organizational objectives) for their attainment, and the expectancies that are held with respect to the employees' ability to influence the first-level outcomes.[4]

Morale

Morale is difficult to define. The word, first used instead of *esprit de corps* by a French general writing about his experiences in World War I, entered the English language in the 1920's, and today there are almost as many definitions as there are writers on the subject. *Esprit de corps,* literally the spirit of the army, is a group phenomenon while morale applies to both individuals and groups.

Wiles defines morale as the mental and emotional reaction of an individual to his job.[5] Lonsdale regards it as a dynamic relationship of equilibrium between an individual and an organization.[6] G. W. Allport defines it as an individual attitude in a group endeavor.[7] Guba thinks of morale as the extra amount of energy needed to carry out institutional tasks but before this extra effort can be evoked over an extended period of time there must exist an optimum degree of satisfaction.

Stogdill considers morale the freedom from restraint exhibited by a group in working towards a goal.[8] Motivation in his view provides the potential for morale; a group may have the incentive to act but lack the morale to do so.

By an analogy with a baseball team, Maier shows the difference between motivation and morale. All the players may be highly motivated and

---

[4]Hunt, J. G. and Hill, J. W., "The New Look in Motivation Theory for Organizational Research," *Human Organization,* Summer 1969, p. 104, quoted in Luthans, Fred, *Organizational Behavior,* New York: McGraw-Hill, 1973, p. 492.

[5]Wiles, Kimball, *Supervision for Better Schools,* Englewood Cliffs, N.J.: Prentice-Hall, 1955, 2nd Ed., p. 50.

[6]Lonsdale, Richard C., "Maintaining the Organization in Dynamic Equilibrium," *Behavioral Science and Educational Administration,* Sixty-third Yearbook of the National Society for the Study of Educational Administration, ed. Daniel E. Griffiths and Herman G. Richey, Chicago: University of Chicago Press, 1964.

[7]Allport, G. W. quoted in Maier, Norman R. F., *Psychology in Industry,* Boston: Houghton Mifflin, 1965, 3rd ed., p. 118.

[8]Stogdill, Ralph M., *Individual Behavior and Group Achievement: a Theory,* New York: Oxford University Press, 1959, pp. 277-278.

their individual attitudes may be favorable. One wants to be a home-run king, another wants to get the most stolen bases, and so on, but unless they are working toward a common goal they lack high morale.[9] The characteristics of high morale, in Maier's view, are team spirit or a helping attitude, perseverance, enthusiasm for the task at hand, and resistance to frustration. Low morale is characterized by apathy, bickering, jealousies, disjointed effort, and pessimism.[10]

In terms of the Getzels-Guba model, morale is a function of three variables: belongingness, rationality, and identification or commitment. Belongingness is the congruence between personal needs and institutional expectations. Rationality is the appropriateness of role expectations to institutional goals. Identification is the integration of institutional goals with individual needs and values.

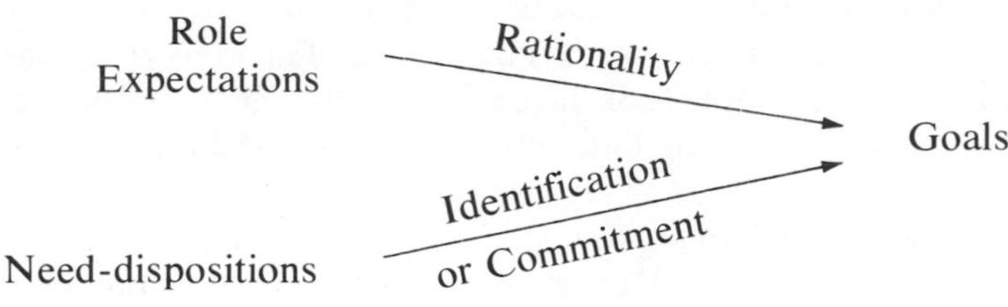

Figure 3

THE DIMENSIONS OF MORALE

Adapted from J. W. Getzels and E. G. Guba, "Social Behavior and the Administrative Process," *School Review,* 65 (1957), 439. University of Chicago Press.

Morale depends on the degree to which individuals integrate organizational goals with their own needs, their perception of the logical relationship between role expectations and organizational goals, and the simultaneous satisfaction of their own needs and organizational role expectations. In mathematical terms, morale is a function of commitment, rationality, and belongingness, $M=f(C \cdot M \cdot B)$.

---

[9] Maier, Norman R. F., *Psychology in Industry,* Boston: Houghton Mifflin, 1965, 3rd ed., p. 119.

[10] Ibid., p. 120.

Group morale. Morale problems vary in small and large groups. It is easier to maintain high morale in a group composed of not more than 12 than in a larger group because individuals find identification with large groups difficult.

There seems to be agreement that morale is heightened when group members have an opportunity to participate in making decisions which affect them and when their achievements are recognized by their associates. Group members feel satisfied and secure when they know they are treated fairly and when the policies which control their work are consistent. The leader behavior of their supervisors particularly affects their sense of well-being. Leaders whose behavior is characterized by high initiating structure and consideration affect group morale positively. (See pp. 136-140) Negative employee behaviors such as absenteeism and grievances are related to low consideration scores coupled with high initiating structure scores.

Individual morale. Individual and group morale usually go together although exceptions are not uncommon. The morale of an individual teacher is often symptomatic of the morale of the entire faculty. Zest, confidence, and cooperation cut across both the individual and group and affect both.

Individual ego and group prestige go hand in hand. There seems to be a relationship between individual pride and group accomplishment. Years ago, when the Yankees dominated baseball, more than one sports writer commented that ball players improved the moment they put on a Yankee uniform.

Morale and productivity. Are high morale and productivity related? This problem, which seems so simple on its face, is quite complex. Research shows two conflicting findings.

Generally individuals with high morale are motivated to work to capacity. Their urge to be productive probably stems from many influences acting upon them rather than a single one. These influences have their roots in the organization, administrative and supervisory behavior, the work group, and individual personality. Some of these may overlap as in the case of a professionally-minded teacher who enjoys stimulating, purposeful leadership and helpful colleagues.

But satisfied individuals are not *necessarily* more productive. Morale and productivity are related only when certain conditions are present. As Herzberg showed, the satisfaction must arise from the work itself rather than the conditions surrounding it. A satisfied worker is a more productive worker only when his satisfaction arises from his work performance. There must be group cohesiveness so that the goals of the work group and the organization are in harmony.[11] There must also be supervisory behavior which sets high standards of performance, gives subordinates a sense of personal worth, and is supportive of their efforts.

A desire for improvement should not be interpreted as a sign of poor morale. True professionals always want to better their performance, no matter how high their morale. Teachers are frequently dissatisfied with courses of study or the methods and results of their teaching, and their dissatisfaction may spur them to improve. Before equating dissatisfaction with low morale we must ask why the worker is dissatisfied. There are different types of dissatisfaction and, paradoxically, some may actually be desirable.

Morale of school administrators. Factors related to high morale in school administrators include community recognition, cooperative relationships with the board of education and other administrators in the district, responsibility and influence in the community, participation in projects to improve education, satisfaction with such material factors as salary and facilities, and attendance at professional meetings.[12] With the exception of the last two, these parallel those of Sergiovanni.

The morale of school administrators tends to be high despite the pressures of their jobs and the accompanying harassments. A survey revealed that 83 out of 105 Massachusetts school superintendents liked the superintendency very much. Only 26 expressed dissatisfaction with many features of it, the most common source of dissatisfaction being the lack of leisure time.[13]

Morale of teachers. Goodwin Watson listed five factors essential for high morale in teachers:

1. A sense of positive goal
2. Mutual support
3. A sense of commitment
4. A sense of contribution

---

[11] Seashore, S. E., *Group Cohesiveness in the Industrial Work Group,* Ann Arbor, Mich.: University of Michigan Survey Research Center, 1954.

[12] Barry, F., "Factors Affecting Administrative Morale," unpublished Ed.D. project, Syracuse University, 1956.

[13] Gross, N., Mason, W. S., and McEachern, A. W., *Exploration and Role Analysis of the School Superintendency Role,* New York: John Wiley & Sons, Inc., 1958, p. 355.

5. A sense of progress and awareness of results. ("Morale is much stronger when the teacher can see that he has the competency to improve existing conditions.")[14]

School administrators need to be aware that teacher morale is not static. It changes from time to time but never suddenly. Just as illness is preceded by small warning signs that all is not well, so too is poor morale. An alert administrator is sensitive to such signs and takes anticipatory action.

Administrators should also be aware that teachers' perceptions of conditions are what matter rather than the actual conditions. Thus, a faculty may grouse about work loads or pupil behavior even though it can be demonstrated that these aspects of school life are superior to those in comparable districts. Conditions must be viewed from the teachers' eyes.

Low standards of performance or permissive discipline instead of helping morale may actually lower it.

Good human relations combined with systematic procedures are crucial. So also are teacher participation in the formulation of policies, especially those relating to curriculum and methods of teaching, and stimulating leadership.

SELECTED READINGS

Griffiths, Daniel E., *Human Relations in School Administration,* New York: Appleton-Centur-Crofts, 1956.

This much-quoted book has a chapter on morale which, although in need of up-dating, is still helpful and informative.

[14] Watson, Goodman, "Five Factors in Morale," Second Yearbook, Society for the Psychological Study of Social Issues, New York: Holt, Rinehart, and Wilson, Inc., 1942, pp. 30-47.

Lane, W. R., Corwin, R. G., and Monahan, W. G., *Foundations of Educational Administration,* New York: Macmillan, 1967.

Chapter 13, "Evaluation and Morale," considers symptoms, personal and situational approaches among administrators, major sources of dissatisfaction among teachers, and the meaningfulness of work.

Wiles, Kimball, *Supervision for Better Schools,* Englewood Cliffs, N.J.: Prentice-Hall, 1955.

Chapter 4, "How Can Staff Morale Be Built?" treats the topic in a popular style but is founded on scholarship and experience.

Vroom, Victor H., *Work and Motivation,* New York: John Wiley & Sons, Inc., 1964.

Vroom's motivational theory, an alternative to Herzberg's, has stirred considerable controversy. Difficult to understand, it underscores the complexities of work motivation. Unlike Herzberg and Maslow, Vroom does not offer specific suggestions for motivating individuals in organizations.

TOPICS FOR DISCUSSION

1. In informal conversations with other teachers in your school, try to find out the most common causes of satisfaction and dissatisfaction. Do your findings correspond to those of Sergiovanni, pp. 376-377? If they differ, can you account for the differences?

2. Interview your school principal to learn what he perceives to be the causes of dissatisfaction among the faculty. Do his perceptions correspond with the teachers'?

3. If you were a school administrator, what action would you take to lessen dissatisfaction among teachers?

4. Morale studies often show that female teachers and older teachers have a higher degree of morale than male teachers and young teachers. How do you account for this?

5. Sometimes it is necessary to depress morale in order to increase productivity. Explain.

6. Show how the results of Herzberg's research are supported by McGregor's Theory Y.

7. What are some signs of poor morale in a school system? In a school? In a class?

8. How might a teacher improve the morale of his students?

9. "Morale is sometimes higher when supervisors are less permissive." a. Do you agree? Why? b. Do teachers interpret directions from supervisors as a criticism of their ability? Is it necessary to admit the superior and technical wisdom of the supervisor?

10. What new insights have you gained from this unit?

THE HERZBERG CONTROVERSY: A CRITICAL REAPPRAISAL

By
Orlando Behling, George Labowitz, and Richard Kosmo

Herzberg's motivator-hygiene theory has been the subject of controversy since its presentation in 1959. The conventional explanation of job satisfaction considers satisfaction and dissatisfaction to be polar extremes in a continuum. Herzberg contended that the factors causing dissatisfaction and those causing satisfaction were different sets and could not be arranged in a continuum. Job satisfaction factors, however, do not become operative until those causing dissatisfaction have been removed or improved.

Critics of Herzberg's theory dispute his duality approach. They submit the findings of 15 research studies as evidence in support of their stand and argue that Herzberg's results are a product of his critical-incident method.

The authors of this article suggest that the difference in results reflects a view of job satisfaction as a single attitudinal entity rather than as many varied and often conflicting evaluations of a job. Moreover, there is no single uniscalar theory. New measuring devices and techniques are needed to provide reliable data.

In 1959 Professor Frederick W. Herzberg fired the first salvo in what has proven to be one of the most heated and durable controversies in modern management theory. The salvo was, of course, the book *The Motivation to Work*[1] in which he and his co-authors first presented his motivator-hygiene theory of job satisfaction. In order to understand the nature of the controversy which has grown up around this approach to the study of job satisfaction, it is necessary to look briefly at the contrast between the Herzberg proposal and what the "conventional wisdom" of management has to say about the topic.

The conventional explanation of job satisfaction considers "satisfac-

[1] F. Herzberg, B. Mausner, and B. Snyderman, *The Motivation to Work* (New York: John Wiley and Sons, 1959).

"The Herzberg Controversy: A Critical Reappraisal," by Orlando Behling, George Labowitz and Richard Kosmo *Academy of Management Journal,* March 1968, pp. 99-108. Copyright © 1968 by Academy of Management Journal and reprinted by their permission.

tion'' and ''dissatisfaction'' to be the extremes of a continuum having a neutral condition in which the individual is ''neither satisfied nor dissatisfied'' as its midpoint. Generally this analysis assumes that individuals shift along this continuum in response to changes in numerous factors, some of which are intrinsic to their jobs, while others make up the environment in which they are performed. The nature of the work itself, the challenge it offers, the behavior of supervisors, pay, working conditions, relations with co-workers, and dozens of other things are all assumed to affect job satisfaction to some degree. The exact way in which these factors interact is usually less clearly expressed. Basically, however, dissatisfaction is seen as the product of an absence of factors causing satisfaction. Deficiencies in supervision, pay, or similar things can result in dissatisfaction or, if their absence is balanced off by the presence of positive factors, in neutrality.

If one of the factors is improved or a new one introduced, the individual is thought to move some distance toward the positive ''satisfied'' end of the scale. If one of them is reduced or eliminated (a well-liked supervisor is replaced or a new and less competent food service crew is moved into the cafeteria), the individual shifts toward the negative ''dissatisfied'' end of the continuum. How far along the scale any given change will move an individual is seen as a function of several factors. The magnitude of the shift along the scale is usually seen as being positively (though generally not perfectly) correlated with the size of the change in the factor generating it. Thus a $40 per month salary increase would be expected to increase job satisfaction more than a $20 one, though not necessarily twice as much. The size of the shift is also seen as being affected by the type of factor being changed. There seems to be little real agreement as to the relative importance of various factors. It is generally accepted, however, that variations do exist and that, for example, a salary increase would have greater positive impact than painting the walls of the work area a new and more cheerful color. It was against the backdrop of general and mostly unquestioning acceptance of this conventional view of job satisfaction that Herzberg exploded his bombshell.

The Herzberg position gained considerable acceptance, in part, perhaps, because it lent support to the emerging ''Theory Y'' idea that factors intrinsic to the job were somehow different and more important than those surrounding the work, in terms of effects on motivation. Equally important in the development of acceptance of the approach, however, was the fact that during the early 1960's Herzberg, as well as a number of other researchers, performed studies which verified the existence of the motivator-hygiene duality. These studies, which were summarized by Herzberg in *Work and the Nature of Man,*[2] flowed out as a steady stream of dissertations, journal articles, and papers at scholarly meetings. Using the

Herzberg critical-incident method or something closely akin to it, these researchers were able to demonstrate the existence of the duality in close to twenty separate studies involving such diverse groups as housekeeping and unskilled food service workers, county agricultural extension workers, women in high-level professional positions, scientists, nurses and engineers — including a group of Hungarian engineers.

Despite the large volume of empirical evidence by supporters of the duality theory and the degree to which the Herzberg theory dovetails with other approaches to the study of job satisfaction, from the very beginning the theory was not without its critics. They have been able to assemble a great deal of evidence in support of a conventional, uniscalar explanation of job satisfaction as an alternative to the Herzberg approach.

Robert B. Ewen, for example, factor-analyzed the responses of 1,021 life insurance agents to a 58-item, four-point attitude scale and was able to extract six major factors. Two of the factors (*work itself* and *prestige*) were motivators in Herzberg's framework, three (*manager interest in agents, company training policies,* and *salary*) were hygienes. The sixth factor appeared to be indicative of overall contentment with the job, and thus was labeled *general satisfaction*. With attributes (motivators or hygienes) held constant at a neutral level when they were not being tested, it was found that the effects of certain motivators and hygienes on general satisfaction varied from those predicted on the basis of Herzberg's theory. In both of the two subgroups making up the total sample, *company training policies* and *manager interest in agents* — both nominally hygienes — actually acted as if they were motivators. *Salary* acted as a motivator in one group, but caused both satisfaction and dissatisfaction in the other. *Prestige* (a motivator) caused satisfaction and dissatisfaction in both groups. Only one factor, *work itself,* acted as a motivator in both samples in accordance with the Herzberg theory.[3]

Charles L. Hulin and Patricia A. Smith tested the Herzberg quality by examining the relative contributions of various motivators and hygienes to satisfaction and dissatisfaction and by examining the effects of their presence on workers' judgments of jobs. The assumption underlying their first hypothesis is that, if the duality theory is correct, there should be no significant correlation between degree of contentment with motivators and overall job dissatisfaction, nor should there be a correlation between degree of

[2]World Publishing Company, 1966.

[3]"Some Determinants of Job Satisfaction: A Study of the Generality of Herzberg's Theory," *Journal of Applied Psychology,* XLVIII (1964), 161-163.

dissatisfaction with hygienes and overall job satisfaction. The logic behind the second hypothesis is drawn from a conventional uniscalar analysis. If an individual is highly satisfied when a particular factor is present in his job, he should be dissatisfied when it is absent and vice versa. Tests of these two hypotheses among a group of home office employees of a large international corporation revealed results which more clearly support the uniscalar approach than they do Herzberg's duality. Satisfaction with *pay received* (a hygiene) and with *advancement* and *work done* (both motivators) correlated significantly with satisfaction, dissatisfaction, and overall satisfaction-dissatisfaction scores for male employees. Similar though less clear results were obtained for female employees. A linear relationship between log (to correct for unequal scale intervals) importance of a factor when it was absent and its importance when it was present for four hygienes and two motivators was uncovered, though the results among the female employees were again not absolutely clear.[4]

These are by no means the only studies which conflict with or do not fully support predictions based on the Herzberg duality. A brief survey of the literature revealed thirteen such studies in addition to the two reported in the preceding paragraphs. These studies treated a variety of populations and involved several different methods of gathering data. In fact, the only truly consistent pattern running through them was a negative one — none of the studies in support of a uniscalar explanation used Herzberg's critical-incident technique. With few exceptions, although the measuring techniques varied, they used some form of structured, scalar device.

Examination of the results of these studies and those reported by Herzberg in his 1966 book reveals a fairly obvious but nonetheless important point: almost without exception, research using the Herzberg critical-incident method gives results supporting the Herzberg duality. Just as constantly, research using other methods of gathering data provides results which conflict with the Herzberg approach and support a uniscalar theory of job satisfaction. This fact has not escaped the proponents of the two types of theories and the argument between them has unfortunately deteriorated to a series of accusations and counteraccusations, revolving for the most part around the relative merits of the two methods of obtaining data. The proponents of the uniscalar theories consider Herzberg's results to be an artifact of the method used.

Only Victor H. Vroom attempts to account for this. He takes the posi-

[4] "An Empirical Investigation of Two Implications of the Two-Factor Theory of Job Satisfaction," *Journal of Applied Psychology,* LI (1967), 396-402.

tion that Herzberg's unstructured format tends to overemphasize the importance of self-controlled actions as sources of satisfaction and things beyond the control of the individual as sources of dissatisfaction. The individual can, according to Vroom, take credit for his successes and blame others for his failures by emphasizing what Herzberg has labeled motivators as sources of satisfaction and what he calls hygienes as sources of dissatisfaction.[5]

Herzberg attempts to refute the Vroom argument by pointing out that it is naive to think that persons wishing to make themselves "look good" would prefer to blame hygienes for dissatisfaction. More frequently, Herzberg states, individuals who want to make themselves "look good" tend to complain about lack of motivators such as *responsibility* and *possibility of growth* rather than problems with petty hygienes. He then attacks the data-gathering techniques used in the non-Herzberg studies pointing out that:

> The "fakeability" of responses and the openness to suggestion that job-attitude scales have shown in the past recommended the motivation-hygiene procedure. While it is not possible to eliminate bias, conscious or unconscious, on the part of the subjects when using verbal methods (written scales or interviews), at least it is much more difficult to conjure up appropriate events in one's life during a patterned interview than it is to respond "appropriately" to items in a questionnaire. The general practice of psychologists of giving lists of factors for employees to rate with respect to their job satisfactions by now should be recognized as one of the most misleading approaches to the study of work feelings.[6]

He then provides a series of alternate interpretations of the results obtained in some of the studies which were seen by their original authors as providing evidence in conflict with the motivator-hygiene duality. When seen through Herzberg's eyes, the results are in line with the duality theory.

Despite these reinterpretations, the contention made in an earlier paragraph still stands to the satisfaction of the authors of this paper: research using open end formats similar to the original critical-incident method used by Herzberg, almost without exception, gives results supporting the Herzberg duality. With a similar degree of certainty, more structured methods of data gathering give uniscalar results. Students of the field have thus far failed to take these results at face value. The fact that dif-

---

[5] *Work and Motivation* (New York: John Wiley and Sons), p. 129.

[6] *Work and the Nature of Man,* op. cit., pp. 130-132.

ferent results are obtained from different techniques is in itself extremely important.

The differences are important because they are indicative of the possibility that the study of job satisfaction in general may be hoisted by its own petard or, more accurately, by its own theoretical construct. The culprit in this case is the theoretical construct "job satisfaction" itself. Because it has so much face validity — that is, it seems so "right" that there should be a single attitudinal entity which represents an individual's overall feelings about his work — and because it is such a convenient concept for the development of theories and the design and analysis of experiments, it has apparently been forgotten that job satisfaction is nothing more than an idea made up by students of the field.

There is no evidence that any single, unitary, overall attitude toward an individual's employment exists. There is, however, considerable evidence to support the idea that the researcher must deal with many varied and often conflicting evaluations of various aspects of a man's job, different parts of which are tapped in different ways by different data-gathering techniques. The argument between the pro- and anti-Herzberg factions itself is evidence in support of this idea. The conflicting results obtained with semistructured critical-incident techniques and more structured scalar approaches provide further support. Even the repeated references of some of the opponents of the duality theory to "*the* uniscalar approach" is incorrect. Close examination reveals that there is *no* single uniscalar theory. The assumption underlying research, the comments made about the nature of job satisfaction and the research results obtained, reveal little consistency from author to author or from study to study. They are talking about different things, measuring them in different ways, and obtaining dissimilar results.

Obviously, if this analysis of the nature of job satisfaction is correct, substantial reorientation in treatment of intervening variables connecting aspects of work and the work environment to employee behaviors is required. It must be recognized that any attempt to produce a single measure of job satisfaction, whether it is based on a conventional uniscalar or a Herzberg duality analysis is doomed to failure. Effort must be devoted to the development of many measuring devices and techniques which will provide reliable and internally consistent data indicative of important parts of the total attitudinal complex. Only then can steps be taken to relate those aspects of the entity we call job satisfaction to aspects of the job, its environment, and individual behavior on the job.

QUESTIONS

1. In your own words summarize the objections to Herzberg's motivator-hygiene theory as expressed in this article.

2. In your own words summarize Herzberg's refutation of Vroom's argument.

FACTORS AFFECTING TEACHER MORALE

By
F. C. Ellenburg

Although research on teacher morale has been copious, reports of it have been scattered and not easily available. This article presents the major conclusions of several studies. The results in many cases are contradictory but the author discerns a general conclusion: that the administrator is a key person in teacher morale. How he works with his staff determines to a great extent the morale of the school. Three implications of this general conclusion for administrators are discussed.

Administrators in every school in America, at one time or another, have faced the problem of teacher morale. There seems to be evidence that when high morale exists, productivity is increased.

One study of 12 secondary public schools in Dearborn, Mich., compared the achievement of students with the morale of their teachers. In conducting the study, Koura[1] found that student achievement increased under teachers with high morale and decreased under teachers of low morale.

MORALE AND A SCHOOL'S CHARACTER

Morale affects more than just productivity or student achievement. It assists in establishing the character of a school. It is one of the factors which may determine whether a school functions at its best, demanding and receiving the utmost from its students, or whether the school plods along happy just to see the passing of another day. Von Burg[2] says, "Call it rapport, morale, spirit, enthusiasm, or what you will. It is something easy to overlook and yet it can make a school stand ahead of the rest."

---

[1]Koura, Hussein S. "An Experimental Study of Students' Achievement in Relation to the Morale of Selected Secondary School Teachers." Unpublished Ph.D. Dissertation, The University of Michigan, 1963.

[2]Von Burg, Fred. "Faculty Morale Rests with Administrators." *Review of Educational Research,* XXXIII (October, 1963), pp. 267-269.

"Factors Affecting Teacher Morale," by F. L. Ellenburg, *Bulletin of the NASSP,* December 1972, pp. 37-44. Copyright © 1972 by the NASSP, and reprinted by their permission.

Why teachers quit the profession was examined by Nelson and Thompson[3]. Out of a list of 17 reasons, the one given most frequently was salary. Others near the top included teaching loads, inadequate supervision, poor assignment during first year at teaching, discipline problems, pressure groups, marriage, and inadequate preparation in the subject field.

Dropkin and Taylor[4] did a similar study with relation to first-year teachers only. The problems that these teachers faced were, in descending order of difficulty: discipline, relations with parents, methods of teaching, evaluation, planning, materials and resources, and classroom routines.

STAFF MORALE AND ADMINISTRATION

The fact that faculty morale is related to democratic school administration was found by Burkett[5]. From his data it can be assumed that the more democratic the administration, the higher the morale. There is, naturally, a limit to this relationship as one can go only so far with either of the two variables.

Redefer[6] polled 5,000 teachers to get their opinion of the factors affecting teacher morale. He learned that the quality of education in the individual schools and superiority ratings of teachers by administrators had some affect on the morale of the faculty. Some of the factors that did not affect morale were thought to be: merited status, sex, age, level of education, and socio-economic status. An interesting outcome of this study was the discovery that salary in the opinion of the teachers surveyed was *not* a factor in determining the morale status of teachers.

Robinson and Connors[7] reported that intellectual stimulation and pay are significantly related to the job *satisfaction* of teachers in general and that clerical work, pay, and supervisory duties are closely related to the job *dissatisfaction* of teachers in general. It is interesting to note here that salary was both satisfying to some teachers and dissatisfying to others. An analysis

---

[3] Nelson, Robert H. and Michael L. Thompson. "Why Teachers Quit." *The Clearing House,* XXXVII (April, 1963), pp. 467-472.

[4] Dropkin, Stanley and Marvin Taylor. "Perceived Problems of Beginning Teachers and Related Factors." *The Journal of Teacher Education,* XIV (December, 1963), pp. 384-390.

[5] Burkett, Clifford A. "The Relationship Between Teacher Morale and Democratic School Administration." Unpublished Ed.D. Dissertation, University of Pittsburgh, 1965.

[6] Redefer, Frederic L. "Factors that Affect Teacher Morale." *Nations Schools,* LXIII (February, 1959), pp. 59-62.

[7] Robinson, H. Alan and Ralph P. Connors. "Jobs Satisfaction Researches of 1961." *Personnel and Guidance Journal,* XLI (November, 1962), p. 240.

of the types of people employed in the profession might explain these results. A married man who is just beginning to teach might be discouraged with his income, whereas a single woman with many years' experience might be delighted.

The morale level of selected schools in Illinois appeared to be a function of their particular organizational climate in a study by Koplyay[8]. His most surprising finding was that where significant differences were found, schools using merit salary policies seemed to have higher morale as reflected in their responses to the Morale Inventory.

Although personal factors are the most important of all factors in determining the individual morale level of the teacher, the principal is the key non-personal factor in the professional environment of the teacher, according to the research of Hood[9]. The teacher's relationship with the principal is more important in determining morale level than is the teacher's relationship with other teachers.

FINDINGS IN SMALL CITIES

Some interesting things for administrators of schools in small cities were found by Lolis[10]. While teacher morale, teacher attitudes to parents, and teacher attitudes to children are found to be intertwined and closely related, no single factors of cause and effect in these relationships emerged. The level of the school system neighborhood, the certainty of administrative support in differences with parents, and the feeling of gap between one's own social status and that of the children are important and contributory but not single factors in teacher morale. The teacher with high morale tends to be the teacher who relates well to parents and children. Perhaps because such a teacher is a more positively oriented person.

Sweat[11] studied the relationship of morale to the authoritarian-

---

[8] Koplyay, Janos B. "Relationships Between Teachers' Morale, Organizational Climate, and School Salary Policies in Selected Schools." Unpublished Ph.D. Dissertation, Northwestern University, 1966.

[9] Hood, Evans C. "A Study of Congruence of Perceptions Concerning Factors Which Affect Teacher Morale." Unpublished Ph.D. Dissertation, East Texas State University, 1965.

[10] Lolis, Kathleen. "Teacher Morale and Teacher Attitudes Toward Parents: A Psychological and Social Analysis of Inter-relationships of Teacher Morale, the Attitudes Teachers Express Towards Parents and Certain Personal Factors in Teachers' Lives in 'Small City'." Unpublished Ph.D. Dissertation, New York University, 1962.

[11] Sweat, Joseph P. "Authoritarian-Democratic Personality Traits of High School Principals and Teacher Morale." Unpublished Ed.D. Dissertation, University of Arkansas, 1963.

democratic traits of high school principals in Arkansas. Although the differences were not statistically significant, he found that the faculties of democratically administered high schools made the highest scores on a morale instrument, the faculties of the neutrally administered high schools made the second highest scores, and the faculties of the authoritarian-administered high schools made the lowest scores.

Greenwald[12] studied the relationship of morale of interpersonal and intrapsychic factors. His conclusion was that feelings have a significant effect upon morale. The interpersonal factors included attitudes toward authority and hostility. The intrapsychic factors included, among others, hopelessness, meaninglessness, and loneliness.

In a study which was related to the one done by Greenwald, Havens[13] found that the degree to which organizational dimensions correlate with the job satisfaction of teachers depends upon the personal dimensions of the teacher. The results of this study indicate that the environmental aspects that are related to job satisfaction are not necessarily the same for all subgroups of teachers. That is to say that the things which might cause job dissatisfaction for one person may not affect the morale of another.

CHARACTERISTICS OF HIGH, LOW MORALE TEACHERS

In a study of morale among teachers, Suehr[14] identified many of the characteristics of teachers with high or low morale. The relationships were found to be significant.

High morale teachers more often: (1) were females, (2) had taught longer, (3) felt they fulfilled their parents' expectation for them, (4) grew up in an urban society, (5) went to bed early and got up early, (6) came from upper or upper-middle class homes, (7) indicated both of their parents were happy in their respective occupations, (8) felt their childhood family was very close, (9) felt they have more close friends, (10) rated their personality type as slightly introverted, (11) indicated a stout or plump body-type.

---

[12] Greenwald, Albert. "A Study of the Relationship of Teacher Morale to Selected Interpersonal and Intrapsychic Factors." Unpublished Ph.D. Dissertation, New York University, 1963.

[13] Havens, Nel Hansen. "The Relationship of Organizational Aspects and Personal Characteristics to Teacher Job Satisfaction." Unpublished Ed.D. Dissertation, Stanford University, 1963.

[14] Suehr, John H. "A Study of Morale in Education." Unpublished Ed.D. Dissertation, University of Colorado, 1961.

Low-morale teachers more often: (1) know or estimate their I.Q. to be higher, (2) taught in schools where parent dissatisfaction is greater, (3) felt in teaching they are not realizing their fullest potential, (4) felt they are stubborn in their personality make-up, (5) worried, (6) missed school, (7) felt they repress their true feelings less, (8) consider themselves more or less in degree of gregariousness rather than average, (9) indicated an opposite-sexed parent had influenced them more, (10) considered their self-confidence to be greater, (11) considered themselves above or below average in degree of perseverance, (12) were the youngest child, (13) felt their personal appearance to be above average, (14) rated their degree of ambition as being greater, (15) indicated more consumption of alcoholic beverages.

Franks[15] reported that teacher morale seems to be related to teachers' ages, age differences from principals, extent of teaching experience with their present principals, degree of closed-mindedness, extent of similarity to principal's general social values, and perceptions of the morale level of their colleagues. The conclusion about the relation of age to morale seems to be in contradiction with the findings of Redefer.

Studying how teachers' perceptions of administrative dimensions relate to their morale was done by Pryor[16]. He concluded that as a teacher's perception of the administrative function increased, his morale increased. A minor conclusion was that the pattern of administration was not significantly related to the morale of the teachers. This is in contradiction to the results found by Burkett. The conflict of results found in these two might be clarified by Leiman[17].

Leiman found that the participation of teachers in administrative decisions was definitely related to morale. Four of his conclusions were:

- Teachers who participate in school administration have higher morale than teachers who do not participate.
- Teachers who participate in school administration have more positive attitudes toward their principals, toward their colleagues, and toward their pupils.

---

[15] Franks, Thomas D. "A Study of Teacher Morale as Related to Selected Personal and Professional Factors." Unpublished Ed.D. Dissertation, Indiana University, 1963.

[16] Pryor, Guy Clark. "The Relationship Between Teachers' Perception of Administrative Dimensions and the Morale Status of Teachers in Certain Texas Schools." Unpublished Ed.D. Dissertation, North Texas State University, 1964.

[17] Leiman, Harold I. "A Study of Teacher Attitudes and Morale as Related to Participation in Administration." Unpublished Ph.D. Dissertation, New York University, 1961.

- Teachers who participate in school administration have higher regard for themselves and for the teaching profession.
- Female teachers seem to have higher morale than male teachers.

FACTORS RAISING, LOWERING MORALE

Factors affecting teacher satisfaction with their jobs, reported by Johnson[18] include: achievement, interpersonal relations, recognition, work itself, and responsibility. Four factors — policy and administration, working condition, status, and personal life — showed statistical relationship to teacher dissatisfaction. It is worthy of note that salary was one of the five factors which *did not* show statistical relation to either satisfaction or dissatisfaction of teachers with their jobs.

Ten significant factors found by Strickland[19] to have a tendency to raise teacher morale in descending order were: (1) cooperation and helpful co-workers who share ideas and materials; (2) a helpful and cooperative principal; (3) appreciative and cooperative parents; (4) adequate supplies and equipment; (5) freedom in classroom teaching; (6) respectful pupils; (7) an adequate school plant; (8) pupils interested in school work; (9) a helpful supervisor; and (10) a well-organized school with formulated policies.

The most significant factors that tend to lower morale were: (1) lack of relief from pupil contact during the school day, (2) clerical duties, (3) lack of cooperation and support of principal, (4) inadequate school plant, (5) lack of staff cooperation, (6) excessive teaching load, (7) low salary, (8) lack of parent cooperation and interest, (9) poor pupil discipline, and (10) lack of proper equipment and supplies.

According to the research by Napier[20], high teacher morale is associated with:

1. the administrator's understanding and appreciation of the teacher as an individual.
2. the confidence the teacher has in the administrator's professional competence.

---

[18] Johnson, Eldon D. "An Analysis of Factors Related to Teacher Satisfaction — Dissatisfaction." Unpublished Ed.D. Dissertation, Auburn University, 1967.

[19] Strickland, Benjamin F. "A Study of Factors Affecting Teachers' Morale in Selected Administrative Units of North Carolina." Unpublished Ed.D. Dissertation. The University of North Carolina, 1962.

[20] Napier, Thomas G. "Teacher Morale." Unpublished Ed.D. Dissertation, The University of Nebraska Teachers College, 1966.

3. the support the teacher receives from the administration regarding discipline problems.
4. teacher participation in the formulation of policies that affect them.
5. adequate facilities and equipment.
6. adequate teaching supplies.
7. teaching assignments which are commensurable with training.
8. fair and equitable distribution of extracurricular assignments.
9. professional training provided through the inservice program.
10. job security.
11. an adequate policy for leaves of absence.
12. a fair and equitable distribution of the teaching load, and
13. salaries that are comparable with professions requiring equal training.

At first glance the findings of these studies seem to indicate nothing except that a statistician can show anything by the use of statistics. In many cases the results are contradictory. After a more in-depth look at the findings, however, one begins to realize that a general conclusion seems to be evident. That is, that the administrator — his attitudes, his policies, his procedures, his understanding of the individual teachers, and his philosophical approach to problems — seems to be the major factor in teacher morale. How he works with his staff, whether he treats them as individuals with worth and dignity or merely as part of the machine, will determine to a great extent the morale of the school.

IMPLICATIONS FOR ADMINISTRATORS

It should be clear that the administrator should strive to keep lines of communication open at all times between himself and his staff as well as within the staff. A lack of communication will most surely prohibit understanding of one another and will deter the proper morale status. Many studies have found that the teacher's morale level was definitely affected by that teacher's opinion of whether he was understood and appreciated by the principal. In communicating with the staff, the principal should be careful to demonstrate his respect for the teacher as an individual with worth and dignity and as a professional person qualified to do the job for which he was hired.

Secondly, the administrator should strive to publicly support his staff as much as possible. Private support is valuable and will aid in building morale, but public support is essential to the well-being of individuals and the staff as a whole. This does not mean that the principal must take the attitude that the teacher is always right and everyone else must be wrong. It does mean, however, that he should be careful in giving criticism or allowing undue criticism of a staff member. He should always strive to build respect for staff members as professional people. Even if criticism is justified, the administrator should be careful in its use. When problems arise due to deficiencies on the part of a staff member, the administrator should earnestly seek ameliorations that will allow the teacher to grow professionally and personally.

Finally, the administrator should involve staff members in the operation of the school. When teachers are involved, their understanding of the functions of the administrator increases and this positively affects teacher morale. Democratic administration can be overdone and should be used carefully. The administrator should remember and frequently remind the staff that he is legally and professionally responsible for making the decisions, but that he respects their opinions and ideas and will use them where possible. Matters that can be decided by the staff and which affect them should be referred to them for consideration and possibly for a decision. When teachers feel that they have had some say in the making of policies by which they work, they will feel more commonality with the goals of the staff as a whole.

From all of this it should be clear that the administrator plays a significant part in the establishment and maintenance of morale among the staff of a school. How well he functions and the degree to which he involves his staff will help determine the morale of his faculty.

QUESTIONS

1. Explain in specific terms how an administrator can keep his lines of communication open at all times "between himself and his staff as well as within the staff." (p. 400)

2. It has often been said that a school reflects its principal. Do you agree? Explain.

FACTORS WHICH AFFECT SATISFACTION AND DISSATISFACTION OF TEACHERS

By
Thomas Sergiovanni

Sergiovanni replicates Herzberg's research on job satisfiers and dissatisfiers, using a sample population of teachers and slightly modifying the original Herzberg design. The critical-incident technique is described and results analyzed.

Achievement, recognition, and responsibility appeared as sources of teacher job satisfaction. Advancement and the work itself did not appear as satisfiers as in Herzberg's study.

Implications of this study for administrative behavior are discussed.

Satisfaction and dissatisfaction of teachers has long been an area of intense interest to researchers in school personnel management. In a recent review of industrial and education job satisfaction research Robinson[1] notes that over 40 per cent of the studies reviewed relate to teachers and their satisfaction or morale. However, the voluminous research in the field to date appears to be lacking in conceptual perspective and may, in fact, be misleading.

An assumption basic to the literature in this area is that factors which account for job satisfaction of teachers and factors which account for job dissatisfaction of teachers are arranged on a conceptual continuum (Figure 1). Thus, a factor identified as a source of dissatisfaction is also likely to be a potential satisfier. The administrative prescription based on this assumption is that if a factor accounting for dissatisfaction is altered or eliminated, job satisfaction will result. Or, failure to maintain a satisfaction condition will result in teacher dissatisfaction.

---

[1] Robinson, Alan. Ralph Conners and Ann Robinson, "Job Satisfaction Researches of 1963." *Personnel and Guidance Journal*. XLIII, 1964. p. 361.

"Factors Which Affect Satisfaction and Dissatisfaction of Teachers," by Thomas Sergiovanni, *Journal of Educational Administration*, Vol. V, No. 1, May 1967. Copyright © 1967 by the Journal of Educational Administration, and is reprinted by their permission.

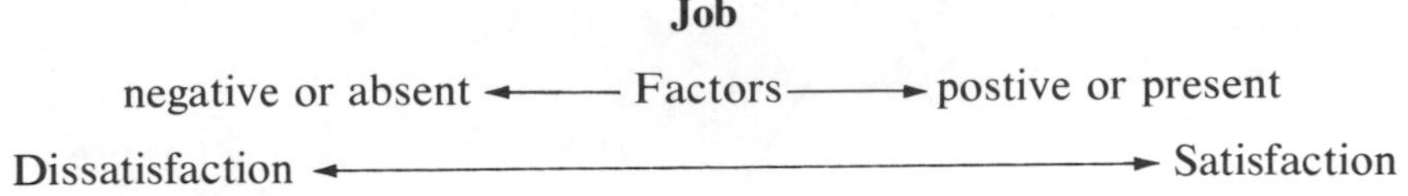

Figure 1

The Continuum Assumption

The Herzberg Study

The impetus for the research reported here comes from the work of Frederick Herzberg, Bernard Mausner, and Barbara Snyderman.[2] In a review of industrial motivation studies Herzberg observed that a difference in the primacy of work factors appeared depending upon whether the investigator was searching for factors which led to job satisfaction or factors which led to job dissatisfaction.[3] This observation led to the concept that some factors in the work situation were "satisfiers" and other factors were "dissatisfiers." Herzberg hypothesized that some factors were satisfiers when present but not dissatisfiers when absent; other factors were dissatisfiers, but when eliminated as dissatisfiers did not result in positive motivation (Figure 2).

Herzberg's research with accountants and engineers[4] tends to confirm the existence of the satisfier and dissatisfier phenomenon. Herzberg found that five factors (achievement, recognition, work itself, responsibility and advancement) tended to affect job attitudes in only a positive direction. The absence of these factors did not necessarily result in job dissatisfaction. The eleven remaining factors, if not present, led to employee dissatisfaction. The absence of these factors tended not to lead to employee satisfaction. Herzberg observed that job factors which resulted in satisfaction were directly related to the work itself. Job factors which resulted in dissatisfaction

[2] Herzberg, Frederick, Bernard Mausner, and Barbara Snyderman. *The Motivation to Work*. New York. John Wiley and Sons. 1959.

[3] Herzberg, Frederick, Bernard Mausner, Richard Peterson and Dora Capewell. *Job Attitudes: Review of Research and Opinion*. Pittsburg. Psychological Service of Pittsburg. 1957.

[4] Herzberg, *The Motivation to Work*.

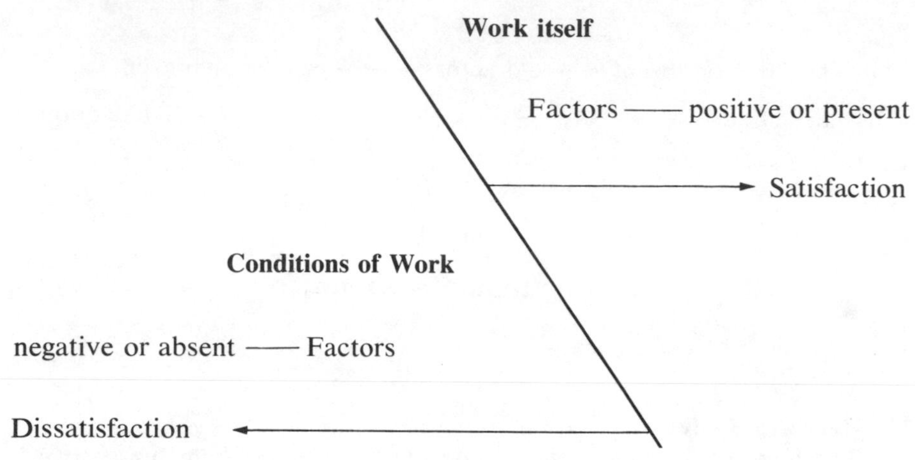

Figure 2

Herzberg hypothesis: Satisfaction factors and dissatisfaction factors are mutually exclusive

tended to be related to the environment of work. The factors in their two sub-categories are as follows.

Satisfiers (found in work itself)	**Dissatisfiers (found in the environment of work)**
1. Achievement	1. Salary
2. Recognition	2. Possibility of growth
3. Work itself	3. Interpersonal relations (subordinates)
4. Responsibility	4. Status
5. Advancement	5. Interpersonal relations (superiors)
	6. Interpersonal relations (peers)
	7. Supervision — technical
	8. Company policy and administration
	9. Working conditions
	10. Personal life
	11. Job security

Though arrived at empirically, the Herzberg findings appear to be consistent with the motivational theory proposed by Maslow.[5] Maslow hypothesized a hierarchy into which needs arranged themselves in order of their appearance. The Maslow hierarchy of needs, from lowest order (most prepotent) to highest order (least basic or prepotent), is as follows: physiological needs, security needs, social needs, esteem needs, and the need for self actualization. Needs that are at or near the top of the hierarchy, assuming that lower order needs are met, will tend to be the focus of an individual's attention. As long as lower order needs are satisfied, they cease to motivate the individual; in our society the physiological and security needs are well met for most people, thus they seldom motivate behavior.

Herzberg identified two levels of needs for his subjects; "hygienic" needs (which tend to focus on the dissatisfaction factors identified in his study) and satisfaction needs (which tend to focus on the satisfaction factors identified). According to Herzberg if "hygienic" needs are not met, the individual is unhappy. Provision for "hygienic" needs, however, does not ensure increased motivation. The satisfaction needs have motivational potential but depend upon reasonable satiation of "hygienic" needs before they become operative.[6]

Herzberg's findings have important implications for educational administration and supervision. They suggest that much of present practice in personnel administration may be directed at controlling the hygienic conditions which have, at best, limited motivating power for professional teachers.

THE PROBLEM

The writer undertook a study to determine whether or not the factors reported by teachers would distribute themselves into mutually exclusive satisfaction and dissatisfaction categories. Further, if the satisfaction-dissatisfaction phenomenon existed for teachers, would the factors resulting in satisfaction be concerned with the work itself, and would the factors resulting in dissatisfaction be concerned with the environment of work?

The following questions were raised:

1. Is there one set of factors which tends to satisfy teachers and another

---

[5] Maslow, A. H. *Motivation and Personality*. New York. Harper & Brothers. 1954.
[6] Herzberg, *The Motivation and Work*. pp. 113-119.

set which tends to dissatisfy teachers? Or are these factors better described as being arranged on a continuum with each being a potential satisfier and dissatisfier?

2. Will the distribution of factors vary for subpopulations of teachers? (Subgroups included: (1) male teachers v. female teachers, (2) tenure teachers v. nontenure teachers, (3) elementary school teachers v. secondary school teachers.)

Methodology

The overall design of this study followed, with some additions and modifications, the design developed and used by Herzberg. Respondents were asked to report incidents judged by them to be representative of their job feelings. Each incident or sequence consisted of three phases: (1) the respondent's attitudes expressed in terms of high job feelings and low job feelings, (2) the first-level and second-level factors[7] which accounted for these attitudes, (3) the effects of these attitudes and factors as reported by respondents. Through content analysis the factors which accounted for the expressed attitudes were sorted into the categories developed, defined, and used by Herzberg in the original study. The effects were sorted and categorized in the same manner.

The Population and Sample

The population for this study consisted of teachers in school districts in Monroe County, New York (the City of Rochester was not included in the sample population). The districts ranged from semi-rural to suburban in orientation and in size from a teaching staff of 36 to a teaching staff of 528. The total sample population consisted of 3,382 teachers.

One hundred and twenty-seven respondents were selected at random from the 3,682 teachers who comprised the study population. The sample was drawn from lists furnished by each of the participating school districts. Administrators, guidance counselors, department chairmen not involved in actual teaching, librarians, supervisors, and other nonteaching personnel were not included in the sample. Seventy-one of the 127 teachers agreed to participate.

The sample included 30 male teachers and 41 female teachers. Elementary school positions were held by 37 respondents and junior high or senior

[7] Herzberg differentiated between the objective events, the actual stories reported by respondents and the subsequent perceptions of respondents of what the objective events meant to them. The actual stories were the basis for the first-level factors and the "interpretation" of the stories by respondents comprised the second-level factors. First-level factors are listed in Table 1 and second-level factors are listed in Table 2.

high school positions were held by 34 respondents. Thirty-seven of the 71 respondents held tenure appointments. Respondents ranged in age from 21 years to 64 years with the average age being 37 and the median age being 32. Years of teaching experience ranged from three months to 36 years with the average experience being nine years and the median experience being seven years.

The Interview

The interview outline and interviewing procedure used in this study was a direct adoption of the Herzberg format. Respondents were told that they could start with either a time when they had felt unusually high or good about their job or a time when they had felt unusually low or bad about their job. After the first unusual sequence each respondent was asked to give another. If he had previously given a high story, he was then asked for a low. The same procedure was followed for most recent high feelings and most recent low feelings.

The objective events, the actual stories, which were reported by respondents as being the source of high or low feelings about their jobs were coded as first-level factors. The second-level factors were categories which constituted respondents' feelings as a result of the objective stories they had related and the attitudes they had identified. The analysis of second level factors came primarily from respondents' answers to two questions: "Can you tell me more precisely why you felt the way you did?" and "What did these events mean to you?" One respondent related a story involving a merit salary increase as a source of good feelings about his job. When asked why he felt the way he did, he replied, "It meant that the administration or whoever was responsible for the increase felt that I was doing a good job." The first-level factor in this sequence was coded as salary. This was the objective occurrence. The second-level factor in this sequence, however, was coded as recognition. The respondent perceived the merit increase as a source of recognition.

Respondents were limited to four specific sequences: an unusual high attitude sequence, an unusual low attitude sequence, a most recent high attitude sequence, and a most recent low attitude sequence. Two hundred and eighty-four sequences were collected for the study. The statistical analysis was based on the number of sequences rather than the number of respondents. Focusing on sequences was consistent with the method used by Herzberg.

Analysis of the Interviews

The technique of content analysis was used in coding each sequence.

Herzberg suggests two basic approaches to content analysis. The first is an *a priori* approach in which the analysis is based upon a predetermined categorical scheme. The second approach extracts the categories from the raw data itself. Herzberg chose the *a posteriori* approach which produced categories specifically related to the data collected in his study. Herzberg noted, however, that the resulting categorical scheme developed through the *a posteriori* approach was not very different from that which could have been derived from an analysis of the literature.[8]

The scheme used for content analysis in this study was a direct adoption of the categories developed and used by Herzberg, and so represents an *a priori* approach, but one based on empirical evidence.

Coding Procedure

The next step in the analysis of the interviews required that the factors contained in the high and low attitude stories of respondents be identified and coded into the categorical scheme. Further, since several factors could appear in a given story, the factor which contributed most to the expressed feeling was to be isolated for subsequent analysis. Each sequence was coded in terms of expressed attitude (high or low), sequence type (unusual or recent), and level (first and second).

Sequences were coded, independently, by three of five judges. A total of 284 sequences were coded for the study. Coding decisions were classified as unanimous choice, majority choice or consensus choice. First-level coding choices of judges for each of the first 160 sequences included 87 unanimous decisions, 69 majority decisions, and 4 consensus decisions. For the second-level factors there were 96 unanimous decisions and 64 majority decisions. Three-way disagreements did not occur for the second-level factors.

Figure 3 summarizes the basic features of the content analysis.

THE ANALYSIS OF RESULTS

The results of the study are presented in two sections. The first reports the results relating to the mutual exclusiveness of factors for the total sample. This section includes an analysis of the first-level and second-level factors which appeared in high attitude sequences and an analysis of

---

[8] Herzberg, *The Motivation to Work.* p. 38.

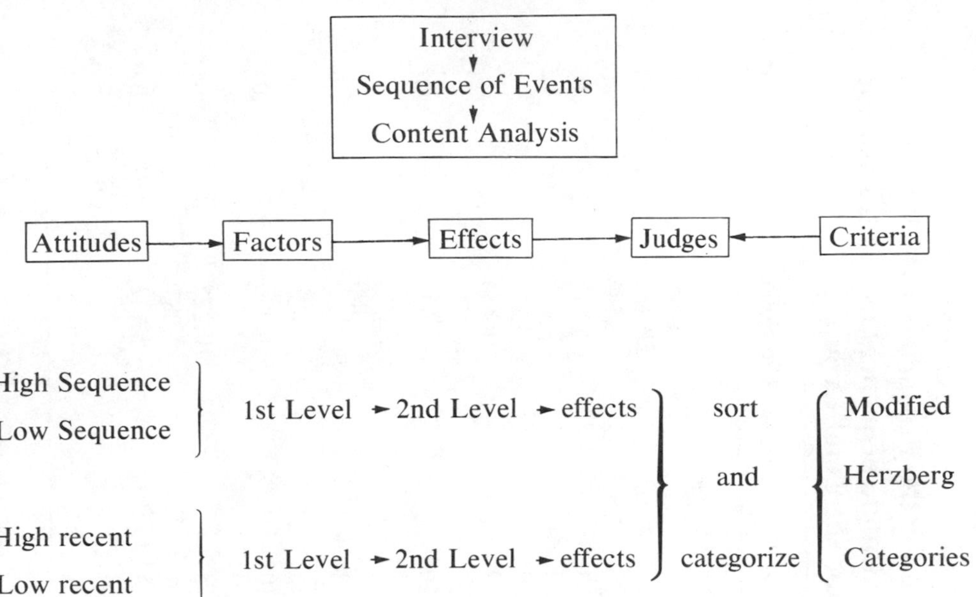

Figure 3

Basic design features of the content analysis

the first-level and second-level factors which appeared in low attitude sequences.

The second section includes a summary of the differences in responses for male teachers as compared with female teachers, tenure teachers as compared with nontenure teachers, and for elementary as compared with secondary teachers.

HIGH ATTITUDE SEQUENCES CONTRASTED WITH LOW ATTITUDE SEQUENCES

Table 1 includes the percentages and values of chi-squared for the frequency with which first-level factors appeared in high attitude sequences as compared with low attitude sequences for the total group.

Sixty-nine percent of the sequences which accounted for high job at-

Table 1

Percentages and Values of Chi Squared for the Frequency with Which Each First-Level Factor Appeared in High Attitude Sequences as Contrasted with Low Attitude Sequences for the Total Group

Factor	High	Low	Chi Squared	P
	+ NS = 142	NS = 142		
1. Achievement —	30*	9	10.500	.01
2. Recognition	28*	2	30.139	.001
3. Work itself	11	8	.346	
4. Responsibility —	7*	1	5.818	.05
5. Advancement	0	1		
6. Salary	2	3		
7. Possibility of growth	6	2	1.454	
8. Interpersonal relations — subordinates)	7	20*	7.605	.01
9. Interpersonal relations (superiors)	3	4	.900	
10. Interpersonal relations — (peers)	1	15*	14.086	.001
11. Supervision — technical —	1	10*	8.470	.01
12. School policy and — administration	2	13*	10.227	.01
13. Working conditions	2	6	2.083	
14. Personal life —	0	5*	5.142	.05
15. Status	0	0		
16. Security	0	1		

+ NS in this table and in Table 2 refers to number of sequences.
Percentages in this table and in Table 2 are approximate but do not vary more than .0075.

* Difference between Highs and Lows is significant. Chi Squared value required for significance at the .05 level is 3.841.

titudes included the first-level factors achievement, recognition, and work itself.Responsibility appeared in seven per cent of the high attitude sequences. Advancement did not appear in the 142 high attitude stories.

First-level factors six through 16 (the environment of work factors) appeared in 24 per cent of the high attitude sequences. The major contributors to the 24 per cent were possibility of growth (6%), and interpersonal relations with subordinates (7%). Personal life, status, and security did not appear in the high attitude sequences.

Interpersonal relations (subordinates), interpersonal relations (peers), supervision technical and school policy and administration appeared in 58 per cent of the low attitude sequences. Achievement, recognition, work itself, responsibility and advancement accounted for 21 per cent of the incidence of factors which appeared in the lows. Status did not appear as a first-level factor in low attitude sequences.

The first-level factors which appeared more often in high attitude sequences were achievement*, recognition*, work itself, responsibility*, and possibility of growth. The first level factors which appeared more often in low attitude sequences were advancement, salary, interpersonal relations (subordinates)*, interpersonal relations (superior), interpersonal relations (peers)*, supervision technical*, school policy and administration*, working conditions, personal life*, and security.

The percentages and values of chi-squared for the frequency with which second-level factors appeared in high attitude and low attitude sequences are reported in Table 2.

Achievement, which appeared in 50 per cent of the sequences, was the dominant second-level factor for the highs. Recognition appeared in 21 per cent of the sequences involving high job feelings. The remaining factors appeared in 29 per cent of the high attitude sequences.

For second-level low attitude sequences feelings of unfairness, with 32 per cent, was the dominant factor. Feelings of guilt and inadequacy, security, and work itself (6%) and possible growth (6%). The second-level factors advancement, status, salary, and fairness did not appear in high attitude sequences.

For second-level low attitude sequences feelings of unfairness, with 32

---

* Difference between Highs and Lows is significant. Minimum P = .05.

Table 2

Percentages and Values of Chi Squared for the Frequency with Which Each Second-Level Factor Appeared in High Attitude Sequences as Contrasted with Low Attitude Sequences for the Total Group

Factor	High	Low	Chi Squared	P
	NS = 142	NS = 142		
1. Recognition	21*	7	9.025	.01
2. Achievement	50*	13	26.677	.001
3. Work itself	6	9	.190	
4. Advancement	0	0		
5. Responsibility	4	4		
6. Group feelings	3	3		
7. Possible growth	6	3	1.230	
8. Status	0	5*	5.1428	.05
9. Security	5	11	1.565	
10. Fairness-unfairness	0	32*	43.022	.001
11. Pride, guilt, inadequacy	5	11	2.782	
12. Salary	0	2		

* Difference between Highs and Lows is significant. Chi squared value required for significance at the .05 level is 3.841.

per cent, was the dominant factor. Feelings of guilt and inadequacy, security, and work itself appeared in 31 per cent of the low sequences. Recognition with seven per cent and lack of achievement with 13 per cent were other contributors to low job feelings. The remaining six factors appeared in 15 per cent of the low sequences. The factor advancement did not appear in the lows.

The second-level factors which appeared more often in high attitude sequences were recognition*, achievement*, and possible growth. The second-level factors which appeared more often in low attitude sequences were work itself, status*, security, feelings of unfairness*, feelings of guilt and inadequacy, and salary.

Summary

The results presented in the first section demonstrate that many of the factors which accounted for high job feelings of teachers and many of the factors which accounted for low job feelings of teachers were mutually exclusive.

The first-level factors which appeared significantly as highs (as contrasted with lows) were recognition, achievement, and responsibility. The first-level factors which appeared significantly as lows (as contrasted with highs) were interpersonal relations (subordinates), interpersonal relations (peers), supervision — technical, school policy and administration, and personal life.

Achievement and recognition were the second-level factors which appeared significantly as highs. Feelings of unfairness and low status were the only second-level factors which appeared significantly as lows.

Subgroup Differences

The analysis of results relating to the second question raised in this study strongly suggests that subgroups of teachers tend not to differ in their responses to sources of high and low job feelings. Significant differences were found in only three of 168 possibilities.

Men teachers tended *not* to respond differently from women teachers to sources of high and low job attitudes. No significant exception to this tendency was found.

Tenure teachers and nontenure teachers tended *not* to differ in their

---

*Difference between Highs and Lows is significant. Minimum P = .05.

responses to sources of high and low job feelings. Three significant exceptions to this tendency were found:

1. The first-level factor interpersonal relations (superior) appeared as a source of low job feelings for tenure teachers in four per cent of the 142 low attitude sequences. This factor did not appear as a source of low job feelings for nontenure teachers.
2. Eleven per cent of the low attitude sequences involved nontenure teachers citing the first-level factor interpersonal relations (peers) as a source of low job attitudes. This was in contrast to four per cent for tenure teachers.
3. Security, a second-level factor, appeared in 11 per cent of the low attitude sequences. Nine of the 11 per cent were cited by nontenure teachers.

Elementary school teachers and secondary school teachers tended *not* to differ in their responses to sources of high job attitudes and low job attitudes. No significant exception to this tendency was found.

DISCUSSION

The Polarity of Factors

The results of this study indicated that achievement, recognition, and responsibility were factors which contributed predominantly to teacher job satisfaction. Interpersonal relations (subordinates), interpersonal relations (peers), supervision — technical, school policy and administration, personal life, and fairness-unfairness were factors which contributed predominantly to teacher job dissatisfaction. The remaining factors appeared to be bi-polar, possessing the potential to contribute to both satisfaction and dissatisfaction (many of the factors did not appear with sufficient frequency to test adequately for polarity).

The Satisfaction Factors

The three dominant factors which appeared in high attitude sequences were achievement, recognition and responsibility. Achievement accounted for nearly one out of three first-level high attitude sequences and for one out of two second-level high attitude sequences. In view of the predominance of the factor achievement, it is interesting to note that most of the teacher achievement-centered stories involved less concrete evidence of actual success and more sensing and feeling by teachers that students had been reached and were presumably affected in some positive way.

This noticeable lack of concrete success reinforces Lortie's notion of psychic gratification as a reward base for teachers. Lortie[9] argues that societal rewards (salary, prestige, and power) are, in general, not perceived by teachers as being in abundance. Thus, teachers tend to focus on psychic gratification as a primary source of reward in their work. One of the major sources of psychic gratification, according to Lortie, is the interaction that the teacher has with individual students and classes where the teacher perceives that something has happened. The teacher senses or believes that, as a result of his activity, a change has taken place in the student or class. Lortie cites the terms "I reached them," "It went today," as being common expressions used by teachers to describe this phenomenon.

This psychic gratification, which is characterized by a task-oriented interaction with some perceived measurable result, was most typical of many of the success stories related by teachers.

Recognition appeared three times as often in high sequences as in low sequences. Sources of recognition for teachers varied. Teachers talked about feedback from principals, supervisors, parents, students, and fellow teachers. Recognition took the form of letters, oral statements, gifts, incentives, and committee appointments.

The need for recognition, the overt bolstering of self-esteem, appears to be important to teachers. The absence of recognition tends not to affect low job attitudes of teachers.

Responsibility, although significantly found to be a high, appeared in only seven per cent of the high attitude sequences. This percentage is small when one considers that teachers do assume a considerable amount of responsibility. As the classroom door closes behind the teacher, it is implied that she assumes responsibility for her own work. This responsibility is limited, however, and falls within the framework of the rules and regulation of the school district, and school board. Further limits are imposed by the state legislature and our society at large. Whatever responsibility a teacher assumes, in terms of what to teach, falls within the framework of the prescribed curriculum.

Perhaps even more interesting than the appearance of achievement, recognition and responsibility as positive polar factors was the absence of

---

[9] Lortie, Dan, "The Changing Role of Teachers as a Result of Such Innovations as Television, Programmed Instruction, and Team Teaching." Richard Lonsdale and Carl Steinhoff (eds.). *The Administrative Analysis of Selected Educational Innovations.* Report of the First Interuniversity Conference for School Administrators. Syracuse University, 1964.

advancement and work itself. These factors did appear as satisfiers in Herzberg's study.

The factor advancement was not mentioned by teachers in high attitude stories. Teaching offers little opportunity for concrete advancement (change in status or position) and in fact any particular teaching assignment could be considered as a terminal position. Whatever potential the factor advancement has as a satisfier appears to be lost for teachers under our present system. Capitalizing on this factor, as a potential source of satisfaction, implies providing overt opportunities for advancement within the ranks of teachers.[10]

Work itself appeared as a bi-polar factor in the study. Although the factor appeared more frequently in teacher high attitude stories, it also appeared as a frequent source of low job feelings. It appears that the job of teacher (although potentially able to provide unlimited opportunity for creative and varied work) requires considerable attention to maintenance type activity. Routine or maintenance tasks range from attendance and scheduling details, daily health checks, study hall assignment, and lunch duty to blowing noses and pouring young scholars into snow suits. The work itself factor, although found to be rich in satisfaction potential, was frequently cited as a source of dissatisfaction for teachers.

The Dissatisfaction Factors

Perhaps of greatest interest among the dissatisfiers was the factor interpersonal relations (subordinates), which appeared in 20 per cent of the low attitude sequences and in seven per cent of the high attitude sequences.

It seems appropriate to assume that since students are the very crux of a teacher's work, they should account for many of the successes and good feelings that teachers have. Indeed, this is so. The students were the raw material for the achievement successes and acts of recognition which teachers perceived as sources of great satisfaction. Establishing an appropriate relationship with students appears to be critical. Once established, the teacher can capitalize on this relationship in pursuit of work-centered or job itself satisfaction. It appears that a happy relationship with students is not in

---

[10] Schools frequently contain an informal promotion system for teachers. Advancement within the informal promotion system may include movement to another grade level, being assigned "quality" students, receiving equipment and facility priorities, and moving to a better school within the district. This informal promotion system was not described in teacher high attitude sequences but did appear in low attitude sequences. Judges coded these low attitude sequences into the factor categories working conditions or school policy and administration.

itself potent enough to be a source of job satisfaction. A poor relationship with students, however, can be a source of considerable teacher dissatisfaction.

Responses of Subgroups Tend Not to Differ

A most interesting finding of the study was that subgroups of teachers — tenure and nontenure, male and female, elementary and secondary — tended not to differ in their responses to sources of job satisfaction and dissatisfaction. There were only three exceptions, out of 168 possibilities, to this tendency. All three involved tenure and nontenure teachers.

One interpretation of this finding is that the satisfaction and dissatisfaction factors identified in this study apply to teachers irrespective of their sex, teaching level or tenure status.

CONCLUSION

This study provides support for the hypothesis that satisfiers and dissatisfiers tend to be mutually exclusive. Further, it was found that factors which accounted for high attitudes of teachers were related to the work itself and factors which accounted for low attitudes of teachers were related to the conditions or environment of work.

Relative to other activities, teachers derive the most satisfaction from work-centered activity. This finding was reflected in the predominance of achievement, recognition and responsibility as sources of teacher job satisfaction. The low attitude sequences, however, revealed factors which were not in themselves work-centered: rather, they focused on the conditions and people which surround the actual work.

Can we conclude that as long as a teacher experiences personal success, and is recognized for this success, the conditions of work need not be considered? It may be possible (although unlikely) for a teacher, who is immersed in an unsatisfactory work environment, to experience personal success and thus achieve considerable job satisfaction. An environment relatively free from sources of dissatisfaction, however, will tend to increase or enhance the appearance of factors which are direct contributors to job satisfaction.

Herzberg refers to the dissatisfaction factors as "hygienic." In describing these factors, Herzberg states:

They act in a manner analagous to the principles of medical hygiene.

> Hygiene operates to remove health hazards from the environment of man. It is not a curative; it is, rather, a preventive.[11]

The "hygienic" factors, according to Herzberg, are essential in preventing dissatisfaction, in making work tolerable. Herzberg describes the satisfaction factors as motivators. These are the job-centered, the task-oriented factors which permit the individual to satisfy his need for self actualization in his work.

The dissatisfaction factors identified for teachers tend to focus on conditions and circumstances which teachers expect to be maintained at acceptable levels. It seems reasonable that teachers should expect fair and adequate supervision, supportive school policies and administrative directives, friendly interpersonal relationships and pleasant working conditions. However, the satisfaction factors focus directly on conditions and circumstances that are not given, which do not come with the job. These factors constitute rewards that must be earned through performance of the job. The reinforcement potential of the satisfiers is dependent upon a teacher's individual performance.

What then are the implications of the study for administrative behavior? The findings suggest that the present emphasis on "teacher-centered" behavior (supportive supervision, interpersonal relations, effective communications, and group effectiveness) is an important perscription for effective administrative behavior. The "teacher-centered" approach, however, is limited in that it tends to concentrate on the elimination of dissatisfaction factors and thus does not contribute directly to teacher job satisfaction.

"Task-oriented" behavior (organizing and planning work, implementing goal achievement) emerges as an important and direct contributor to teacher job satisfaction. Such behavior, on the part of the administrator, would include increasing the opportunities for teachers to experience personal and professional success. Basic to this undertaking is the proposition that administrators will permit and encourage teachers to (1) exercise more autonomy in making decisions, (intensifying collaborative efforts and consultative management would be a good start), (2) increase individual responsibility in developing and implementing teaching programs, and (3) develop professional skills. These variables will serve to increase individual identification with the task.[12] Task identification appears to be a prerequisite for

---

[11] Herzberg, *The Motivation to Work,* p. 113.

[12] March, John and Herbert Simon. *Organizations*. New York. John Wiley and Sons. 1958. p. 77.

focusing on achievement as a means to personal and professional success and subsequent job satisfaction.

A corollary to personal success is recognition for such success. Although recognition was not found to be as potent as actual success, it was perceived by teachers as a measure of success. Capitalizing on recognition, as a satisfier for teachers, implies that dispensing of recognition should be as closely associated with successful teacher task-oriented behavior as possible.

Finally, effective administrative behavior would not exclude or ignore the sources of job dissatisfaction. Supervisory behavior, interpersonal relationships, and other factors relating to the conditions of work are necessary components in promoting an environment which will enhance job itself satisfaction for teachers. Teachers whose energies are taxed in coping with sources of job dissatisfaction will tend not to be vigorous and dynamic pursuers of work-centered satisfaction.

An inherent assumption, in the discussion above, has been that job satisfiers are reinforcers of behavior and motivators of performance. Considerable evidence has been accumulated which disputes the claim that a satisfied worker is more productive than a dissatisfied one. However, when satisfaction is dependent upon performance in work, satisfaction and productivity are related.[13]

The satisfaction factors identified for teachers cannot be separated from performance and, in fact, are dependent upon performance. It was successful performance which accounted for the high attitudes expressed in achievement-centered stories. Performance was also the basis for recognition-centered sequences. If performance is rewarded in terms of intrinsic personal success and extrinsic recognition for success, it will tend to be repeated.

SUMMARY

The assumption that factors which tend to satisfy teachers and factors which tend to dissatisfy teachers are arranged on a conceptual continuum tends *not* to be supported by this study. Factors which appeared as sources of high job feelings for teachers, tended to differ from factors which appeared as sources of low job feelings. Further, the satisfaction factors

[13] Bass, Bernard. *Organizational Psychology*. Boston. Allyn and Bacon, Inc. 1965. p. 38.

tended to focus on the work itself, and the dissatisfaction factors tended to focus on the conditions of work.

It was concluded that the elimination of the dissatisfiers would tend not to result in job satisfaction. However, it does not appear likely that one can experience work satisfaction *without* the elimination or tempering of the dissatisfiers. Deriving satisfaction from work-centered activity assumes that one's energies and efforts are not taxed or depleted by unsatisfactory conditions of work. The point is not whether satisfiers are more crucial than dissatisfiers, or *vice versa,* but rather the dependence of the satisfiers on the elimination or tempering of the dissatisfiers.

QUESTIONS

1. How do you account for the absence of advancement and the work itself as satisfiers in Sergiovanni's study?

2. According to Sergiovanni, a satisfied worker is not more productive than a dissatisfied one except when satisfaction is dependent on performance in work. Explain.

UNIT VIII

EVALUATION OF TEACHER COMPETENCE

EVALUATION OF TEACHING COMPETENCE

OVERVIEW

In all but the smallest school districts teachers are formally evaluated, usually by their principal, at the end of the school year. Some districts evaluate probationary teachers more often than tenured teachers and some do not evaluate tenured teachers at all. Generally teachers do not actively participate in the evaluation process; they are passive subjects. Consequently the process has an undesirable concomitant outcome — fear. Nevertheless nine out of ten teachers approve of regular evaluations.[1]

Conscientious school administrators have reservations about the validity and usefulness of the evaluation process as currently practiced. Moreover they find themselves in a dilemma: they want their reports to reflect actuality yet at the same time they do not want to damage the morale of their staffs.

---

[1]*NEA Research Bulletin,* Washington, D.C.: National Education Association, Vol. 47, No. 3, Oct. 1969, p. 72.

Why evaluate? The answer usually given is that evaluation improves teaching. There is no hard evidence that it does. Too often it is a perfunctory procedure, an end-of-year routine which effects no change in classroom performance. In practice, evaluation is used only to maintain personnel records and to grant or deny tenure. Most evaluative instruments are check lists or rating scales which do not offer specific suggestions for improvement although they sometimes provide space for the evaluator to make brief notations.

The prime purpose of evaluation should be to promote the professional growth of the teacher so that he may in turn stimulate and guide the growth of his pupils in socially desirable ways. Its raison d'etre is its effect on a teacher's future work. Past performance is appraised for the purpose of changing future performance. Unfortunately school districts pay lip service to this ideal but fail to put it into practice.

Evaluation procedures. Two-thirds of the 603 comprehensive agreements on file with the NEA Research Division in 1968 contained clauses on the procedures to be followed in the evaluation of teachers.[2] Among the most frequently mentioned items were:

1. Designation of the evaluator, usually the teacher's immediate supervisor or school principal.
2. Statement that all observations must be made with the knowledge of the teacher.
3. Requirement that all evaluations be in writing on a standard form.
4. Provision for the teacher's review of the written evaluation report and opportunity to respond to any adverse comments before the report is placed in his personal file.
5. Statement that teachers may be accompanied by an organization representative when discussing evaluation reports with supervisors.
6. Establishment of a grievance procedure to resolve objections a teacher may have to his evaluation.
7. Provision for special assistance to teachers receiving unsatisfactory evaluations to help them improve their performance.

Theory base. Implicit in the evaluation of teaching competence are certain assumptions. Teaching is behavior. It is what a teacher does and what his students do in interaction. It is observable and describable and hence subject to analysis and appraisal. These assumptions seem unexceptionable.

---

[2] **Ibid.**

However, two further assumptions would be challenged by many. First, teaching cannot be evaluated apart from its results. The measure of a teacher's performance is what his students learn. Secondly, good teaching can be defined.

Laymen see no difficulty in evaluating teachers on the basis of what their students learn. To them evaluation is simply a matter of measuring what students know at the beginning of a school year and again at the end, and the difference between the two is a measure of the teacher's ability. If the students haven't learned, the teacher hasn't taught.

Teachers oppose this solution as simplistic. Admittedly it is possible to measure a knowledge of subject matter with reasonable accuracy. However, modern education is concerned not only with facts and skills but also with attitudes, habits, and appreciations which are not so easily measured. Besides, even the learning of facts and skills is dependent on many variables not under the teacher's control, including the intellectual ability, emotional stability, socio-economic status, and family backgrounds of the students. Even superior teachers achieve comparatively less with youngsters who are handicapped mentally, emotionally, economically, and socially. Moreover, some learnings may occur despite poor teaching so that a teacher may be given credit for results for which he is not responsible.

Nevertheless, a number of individual researchers and professional associations support the position that it is possible to discover the effectiveness of teachers by their impact on students.[3] There are technical problems in measuring learner growth — for example, the adequacy of instruments for assessing a wide range of attitudes and achievement at different educational levels and in diverse subject matter areas, failure to account for instructional variables that the teacher does not control, and the inconsistent progress of students under the same teacher. But these problems are not insuperable.

Who's a good teacher? Evaluation implies a criterion, a standard against which to judge who is a good teacher and what is good teaching. But there is no such yardstick. There are probably many kinds of good teachers just as there are many kinds of learners. There is no one best way of teaching, no set of competencies that every teacher should possess.

Having said that, it must be admitted that it's easy to identify the poor

---

[3] McNeil, J. D. and Popham, J. W., "The Assessment of Teacher Competence," in Travers, Robert M. W., *Second Handbook of Research in Teaching*, Chicago, Ill: Rand McNally, 1973, p. 218.

teacher and fairly easy to identify the truly outstanding teacher. But the nice discriminations made on evaluation forms about the great mass of in-betweens are fanciful.

Research on evaluation. The extensive research on teacher effectiveness has not been helpful. In 1954 Morsh and Wilder conducted a comprehensive analysis of all existing evidence on the subject for the United States Air Force but came up with almost nothing positive.[4]

Prof. A. S. Barr, after a lifetime of research on the subject, said that — like Edison searching for a good light-bulb filament — the best contribution he had made was that he identified many things that did not work.[5]

Ryans' massive research project, *Characteristics of Teachers*, offers a promising approach.[6] Ryans and his staff focussed on the teacher himself more than on his practices and found that teacher characteristics could be grouped along three major scales:

1. From warm, understanding, friendly teacher behavior toward aloof, egocentric, restricted behavior.
2. From systematic, responsible, businesslike behavior toward evading, unplanned, slipshod behavior.
3. From stimulating, imaginative, surgent behavior toward routine, dull behavior.

These scales might readily be adapted for evaluative purposes although Ryans did not make such a suggestion. The three elements do not overlap; they are clinically descriptive; and each measures something distinctive.

Validity. Do evaluative instruments yield a true measure of teaching performance?

An evaluative form is basically a district's definition of what constitutes a good teacher. It lists the personal attributes and professional competencies assumed to be essential for teaching success. Since no research has established such a relationship, the validity of the instrument is suspect.

---

[4] Morsh, J. E. and Wilder, E. W., *Identifying the Effective Instructor: A Review of the Quantitative Studies, 1900-1952*, USAF Personnel Training Research Center, Research Bulletin No. AFPTRC-RE-54-44, 1954.

[5] *Spotlight*, Washington D.C.: National Association of Secondary School Principals, No. 62, March-April 1964, p. 2.

[6] Ryans, D. G., *Characteristics of Teachers, Their Description, Comparison, and Appraisal*, Washington, D.C., American Council on Education, 1960.

The best criteria for assessing teacher competence are behavioral changes in the learner, that is, product criteria. However, the use of product criteria presents difficulties, so evaluators have resorted to process criteria, that is, instructional procedures assumed to be related to student growth. Process criteria are easily accessible but the assumption that they are related to outcomes is questionable and weakens the validity of the instrument.

Other deficiencies which adversely affect validity include failure to
. . . define terms operationally so that they have identical meaning for all evaluators
. . . weight items to reflect their relative significance
. . . require supporting evidence
. . . differentiate between the levels of competence for each item.

Reliability. Do evaluative instruments consistently measure what they purport to measure?

Agreement among observers, the most common form of reliability, is difficult to attain. When different evaluators apply the same observational device to the same teacher, the results are divergent. The divergence may be caused by deficiencies in the instrument or by bias and selective perception on the part of the evaluator. All evaluators are subject to some degree of personal bias, some are more lenient or severe than others, and some have had more training and experience than others. The halo phenomenon — the tendency to allow a high or low rating on one trait to influence ratings on others — may also affect reliability. In effect, the evaluator becomes the evaluating instrument.

The evaluative instrument calls for subjective, qualitative judgments. Even when these judgments are converted into quantitative scores, there is no increase in objectivity and reliability. Subjectivity is merely quantified.

Moreover, the sample of classroom observations may not be representative of a teacher's total behavior. When comparing one *group* of teachers with another *group*, the number of observations necessary for a representative sample can be relatively small, but when relating a teacher's instructional activities to outcomes, a larger sample is required. Just how large is a perplexing problem.

Reliability can be improved by training. Courses in psychology and educational testing and measurement may narrow the range of differences among observers. Group training sessions in observation and evaluation can bring about agreement on the meaning of each items and evidences of its presence.

The evaluation conference. A conference between the teacher and school principal or other evaluating official would seem to be an indispensable part of any evaluative procedure if the aim of evaluation is to improve teaching, but apparently many teachers are evaluated annually without one. An NEA survey of the number of conferences of more than ten minutes duration which teachers had with an evaluator revealed that the median number for an entire school year for probationary, continuing, and elementary school teachers was only two, and for secondary school teachers, one. Many teachers who received a written evaluation — 22 percent — had no conference at all.[7]

An evaluation conference can be a helpful procedure if rightly conducted, perhaps the most helpful of all supervisory techniques. The teacher benefits from conferring with an experienced and knowledgeable colleague. The supervisor benefits because he gains insights into the problems his teachers are facing and can adjust his supervisory program accordingly.

From the teacher's viewpoint the conference has several shortcomings. It is looked upon as a judgmental procedure in which the teacher is a passive listener, a recipient of criticism and advice. Since his continued employment may rest upon the outcome, it is accompanied by anxiety. It accentuates the superior-inferior relationship between evaluator and teacher. If its emphasis is on finding faults and correcting them, it is an unpleasant situation and may degenerate into a debate in which the teacher tries to justify his actions and the evaluator tries to defend his criticisms. It is a uni-directional procedure with the flow of information and opinion mainly from the evaluator to the teacher.

From the evaluator's viewpoint it is a time-consuming procedure and it is distasteful because no one likes to sit in judgment on people with whom he works closely every day.

Neither participant sees it as a joint examination of past performance for the purpose of improving future performance or as an exchange of facts and views in an atmosphere of mutual trust and respect.

A new approach to the appraisal conference should minimize these difficulties and perhaps eliminate them. The emphasis should be on analysis rather than appraisal. The teacher's role should be active rather than passive, for he learns from the conference in direct proportion to his degree of

---

[7]*Evaluation of Teachers,* Research Report 1964-R 14, Washington, D.C.: 1964, p. 41.

independence. Independence, in turn, varies in relation to the evaluator's use of direct or indirect influence; the more direct his influence, the less the teacher learns.

The subject matter should be performance and results, not the teacher. The focus should be on problems and their solution. The discussion should be two-directional, characterized by the free flow of information and opinion between the two participants. The dialogue should be informal, like a social conversation only more purposive — and it will be if the discussion centers on observed behavior rather than personal traits.

The analysis addresses itself to such matters as goals, curriculum, organization of materials, methods, evidences of pupil growth, and instructional problems, especially those which the teacher perceives to be important. Are goals stated in behavioral terms? Is the subject matter appropriate to the class level? What curriculum changes are desirable? How are the materials of instruction organized? What provisions are made for individual differences? What methods of evaluation are used? What can pupils do at the end of the school year that they couldn't do at the beginning? What are the results of standardized and teacher-constructed tests? What problems do the teacher and supervisor see as most in need of solution? What area does the teacher perceive to be the one in which he most needs to improve? How does he plan to bring about this improvement? These are only a sample of questions to show the shift from fault-finding or praising to clinical analysis and cooperative planning.

The discussion is characterized by professional objectivity in a friendly atmosphere. While there is inequality of status between the two participants, both are professionals actuated by concern for the betterment of instruction. Any pretence of equality by the evaluator will be perceived as bogus by the teacher.

The give-and-take between the two is largely non-evaluative, but not completely so. Some value judgments will be made by the evaluator, necessarily so, and some will be explicitly stated or inferred by the teacher from the evaluator's objective description of pupil activities and their outcomes. Behavior rather than personality, observation rather than inference, and the exploration of alternative procedures rather than the prescription of a single method are some of the hallmarks of a productive conference. The evaluator's role is that of a catalyst attempting to lead a teacher to discover for himself what the realities are and to formulate his own program of self-improvement. A teacher is more likely to put remedial measures into action if he has worked them out for himself.

Conferences with beginning teachers will tend to be directive because the usual beginner lacks the knowledge and experience to judge his own performance objectively. He has so much to learn that he looks for direction. He wants to be told and shown what to do. After he has learned to stand on his own two feet, his principal can use a different approach — joint assessment rather than unilateral rating.

Work planning and review. A spokesman for the American Association of School Administrators, George B. Redfern, suggests a plan for evaluating teacher performance under which evaluator and evaluatee would:

. . . Agree upon specific, relevant performance objectives
. . . Plan a cooperative course of action to achieve the objectives
. . . Establish ways to check periodically on the extent to which instructional procedures are achieving desired results
. . . Make a joint assessment of results achieved
. . . Hold a conference to discuss the extent of achievement and decide the follow-up that is called for.

According to Mr. Redfern, this approach, known in industry as WPR, work planning and review, "makes more sense than unilateral evaluation wherein the evaluator attempts to assess performance in the typical framework of observations and ratings without reference to predetermined goals."[8]

Self-evaluation. Video-taping provides teachers with a means of viewing their own classroom behavior and informally appraising it. It has not been shown, however, that they can appraise their work and achieve better results by observing video-tapes of their own lessons. Without training in how to analyze their teaching, they criticize superficialities — their personal mannerisms, appearance, voice, and the like — and they tend to overrate themselves.[9]

Formal self-evaluation is rarely used. It is based on the premise that no teacher will begin to improve himself unless he is dissatisfied with his performance, a premise that seems unexceptionable.

A self-evaluation form appears below. Whether teachers should be required to complete and submit such a form is disputable. Perhaps its use

---

[8]*Teacher's Letter*, New London, Conn.: Croft Educational Services, Inc., Vol. 18, No. 16, April 15, 1969.

[9]Travers, op. cit., p. 231.

should be optional; those who wish to do so may submit their report for examination and inclusion in their personnel folder.

TEACHER'S SELF-EVALUATION[10]

1. Teaching and related activities
   a. I introduced the following new techniques into my teaching this year:

   b. I used these major visual aids during the school year (names of films, filmstrips, and recordings):

   c. I made use of these resources (people, places, and things) from my neighborhood and community:

   d. I tried out these varied home assignment projects:

   e. I helped identify these exceptionally able children (name of child and special ability) for further attention:

   f. As I look back I am most pleased with these teaching activities:

   g. I gave the following uncompensated remedial instruction after school on a voluntary basis:

2. Special departmental service
   a. I served on the following departmental committees:

   b. I participated in thc following departmental activities:

   c. I participated in curriculum revision in the following area:

3. Special school service
   a. I served on the following school or systemwide committees:

   b. I volunteered for the following student extraclass activities:

   c. I made these suggesions for improving procedure in school operations (other than classroom):

---

[10] Adapted from *Teachers Letter*, New London, Conn.: Croft Educational Services, Inc., Vol. 12, No. 17, May 12, 1963.

4. Community services which enhance the school's reputation
   a. I took part in these community activities:

   b. I spoke at the following meetings of community organizations:

5. Professional activities
   a. I served on these committees of my local professional organizations:

   b. I took part in the following professional conventions and meetings:

   c. I read these professional works:

   d. I contributed the following materials to professional magazines:

   e. I successfully completed the following courses:

   f. I supervised the following student teachers:

   g. I engaged in research projects having to do with these problems:

Conclusions and recommendations. From the extensive literature on the evaluation of teaching, the following conclusions and recommendation can be drawn:

1. The primary purpose of evaluation is the improvement of teaching. It is also essential for the traditional purpose of maintaining personnel records since there is a large turnover annually of teacher personnel. A district must have some indication of a teacher's merit and accomplishment to answer inquiries from prospective employers, if for no other reason.

   Evaluation is not an end in itself: it is a means to an end. It should be designed to bring about change in the classroom so that a teacher may become increasingly effective. It is a procedure for the improvement of the product, process, and goals of teaching.
2. Teachers should know beforehand the basis on which they are to be evaluated.
3. The core of all evaluative devices should be classroom performance. However, the teacher's contribution to the entire life of the school should also be considered.
4. Evaluation should be based on more than one classroom observation. The minimum number should be determined locally. Non-

tenured teachers should be observed more frequently than tenured teachers.

5. Research has failed to substantiate links between teacher effectiveness and intelligence, age, experience, cultural background, socioeconomic background, sex, marital status, scores on aptitude tests, job interest, voice quality, and special talents.
6. There are some indications of slight positive correlations between scholarship and teaching effectiveness; professional knowledge seems to be a valid predictor of the quality of teaching performance.
7. Two or more raters using the same instrument in rating the same teachers will not produce the same results.
8. Supervisors and administrators should be trained in the use of the evaluative instrument to reduce subjectivity.
9. Evaluation should include an extended conference between supervisor and teacher.
10. If an evaluation is unfavorable or doubtful, several supervisors should participate, each rating independently.
11. The evaluative instrument should contain only items which are valid, observable, and the result of a teacher-created condition. The items should be defined in behavioral terms.
12. Evaluation is an administrative responsibility. It should be performed by the principal or superintendent. A supervisor's function is to help and guide a teacher so that he may be favorably evaluated.

SELECTED READINGS

American Federation of Teachers A.F.L.-C.I.O., Chicago, Ill., *Merit Rating*, 1958.

The proposal that teachers be paid on the basis of merit or evaluation of individual service is not yet a dead issue although it is not as frequently discussed as it used to be. This pamphlet argues that it is a dangerous mirage.

Bolton, Dale L., *Selection and Evaluation of Teachers,* Berkeley, Cal.: McCutchan Publishing Corporation, 1973.

Adapted from the report of a study made for the U.S. Office of

Education. The general purpose of the study was to acquire and synthesize research and development information regarding selection and evaluation of teachers so that the information could be used by practicing administrators, teachers, and board of education members to improve school personnel practices.

Lewis, James, *Appraising Teacher Performance,* West Nyack, N.Y.: Parker Publishing Co., 1973.

The author recommends that the comparative rating of teachers be discontinued and that the administrator aim to establish agreement with the teachers on whether the teacher's performance meets local expectancies, including the teacher's own. The focus is on teacher improvement rather than teacher shortcomings.

McNeil, John D. and Popham, James W., "The Assessment of Teacher Competence," in Travers, Robert M. W., ed., *Second Handbook of Research in Teaching,* Chicago, Ill.: Rand McNally, 1973.

A comprehensive survey of research on the problem of assessing teacher effectiveness. Includes a critique of widely used criteria and a helpful bibliography.

National Education Association, Washington, D.C., *Evaluation of Classroom Teachers,* 1964.

This report is based on three questionnaires: one to superintendents on the administrative requirements in their school systems, one to principals on their responsibilities for evaluating teaching, and one to classroom teachers on how their work is evaluated and how they feel about the evaluation programs in their schools. Probably the most extensive survey to date of evaluation procedures.

National Education Association, Washington, D.C., *NEA Research Bulletin.*

From time to time this little bulletin, published four times yearly, contains reports of research on teacher evaluation. The reports are unfailingly informative and concise.

Redfern, George B., *How to Appraise Teaching Performance*, Columbus, O.: School Management Institute, Inc., 1963.

A brief, helpful paperback handbook which considers the following topics among others: "tooling-up" for appraisal, materials and tools of appraisal, the appraisal process, utilization of the outcomes of appraisal, and the principal's role.

Stinnett, T. M., *Professional Problems of Teachers,* 3rd Ed., New York: Macmillan, 1968.

Chapter 8 treats of teacher evaluation and merit pay. Sub-topics include a history of rating, policy statements of educational associations, basis for teacher evaluation, and the future of teacher salary scheduling.

TOPICS FOR DISCUSSION

1. Report on the evaluation form used in your school district. What is its purpose? What are its merits and shortcomings? Are its items concerned with instructional procedures, teachers' personality traits, or outcomes of teaching? What changes would you suggest?

2. If you were an evaluator using Ryans three scales (p. 426) as a basis for evaluation, what *specific* behaviors would you look for?

3. Report on an evaluation conference in which you were recently involved, either as an evaluator or as an evaluatee. Was the conference a unilateral procedure? Did it offer insights into teaching practices? Did it improve subsequent teaching?

4. Criticize, favorably or unfavorably, Redfern's plan for evaluating teacher competence. (p. 430)

5. From your own experience, has your viewing of video tapes of your own lessons improved your teaching? Explain.

6. What are the merits and shortcomings of the self-evaluation form on p. 431-432?

7. The list of conclusions and recommendations, p. 432-433, is necessarily in complete. Add recommendations that you think should be included.

A HISTORICAL APPROACH TO TEACHER EVALUATION

By
Michael L. Thompson

Since good teaching must be defined before it is evaluated, evaluation becomes almost impossible because good teaching cannot be defined without resorting to circular argument.

Since 1918 researchers have investigated five methods of evaluating teachers: pupil achievement, supervisory ratings, student evaluations, teacher self-evaluation, and teacher accomplishments. Each of these is discussed and studies cited to show their inadequacy.

Today there is more consideration given to all the variables influencing efficiency and more effort to elevate the quality and widen the range of evaluative instruments.

Despite the belief that teachers are better trained today than ever before, the major problem that continues to confront researchers is teacher evaluation. How are they better? Can teaching ability be measured? What makes one teacher more capable than another? What quality assets should the good teacher have?

These questions are not new to the present generation of teachers and researchers. Years of work have been expended in seeking a solution of this age-old enigma. Since good teaching must first be defined before it can be evaluated, the task becomes almost impossible at the outset. A review of past writings immediately reveals the fact that teachers may be good or efficient for numerous reasons.

Mr. A. may be a "good" teacher because of the way he manipulates his students. He is firm because it is his belief that students learn more with this approach. Mr. A's needs have been satisfied. Mr. B. gives unstintingly of his time and energy to the school's extracurricular programs. Miss C. has achieved untold recognition on the basis of her participation in community activities. Mr. D. concentrates all his efforts in the direction of proper

"A Historical Approach to Teacher Evaluation," Michael L. Thompson, *The Clearing House*, November 1962. Copyright © 1962 by *The Clearing House*. Reprinted by permission of Heldref Publications.

personality development. Mr. E. and Miss F. are officers in several national and professional associations and therefore are considered good teachers. Finally, there is Mr. G., who is considered a good teacher mainly on the basis of publications. This evaluation of teaching "goodness" was not on how valuable his research was but solely on the grounds that he is publishing. Many other examples could be listed for further illustration, but I believe the point has been made. It doesn't seem probable that all teachers can carry on all the aforementioned activities. It is much more reasonable to believe that each possesses one or two of these abilities. It is simply impossible to define good teaching without resorting to circular argument. Small wonder our evaluation scales and other instruments have yielded rather poor results for lack of validating criteria.

The researcher is confronted with an even more formidable task when, to the difficulty of defining good teaching, he adds the problem of appraising those characteristics that are related to successful teaching. During the last half century innumerable studies have been made to show the relationship between effective teaching and such traits as interest in people, sympathy, enthusiasm for the material taught, good judgment, self-control or restraint, and the like. But do we need all these data of research to point up the fact that a good teacher needs such qualities to enable him to get along with others?

To confound the problem even more, academic success, health, and personality are constantly found to be influencing factors. Of course these may be minimized, but when they are combined with other components of teaching effectiveness the outcomes of any study will yield only limited results upon which interpretations can be made.

As stated before, many studies have been made to improve our understanding of the factors that influence teaching and to assist us in the evaluation of teachers. The methods described in these studies are varied, but several have been used consistently enough to warrant additional discussion. The first bases judgment on an evaluation of achievement or changes brought about in a teacher's students; the second stresses the ratings accorded classroom teachers by their superiors or administrators; the third utilizes student evaluation of a teacher's proficiency; the fourth is the teacher self-evaluation technique; and the fifth stresses the teacher's accomplishments (training, affective characteristics, and the like)[1]. Other methods might be listed, but they would merely be a rewording of the tech-

---

[1] Downie, N. M. *Fundamentals of Measurement: Techniques and Practices*. New York: Oxford University Press, 1959, p. 362.

niques mentioned above. Following are several studies which will illustrate each of these evaluation procedures, and the weaknesses in them which hinder sound teacher evaluation.

The first major attempt to use pupil achievement as a criterion of teaching efficiency was made by Crabbs[2] in 1925. By measuring pupil achievement at the beginning and end of a fixed period, Crabbs was able to obtain "accomplishment quotients." Correlations between this criterion and ratings by supervisors were generally low and negative in some cases. Subsequent research of this type has borne out this low degree of relationship between the two. It should not be inferred here that teacher evaluation is as simple as just testing and retesting. This procedure is much more complicated than the above illustration indicates. After all the data have been collected, the researcher is still left with a constellation of problems. Did the student learn in spite of the teacher? Could the growth be credited to another instructor? How much may be attributed to maturation? How many more reading opportunities did one class have than another? Was the home environment responsible for much of the progress? Many other questions would only increase the impossibility of saying that the child's achievement was related to any one teacher.

Measuring changes demands a definition of exactly what is important in terms of change. Observing changes in terms of class and school objectives is difficult because of the time and planning that are necessary. There are no simple, ready-made instruments to assist in this undertaking. Objectives are usually related to future activities, and unless the opportunities are present to allow the application of learned material, we have no outside criteria on which we may validly evaluate. These may be highly "remote," to say the least. In 1945 three related studies from the University of Wisconsin, using quality of pupil growth as a valid criterion of teaching efficiency, gave conflicting evidence which only corroborates how difficult this method of evaluation has been.[3,4,5]

The second method, "supervisor ratings," is still heatedly debated

---

[2]Crabbs, Lelah Mae. "Measuring Efficiency in Supervision and Teaching." *Contributions to Education,* No. 175. New York: Bureau of Publications, Teachers College, Columbia University, 1925.

[3]LaDuke, C. V. "The Measurement of Teaching Ability, Study Number Three." *Journal of Experimental Education,* 14:74-100 (September, 1945).

[4]Rolfe, J. F. "The Measurement of Teaching Ability, Study Number Two." *Journal of Experimental Education,* 14:52-74 (September, 1945).

[5]Rostker, L. E. "The Measurement of Teaching Ability, Study Number One." *Journal of Experimental Education,* 14:6-51 (September, 1945).

today and from all indications there doesn't appear to be any immediate end to the debate. The basic argument against the method is low reliability and questionable validity of rating instruments. The term "merit rating" is the most popular term in vogue today to describe this method, which is used in many systems across the country as a basis for promotion and salary increases. However, many problems are found which interfere with sound evaluations by supervisors. Is there a cooperative and democratic approach? How often should the instructor be observed? How was the instrument constructed? Are there qualified personnel to use the tool? How are finished products evaluated? Does the instrument actually bring about improved teaching? There are many other questions that could be added.

Teachers have been emotionally and bitterly opposed to these ratings and still shout "unreliable" or "invalid." Nevertheless, some form of rating is necessary even if the objections are true. In 1952 McCall[6] made an intensive study of 73 sixth-grade classes (including 2,164 students) as part of an investigation sponsored by the North Carolina Assembly. His findings were based on records of student growth over a school year, measured by a wide variety of tests, with corrections for factors affecting the capacity of each class to grow. The analysis of his research failed to find any system of measuring teacher merit which could be used as a basis of recommending salary increases. He found that the system of merit rating by official superiors was without value.

Much has been written about the third method of evaluating teacher efficiency, student evaluation of teaching. This procedure might be rated second only to merit rating in terms of its kindling point for beginning heated arguments. The difficulties posed by student evaluation involve the rating scale used, prejudice, inability to rate, required courses v. electives, sex of the instructor, intelligence of the student, low achievers, fear, and many other variables that affect the ratings received by instructors. Domas[7] used the "critical incident technique" to collect from teachers and principals descriptions of outstanding incidents of teacher efficiency and inefficiency. However, he was unable to develop a valid classification of the incidents which would be short enough for practical uses.

The fourth procedure, teachers' rating themselves, is almost self-explanatory. However, it might be pertinent to point out the problem that

---

[6] McCall, W. A. "Measurement of Teacher Merit." North Carolina State Department of Public Instruction, 1952, p. 40.

[7] Domas, S. J. *Report of an Exploratory Study of Teacher Competence.* Cambridge, Mass.: New England School Development Council, 1950.

exists today as not being new because it has been one for years. In 1920 Rugg[8] constructed an instrument with which teachers might rate themselves and in turn encourage self-evaluation and improvement. He pointed out the inadequacies of rating scales then in use by citing a distribution of the efficiency ratings of 7,131 teachers in a number of cities which manifested a skewed curve to the extent that 96 percent of all the teachers were rated either "superior," "excellent," or "good." A rating scale consisting of two forms was proposed. On the first form, the teacher was rated by the supervisor; on the second form, the teacher rated himself. This instrument had a particular significance: In placing a major emphasis upon self-evaluation and improvement, it preceded an important use of the modern rating scale. These scales as yet have not completely done away with the skewing of high ratings found in this study by Rugg.

Finally, the measurement of teacher ability in terms of attitudes and knowledge of educational practices and principles completes the picture of how difficult teacher evaluation has become. Some thirty years ago, tests to measure the above were quite common. Their basis was mainly to predict teacher efficiency. Later many other variables were combined with the hope of increasing prediction accuracy. One of the earliest was the Coxe-Orleans prognosis test of teaching ability[9]. This test of teaching ability was made up of five subtests, three of which were designed to measure content of a professional nature. The authors reported a reliability of .98 for the test and an average correlation index of .545 with scholastic achievement in the study. This battery is no longer used today. Franchi[10] studied county examinations in California and found the number of counties offering examinations decreased from 33 in 1913 to 7 in 1941 as did the number of individuals taking the examinations. In this study he found large variations in difficulty levels from county to county and concluded that the examinations, as a group, were poorly constructed technically and were limited in scope. The problems that exist with these and other instruments are complex. Different schools, philosophies, standards, course work, and immediate criteria limit these measurements.

Summary

Since 1918, there has been a notable increase by researchers to develop and apply objective instruments of measurement and to secure a more dependable criterion of teacher efficiency. In the 1920's research centered

[8] Rugg, H. O. "Self-Improvement of Teachers Through Self-Rating: a New Scale for Rating Teachers' Efficiency." *Elementary School Journal,* 20:670-84 (May, 1920).

[9] Coxe, W. W. and Orleans, J. S. *Coxe-Orleans Prognosis Test of Teaching Ability.* Yonkers-on-Hudson, N.Y.: World Book Co., 1930.

[10] Franchi, E. H. "Teachers Examinations," *Sierra Education News,* 40:20-21 (June, 1944).

around the identification of single factors or combinations of them which would give more reliable prediction of teaching success. A more intensive study of the qualities of instructors followed this period. Today there is a growing respect for the teaching complexities and more consideration given to all the variables in a teaching position which influence a teacher's efficiency. More effort is being given to define the criteria of this phenomenon and to elevate the quality and widen the range of the evaluative instruments.

QUESTIONS

1. "It is simply impossible to define good teaching without resorting to circular argument." Explain.

2. Briefly summarize the objections to each of the five methods of evaluation used over the years.

AN UNEASY LOOK AT PERFORMANCE APPRAISAL

By
Douglas McGregor

The conventional approach to performance appraisal which requires an administrator to pass judgment on a subordinate is examined and found unworkable. Managerial resistance to it reflects an unwillingness to treat human beings like physical objects.

McGregor proposes a new approach which calls on a subordinate to establish short-term performance goals for himself. The administrator's role is to help the subordinate relate his self-appraisal, goals, and plans for the ensuing period to the realities of the organization. Thus the emphasis shifts from appraisal to analysis.

The advantages and difficulties of the proposed approach are discussed. While it requires more managerial skill and time, the greater motivation and more effective development of subordinates justify the added costs.

Performance appraisal within management ranks has become standard practice in many companies during the past twenty years, and is currently being adopted by many others, often as an important feature of management development programs. The more the method is used, the more uneasy I grow over the unstated assumptions which lie behind it. Moreover, with some searching, I find that a number of people both in education and in industry share my misgivings. This article, therefore, has two purposes:

- To examine the conventional performance appraisal plan which requires the manager to pass judgment on the personal worth of subordinates.
- To describe an alternative which places on the subordinate the primary responsibility for establishing performance goals and appraising progress toward them.

"An Uneasy Look at Performance Appraisal" by Douglas MacGregor, May-June 1957, *Harvard Business Review*. Copyright © 1957 by the President and Fellows of Harvard College; all rights reserved. Reprinted by permission of Harvard Business Review.

CURRENT PROGRAMS

Formal performance appraisal plans are designed to meet three needs, one for the organization and two for the individual:

(1) They provide systematic judgments to back up salary increases, promotions, transfers, and sometimes demotions or terminations.
(2) They are a means of telling a subordinate how he is doing, and suggesting needed changes in his behavior, attitudes, skills, or job knowledge; they let him know "where he stands" with the boss.
(3) They also are being increasingly used as a basis for the coaching and counseling of the individual by the superior.

Problem of Resistance

Personnel administrators are aware that appraisal programs tend to run into resistance from the managers who are expected to administer them. Even managers who admit the necessity of such programs frequently balk at the process — especially the interview part. As a result, some companies do not communicate appraisal results to the individual, despite the general conviction that the subordinate has a right to know his superior's opinion so he can correct his weaknesses.

The boss's resistance is usually attributed to the following causes:

- A normal dislike of criticizing a subordinate (and perhaps having to argue about it).
- Lack of skill needed to handle the interviews.
- Dislike of a new procedure with its accompanying changes in ways of operating.
- Mistrust of the validity of the appraisal instrument.

To meet this problem, formal controls — scheduling, reminders, and so on — are often instituted. It is common experience that without them fewer than half the appraisal interviews are actually held. But even controls do not necessarily work. Thus:

In one company with a well-planned and carefully administered appraisal program, an opinion poll included two questions regarding appraisals. More than 90% of those answering the questionnaire approved the idea of appraisals. They wanted to know how they stood. Some 40% went on to say that they had never had the experience of being told — yet the files showed that over four-fifths of them had signed a form testifying that they had been through an appraisal interview, some of them several times!

> The respondents had no reason to lie, nor was there the slightest supposition that their superiors had committed forgery. The probable explanation is that the superiors, being basically resistant to the plan, had conducted the interviews in such a perfunctory manner that many subordinates did not recognize what was going on.

Training programs designed to teach the skills of appraising and interviewing do help, but they seldom eliminate managerial resistance entirely. The difficulties connected with "negative appraisals" remain a source of genuine concern. There is always some discomfort involved in telling a subordinate he is not doing well. The individual who is "coasting" during the few years prior to retirement after serving his company competently for many years presents a special dilemma to the boss who is preparing to interview him.

Nor does a shift to a form of group appraisal solve the problem. Though the group method tends to have greater validity and, properly administered, can equalize varying standards of judgment, it does not ease the difficulty inherent in the interview. In fact, the superior's discomfort is often intensified when he must base his interview on the results of a *group* discussion of the subordinate's worth. Even if the final judgments have been his, he is not free to discuss the things said by others which may have influenced him.

The Underlying Cause

What should we think about a method — however valuable for meeting organizational needs — which produces such results in a wide range of companies with a variety of appraisal plans? The problem is one that cannot be dismissed lightly.

Perhaps this intuitive managerial reaction to conventional performance appraisal plans shows a deep but unrecognized wisdom. In my view, it does not reflect anything so simple as resistance to change, or dislike for personnel technique, or lack of skill or mistrust for rating scales. Rather, managers seem to be expressing very real misgivings, which they find difficult to put into words. This could be the underlying cause:

> The conventional approach, unless handled with consummate skill and delicacy, constitutes something dangerously close to a violation of the integrity of the personality. Managers are uncomfortable when they are put in the position of "playing God." The respect we hold for the inherent value of the individual leaves us distressed when we must take responsibility for judging the personal worth of a fellow man. Yet the conventional approach to performance appraisal forces us, not only to make such judgments and to see them acted upon, but also to communi-

cate them to those we have judged. Small wonder we resist!

The modern emphasis upon the manager as a leader who strives to *help* his subordinates achieve both their own and the company's objectives is hardly consistent with the judicial role demanded by most appraisal plans. If the manager must put on his judicial hat occasionally, he does it reluctantly and with understandable qualms. Under such conditions it is unlikely that the subordinate will be any happier with the results than will the boss. It will not be surprising, either, if he fails to recognize that he has been told where he stands.

Of course, managers cannot escape making judgments about subordinates. Without such evaluations, salary and promotion policies cannot be administered sensibly. But are subordinates like products on an assembly line, to be accepted or rejected as a result of an inspection process? The inspection process may be made more objective or more accurate through research on the appraisal instrument, through training of the "inspectors," or through introducing group appraisal; the subordinate may be "reworked" by coaching or counseling before the final decision to accept or reject him; but as far as the assumptions of the conventional appraisal process are concerned, we still have what is practically identical with a program for product inspection.

On this interpretation, then, resistance to conventional appraisal programs is eminently sound. It reflects an unwillingness to treat human beings like physical objects. The needs of the organization are obviously important, but when they come into conflict with our convictions about the worth and the dignity of the human personality, one or the other must give.

Indeed, by the fact of their resistance managers are saying that the organization must yield in the face of this fundamental human value. And they are thus being more sensitive than are personnel administrators and social scientists whose business it is to be concerned with the human problems of industry!

A NEW APPROACH

If this analysis is correct, the task before us is clear. We must find a new plan — not a compromise to hide the dilemma, but a bold move to resolve the issue.

A number of writers are beginning to approach the whole subject of management from the point of view of basic social values. Peter Drucker's concept of "management by objectives"[1] offers an unusually promising framework within which we can seek a solution. Several companies, notably General Mills, Incorporated, and General Electric Company, have been exploring different methods of appraisal which rest upon assumptions consistent with Drucker's philosophy.

Responsibility on Subordinate

This approach calls on the subordinate to establish short-term performance goals *for himself*. The superior enters the process actively only *after* the subordinate has (a) done a good deal of thinking about his job, (b) made a careful assessment of his own strengths and weaknesses, and (c) formulated some specific plans to accomplish his goals. The superior's role is to help the man relate his self-appraisal, his "targets," and his plans for the ensuing period to the realities of the organization.

The first step in this process is to arrive at a clear statement of the major features of the job. Rather than a formal job description, this is a document drawn up *by the subordinate* after studying the company-approved statement. It defines the broad areas of his responsibility as they actually work out in practice. The boss and employee discuss the draft jointly and modify it as may be necessary until both of them agree that it is adequate.

Working from this statement of responsibilities, the subordinate then establishes his goals or "targets" for a period of, say, six months. These targets are *specific* actions which the man proposes to take, i.e., setting up regular staff meetings to improve communication, reorganizing the office, completing or undertaking a certain study. Thus, they are explicitly stated and accompanied by a detailed account of the actions he proposes to take to reach them. This document is, in turn, discussed with the superior and modified until both are satisfied with it.

At the conclusion of the six-month period, the subordinate makes *his own* appraisal of what he has accomplished relative to the targets he had set earlier. He substantiates it with factual data wherever possible. The "interview" is an examination by superior and subordinate together of the subordinate's self-appraisal, and it culminates in a resetting of targets for the next six months.

Of course, the superior has veto power at each step of this process; in an organizational hierarchy anything else would be unacceptable. However, in practice he rarely needs to exercise it. Most subordinates tend to under-

---

[1]See Peter Drucker, *The Practice of Management* (New York, Harper & Brothers, 1954).

estimate both their potentialities and their achievements. Moreover, subordinates normally have an understandable wish to satisfy their boss, and are quite willing to adjust their targets or appraisals if the superior feels they are unrealistic. Actually, a much more common problem is to resist the subordinates' tendency to want the boss to tell them what to write down.

Analysis vs. Appraisal

This approach to performance appraisal differs profoundly from the conventional one, for it shifts the emphasis from *appraisal* to *analysis*. This implies a more positive approach. No longer is the subordinate being examined by the superior so that his weaknesses may be determined; rather, he is examining himself, in order to define not only his weaknesses but also his strengths and potentials. The importance of this shift of emphasis should not be underestimated. It is basic to each of the specific differences which distinguish this approach from the conventional one.

The first of these differences arises from the subordinate's new role in the process. He becomes an active agent, not a passive "object." He is no longer a pawn in a chess game called management development.

Effective development of managers does not include coercing them (no matter how benevolently) into acceptance of the goals of the enterprise, nor does it mean manipulating their behavior to suit organizational needs. Rather, it calls for creating a relationship within which a man can take responsibility for developing his own potentialities, plan for himself, and learn from putting his plans into action. In the process he can gain a genuine sense of satisfaction, for he is utilizing his own capabilities to achieve simultaneously both his objectives and those of the organization. Unless this is the nature of the relationship, "development" becomes a euphemism.

Who Knows Best?

One of the main differences of this approach is that it rests on the assumption that the individual knows — or can learn — more than anyone else about his own capabilities, needs, strengths and weaknesses, and goals. In the end, only he can determine what is best for his development. The conventional approach, on the other hand, makes the assumption that the superior can know enough about the subordinate to decide what is best for him.

No available methods can provide the superior with the knowledge he needs to make such decisions. Ratings, aptitude and personality tests, and the superior's necessarily limited knowledge of the man's performance yield at best an imperfect picture. Even the most extensive psychological counseling (assuming the superior possesses the competence for it) would not solve the problem because the product of counseling is self-insight on the part of the *counselee*.

(Psychological tests are not being condemned by this statement. On the contrary, they have genuine value in competent hands. Their use by professionals as part of the process of screening applicants for employment does not raise the same questions as their use to "diagnose" the personal worth of accepted members of a management team. Even in the latter instance the problem we are discussing would not arise if test results and interpretations were given *to the individual himself,* to be shared with superiors at his discretion.)

The proper role for the superior, then, is the one that falls naturally to him under the suggested plan: helping the subordinate relate his career planning to the needs and realities of the organization. In the discussions the boss can use his knowledge of the organization to help the subordinate establish targets and methods for achieving them which will (a) lead to increased knowledge and skill, (b) contribute to organizational objectives, and (c) test the subordinate's appraisal of himself.

This is help which the subordinate wants. He knows well that the rewards and satisfactions he seeks from his career as a manager depend on his contribution to organizational objectives. He is also aware that the superior knows more completely than he what is required for success in this organization and *under this boss*. The superior, then, is the person who can help him test the soundness of his goals and his plans for achieving them. Quite clearly the knowledge and active participation of *both* superior and subordinate are necessary components of this approach.

If the superior accepts this role, he need not become a judge of the subordinate's personal worth. He is not telling, deciding, criticizing, or praising — not "playing God." He finds himself listening, using his own knowledge of the organization as a basis for advising, guiding, encouraging his subordinates to develop their own potentialities. Incidentally, this often leads the superior to important insights about himself and his impact on others.

Looking to the Future

Another significant difference is that the emphasis is on the future rather than the past. The purpose of the plan is to establish realistic targets and to seek the most effective ways of reaching them. Appraisal thus becomes a means to a *constructive* end. The 60-year-old "coaster" can be encouraged to set performance goals for himself and to make a fair appraisal of his progress toward them. Even the subordinate who has failed can be helped to consider what moves will be best for himself. The superior rarely finds himself facing the uncomfortable prospect of denying a subordinate's personal worth. A transfer or even a demotion can be worked out without the connotation of a "sentence by the judge."

Performance vs. Personality

Finally, the accent is on *performance,* on actions relative to goals. There is less tendency for the personality of the subordinate to become an issue. The superior, instead of finding himself in the position of a psychologist or a therapist, can become a coach helping the subordinate to reach his own decisions on the specific steps that will enable him to reach his targets. Such counseling as may be required demands no deep analysis of the personal motivations or basic adjustment of the subordinate. To illustrate:

> Consider a subordinate who is hostile, short-tempered, uncooperative, insecure. The superior need not make any psychological diagnosis. The "target setting" approach naturally directs the subordinate's attention to ways and means of obtaining better interdepartmental collaboration, reducing complaints, winning the confidence of the men under him. Rather than facing the troublesome prospect of forcing his own psychological diagnosis on the subordinate, the superior can, for example, help the individual plan ways of getting "feedback" concerning his impact on his associates and subordinates as a basis for self-appraisal and self-improvement.

There is little chance that a man who is involved in a process like this will be in the dark about where he stands, or that he will forget he is the principal participant in his own development and responsible for it.

A NEW ATTITUDE

As a consequence of these differences we may expect the growth of a different attitude toward appraisal on the part of superior and subordinate alike.

The superior will gain real satisfaction as he learns to help his subordinates integrate their personal goals with the needs of the organization so that both are served. Once the subordinate has worked out a mutually satisfactory plan of action, the superior can delegate to him the responsibility for putting it into effect. He will see himself in a consistent managerial role rather than being forced to adopt the basically incompatible role of either the judge or the psychologist.

Unless there is a basic personal antagonism between the two men (in which case the relationship should be terminated), the superior can conduct these interviews so that both are actively involved in seeking the right basis for constructive action. The organization, the boss, and the subordinate all stand to gain. Under such circumstances the opportunities for learning and for genuine development of both parties are maximal.

The particular mechanics are of secondary importance. The needs of the organization in the administration of salary and promotion policies can easily be met within the framework of the analysis process. The machinery of the program can be adjusted to the situation. No universal list of rating categories is required. The complications of subjective or prejudiced judgment, of varying standards, of attempts to quantify qualitative data, all can be minimized. In fact, *no* formal machinery is required.

Problems of Judgment

I have deliberately slighted the many problems of judgment involved in administering promotions and salaries. These are by no means minor, and this approach will not automatically solve them. However, I believe that if we are prepared to recognize the fundamental problem inherent in the conventional approach, ways can be found to temper our present administrative methods.

And if this approach is accepted, the traditional ingenuity of management will lead to the invention of a variety of methods for its implementation. The mechanics of some conventional plans can be adjusted to be consistent with this point of view. Obviously, a program utilizing ratings of the personal characteristics of subordinates would not be suitable, but one which emphasizes *behavior* might be.

Of course, managerial skill is required. No method will eliminate that. This method can fail as readily as any other in the clumsy hands of insensitive or indifferent or power-seeking managers. But even the limited experience of a few companies with this approach indicates that managerial *resistance* is substantially reduced. As a consequence, it is easier to gain the collaboration of managers in developing the necessary skill.

Cost in Time

There is one unavoidable cost: the manager must spend considerably more time in implementing a program of this kind. It is not unusual to take a couple of days to work through the initial establishment of responsibilities and goals with each individual. And a periodic appraisal may require several hours rather than the typical 20 minutes.

Reaction to this cost will undoubtedly vary. The management that considers the development of its human resources to be the primary means of achieving the economic objectives of the organization will not be disturbed. It will regard the necessary guidance and coaching as among the most important functions of every superior.

CONCLUSION

I have sought to show that the conventional approach to performance appraisal stands condemned as a personnel method. It places the manager in the untenable position of judging the personal worth of his subordinates, and of acting on these judgments. No manager possesses, nor could he acquire, the skill necessary to carry out this responsibility effectively. Few would even be willing to accept if if they were fully aware of the implications involved.

It is this unrecognized aspect of conventional appraisal programs which produces the widespread uneasiness and even open resistance of management to appraisals and especially to the appraisal interview.

A sounder approach, which places the major responsibility on the subordinate for establishing performance goals and appraising progress toward them, avoids the major weaknesses of the old plan and benefits the organization by stimulating the development of the subordinate. It is true that more managerial skill and the investment of a considerable amount of time are required, but the greater motivation and the more effective development of subordinates can justify these added costs.

QUESTIONS

1. Informally discuss McGregor's proposal with some of your teacher colleagues and with your principal or superintendent. Report on their reactions.

2. Are there other difficulties in the operation of this plan besides those mentioned in the article?

IN DEFENSE OF PERFORMANCE APPRAISAL

By
Harold Mayfield

Replying to McGregor and others who have criticized conventional appraisal systems, Mayfield asserts that the bad results conjured up by critics rarely occur. He makes this assertion on the basis of his participation in thousands of individual appraisals and several years' association with interviewers and interviewees.

The appraisal interview is described as a round-table discussion among several administrators without the participation of the person who is being evaluated. The subsequent progress interview involves only the evaluator and evaluatee.

Reasons for managerial resistance to the progress interview are discussed. Its problems are overestimated. A certain amount of system and pressure is necessary if it is to be applied generally in an organization.

People do not invariably resent suggestions. Although there are limits to candor, most people can take more than they get. The supervisor's greatest need for learned skill is in the art of listening.

By this time readers of HBR articles[1] should be fully aware of, if not alarmed about, the dangers in thinking systematically about their subordinates (i.e., *appraisal*) and talking with them about their work (i.e., *progress interview*). Now I believe the time has come for a word of reassurance from someone in business who has used these tools over a period of years and found the difficulties largely illusory.

I am particularly moved to make a statement because I believe there are readers who will remember each author's fears much longer than they re-

---

[1] Douglas McGregor, "An Uneasy Look at Performance Appraisal," HBR May — June 1957, p. 89; Philip R. Kelly, "Reappraisal of Appraisals," HBR May — June 1958, p. 59; Robert N. McMurry, "Mental Illness in Industry," HBR March — April 1959, p. 79; Rensis Likert, "Motivational Approach to Management Development," HBR July — August 1959, p.75; Arch Patton, "How to Appraise Executive Performance," HBR January — February 1960, p. 63.

"In Defense of Performance Appraisal", by Harold Mayfield. March-April 1960, *Harvard Business Review*. Copyright © 1960 by the President and Fellows of Harvard College; all rights reserved. Reprinted by permission of Harvard Business Review.

member his remedies. And, worse, the misgivings expressed so thoughtfully, taken out of context, may provide ready-made justification for continued inaction by managers who have little heart for the human side of their jobs.

CONVENTIONAL SYSTEMS

Let me state, first, that I have great respect for the authors who have written on this subject in these pages. In fact, I am in substantial agreement with them on most points. But, while they are mainly concerned with avoiding the dangers through new approaches, I maintain that the conventional tools of appraisal and of progress interview are surprisingly effective and free from difficulties when used with reasonable judgment.

The prime objective of conventional appraisal systems is to help each individual do a better job in his present position. There are also secondary objectives, such as identifying promotable men in a far-flung organization and achieving a comprehensive view of a group as an aid to organization planning. So that what I am defending is clear to all readers, here is a summary of the basic procedure:

- The process of appraisal begins with a roundtable discussion between the immediate supervisor and one or two other people of higher rank than the person being appraised (usually the manager next in rank to the immediate supervisor is included). This discussion, summarized briefly in writing for the record, need not center around such indefensible features as those "mainly concerned with personality and character traits" described and justly condemned by Kelly in his article.
- On completing this preparation, the supervisor holds a progress interview with each subordinate. In it the two people talk over job problems and future plans more broadly than they could in the ordinary course of their work. These actions, plus the innumerable and mostly individual steps resulting from them, constitute the conventional approach to management development.

Groundless Fears

When I earlier referred to the conventional systems as "surprisingly effective," I was actually reflecting the development of my present viewpoint. I, too, at one time had serious doubts, especially about the ability of some supervisors to conduct successful interviews. Indeed, if we sit down and contemplate all the barbarities that could be perpetrated in the name of appraisal and interview, we may well shudder. But do they actually occur?

My answer, based on participation in thousands of individual appraisals and several years' association with people interviewing and interviewed in one company, is that bad results rarely occur — and certainly not more often than they do in other man-to-man dealings between supervisor and subordinate. True, what is said in the privacy of the interview might occasionally give chills to the professional counselor if he could overhear it. But, as proof of the pudding, I set observed accomplishments and find it hard to scratch up any evidence of harm.

Even the critics of the conventional approach concede that 90% of the people who have been interviewed express satisfaction with the procedure. (In one study, our company found that among people who had been interviewed only 2% checked *"no"* and 6% checked *"undecided"* in an anonymous questionnaire asking, "Should these discussions be continued?") There are few actions of management that would get this degree of endorsement from salaried people.

So, in spite of the forebodings of people contemplating these steps *in advance*, we find both supervisors and subordinates in favor of these procedures *after they have tried them*. Why? To understand in part how the obvious pitfalls are avoided, let us look at how these matters work out in actual practice.

WHAT IS APPRAISAL?

First, consider appraisal. Stripped of all jargon it is simply an attempt to think clearly about each person's performance and future prospects against the background of his total work situation. Performance can be appraised succinctly by describing the best aspects of the individual's work and suggesting possible areas for improvement. Future prospects can be reviewed constructively when the supervisors attempt to name jobs the individual could perform if given the opportunity.

McGregor suggests this process may be disturbing to the manager because it puts him in the position of "playing God." He sees the manager putting on "his judicial hat . . . reluctantly and with understandable qualms . . . distressed . . . to take the responsibility for judging the personal worth of a fellow man." I suppose appraisal could be conducted in such a way as to call up these emotions, but my experience has been quite different. Typically, I have found just the reverse to be true. Supervisors emerge from an appraisal session with a sense of satisfaction — not with the weight of embarrassment that would be expected had they been engaged in pillorying friends.

Supervisors find they have indeed achieved both a deeper understanding and a warmer appreciation of their people. Further, they come out with new ideas for dealing with long-standing but perhaps vaguely recognized problems. And, especially important, since their own supervisor is usually present, they now have a better understanding of the attitude of higher management. In our company we frequently describe this searching process as a *personnel inventory* — that is, taking stock not only of people but also of ideas for actions which affect people.

Critics who are distressed by the cold analysis they read into appraisal often underestimate the values of thoughtful consideration which I see in appraisal. Impressions of people are already rife. Snap judgments are the rule in business and, in the absence of anything better, they become too frequently the basis for grave decisions. The process of bringing opinions out in the open and examining them is corrective — not damaging. It dispels shadows, lights dark corners.

McGregor concedes that "managers cannot escape making judgments about subordinates." I would express it more strongly:

> Nearly every action affecting people is based in part on judgments about them, conscious or unconscious. In my experience, intuitive, unexpressed judgments are much less likely to be considerate or sound than those which result from examination and discussion.

THE PROGRESS INTERVIEW

The step called appraisal is clearly just a preliminary. It is not even complete, because a vital ingredient is missing — the man himself. Many of the appraisal comments are just speculations or provisional suggestions until endorsed or modified by the man involved. For example, it is idle to suggest that a man ought to be given a sales assignment if he is not willing to travel.

Thus, to use appraisal for development we are brought inescapably to the second step: talking with the man, preferably after he too has had a chance to collect his thoughts and questions. This is the *progress interview*.

Reasons for Resistance

At this point, as has been noted by others, resistance often develops — principally from managers who have never conducted progress interviews. McGregor charitably suggests that resistors may be moved by a "deep but unrecognized wisdom," arising from an intuitive sense of delicacy in their relations with subordinates. Perhaps this is true, but there are two other factors that I am sure are more potent with the managers I know: (1) fear of opening a situation they cannot cope with, and (2) lack of urgency. For instance:

- The supervisor not only dreads talking with people about their shortcomings but also dreads their questions. The prospect of sitting down with each subordinate and talking about ''anything on *his* mind' fills many supervisors with vague alarms. Fearful of opening a Pandora's box of troubles, they may be painfully aware of areas they would like to avoid. ''What if the man asks for a raise?'' ''Suppose he wants a transfer to another department?'' ''What if he questions the way I have been running the department?'' The nature of the questions found most threatening will vary from one supervisor to another but the possible list is endless. Almost every supervisor has some qualms about exposing himself in such an unfamiliar situation, and some would frankly prefer to ''let sleeping dogs lie.''

- Further, many people in management are harassed men. They are at the focal point of pressures from many directions. Their daily work is a succession of crises; they are forever putting out fires. It is not surprising, therefore, that they respond to most stimuli according to urgency — or immediate satisfactions. Against most long-range considerations there is always the pressure of the ringing telephone, today's emergency, and tomorrow's deadline. Hence, any proposal that asks for a part of the manager's time, and promises no immediate payoff, is likely to be resisted or quietly laid to rest in the bottom drawer.

The process of seeking a better understanding among people is slow and unspectacular; often it calls for painful self-searching. It takes time from people who feel they have no time to spare. The real go-getter may conclude he ought to exert himself in another direction where there is a better chance of producing a dramatic ''critical incident'' to adorn his reputation.

It is not the progress interview alone that is resisted on this score. Many years ago I discovered that most training proposals are commonly greeted in a similar way. Even proposals when developed by the manager himself tend to be deferred until some more propitious time that never comes — unless something makes them urgent, such as a painful problem or an edict from the boss. The same is true of many other desirable actions. Indeed, how many managers would prepare a financial budget if not under compulsion to do so. Somewhere Lawrence Appley has said that people in business tend to do what the boss *inspects*.

Thus, I believe that a program such as the progress interview, which does not promise unalloyed pleasure or a dramatic payoff, needs a certain amount of system and pressure if it is to be applied generally in a company.

Periodic Interviews

How much system is desirable? There is room for disagreement here. Personally, I believe the program should be structured only to the minimum extent required to ensure that managers will (1) give individual thought to the present performance and future prospects of each of their people, and (2) hold periodic individual interviews with them. In my opinion, the mechanics of the program are important only if they help accomplish these steps and are likely to become detrimental if they specify in fine detail exactly how the manager is to conduct himself in each phase.

I have come to realize, reluctantly, that interviews of this kind will not be held by most supervisors unless they are built into the schedule as a part of standard operations. Such an interview once or twice a year, considered as an isolated event, is a very small ingredient in the total relationship between supervisor and subordinate. We all know that the day-to-day contacts build the substance of a relationship.

To hold that this obviates the need for periodic, scheduled interviews is to ignore certain realities. I have become suspicious of this argument, because it seems to be advanced so often by supervisors who are deficient in their relationships with their people. It is easy to find a supervisor who says, "I am in such close touch with my men that they do not need any special interview," but it is difficult to find a man who would not welcome a chance for a little better understanding with the boss. As Likert points out, "superiors think they understand subordinates' problems well but subordinates disagree." Similarly, many of us have come to greet with a smile the statement, "My door is always open."

Different Perceptions

Why do supervisors and subordinates perceive the same situation so differently? There are several reasons:

(1) The supervisor, who deals with many people, assumes he imparts more of his viewpoint to each person than he does. Aware of the approaches of an aggressive minority — and perhaps annoyed by them — he can easily convince himself that everyone with something on his chest runs to the boss. Dealing with a myriad of specific work items at the moment — commending good performance, correcting poor performance — the manager may look back over the

months and feel there is nothing more to say.

(2) His people rarely share this view. Every event appears important at the time, but it is quite difficult for people looking back from a distance to put things into perspective. The reprimand that seemed earth shaking at the moment may seem trivial six months later. And the event that passed unnoticed when it happened sometimes takes on great significance in the light of later events. There is a need for a summing up. In this process the supervisor plays an indispensable role, because from his higher perch on the management ladder, he can see larger implications.

(3) Questions also arise that are only indirectly related to the work at hand. There are worried questions and hopeful questions. Even though the person feels great concern, his own tact and shyness, and the manifest preoccupation of the boss, are impediments sufficient to keep the person silent. So the overture must be made by the supervisor, who alone can provide the opportunity — the time, the climate, the privacy — for the subordinate to express his deeper feelings. For most people this opportunity does not occur in the ordinary course of the job, and unless they are greatly disturbed, they will not force an audience with their boss.

I will readily concede there may be a supervisor somewhere who conducts himself in such a way as to make a scheduled interview superfluous. But until I find him, I shall continue to recommend interviews to all.

Actually, the scheduled interview, far from supplanting the daily contacts, often enriches them. Although seemingly a small event in itself, the interview — particularly the first with a supervisor — may have startling importance. I have heard the following statement too many times to take lightly its possible impact: "This is the first time in 15 years anybody has sat down with me and told me how I was getting along or asked my viewpoint on things." In some cases, I suspect the very fact the interview is being held means much to the individual, even though nothing very profound is said in it. It represents the opening of a door, and its full effects may not be seen until some time later.

COUNSELING FOR IMPROVEMENT

Too much, I believe, has been made of the difficulty of talking with subordinates about their shortcomings. Likert quotes Mark Twain to the effect that amateur writers, when they ask for advice, are really seeking praise and reassurance. But is not this attitude particularly expected from the amateur? It is my impression that many professional writers acknowledge with gratitude the training they received from severe taskmasters; and,

I believe, respect for the blue pencil of the editor is a mark of a successful writer.

In business, a great deal more than reassurance goes into the development of a man. I have heard from Likert's own research staff that, regardless of differing leadership styles, outstanding results rarely if ever come from groups where the leader does not hold up high standards. It is a corollary that the members of such a group must know about their departures from these standards — surely in many instances through plain speaking. There is also research with which Likert is doubtless familiar showing that when firmer pressure is put on a working group which has been under lax supervision, the immediate effect is good both for morale and production.

I am not for an instant advocating callousness toward the feelings of others, but I believe it is a mistake to assume that people invariably resent suggestions. True, there are people who seem to be untouchable; also some people can be dealt with more directly than others. But is is my belief that most people can take more candor than they get. It is a grave mistake to shy away from straightforwardness with *all* merely because a *few* might wither before it. It is my experience that most supervisors err on the side of reticence rather than frankness.

Limits to Candor

On the other hand, there are limits to what a supervisor should say, but he must decide these limits for himself in the light of his relationship with the person interviewed. Although urging him to open up with his people, I do not ask that he surrender his judgment. In fact, I have more confidence in his judgment about what can be said with good effect that I have in any rule I could lay down. Therefore, any guidelines I offer are quite general in nature. For example, the supervisor might well ask himself, "Will what I am about to say *help* this man?" If the answer is *"no,"* then he should not say it.

To tell a man the whole bitter truth in a "hammer and tongs" fashion is an offense against common courtesy. Giving a "piece of our mind" "straight from the shoulder" is the way we deal with enemies not friends. This is candor to the point of brutality. I am happy to say that I have never known it to occur in a progress interview.

Some argue that the supervisor is a poor judge of what can be said to good effect. I reply that he is the best judge available. Indeed, I would despair of getting managers to say anything against their better judgments, even in the privacy of their offices. But far from deploring this fact, I am reassured by it. One of the reasons we have so few bad repercussions from progress interviews, I am sure, is that the good judgment of the interviewer

— and the interviewee — tends to intervene before anything unfortunate occurs.

So I accept the intuitive feeling of the supervisor as a guide to action in the privacy of the interview, even though, unlike McGregor, I am not willing to let the supervisor reject the whole program untried, on intuitive grounds.

Price of Communication

True, not all goes smoothly. Likert tells of one manager who expressed his distress over an interview with the words, "What I would give to have that hour back!" This is most interesting to me because in my close relationship with scores of managers who have conducted such interviews over a nine-year period, I have not encountered this comprehensive sense of failure. Therefore, I am inclined to believe it is very rare indeed — and not more frequent in the progress interview than in other purposeful contacts between people in business.

Is there a salesman who has not regretted an unfortunate call? Is there a supervisor who would not have liked at some time to call back the words he used in conveying an order or answering a question? Is there one of us who has not kicked himself for some inglorious episode in our human relationships? This risk I believe to be one of the prices we must pay for any attempt at serious communications. Against it, we must weigh the cost of silence. It, too, leaves scars.

EACH IN HIS OWN WAY

Since I have confidence in the good judgment of the manager interviewing his people, I make no attempt to dictate his words from an ivory tower. On the contrary, I am convinced that there are many approaches which will work, including some that might appear completely unacceptable to me. The relationships between people are infinitely various, and I do not pretend to understand them all. One supervisor can say things to his people which no one else could say. One subordinate will accept gratefully what another would reject in anger. Few men who have succeeded in the social interplay of business well enough to achieve managerial rank are oblivious to such nuances of feeling, especially on their home ground.

If left to his own devices, the manager will deal quite differently, on the one hand, with the young man who looks up to him as to an older member of the family and, on the other hand, with the personal rival who now finds himself a subordinate. In the first case, the supervisor may talk to the youngster at times like the proverbial Dutch uncle, but to the erstwhile rival, with all the tact he can muster.

Feeling for Intent

In my experience, I have been surprised, not with the reluctance of subordinate to accept constructive advice, but with their readiness to listen. I believe this is explainable, in part, by their feeling for intent. If the supervisor genuinely means to be helpful, they will make allowances for words which in another context would be unforgivable. I fully endorse Kelly's observation that, " . . . men *do* welcome fair and even unflattering comments if made in a total context of friendship and trust." Conversely, a steady flow of praise does not bespeak real interest.

Thus, the right climate for the interview calls for sincerity more than technique. It calls for each supervisor to be himself. His manner in the interview must be an extension of his manner on the job. The straight-talking supervisor will pull few punches in the interview; the man of few words will not waste them here; the garrulous will interview wordily; the devious will use strategy. To be otherwise is to be false. Our subordinate will weigh our words in the light of what they know about us. Overconcern for technique may stand in the way of successful communication.

When people speculate about alarming possibilities in the progress interview, I believe they tend to overestimate its problems. More precisely, they tend to attribute to the interview alarming consequence that are already abundantly present in the working situation and are more likely to be eased than intensified by an interview. If a man is so constituted that his ego is shattered by a breath of criticism, I believe the give-and-take of business life will be so unsettling to him that he will need more than the usual amount of attention and understanding from this supervisor; in short, he will need more than the usual number of progress interviews (call them what you will).

McMurry deplores attempts by supervisors to "counsel" with "problem employees," pointing out that if the employee is mentally ill, the fumbling efforts of an amateur may be harmful. He recommends wisely that the mentally ill be referred to professional care. But, I submit respectfully, the supervisor is in a much better position to identify the cases that are beyond his abilities after he has made an attempt to understand the individual in the privacy of an interview than he is in the hurly-burly of the job.

Toward Understanding

Human problems are ever present in the business scene. Subordinates are problems to supervisors, and supervisors themselves are problems to subordinates. Fortunately, most of these problems can be worked out reasonably well through mutual effort without any remolding of basic personality.

Much of the content of progress interviews, however, is not to be described in terms of problems. Rather, the interview is mostly an attempt toward *understanding,* and, for the most part, the need for it lies in areas that are nonthreatening to either party. For example, typical subjects treated are as follows:

- Objectives (McGregor likewise endorses this topic, but I would not limit the interview to this alone).
- Recognition of good work.
- Suggestions for improvement — on both sides.
- Agreement on top-priority job elements.
- Clarification of responsibilities.
- Verifying or correcting rumors.
- Personal long-range goals.
- And a myriad of other topics that may seem important to someone at some time.

Art of Listening

I fully share Kelly's and McGregor's distrust of technique, but believe the supervisor's greatest need for learned skill is in the art of listening. An interview, by definition, is an interchange of ideas. A lecture or monologue is not an interview. And, more profoundly, understanding is a two-way street. But the dynamic, self-asertive individual brought to the top by the selective processes of business is often unprepared by experience or inclination for patient listening. We would despair of making nondirective counselors out of many of these men, but we can at least coach them to pose a few questions and to ask themselves at the close of the interview if the other person did at least half the talking.

CONCLUSION

Although a number of authors have suggested recently that there are serious problems in conventional procedures for appraising and interviewing subordinates, my experiences indicate that while these dangers exist they are more theoretical than real. Furthermore, the possible trouble areas are minimized when the basic tools of management development are used with moderate judgment.

Thus, in this article I have expressed my belief that every supervisor should *appraise* his subordinates periodically — that is, he should review thoughtfully each person's performance and potential. Following this preparation, he should talk with each subordinate, who should, likewise, be encouraged to prepare for the occasion. The immediate goal of such conversation is better understanding on both sides, and the ultimate goal is to set in motion mutually agreed on steps that will help the subordinate improve his effectiveness on his present job. These ingredients comprise what I regard as the basic elements of a conventional plan of appraisal and progress interview.

Nearly all supervisors who have experienced this process will witness to its wholesome effects; nevertheless, a great many of them will tend to defer it or avoid it completely under the manifold pressures of business unless it is made *urgent* by the insistence of higher management and the establishment of certain routines. And when need for administering the conventional plan is made urgent, management can feel certain it will work, despite chants of the nay-sayers.

In the conventional system of management development, we have the proverbial goose that has been laying golden eggs for years. For fear of an egg possibly being stolen, should we kill the goose? That, I fear, is what the opponents of performance appraisals basically recommend.

QUESTIONS

1. To what extent are McGregor and Mayfield in agreement? On what points do they disagree? With which of the two presentations do you concur? Why?

2. Are McGregor and Mayfield talking about the same thing? Do they both ascribe the same meaning to appraisal interview? Does Mayfield's progress interview correspond to McGregor's analysis approach?

EVALUATE TEACHERS?

By
David Selden

David Selden, formerly president of the American Federation of Teachers, argues that teacher evaluation is a red herring because it turns the attention of teachers against themselves instead of against the educational mores and economic forces which block educational improvement.

Teacher evaluation costs nothing but raising selection and certification requirements, lowering class size, reducing teaching hours, and increasing the number of teachers necessitates more money for schools. There will be little need for teacher evaluation if the process of teacher selection is properly carried out.

The evaluation process is a weapon for enforcing discipline and conformity among teachers. When evaluation is necessary it should be conducted by panels of outside educators. Objections to this plan are considered and rejected.

A perennial, educational red herring is the question of "teacher evaluation." It usually arises from the anguish of superintendents and school boards over the problem of How-to-Get-Quality-Education-Without-Really-Paying-for-It. A good teacher is a pearl without price, they say, but some teachers are better than others. The problem is to find and reward the good teachers, meanwhile continuing to depend on the average and bad teachers to carry on most of the enterprise of teaching — but at a lower salary.

Most teachers have learned to recognize merit rating salary schedules and "professional advancement" schemes and are wary of them. We are agreed that the salary of a teacher must not be tied to an evaluation of his pedagogical worth. However, many of us are still susceptible to the idea that if we really purify our own ranks, our sanctity will be recognized by the public and our employers, and we will be appropriately rewarded. We must "cleanse our own ranks." This puritanical proclamation leads to the conclu-

---

"Evaluate Teachers?" by David Seldon, *Changing Education*, Vol. 1, No. 2, Spring 1969. Reprinted by permission of David Seldon.

sion that we must devise more stringent ways for evaluating teachers. Very often we are led to the further conclusion that the hand of the administration must be strengthened in weeding out the unfit. The higher one's status in the educational power pyramid, the more self-righteous one is apt to be in calling for more rigorous evaluations.

Preoccupation with teacher evaluation is a red herring because it turns the attention and energies of teachers inward, against themselves, rather than outward against the complex of educational mores and economic forces which are the real obstacles to improving the quality of education.

EDUCATIONAL QUALITY CANNOT BE SIGNIFICANTLY IMPROVED BY TEACHER EVALUATION

The basic attitude of school boards and administrators is that the schools must be operated regardless of the amount of money and manpower provided by state legislatures and local taxpayers. When it comes to a choice between maintaining teacher certification standards and professionally sound teaching conditions or evading standards and "making do," the rulers of the Establishment will try to make do every time. Massive restriction of educational quality results from the failure of our school managers to demand more money and higher standards. In comparison, the amount of bad teaching, which can be eliminated through more stringent evaluation, has little significance.

It is much easier, of course, to indulge in moralistic exercises against ourselves than to demand solutions of the basic problems confronting education. Raising certification standards and enforcing them necessitates finding more money for schools, because better qualified people command higher salaries. When you try to obtain more money for schools, you have a fight on your hands. On the other hand, teacher "evaluation" costs nothing.

WHAT IT TAKES TO IMPROVE EDUCATIONAL QUALITY

Raising the level of teaching performance nationwide will require, roughly, a doubling of labor costs. To establish a maximum class size of 20 pupils requires setting the average at about 15 pupils. A teacher will be able to give little individual attention to pupils in a class as large as 20. Yet, there is not a major school district in the country with a true average class size of even 30, let alone 20. On the elementary level where small classes are needed most, the averages are much higher than for systems as a whole. Thus, teaching staffs must be increased at least 50% to bring class sizes within professionally sound limits. This will cost something!

Add another 50% to reduce teaching hours. College teachers are expected to teach 9 to 12 hours a week, so that out-of-class time can be devoted to study and research. Perhaps there is less need for elementary and secondary school teachers to be as scholarly, but certainly they should not be placed in a situation where 25 to 35 hours must be spent in classroom instruction. In addition to these responsibilities, there are 10 to 30 hours of out-of-class paper marking and lesson preparation. It is clear that under present conditions, teachers do not have the time or energy to be true professionals.

Considering the lower class size and the reduction of teaching hours together, the teaching force of the nation must be vastly increased before we can expect much improvement of educational quality. In addition to this expansion of the teaching force, wemust also become more selective in choosing individuals who will enter the profession. We cannot be more selective unless the number of people who want to become teachers is greater than the number of teaching jobs available. This condition can not be realized until the teaching profession appears as attractive to people of intellectual attainment as other career opportunities.

Today, most people concede that the finest teachers emerged during the depression era, when teaching was in a superior competitive position among career choices. Certainly we can not advocate another depression as the solution to the selectivity problem. The only alternative is to make teaching more attractive, and this will require finding more money for teachers' salaries.

RAISE ENTRY STANDARDS BEFORE GOING FOR STRICTER EVALUATION

Certainly the teaching profession, as distinguished from the administering or supervising professions of the "educator," has the primary obligation of insisting on professional certification standards and professional teaching conditions, before it can become involved in developing a more stringent system of teacher evaluation. When we begin to select teachers of true professional potential, and when we begin to establish conditions which will permit successful teaching, then we can begin to consider other ways of improving teacher performance.

If and when we are in a position to set up a system of teacher evaluation, what would it be like? In the first place, there must be a new approach to the problem of teacher selection and certification. The main elements of an improved process of teacher selection should include: greater academic content in teacher training; a Master's degree; an examination before going into internship; and, a two or three year internship with a gradual assumption of full teaching load and supervision by training teachers who also teach a reduced load.

A teacher who survives such a rigorous selection process will not require a yearly evaluation. Nor should he be subject to an indefinite "continuing evaluation." The continuing evaluation process is often a matter of permitting an antagonistic supervisor or administrator enough time to compile a record against a teacher he wishes to attack.

Evaluation is now required for the purpose of deciding whether or not a teacher will achieve tenure. If the process of teacher selection, including the probationary period, is properly carried out, there should be little need for further evaluations.

ADMINISTRATORS ABUSE EVALUATION POWER

Most abuses of the evaluation process arise from attempts by administrators and supervisors to use their evaluative power to enforce discipline and conformity within the school bureaucracy. It is often the teacher who criticizes school policies or the actions of members of the school hierarchy, wears a beard, does not submit a detailed planbook, is consistently tardy, or simply does not like his supervisor, who receives a negative evaluation. These acts of nonconformity may be contrary to the rules of the bureaucracy, and they may even be indicators of personality weaknesses which raise doubts about the ability of the teacher, but they are not indicators of teaching *performance*.

The work perspectives and value systems of supervisors and administrators are different from those of teachers. Supervisors and administrators have as their primary interest the functioning of the bureaucracy which supports and nourishes them, while teachers have as their primary work interest the solving of educational problems. The success of a teacher is dependent on the success of his pupils in a very direct, emotional way. The success of the administrator and supervisor, while remotely dependent on the aggregate scholarly success of the pupils, is measured more by the orderliness of the school and the success of activities which require organization, such as the athletic program, the school play, band, and orchestra, building new schools, or getting the annual budget approved.

A PROPOSAL FOR INDEPENDENT EVALUATION

One way to avoid the abuse of the power to evaluate teachers might be to take this function away from supervisors and administrators altogether. Experimentation should be instituted to devise an independent means of evaluation, where evaluation is necessary. Although the procedures of the great school evaluation associations (the North Central and others) certainly are not foolproof, they provide a guide for establishing teacher evaluation procedures. Panels of evaluators consisting of teachers, supervisors, and college faculty could be made available for this purpose. None would be regularly employed by the district of the teacher being evaluated. A team would observe the teacher for perhaps a week, interview him, look over his records, and give a written evaluation which would be available to the teacher. Members of the panel from which the evaluating team is selected would be practicing teachers and supervisors in the geographical area, and approved by the teachers organization and the various administrator organizations. They would, of course, be freed from their regular duties when evaluations would be performed at least once every five years, at the request of the teacher.

Three objections to this proposal will be raised immediately. First, the independent committee would be a more cumbersome device than simply allowing the supervisor or administrator to do the evaluating. Second, could an adequate evaluation be made in a week of observation and interview? Finally, many teachers would rather be evaluated by someone with whom they have a personal relationship than by a committee of outsiders.

These objections are not overriding, however. A committee is certainly more cumbersome than one individual. However, since evaluations would be made far less frequently, the added inconvenience woud not be an insurmountable handicap. As for the length of time needed to analyze the technique of a teacher, further experimentation might show whether more or less time would be needed. One advantage of the proposal is that it eliminates the continuous evaluation practice. Perhaps the third objection — "evaluation by strangers" could be overcome by giving the teacher the option of being evaluated by his supervisor or by the evaluation committee. However, one function of the independent evaluation would be to reduce any tendency on the part of teachers to prejudice their supervisors and administrators.

ACCENT THE POSITIVE

Those who advocate a more rigid evaluation of teachers stress the constructive function which criticism can serve. They agree that evaluation should not be used as a disciplinary or punitive device. Certainly no benefit can be gained from merely passing judgment on the worth of a teacher. The emphasis in an evaluation should be on the analysis of the teacher's strengths and weaknesses. Perhaps the term "evaluation" should be dropped altogether, and the term "critique" or "analysis" substituted.

Judging from discussions at recent conferences on educational problems, we can expect a renewed emphasis on evaluation and salaries based on a merit rating, regardless of the uselessness of present evaluative procedures. For instance, graded certification and differentiated staffing are essentially merit pay schemes. The American Federation of Teachers has taken various actions to oppose merit salary schedules, master teachers, and secret files on teachers. Yet, we have never developed a comprehensive philosophy which effectively answers the proevaluation advocates. It is hoped that this article will provoke discussion among teachers and supervisors, and will assist in the development of such a comprehensive policy.

QUESTIONS

1. "Supervisors and administrators have as their primary interest the functioning of the bureaucracy which supports and nourishes them, while teachers have as their primary work interest the solving of educational problems." Do you agree? Defend your point of view.

2. Discuss Selden's proposal for independent evaluation by panels of evaluators from outside a teacher's school district.